George Daniel

Merrie England in the Olden Time

e-artnow 2020

George Daniel

Merrie England in the Olden Time

Complete Edition (Vol. 1&2)

e-artnow, 2020
Contact: info@e-artnow.org

ISBN 978-80-273-0845-3

Contents

VOLUME 1

Table of Contents

MERRIE ENGLAND IN THE OLDEN TIME.

INTRODUCTION.

Youth is the season of ingenuousness and enjoyment, when we desire to please, and blush not to own ourselves pleased. At that happy period there is no affectation of wisdom; we look only to the bright and beautiful: we inquire not whether it be an illusion; it is sufficient that fairy land, with its flowers of every hue, is the path on which we tread. To youth succeeds manhood, with its worldly prudence: then we are taught to take nothing, not even happiness, upon trust; to investigate until we are lost in the intricacies of detail; and to credit our judgment for what is due only to our coldness and apathy. We lose all sympathy for the past; the future is the subject of our anxious speculation; caution and re serve are our guardian angels; and if the heart still throb with a fond emotion, we stifle it with what speed we may, as detrimental to our interests, and unworthy our new-born intelligence and philosophy. A short acquaintance with the world will convince the most sanguine that this stage is not the happiest; that ambition and mercenary cares make up the tumultuous scene; and though necessity compel a temporary submission, it is good to escape from the toils, and breathe a purer air. This brings us to another period, when reflection has taught us self-knowledge, and we are no longer overwise in our own esteem. Then returns something of the simplicity that characterised our early days. We welcome old friends; have recourse to old amusements, and the fictions that enchained our youthful fancy resume their wonted spell.

We remember the time when just emerging from boyhood, we affected a disdain for the past. We had put on the man, and no urchin that put on for the first time his holiday suit, felt more inexpressible self-complacency. We had roared at pantomime, and gaped with delight at the mysteries of melodrame-but now becoming too sober to be amused, "puerile!"

"ridiculous!" were the critical anathemas that fulminated from our newly-imbibed absolute wisdom! It might be presumption to say that we have since grown wiser; certain it is, we are become less pleased with ourselves, and consequently more willing to be pleased.

Gentle Reader, we are old enough to have enjoyed, and young enough to remember many of the amusements, wakes, and popular drolleries of *Merrie England* that have long since submitted to "the tooth of time and razure of oblivion." Like Parson Adams, we have also been a great traveller-in our books! Reversing the well-known epigram,

> "Give me the thing that's pretty, smart, and new:
>
> All ugly, old, odd things, I leave to you,"

we have all our life been a hunter after oddities. We have studied attentively the past. For the future we have been moderately solicitous; there being so many busy economists to take the unthankful task off our hands. We have lost our friend rather than our joke, when the joke has been the better of the two; and have been free of discourse where it has been courteously received, preferring (in the cant of pompous ignorance, which is dear at any price!) to make ourselves "*cheap*" rather than be set down as exclusive and unkind. Disappointments we have had, and sorrows, with ample experience of the world's ingratitude. But life is too short to harbour enmities; and to be resentful is to be unhappy. This may have cast a transient shade over our lucubrations, which let thy happier humour shine upon and dispel! Wilt thou accept us for thy Cicerone through a journey of strange sights? the curiosities of nature, and the whimsicalities of art. We promise thee faster speed than steam-boat and railroad: for thou shalt traverse the ground of two centuries in two hours! With pleasant companions by the way, free from the perils of fire and flood,

"Fancy, like the finger of a clock,

Runs the great circuit, and is still at home."

CHAPTER I.

Dost thou think because thou art virtuous there shall be no more cakes and ale?" was the admirable reply of Sir Toby Belch to Malvolio when he would have marred his Christmas * merrymaking with Sir Andrew and the Clown. And how beautiful is Olivia's reply to the self-same precisian when the searching apophthegms of the "foolish wise man, or wise foolish man," sounded like discords in his ears. "O, you are sick of selflove, Malvolio, and taste all with a distempered appetite. To be generous, guiltless, and of free disposition, is to take those things for bird-bolts that you deem cannon-bullets. There is no slander in an allowed fool, though he do nothing but rail; nor no railing in a known discreet man, though he do nothing but reprove."

   * Christmas being the season when Jack Frost commonly takes
us by the nose, the diversions are within doors, either in
exercise, or by the fire-side. Viz. a game at blind-man's-
buff, puss-in-the-corner, questions and commands, hoop-and-
hide; stories of hobgoblins, Tom-pokers, bull-beggars,
witches, wizards, conjurors, Doctor Faustus, Friar Bacon,
Doctor Partridge, and such-like horrible bodies, that
terrify and delight!
"O you merry, merry souls,

Christmas is a-coming:
We shall have flowing bowls,
Dancing, piping, drumming.
Delicate minced pies,
To feast every virgin;
Capon and goose likewise,
Brawn, and dish of sturgeon.

We hate to be everlastingly bewailing the follies and vices of mankind; and gladly turn to the pleasanter side of the picture, to contemplate something that we can love and emulate. We know

Then for Christmas-box,

Sweet plum-cake and money;

Delicate holland smocks,

Kisses sweet as honey.

Hey for Christmas ball,

Where we will be jolly;

Coupling short and tall,

Kate, Dick, Ralph, and Molly.

To the hop we go,

Where we'll jig and caper;

Cuckolds all a-row—

Will shall pay the scraper.

Tom must dance with Sue,

Keeping time with kisses;

We'll have a jolly crew

Of sweet smirking Misses!" —Old Song.

There are such things as opaque wits and perverse minds, as there are squinting eyes and crooked legs; but we desire not to entertain such guests either as companions or foils. We come not to the conclusion that the world is split into two classes, *viz.* those who *are* and those who *ought to be* hanged; that we should believe every man to be a rogue till we find him honest. There is quite virtue enough in human life to make our journey moderately happy. We are of the hopeful order of beings, and think this world a very beautiful world, if man would not mar it with his pride, selfishness, and gloom.

It has been a maxim among all great and wise nations to encourage public sports and diversions. The advantages that arise from them to a state; the benefit they are to all degrees of the people; the right purposes they may be made to serve in troublesome times, have generally been so well understood by the ruling powers, that they have seldom permitted them to suffer from the assaults of narrow-minded and ignorant reformers.

Our ancestors were wise when they appointed amusements for the people. And as religious services (which are the means, not the end-the road to London is not London) were never intended for a painful duty, the "drum ecclesiastic," which in latter times called its recruits to pillage and bloodshed, often summoned Punch, Robin Hood, and their merry crew, to close the motley ceremonies of a holy-appointed day! Then was the calendar Devotion's diary and Mirth's manual! Rational pleasure is heightened by participation; solitary enjoyment is always selfish. Who ever inquires after a sour recluse, except his creditors and next heir? Nobody misses him when there are so many more agreeable people to supply his place. Of what use is such a negative, "crawling betwixt earth and heaven?" If he hint that Diogenes, * dying of the dumps, may be found at home in his tub, who cares to disinter him? Oh, the deep solitude of a great city to a morose and selfish spirit! The Hall of Eblis is not more terrible. Away, then, with supercilious exclusiveness! 'Tis the grave of the affections! the charnel-house of the heart! What to us is the world, if to the world we are nothing?

We delight to see a fool ** administer to his brethren.

* Diogenes, when he trod with his dirty cobbled shoes on the beautiful carpets of Plato, exclaimed triumphantly, "I tread upon the pride of Plato!" —"Yes," replied Plato, "but with a greater pride!"

** "A material fool," as Jacques describes Touchstone. Such

was Dr. Andrew Borde, the well-known progenitor of Merry Andrews; and the presumed author of the "Merry Tales of the Wise Men of Gotham," composed in the early part of the sixteenth century. "In the time of Henry VIII. and after," (says Anthony à Wood,) "it was accounted a book full of wit and mirth by the scholars and gentlemen." It is thus referred to in an old play of 1560: —
"Ha! ha! ha! ha! ha!

I must needs laughe in my slefe.
The wise men of Gotum are risen againe."

If merriment sometimes ran riot, it never exhibited itself in those deep-laid villanies so rife among the pretenders to sanctity and mortification. An appeal to "clubs" among the London apprentices; the pulling down of certain mansions of iniquity, of which *Mrs. Cole,* * in after days, was the devout proprietress; a few broken heads at the Bear Garden; the somewhat opposite sounds of the "belles tolling for the lectorer, and the trumpets sounding to the stages," ** and sundry minor enormities, were the only terrible results of this national licence. Mark what followed, when masking, morris-dancing, ***

* Foote's "Minor." Act i. scene 1.
** Harleian MSS. No. 286.

*** The morris-dance was one of the most applauded

merriments of Old England. Robin Hood, Little John, Friar Tuck, Maid Marian, the Queen or Lady of the May, the fool, the piper, to which were afterwards added a dragon, and a hobbyhorse, were the characters that figured away in that truly ancient and grotesque movement. Will Kempe, "the comical and conceited jest-monger, and vicegerent to the ghost of Dicke Tarleton," who "raised many a roar by making faces and mouths of all sorts," danced the morris with his men of Gotham, in his "Nine daies' wonder from London to Norwich." Kempe's "new jigg," rivalled in popularity his Peter in Romeo and Juliet; Dogberry, in "Much ado about nothing;" and
Justice Shallow, of which he was the original performer. In

"Jacke Drum's Entertainment," 4to. 1601, is the following song:
ON THE INTRODUCTION OF A WHITSUN MORRIS-DANCE.

"Skip it and trip it nimbly, nimbly,

Tickle it, tickle it lustily,
Strike up the tabour for the wenches' favour,
Tickle it, tickle it, lustily.
Let us be seene on Hygate Greene,
To dance for the honour of Holloway.
Sing we are come hither, let us spare for no leather,
To dance for the honour of Holloway."

May games, stage-plays, * fairs, and the various pastimes that delighted the commonalty, were sternly prohibited. The heart sickens at the cant and cruelty of these monstrous times, when fanaticism, with a dagger in one hand, and *"Hooks and Eyes for an Unbeliever's Breeches,"* in the other, revelled in the destruction of all that was intellectual in the land.

   * Plays were suppressed by the Puritans in 1633. The actors
were driven off the stage by the soldiers; and the only
pleasantry that Messrs. "Praise-God-Barebones" and "Fight-
the-good-fight," indulged in, was "Enter red coat, exit hat
and cloak;" a cant phrase in reference to this devout
tyranny. Randolph, in "The Muses' Looking-glass," makes a
fanatic utter this charitable prayer:
"That the Globe,

Wherein (quoth he) reigns a whole world of vice,
Had been consum'd, the Phoenix burnt to ashes;
The Fortune whipp'd for a blind-Blackfriars!
He wonders how it 'scap'd demolishing I' the time of

Reformation: lastly, he wished The Bull might cross the
Thames to the Bear Gardens, And there be soundly baited.
In 1599 was published "The overthrow of Stage Playes, by way

of controversie betwixt D. Gager and D. Rainolde, wherein all the Reasons that ean be made for them are notably
refuted, the objections answered, and the case so clear and
resolved as that the judgment of any man that is not froward
and perverse may casilie be satisfied; wherein is
manifestly proved that it is not onely unlawfull to bee an
actor, but a beholder of those vanities, &c. &c."

When the lute, the virginals, the viol-de-gambo, were hushed for the inharmonious bray of their miserable conventicles, * and the quaintly appropriate signs ** of the ancient taverns and music shops were pulled down to make room for some such horrible effigy as we see dedicated to their high priest, *John Knox*, on a wall in the odoriferous Canongate of *Modern Athens.* ***

   * "What a poor pimping business is a Presbyterian place of
worship; dirty, narrow and squalid: stuck in the corner of
an old Popish garden such as Linlithgow, and much more,
Melrose." —Robert Burns.
** Two wooden heads, with this inscription under it: "We

three loggerheads be." The third was the spectator. The
tabor was the ancient sign of a music shop. Tarleton kept an
eating-house with this sign. Apropos of signs-Two Irishmen
beholding a hatchment fixed against a house, the one
inquired what it was? "It's a bad sign!" replied the other
mysteriously. Paddy being still at fault as to the meaning,
asked for further explanation. —"It's a sign," cried his
companion with a look of immeasurable superiority, "that
somebody is dead!"
*** Those who would be convinced of the profaneness of the

Cameronians and Covenanters have only to read "Scotch
Presbyterian Eloquence displayed, or the Folly of their
teaching discovered from their Books, Sermons, and Prayers,"
1738 —a volume full of ludicrous impieties. We select one
specimen.
Mr. William Vetch, preaching at Linton, in Tiviotdale, said,

"Our Bishops thought they were very secure this long time.
"Like Willie Willie Wastel,

I am in my castel.
All the dogs in the town
Dare nor ding me down.
"Yea, but there is a doggie in Heaven that has dung them all

down."

Deep was the gloom of those dismal days! The kitchens were cool; the spits motionless. * The
green holly and the mystic mistletoe ** were blooming abominations. The once rosy cheeks of
John Bull looked as lean as a Shrove-Tuesday pancake, and every rib like the tooth of a saw.
   * "The Lamentable Complaints of Nick Froth the Tapster, and
Ruleroast the Cook," 4to. 1641.
* The magical properties of the mistletoe are mentioned both

by Virgil and Ovid; and Apuleius has preserved some verses
of the poet Lelius, in which he mentions the mistletoe as
one of the things necessary to make a magician. In the dark
ages a similar belief prevailed, and even to the present day
the peasants of Holstein, and some other countries, call the
mistletoe the "Spectre's Wand," from a supposition that
holding a branch of mistletoe in the hand will not only
enable a man to see ghosts, but to force them to speak to
him! The mistletoe is peculiar to Christmas.

Rampant were those times, when crop-ear'd Jack Presbyter was as blythe as shepherd at a wake. *
Down tumbled the Maypoles ** —no more music
   * "We'll break the windows which the whore Of Babylon hath
planted,
And when the Popish saints are down,
Then Burges shall be sainted;

We'll burn the fathers' learned books,
And make the schoolmen flee;
We'll down with all that smells of wit,
And hey, then, up go we!"
** The downfall of May-games, 4to. 1660. By Thomas Hall, the

canting parson of King's-Norton. —Hear the caitiff,
"There's not a knave in all the town,

Nor swearing courtier, nor base clown,
Nor dancing lob, nor mincing quean,
Nor popish clerk, be't priest or dean,
Nor Knight debauch'd nor gentleman,
That follows drab, or cup, or can,
That will give thee a friendly look,
If thou a May-pole canst not brook."
On May 1, 1517, the unfortunate shaft, or May-pole, gave

rise to the insurrection of that turbulent body, the London
apprentices, and the plundering of the foreigners in the
city, whence it got the name of Evil May-day. From that time
the offending pole was hung on a range of hooks over the
doors of a long row of neighbouring houses. In the 3rd of
Edward VI. an over-zealous fanatic called Sir Stephen began
to preach against this May-pole, which inflamed his audience
so greatly, that the owner of every house over which it hung
sawed off as much as depended over his premises, and
committed piecemeal to the flames this terrible idol!
The "tall May-pole" that "onee o'erlooked the Strand,"

(about the year 1717,) Sir Isaac Newton begged of the
parish, and it was carried to Wanstead in Essex, where it
was erected in the park, and had the honour of raising the
greatest telescope then known. The New Church occupies its
site.
"But now (so Anne and piety ordain),

A church collects the saints of Drury Lane."

and dancing! * For the disciples of *Stubbes* and *Prynne* having discovered by their sage oracles,
that *May-games* were derived from the Floralian Feasts and interludes of the pagan Romans,
which were solemnised on the first of May; and that dancing round a May-pole, adorned with
garlands of flowers, ribbons, and other ornaments, was idolatry, after the fashion of Baal's wor-
shippers, who capered about the altar in honour of their idol; resolved that the Goddess Flora
should no longer receive the gratulations of Maid Marian, Friar Tuck, and Robin Hood's merry
men, on a fine May morning; a superstition derived from the Sibyl's books, horribly papistical
and pagan.
   * "Good fellowes must go learne to daunce
The brydeal is full near a:
There is a brail come out of Fraunce,
The fyrst ye harde this yeare a.

For I must leape, and thou must hoppe,
And we must turne all three a;
The fourth must bounce it like a toppe,
And so we shall agree a.
praye the mynstrell make no stoppe,
For we wyll merye be a."
From an unique black letter ballad, printed in 1569,

"Intytuled, 'Good Fellowes must go learne to Daunce.'"

Nor was the "precise villain" less industrious in confiscation and sacrilege. * Painted windows-
Lucifer's Missal drawings! —he took infinite pains to destroy; and with his long pike did the
devil's work diligently. He could endure no cross ** but that on silver; hence the demolition
of those beautiful edifices that once adorned Cheapside, and other remarkable sites in ancient
times.

   * Sir Robert Howard has drawn an excellent picture of a
Puritan family, in his comedy of "The Committee." The
personages are Mr. Day, chairman to the committee of
sequestrations; Mrs. Day, "the committee-man's utensil,"
with "curled hair, white gloves, and Sabbath-day's cinnamon
waistcoat;" Abel, their booby son, a fellow "whose heart is
down in his breeches at every turn and Obadiah, chief clerk,
dull, drawling, and heinously given to strong waters. We are
admitted into the sanctum sanctorum, of pious fraud, where
are seated certain honourable members, whose names cannot
fail to enforce respect. Nehemiah Catch, Joseph Blemish,
Jonathan Headstrong, and Ezekiel Scrape! The work of plunder
goes bravely on. The robbing of widows and orphans is
"building up the new Zion." A parcel of notched rascals
laying their heads together to cheat is "the cause of the
righteous prospering when brethren dwell together in unity
and when a canting brother gives up lying and the ghost, Mr.
Day remarks that "Zachariah went off full of exhortation!"
It was at the sacking of Basing House, the seat of the

venerable Marquis of Winchester, that Harrison, the regicide
and butcher's son, shot Major Robinson, exclaiming as he did
the deed, "Cursed is he that doeth the work of the Lord
negligently." Hugh Peters, the buffooning priest, was of the
party.
** The erection of upright stone crosses is generally

supposed to have dated its origin from the custom which the
first Christians in this island adopted of inscribing the
Druid stones with a cross, that the worship of the converted
idolator might be transferred from the idol to the emblem of
his faith; and afterwards the Saxon kings frequently erected
crosses previously to a battle, at which public prayers were
offered up for victory. After the Norman conquest crosses
became common, and were erected in market-places, to induce
honesty by the sanction of religion: in churchyards, to

inspire devout and pious feelings; in streets, for the
deposit of a corpse when borne to its last home; and for
various other purposes. Here the beggar stationed himself,
and asked alms in the name of Him who suffered on the cross.
They were used for landmarks, that men might learn to
respect and hold sacred the boundaries of another's
property. Du Cange says that crosses were erected in the
14th Richard II. as landmarks to define the boundaries
between Kesteven and Holland. They were placed on public
roads as a check to thieves, and to regulate processions. At
the Reformation (?!!) most of the crosses throughout the
kingdom were destroyed, when the sweeping injunction of
Bishop Horne was formally promulgated at his Visitation in
1571, that all images of the Trinity in glass windows, or
other places of the church, be put out and extinguished,
together with the stone cross in the churchyard! We devoutly
hope, as Dr. Johnson hoped of John Knox, that Bishop Horne
was buried in a cross-road.

The sleek rogue read his Bible * upside down, and hated his neighbour: his piety was pelf;
his godliness gluttony.
    * "They like none but sanctified and shuttle-headed weavers,
long-winded boxmakers, and thorough-stitching cobblers,
thumping felt-makers, jerking coachmen, and round-headed
button-makers, which spoyle Bibles while they thumb over the
leaves with their greasie fingers, and sit by the fireside
scumming their porridge-pot, while their zeal seethes over
in applications and interpretations of Scripture delivered
to their ignorant wives and handmaids, with the name and
title of deare brethren and especially beloved sisters." —
The doleful Lamentation of Cheapside Crosse, or Old England
sick of the Staggers, 1641.

His grace * was as long as his face. The gnat, like Macbeth's "Amen," stuck in his throat; but
the camel slid down merrily. What a weary, working-day world would this have been under
his unhospitable dominion! ** How unlovely and lachrymose! how sectarian and sinister! A
bumper of bitters, to be swallowed with a rising gorge, and a wry face! All literature would
have resolved itself into —
    * One Lady D'Arcy, a well-jointured, puritanical widow,
having invited the next heir in the entail to dine with her,
asked him to say grace. The young gentleman, thinking that
her ladyship had lived quite long enough, expressed his
wishes thus graciously: —
"Good Lord of thy mercy,

Take my good Lady D'Arcy
Unto her heavenly throne;
That I, little Frank,
May sit in my rank,
And keep a good house of my own!"
** John Knox proclaimed the mild sentence, which was loudly

re-echoed by his disciples, that the idolator should die the death, in plain English (or rather, God be thanked! in plain Scotch) that every Catholic should be hanged. The bare toleration of prelacy-of the Protestant prelacy! —was the guilt of soul-murder. These were the merciful Christians! the sainted martyrs! who conducted the inquisitorial tyranny of the high commission, and imposed the test of that piece of impious buffoonery, the "Holy League and Covenant!!" who visited the west of Scotland with the free quarters of the military, and triumphed so brutally over the unfortunate, patriotic and gallant Montrose. The Scotch Presbyterians enacted that each episcopalian was liable to transportation who should baptize a child, or officiate as a clergyman to more than Jour persons, besides the members of his own family!

—*"The plain Pathway to Penuriousness;" Peachums "Worth of a Penny, or a caution to keep Money;" and the "Key to unknowne Knowledge, or a Shop of Five Windows"*

"Which if you do open, to cheapen and copen,

You will be unwilling, for many a shilling,

To part with the profit that you shall have of it;"

and the drama, which, whether considered as a school of eloquence or a popular entertainment, is entitled to national regard, would have been proscribed, because-having neither soul for sentiment, eye for beauty, nor ear for poetry, it was his pleasure to be displeased. His humanity may be summed up in one short sentence, "I will take care, my dear brother, you shall not keep your bed in sickness, for I will take it from under you." There are two reasons why we don't trust a man-one, because we don't know him, and the other because we do. Such a man would have shouted "*Hosan-nah!*" when the Saviour entered Jerusalem in triumph; and cried "*Crucify him!*" when he went up the mountain to die.

Seeing how little party spirit, religious controversy, and money-grubbing have contributed to the general stock of human happiness-that pre-eminence in knowledge is

"Only to know how little can be known,

To see all others' faults, and feel our own,"

we cry, with St. Patrick's dean, "*Vive la bagatelle!*" Democritus lived to an hundred. Death shook, not his dart, but his sides, at the laughing philosopher, and "delay'd to strike" till his lungs had crowed their second jubilee: while Heraclitus was Charon's passenger at threescore. But the night wanes apace; to-morrow we must rise with the lark. Fill we a cup to Mercury, *à bon repos!*

A bumper at parting! a bumper so bright,

Though the clock points to morning, by way of good

night!

Time, scandal, and cards, are for tea-drinking souls!

Let them play their rubbers, while we ply the bowls!

Oh who are so jocund, so happy as we?

Our skins full of wine, and our hearts full of glee!

Not buxom Dame Nature, a provident lass!

Abhors more a vacuum, than Bacchus's glass,

Where blue-devils drown, and where merry thoughts

        swim —

As deep as a Quaker, as broad as his brim!

Like rosy fat friars, again and again

Our beads we have told, boys I —in sparkling champagne!

Our gravity's centre is good vin de grave,

Pour'd out to replenish the goblet concave;

And tell me what rubies so glisten and shine,

Like the deep blushing ruby of Burgundy wine?

His face in the glass Bibo smiles when he sees;

For Fancy takes flight on no wing like the bee's!

If truth in a well lie-ah! truth, well-a-day! —

I'll seek it in "Fmo," —the pleasantest way!

Let temperance, twankay, teetotallers trump;

Your sad, sober swiggers at "*Veritas*" pump!

If water flow hither, so crystal and clear,

To mix with our wine —'tis humanity's tear.

When Venus is crusty, and Mars in a miff,

Their tipple is prime nectar-toddy and stiff—

And shall we not toast, like their godships above,

The lad we esteem, and the lady we love?

Be goblets as sparkling, and spirits as light,

Our next merry meeting! A bumper-good night!

CHAPTER II.

> "The flow'ry *May*, who from her green lap throws
>
> The yellow cowslip and the pale primrose."

'Tis Flora's holiday, and in ancient times the goddess kept it with joyous festivity. Ah! those ancient times, they are food for melancholy. Yet may melancholy be made to "discourse most eloquent music," —

> "O why was England 'merrie' called, I pray you tell
>
> me why? —
>
> Because Old England merry was in merry times gone by!
>
> She knew no dearth of honest mirth to cheer both son
>
> and sire,
>
> But kept it up o'er wassail cup around the Christmas
>
> fire.
>
> When fields were dight with blossoms white, and leaves
>
> of lively green,
>
> The May-pole rear'd its flow'ry head, and dancing round
>
> were seen
>
> A youthful band, join'd hand in hand, with shoon and
>
> kirtle trim,
>
> And softly rose the melody of Flora's morning hymn.
>
> Her garlands, too, of varied hue the merry milkmaid
>
> wove,
>
> And Jack the Piper caprioled within his dancing grove;
>
> Will, Friar Tuck, and Little John, with Robin Hood
>
> their king,
>
> Bold foresters! blythe choristers! made vale and moun

tain ring.

On every spray blooms lovely May, and balmy zephyrs

breathe —

Ethereal splendour all above! and beauty all beneath!

The cuckoo's song the woods among sounds sweetly as of

old;

As bright and warm the sunbeams shine-and why

should hearts grow cold?" *

* This ballad has been set to very beautiful music by Mr. N.
I. Sporle. It is published by T. E. Purday, 50, St. Paul's
Church Yard.

"A sad theme to a merry tune! But had not May *another* holiday maker? when the compassion-ate Mrs. Montague walked forth from her hall and bower to greet with a smile of welcome her grotesque visitor, the poor little sweep."

Thy hand, Eugenio, for those gentle words! *Elia* would have taken thee to his heart. Be the turf that lies lightly on his breast as verdant as the bank whereon we sit. On a cold, dark, wintry morning, he had too often been disturbed out of a peaceful slumber by his shrill, mournful cry; and contrasting his own warm bed of down with the hard pallet from which the sooty little chorister had been driven at that untimely hour, he vented his generous indignation; and when a heart so tender as *Elia's* could feel indignation, bitter must have been the provocation and the crime! But the sweep, with his brilliant white teeth, and Sunday washed face, is for the most part a cheerful, healthy-looking being. Not so the squalid, decrepit *factory lad*, broken-spirited, overworked, and half-starved! The little sweep, in process of time, may become a master "chum-mie," and have (without being obliged to sweep it,) a chimney of his own: but the factory lad sees no prospect of ever emerging from his heart-sickening toil and hopeless dependance; he feels the curse of Cain press heavily upon him. The little sweep has his merry May-day, with its jigs, rough music, gingling money-box, gilt-paper cocked-hat, and gay patchwork paraphernalia. All days are alike to the factory lad —"E'en Sunday shines no Sabbath-day to him." *His* rest will be the Sabbath of the tomb!

Nothing is better calculated to brace the nerves and diffuse a healthful glow over body and mind than outdoor recreations. What is *ennui?* Fogs, and over-feeding, content grown plethoric, the lethargy of superabundance, the want of some rational pursuit, and the indisposition to seek one. What its cure?

"'Tis health, 'tis air, 'tis exercise —

Fling but a stone, the giant dies!"

The money-grub, pent up in a close city, eating the bread of carefulness, and with the fear of the shop always before his eyes, is not industrious. He is the droning, horse-in-a-mill creature of habit-like a certain old lady of our acquaintance, who every morning was the first up in the house, and good-for-nothing afterwards. A century ago the advantages of early rising to the citizen were far more numerous than at present. A brisk walk of ten minutes brought him into the fields from almost any part of the town; and after luxuriating three or four miles amidst clover, sorrel, buttercups, aye, and corn to boot! the fresh breeze of morn, the fragrance of the flowers, and the pleasant prospect, would inspire happy thoughts: and, as nothing better sharpens the appetite than these delightful companions, what was wanting but a substantial breakfast to prepare him for the business of the day? For this certain frugal houses of entertainment were established in the rural outskirts of the Metropolis, *

* "This is to give notice to all Ladies and Gentlemen, at
Spencer's original Breakfasting-Hut, between Sir Hugh
Middleton's Head and St. John Street Road, by the New River
side, fronting Sadler's Wells, may be had every morning,
except Sundays, fine tea, sugar, bread, butter, and milk, at
four-penee per head; coffee at threepence a dish. And in the
afternoon, tea, sugar and milk, at threepence per head, with
good attendance. Coaches may come up to the farthest gar-
den-door next to the bridge in St. John Street Road, near
Sadler's Wells back gate. —Note. Ladies, &c. are desired to
take notice that there is another person set up in
opposition to me, the next door, which is a brick-house, and
faces the little gate by the Sir Hugh Middleton's, and
therefore mistaken for mine; but mine is the *little boarded
place* by the river side, and my backdoor faces the same as
usual; for
I am not dead, I am not gone,

Nor liquors do I sell;
But, as at first, I still go on,
Ladies, to use you well.
No passage to my hut I have,
The river runs before;
Therefore your care I humbly crave,
Pray don't mistake my door.
"Yours to serve,
Daily Advertiser, May 6, 1745. "S. Spencer."

where every morning, "except Sundays, fine tea, sugar, bread, butter, and milk," might be had at fourpence per head, and coffee "at three halfpence a dish.'" And as a walk in summer was an excellent recruit to the spirits after reasonable toil, the friendly hand that lifted the latch in the morning repeated the kind office at evening tide, and spread before him those refreshing elements that "cheer, but not inebriate;" with the harmless addition of music and dancing. Ale, wine, and punch, were subsequently included in the bill of fare, and dramatic representations. But of latter years the town has walked into the country, and the citizen can just espy at a considerable distance a patch of flowery turf, and a green hill, when his leisure and strength are exhausted, and it is time to turn homeward.

The north side of London was famous for suburban houses of entertainment. Midway down Gray's Inn Lane stands Town's End Lane (so called in the old maps), or Elm Street, which takes its name from some elms that once grew there. To the right is Mount Pleasant, and on its summit is planted a little hostelrie, which commanded a delightful prospect of fields, that are now annihilated; their site and our sight being profaned by the House of Correction and the Treadmill! Farther on, to the right, is Warner Street, which the lover of old English ballad poetry and music will never pass without a sigh; for there, while the town were applauding his dramatic drolleries-and his beautiful songs charmed alike the humble and the refined-their author, Henry Carey, in a fit of melancholy destroyed himself. *

* October 4, 1743.

Close by stood the old Bath House, which was built over a *Cold Spring* by one Walter Baynes, in 1697. * The house is razed to the ground, but the spring remains. A few paces forward is the Lord Cobham's Head, ** transmogrified into a modern temple for tippling; its shady gravel walks, handsome grove of trees, and green bowling alleys, are long since destroyed. Its opposite neighbour *was* (for not a vestige of the ancient building remains) the Sir John Oldcastle, *** where the wayfarer was invited to regale upon moderate terms.

* According to tradition, this was once the bath of Nell Gwynn. In Baynes's Row, close by, lived for many years the celebrated clown Joe Grimaldi.
** "Sir-Coming to my lodging in Islington, I called at the

Lord Cobham's Head, in Cold Bath Fields, to drink some of their beer, which I had often heard to be the finest, strongest, and most pleasant in London, where I found a very handsome house, good accommodation, and pleasantly situated. I afterwards walked in the garden, where I was greatly surprised to find a very handsome grove of trees, with gravel walks, and finely illuminated, to please the company that should honour them with drinking a tankard of beer, which is threepence. There will be good attendance, and music of all sorts, both vocal and instrumental, and will begin this day, being the 10th of August.
"I am yours,

"Tom Freeman."

Daily Advertiser, 9th August 1742.

*** "Sir —A few days ago, invited by the serenity of the

evening, I made a little excursion into the fields. Returning home, being in a gay humour, I stopt at a booth near Sir John Oldcastle's, to hear the rhetoric of Mr. Andrew. He used so much eloquence to persuade his auditors to walk in, that I (with many others) went to see his entertainment; and I never was more agreeably amused than with the performances of the three Bath Morris Dancers. They showed so many astonishing feats of strength and activity, so many amazing transformations, that it is impossible for the most lively imagination to form an adequate idea thereof. As the Fairs are coming on, I presume these admirable artists will be engaged to entertain the town; and I assure your readers they can't spend an hour more agreeably than in seeing the performances of these wonderful men.
"I am, &c.

Daily Advertiser, 27th July 1743.

See a rare print, entituled "A new and exact prospect of

the North side of the City of London, taken from the Upper Pond near Islington. Printed and sold by Thomas Bake-well, Print and Map-seller, over against Birching Lane, Corn-hill, August 5, 1730."

Show-booths were erected in this immediate neighbourhood for Merry-Andrews and mor-ris-dancers. Onward was the Ducking Pond; * ("Because I dwell at Hogsden," says *Master Stephen, in Every Man in his Humour*, "I shall keep company with none but the archers of Finsbury or the citizens that come a ducking to Islington Ponds;") and, proceeding in almost a straight line towards "*Old Iseldon*," were the London Spa, originally built in 1206; Phillips's New Wells; *

Original

* "By a company of English, French, and Germans, at
Phillips's New Wells, near the London Spa, Clerkenwell, 20th
August 1743.
"This evening, and during the Summer Season, will be

performed several new exercises of Rope-dancing, Tumbling,
Vaulting, Equilibres, Ladder-dancing, and Balancing, by Ma —
dame Kerman, Sampson Rogetzi, Monsieur German, and Monsieur
Dominique; with a new Grand Dance, called Apollo and Daphne,
by Mr. Phillips, Mrs. Lebrune, and others; singing by Mrs.
Phillips and Mrs. Jackson; likewise the extraordinary
performance of Herr Von Eeekenberg, who imitates the lark,
thrush, blackbird, goldfinch, canary-bird, flageolet, and
German flute; a Sailor's Dance by Mr. Phillips; and Monsieur
Dominique flies through a hogshead, and forces both heads
out. To which will be added The Harlot's Progress. Harlequin
by Mr. Phillips; Miss Kitty by Mrs. Phillips. Also, an exact
representation of the late glorious victory gained over the
French by the English at the battle of Dettingen, with the
taking of the White Household Standard by the Scots Greys,
and blowing up the bridge, and destroying and drowning most
part of the French army. To begin every evening at five
o'clock. Every one will be admitted for a pint of wine, as
usual."
Mahommed Caratha, the Grand Turk, performed here his

"Surprising Equilibres on the Slack Rope."
In after years, the imitations of Herr Von Eeekenberg were

emulated by James Boswell. (Bozzy!)
"A great many years ago, when Dr. Blair and I (Boswell) were

sitting together in the pit of Drury Lane Playhouse, in a
wild freak of youthful extravagance, I entertained the
audience prodigiously by imitating the lowings of a cow. The
universal cry of the galleries was, 'Encore the cow!' In the
pride of my heart I attempted imitations of some other
animals, but with very inferior effect. My revered friend,
anxious for my fame, with an air of the utmost gravity and
earnestness, addressed me thus, My dear sir, I would confine
myself to the cow!'"

the New Red Lion Cockpit; * the Mulberry Gardens; **
    * "At the New Red Lion Cockpit, near the Old London Spaw,
Clerkenwell, this present Monday, being the 12th July 1731,
will be seen the Royal Sport of Cock-fighting, for two
guineas a-battle. To-morrow begins the match for four
guineas a-battle, and twenty guineas the old battle, and
continues all the week, beginning at four o'clock."

** "Mulberry Gardens, Clerkenwell. —The gloomy clouds that

obscured the season, it is to be hoped, are vanished, and
nature once more shines with a benign and cheerful
influence. Come, then, ye honest sons of trade and industry,
after the fatigues of a well-spent day, and taste of our
rural pleasures! Ye sons of care, here throw aside your
burden! Ye jolly Bacchanalians, here regale, and toast your
rosy god beneath the verdant branches! Ye gentle lovers,
here, to soft sounds of harmony, breathe out your sighs,
till the cruel fair one listens to the voice of love! Ye who
delight in feats of war, and are anxious for our heroes
abroad, in mimic fires here see their ardour displayed!
"Note. —The proprietor being informed that it is a general

complaint against others who offer the like entertainments,
that if the gentle zephyrs blow ever so little, the company
are in danger of having their viands fanned away, through
the thinness of their consistence, promises that his shall
be of such a solidity as to resist, the air!" —Daily
Advertiser, July 8, 1745.
The latter part of this picturesque and poetical

advertisement is a sly hit at what, par excellence, are
called, "Vauxhall slices."

the Shakspeare's Head Tavern and Jubilee Gardens; * the New Tunbridge Wells, **
    * In 1742, the public were entertained at the "Shakspeare's
Head, near the New Wells, Clerkenwell,', with refreshments
of all sorts, and music; "the harpsichord being placed in so
judicious a situation, that the whole company cannot fail of
equally receiving the benefit." In 1770, Mr. Tonas exhibited
"a great and pleasing variety of performances, in a
commodious apartment," up one pair.
** These once beautiful tea-gardens (we remember them as

such) were formerly in high repute. In 1733, their Royal
Highnesses the Princesses Amelia and Caroline frequented
them in the summer time, for the purpose of drinking the
waters. They have furnished a subject for pamphlets, poems,
plays, songs, and medical treatises, by Ned Ward, George
Col-man the elder, Bickham, Dr. Hugh Smith, &c. Nothing now
remains of them but the original chalybeate spring, which is
still preserved in an obscure nook, amidst a poverty-
stricken and squalid rookery of misery and vice.

a fashionable morning lounge of the nobility and gentry during the early part of the eighteenth
century; the Sir Hugh Middleton's Head; the Farthing Pie House; * and Sadler's Music House
and "Sweet Wells." ** A little to the left were Merlin's Cave,
    * Farthing Pie Houses were common in the outskirts of London
a century ago. Their fragrance caught the sharp set citizen

by the nose, and led him in by that prominent member to feast on their savoury fare. One solitary Farthing Pie House (the Green Man) still stands near Portland Road, on the way to Paddington.

** Originally a chalybeate spring, then a music-house, and

afterwards a "theatre-royal!" Cheesecakes, pipes, wine, and punch, were formerly part of the entertainment.

"If at Sadler's sweet Wells the wine should be thick,

The cheesecakes be sour, or Miss Wilkinson sick,
If the fume of the pipe should prove pow'rful in June,
Or the tumblers be lame, or the bells out of tune,
We hope you will call at our warehouse at Drury-We've a

curious assortment of goods, I assure you." Foote's Prologue to All in the Wrong, 1761.

Its rural vicinity made it a great favourite with the play-

going and punch-drinking citizens. See Hogarth's print of "Evening."

"A New Song on Sadler's Wells, set by Mr. Brett, 1740.

'At eve, when Sylvan's shady scene

Is clad with spreading branches green,
And varied sweets all round display'd,
To grace the pleasant flow'ry meads,
For those who're willing joys to taste,
Where pleasures flow and blessings last,
And God of Health with transport dwells,
Must all repair to Sadler's Wells.
The pleasant streams of Middleton
In gentle murmurs glide along,
In which the sporting fishes play,
To close each weary summer's day;
And music's charm, in lulling sounds,
With mirth and harmony abounds;
While nymphs and swains, with beaus and belles,
All praise the joys of Sadler's Wells.'"

Bagnigge Wells, * the English Grotto (which stood near the New River Water-works in the fields), and, farther in advance, White Conduit House. **

  * Once the reputed residence of Nell Gwynn, which makes the tradition of her visiting the "Old Bath House" more than probable. F or. upwards of a century it has been a noted place of entertainment.'Tis now almost a ruin! Pass we to its brighter days, as sung in the "Sunday Ramble," 1778: —

"Salubrious waters, tea, and wine,

Here you may have, and also dine;

But as ye through the gardens rove,
Beware, fond youths, the darts of love!"
** So called after an ancient conduit that once stood hard

by. Goldsmith, in the "Citizen of the World," celebrates the
"hot rolls and butter' of White Conduit House. Thither
himself and a few friends would repair to tea, after having
dined at Highbury Barn. A supper at the Grecian, or Temple
Exchange Coffeehouses, closed the "Shoemaker's Holiday" of
this exquisite English Classic-this gentle and benignant
spirit!

Passing by the Old Red Lion, bearing the date of 1415, and since brightened up with some
regard to the taste of ancient times; and the Angel-now a *fallen* one! —a huge structure, the
architecture of which is anything but angelic, having risen on its ruins, we enter Islington, described by Goldsmith as "a pretty and neat town." In ancient times it was not unknown to fame.

"What village can boast like fair Islington town

Such time-honour'd worthies, such ancient renown?

Here jolly Queen Bess, after flirting with Leicester,

'*Undumpish'd"* herself with Dick Tarleton her jester.

Here gallant gay Essex, and burly Lord Burleigh,

Sat late at their revels, and came to them early;

Here honest Sir John took his ease at his inn —

Bardolph's proboscis, and Jack's double chin!

Here Finsbury archers disported and quaff'd,

Here Raleigh the brave took his pipe and his draught;

Here the Knight of St. John pledged the Highbury Monk,

Till both to their pallets reel'd piously drunk." *

In "The Walks of Islington and Hogsdon, with the Humours of Wood Street Compter," a
comedy, by Thomas Jordan, 1641, the scene is laid at the Saracen's Head, Islington; and the
prologue celebrates its "bottle-beer, cream, and (gooseberry) fools and the "Merry Milkmaid
of Islington,
    * "The Islington Garland."

or the Rambling Gallant defeated," a comedy, 1680, is another proof of its popularity. Poor
Robin, in his almanac, 1676, says,

"At Islington

A Fair they hold,

Where cakes and ale

Are to be sold.

At Highgate and

At Holloway

The like is kept

Here every day.

At Totnam Court

And Kentish Town,

And all those places

Up and down."

Drunken Barnaby notices some of its inns. Sir William d'Avenant, describing the amusements of the citizens during the long vacation, makes a "husband gray" ask,

"Where's Dame? (quoth he.) Quoth son of shop

She's gone her cake in milk to sop —

Ho! Ho! —to *Islington* —enough!"

Bonnel Thornton, in "The Connoisseur," speaks of the citizens smoking their pipes and drinking their ale at Islington; and Sir William Wealthy exclaims to his money-getting brother, "What, old boy, times are changed since the date of thy indentures, when the sleek crop-eared 'prentice used to dangle after his mistress, with the great Bible under his arm, to St. Bride's on a Sunday, bring home the text, repeat the divisions of the discourse, dine at twelve, and regale upon a gaudy day with buns and beer at *Islington* or Mile-end." *

Among its many by-gone houses of entertainment, the *Three Hats* has a double claim upon our notice. It was the arena where those celebrated masters, Johnson, ** Price, Sampson, *** and Coningham exhibited their feats of horsemanship, and the scene of Mr. Mawworm's early back-slidings. "I used to go," (says that regenerated ranter to old Lady Lambert,) "every Sunday evening to the Three Hats at Islington; it's a public house; mayhap your Ladyship may know it.

* "The Minor," Act I.
** Johnson exhibited in 1758, and Price, at about the same

time-Coningham in 1772. Price amassed upwards of fourteen
thousand pounds by his engagements at home and abroad.
*** "Horsemanship, April 29, 1767.

Mr. Sampson will begin his famous feats of horsemanship next

Monday, at a commodious place built for that purpose in a
field adjoining the Three Hats at Islington, where he
intends to continue his performance during the summer
season. The doors to be opened at four, and Mr. Sampson will
mount at five. Admittance, one shilling each. A proper band
of music is engaged for the entertainment of those ladies
and gentlemen who are pleased to honour him with their
company."

I was a great lover of skittles, too; but now I can't bear them." At Dobney's Jubilee Gardens (now
entirely covered with mean hovels), Daniel Wildman * performed equestrian exercises; and, that
no lack of entertainment might be found in this once merry village, "a new booth, near Islington
Turnpike," for tricks and mummery, was erected in September 1767; "an insignificant erection,
calculated totally for the lowest classes, inferior artisans, superb apprentices, and journeymen."

Fields,
 * "The Bees on Horseback!" At the Jubilee Gardens, Dobney's,
1772. "Daniel Wildman rides, standing upright, one foot on
the saddle, and the other on the horse's neck, with a
curious mask of bees on his face. He also rides, standing
upright on the saddle, with the bridle in his mouth, and, by
firing a pistol, makes one part of the bees march over a
table, and the other part swarm in the air, and return to
their proper places again."
** Animadvertor's letter to the Printer of the Daily

Advertiser, 21st September 1767.
*** August 22nd, 1770, Mr. Craven stated in an

advertisement, that he had "established rules for the
strictest maintenance of order" at the Pantheon. How far
this was true, the following letter "To the Printer of the
St. James's Chronicle" will show: —
"Sir-Happening to dine last Sunday with a friend in the

city, after coming from church, the weather being very
inviting, we took a walk as far as Islington. In our return
home towards Cold Bath Fields, we stepped in to view the
Pantheon there; but such a scene of disorder, riot, and
confusion, presented itself to me on my entrance, that I was
just turning on my heel in order to quit it, when my friend
observing that we might as well have something for our money

(for the doorkeeper obliged each of us to deposit a tester before he granted us admittance), I acquiesced in his proposal, and became one of the giddy multitude. I soon, however, repented of my choice; for, besides having our sides almost squeezed together, we were in danger every minute of being scalded by the boiling water which the officious Mercuries were circulating with the utmost expedition through their respective districts. We therefore began to look out for some place to sit down in, which with the greatest difficulty we at length procured, and producing our tickets, were served with twelve-penny worth of punch. Being seated towards the front of one of the galleries, I had now a better opportunity of viewing this dissipated scene. The male part of the company seemed to consist chiefly of city apprentices and the lower class of tradesmen. The ladies, who constituted by far the greater part of the assembly, seemed most of them to be pupils of the Cyprian goddess, and I was sometimes accosted with, 'Pray, sir, will you treat me with a dish of tea?' Of all the tea-houses in the environs of London, the most exceptionable that I have had occasion to be in is the Pantheon.

"I am sir, your constant reader,

"Speculator."

"Chiswick, May 5, 1772."

near Islington," * was opened in 1770 for the sale of tea, coffee, wine, punch, &c., a "tester" being the price of admission to the promenade and galleries. It was eventually turned to a very different use, and converted into a lay chapel by the late Countess of Huntingdon.

* Spa-Fields (like "Jack Plackett's Common" the site of Dalby Terrace, Islington) was famous for duck-hunting, bull-baiting, and other low sports. "On Wednesday last, two women fought for a new shift valued at half-a-guinea, in the Spaw-Fields near Islington. The battle was won by a woman called Bruising Peg, who beat her antagonist in a terrible manner." —22nd June 1768.

But by far the most interesting ancient hostelrie that has submitted to the demolishing mania for improvement is the *Old Queen's Head*, formerly situate in the Lower Street, Islington. This stately edifice was one of the most perfect specimens of ancient domestic architecture in England. Under its venerable roof Sir Walter Raleigh, it is said, "puffed his pipe;" and might not Jack Falstaff have taken his ease there, when he journeyed to string a bow with the Finsbury archers? For many years it was a pleasant retreat for retired citizens, who quaffed their nut-brown beneath its primitive porch, and indulged in reminiscences of the olden time. Thither would little Quick, King George the Third's favourite actor, resort to drink cold punch, and "babble" of his theatrical contemporaries. Plays * were formerly acted there.

* The following curious "Old Queen's Head" play-bill, temp. George the Second, is presumed to be unique: —

G. II. R.

By a Company of Comedians, at the Queen's Head, in the Lower

Street, Islington,
This present evening will be acted a Tragedy, called the

Fair Penitent.
Sciolto, Mr. Malone. —Horatio, Mr. Johnson.

Altamont, Mr. Jones. —Lothario, Mr. Dunn.
Rosano, Mr. Harris. —Calista, Mrs. Harman.
Lavinia, Mrs. Malone. —Lucilla, Miss Platt.
To which will be added, a Farce called The Lying Valet.
Prices-Pit, 2s.; Gallery, Is. To begin at 7 o'clock."

On Monday, October 19, 1829, it was razed to the ground, to make room for a misshapen mass of modern masonry. The oak parlour has been preserved from the wreck, and is well worth a visit from the antiquary. Canonbury Tavern and Highbury Barn still maintain their festive honours. Farther a-field are the Sluice, or Eel-pie House; Copenhagen House; Hornsey-wood House, formerly the hunting seat of Queen Elizabeth; Chalk Farm; Jack Straw's Castle; the Spaniards, &c. as yet undefiled by pitiful prettinesses of bricks and mortar, and affording a delightful opportunity of enjoying pure air and pastime. The canonised Bishop of Lichfield and Mademoiselle St. Agnes have each their wells. What perambulator of the suburbs but knows St. Chad, in Gray's Inn Lane, and St. Agnes le Clair, * at Hoxton? Paneras **

* Whit, in Jonson's Bartholomew Fair, promises to treat his
company with a clean glass, washed with the water of Agnes
le Clare.
** "At Edward Martin's, at the Hornes at Pancrass, is that

excellent water, highly approved of by the most eminent phy-
sitians, and found by long experience to be a powerful
antidote against rising of the vapours, also against the
stone and gravel. It likewise cleanses the body, purifies
and sweetens the blood, and is a general and sovereign help
to nature. I shall open on Whitson-Monday, the 24th of May
1697; and there will be likewise dancing every Tuesday and
Thursday all the summer season at the place aforesaid, The
poor may drink the waters gratis." Then follow sixteen lines
of rhyme in praise of "this noble water," and inviting
ladies and gentlemen to drink of it. Of this rare hand-bill
no other copy is known.
"And although this place (Paneras) be as it were forsaken of

all, and true men seldome frequent the same but upon de-vyne
occasions, yet is it visyted and usually haunted of roages,
vagabondes, harlettes and theeves, who assemble not ther to
pray, but to wayte for praye, and manie fall into their
hands clothed, that are glad when they are escaped naked.
Walke not ther too late." —Speculi Britannio Pars, by John
Norden, MS. 1594.

and Hampstead Wells, renowned for their salubrious waters, are dried up. Though the two latter were professed marts for *aqua pura*, liquids more exhilarating were provided for those who relished stronger stimulants. We may therefore fairly assume that John Bull anciently travelled northward ho! when he rambled abroad for recreation.

As population increased, houses of entertainment multiplied to meet the demand. South, east, and west they rose at convenient distances, within the reach of a short stage, and a long pair of legs. Apollo Gardens, St. George's Fields; Bohemia's Head; Turnham Green; Cuper's Gardens, Lambeth; China Hall, Rotherhithe; Dog and Duck, St. George's Fields; Cherry Gardens Bowling-green, Rotherhithe; Cumberland Gardens, Vaux-hall; Spa Gardens, Bermondsey; Finch's Grotto Garden's, St. George's Fields; Smith's Tea Gardens, Vauxhall; Kendal House, Isleworth; New Wells, Goodman's Fields; Marble Hall, Vaux-hall; Staton's Tea-House, opposite Mary-le-bone Gardens; the Queen's Head and Artichoke, Mary-le-bone Fields; Ruckholt House, in Essex, of which facetious Jemmy Worsdale was the Apollo; Old Chelsea Bun-house; Queen Elizabeth's Cheesecake House, in Hyde Park; the Star and Garter Tavern, * and Don Saltero's coffeehouse, **

* "Star and Garter Tavern, Chelsea, 1763. Mr. Lowe will
display his uncommon abilities with watches, letters, rings,
swords, cards, and enchanted clock, which absolutely tells
the thoughts of any person in the company. The astonishing
Little Man, only four inches high, pays his respects to the
company, and vanishes in a flash of fire. Mr. Lowe commands
nine lighted candles to fly from the table to the top of the
ceiling! Added, a grand entertainment, with musick and
dancing, &c. &c."
** The great attraction of Don Saltero's Coffeehouse was its

collection of rarities, a catalogue of which was published
as a guide to the visitors. It comprehends almost every
description of curiosity, natural and artificial. "Tigers'
tusks; the Pope's candle; the skeleton of a Guinea-pig; a
fly-cap monkey; a piece of the true Cross; the Four
Evangelists' heads cut on a cherry-stone; the King of
Morocco's tobacco-pipe;
Mary Queen of Scot's pincushion; Queen Elizabeth's prayer-

book; a pair of Nun's stockings; Job's ears, which grew on a
tree; a frog in a tobacco stopper," and five hundred more
odd relies! The Don had a rival, as appears by "A Catalogue
of the Rarities to be seen at Adams's, at the Royal Swan, in
Kingsland Road, leading from Shoreditch Church, 1756." Mr.
Adams exhibited, for the entertainment of the curious, "Miss
Jenny Cameron's shoes; Adam's eldest daughter's hat; the
heart of the famous Bess Adams, that was hanged at Tyburn
with Lawyer Carr, January 18, 1736-7; Sir Walter Raleigh's
tobacco-pipe; Vicar of Bray's clogs; engine to shell green
pease with; teeth that grew in a fish's belly; Black Jack's
ribs; the very comb that Abraham combed his son Isaac and
Jacob's head with; Wat Tyler's spurs; rope that cured
Captain Lowry of the head-ach, ear-ach, tooth-ach and belly-
ach; Adam's key of the fore and back door of the Garden of
Eden, &e. &e." These are only a few out of five hundred

others equally marvellous. Is this strange catalogue a quiz
on Don Saltero?

Chelsea; Mary-le-bone and Ranelagh Gardens; *
  * The Rotunda was first opened on the 5th of April, 1742,
with a public breakfast. At Ranelagh House (Gentleman's
Magazine for 1767) on the 12th of May, were performed the
much-admired catches and glees, selected from the curious
collection of the Catch Club; being the first of the kind
publickly exhibited in this or any other kingdom. The
entertainment consisted of the favourite catches and glees,
composed by the most eminent masters of the last and present
age, by a considerable number of the best vocal and
instrumental performers. The choral and instrumental parts
were added, to give the catches and glees their proper
effect in so large an amphitheatre; being composed for that
purpose by Dr. Arne. The Masquerades at Ranelagh are
represented in Fielding's "Amelia" as dangerous to morals,
and the "Connoisseur" satirises their Eve-like beauties with
caustic humour.

and the illuminated saloons and groves of Vauxhall. * These, and many others, bear testimony
to the growing spirit of national jollity during a considerable part of the eighteenth century.
How few now remain, "the sad historians of the pensive tale," of their bygone merriments!
  * "The extreme beauty and elegance of this place is well
known to almost every one of my readers; and happy is it for
me that it is so, since to give an adequate idea of it would
exceed my power of description. To delineate the particular
beauties of these gardens would indeed require as much
pains, and as much paper too, as to rehearse all the good
actions of their master; whose life proves the truth of an
observation which I have read in some other writer, that a
truly elegant taste is generally accompanied with an
excellency of heart; or in other words, that true virtue is

  indeed nothing else but true taste." Amelia, b. ix. c. ix.

CHAPTER III.

The Genius of Mirth never hit upon a happier subject than the humours of Cockneyland. "Man made the town and a pretty sample it is of the maker! Behind or before the counter, at home and abroad, the man of business or the beau, the Cockney is the same whimsical original, baffling imitation, and keeping description in full cry. See him sally forth on a fine Sunday to inhale his weekly mouthful of fresh air, * the world all before him, where to choose occupying his meditations, till he finds himself elevated on High-gate Hill or Hampstead Heath. From those magnificent summits he beholds in panorama, woods, valleys, lofty trees, and stately turrets, not forgetting that glorious cupola dedicated to the metropolitan saint, which points out the locality where, six days out of the seven, his orisons are paid to a deity not contemplated by the apostle.

* Moorfields, Pimlico Path, and the Exchange, were the fashionable parades of the citizens in the days of Elizabeth and James I.

He lays himself out for enjoyment, and seeks good entertainment for man and (if mounted, or in his cruelty-van) for horse. Having taken possession of a window that commands the best prospect, the waiter is summoned, the larder called over, the ceremony of lunch commenced, and, with that habitual foresight which marks his character, the all-important meal that is to follow, duly catered for. The interval for rural adventure arrives; he takes a stroll; the modest heath-bell and the violet turn up their dark blue eyes to him; and he finds blackberries enough (as Falstaff's men did *linen!*) on every hedge. Dinner served up, and to his mind, he warms and waxes cosey, jokes with the waiter, talks anything, and to anybody,

Drinks a glass

To his favourite lass!"

pleased with himself, and willing to please. If his phraseology provoke a laugh, he puts it to the account of his smart sayings, and is loudest in the chorus; for when the ball of ridicule is flying about, he ups with his racket and strikes it off to his neighbour.

He is the worst mortal in the world to be put out of his way. The slightest inconvenience, the most trifling departure from his wonted habits, he magnifies into a serious evil. His well-stocked larder and cheerful fireside are ever present to his view: beef and pudding have taken fast hold of him; and, in default of these, his spirits flag; he is hipped and melancholy. Foreign travel exhibits him in his natural light; his peculiarities break forth with whimsical effect, which, though not always the most amiable, are nevertheless entertaining. He longs to see the world; and having with due ceremony arranged his wardrobe, put money in his purse, and procured his passport to strange lands, he sets forward, buttoned up in his native consequence, to the capital of the grand monarque, to rattle dice, and drink champagne. His expectations are not the most reasonable. Without considering the different manners and customs of foreign parts, he bends to nobody, yet takes it as an affront if everybody bend not to him! His baggage is subjected to rigorous search. The infernal *parlez-vous!* —nothing like *this* ever happens in old England! His passport is inspected, and his person identified. The inquisitors! —to take the length and breadth of a man, his complexion and calling! The barriers are closed, and he must *bivouac* in the Diligence the live-long night. Monstrous tyranny! Every rogue enjoys free ingress and egress in a land of liberty! He calls for the bill of fare, the "*carte,*" and in his selection puts the cart before the horse! Of course there is a horrible conspiracy to poison him! The wines, too, are sophisticated. The champagne is gooseberry; the Burgundy, Pontac; and the *vin ordinaire* neither better nor worse than a dose of "Braithwait's Intermediate." The houses are dirty and dark; the streets muddy and gay; the madames and mademoiselles pretty well, I thank'e; and the Mounseers a pack of chattering mountebanks, stuck over with little bits of red ribbon, and blinded with snuff and whiskers! Even the air is too thin: he misses his London smoke! And but one drunken dog has he encountered (and *he* was his countryman!) to bring to fond remembrance the land we live in! * What wonder, then, if he sigh for luxurious bachelorship in a Brighton boarding-house? Beds made, dinner provided, the cook scolded by proxy, and all the agreeable etceteras incidental to good living set before him, without the annoyance of idle servants, and the trouble of ordering, leaving him to the delightful abandonment of every care, save that of feasting and pleasure-taking!

* Beware of those who are homeless by choice. Show me the
man who cares no more for one place than another, and I will
show you in the same person one who loves nothing but
himself. Home and its attachments are dear to the ingenuous
mind-to cherish their remembrance is the surest proof of a
noble spirit.

With moderate gastronomical and soporific powers, he may manage to eat, drink, and sleep out three guineas a-week; for the sea is a rare provocative to feeding and repose. Besides, a Brighton boarding-house is a change both of air and condition; bachelors become Benedicks, and widows wives, for three guineas a-week, more or less! It furnishes an extensive assortment of acquaintance, such as nowhere else can be found domiciled under the same roof. Each finds it necessary to make himself and herself agreeable. Pride, *mauvaise honte*, modesty? that keep people apart in general society, all give way. The inmates are like one family; and when they break up for the season, 'tis often in pairs!

"Uncle Timothy to a T! Pardon me, sir, but he must have sat to you for the portrait. If you unbutton his native consequence a little, and throw a jocular light over his whim-whams and caprices, the likeness would be perfect."

This was addressed to us by a lively, well-to-do-in-the-world-looking little gentleman, who lolled in an arm-chair opposite to an adjoining window, taking things in an easy pick-tooth way, and coquetting with a pint of old port.

"The picture, sir, that you are pleased to identify is not an individual, but a species —a slight off-hand sketch, taken from general observation."

"Indeed! That's odd."

"Even so."

"Never knew Uncle Tim was like all the world. Would, for all the world's sake, that all the world were like Uncle Tim!"

"A worthy character."

"Sir, he holds in his heart all the four honours-Truth, Honesty, Affection, and Benevolence-in the great game of humanity, and plays not for lucre, but love! I fear you think me strangely familiar-impertinent too, perhaps. But that portrait, so graphical and complete, was a spell as powerful as Odin's to break silence. Besides, I detest your exclusives-sentimentalising! soliloquising! —Their shirt-collars, affectedly turned down, puts my choler up! Give *me* the human face divine, the busy haunts of men, the full tide of human existence."

The little gentleman translated the "full tide" into a full glass to our good healths and better acquaintance, at the same time drawing his chair nearer, and presenting a handsomely embossed card, on which was inscribed, in delicate Italian calligraphy, "Mr. Benjamin Bosky, Dry-salter, Little Britain."

Drysalter —he looked like a thirsty soul!

"Pleasant prospect from this window; you may count every steeple in London. There's the 'tall bully,' —how gloriously his flaming top-knot glistens in the setting sun! Wouldn't give a fig for the best view in the world, if it didn't take in the dome of St. Paul's! Beshrew the Vandal architect that cut down those beautiful elms. —

'The rogue the gallows as his fate foresees,

And bears the like antipathy to trees,'

and run up the wigwam pavilions, the Tom-foolery baby-houses, the run mad, shabby-genteel, I-would-if-I-could-but-I-can't cottages *ornée-ornée?* —horney! —the cows popping in their heads at the parlour windows, frightening the portly proprietors from their propriety and port!"

It was clear that Mr. Bosky was not to be so frightened; for he drew another draught on his pint decanter, though sitting beneath the umbrage of a huge pair of antlers that were fixed against the wall, under which innumerable Johnny New-comes had been sworn, according to ancient custom, at the Horns at Highgate. It was equally clear, too, that Mr. Bosky *himself* might have sat for the portrait that he had so kindly appropriated to Uncle Timothy.

A fine manly voice without was heard to troll with joyous melody —

"The lark, that tirra-lirra chants —

With hey! with hey! the thrush and the jay,

Are summer songs for me and my aunts,

While we lie tumbling in the hay."

"Uncle Tim! Uncle Tim!" shouted the mercurial little Drysalter, and up he started as if he had been galvanised, scampered out of the room, made but one leap from the top of the stairs to the bottom, descended *à plomb*, was up again before we had recovered from our surprise, and introduced a middle-aged, rosy-faced gentleman, "more fat than bard beseems," with a perforating eye and a most satirical nose. "Uncle Timothy, gentlemen. —A friend or two, (if I may presume to call them so,) Uncle Timothy, that I have fallen in with most unexpectedly and agreeably."

There is a certain "I no *not* like thee, *Doctor Fell*," feeling, and an "I do," that have rarely deceived us. With the latter, the satirical-nosed gentleman inspired us at first sight. There was the humorist, with a dash of the antiquary, heightened with a legible expression that nature sometimes stamps on her higher order of intelligences. What a companion, we thought, for *"Round about our coal fire"* on a winter's evening, or, *"Under the green-wood tree"* on a summer's clay!

We were all soon very good company; and half a dozen tea-totallers, who had called for a pint of ale and six glasses, having discussed their long division and departed, we had the room to ourselves.

"Know you, Uncle Timothy," cried Mr. Bosky, with a serio-comic air, "that the law against vagabonds and sturdy beggars is in full force, seeing that you carol in broad daylight, and on the King's highway, a loose catch appertaining to one of the most graceless of their fraternity?"

"Beggars! varlet! I beg nothing of thee but silence, which is gold, if speech be silver. * Is there aught unseemly in my henting the stile with the merry Autolycus? Vagabonds! The order is both ancient and honourable. Collect they not tribute for the *crown?* Take heed, Benjamin, lest thine be scored on! Are they not solicitors as old as Adam?"

* A precept of the Koran.

"And thieves too, from Mercury downwards, Uncle Timothy."

"Conveyancers, sirrah! sworn under the Horns never to beg when they can steal. Better lose my purse than my patience. Thou, scapegrace! rob best me of my patience, and beggest nought but the question."

"Were not the beggars once a jovial crew, sir?" addressing ourselves to the middle-aged gentleman with the satirical nose.

"Right merry! Gentlemen —

'Sweeter than honey

Is other men's money.'

"The joys of to-day were never marred by the cares of to-morrow; for to-morrow was left to take care of itself; and its sun seldom went down upon disappointment. The beggar, * though his pockets be so low, that you might dance a jig in one of them without breaking your shins against a halfpenny; while from the other you might be puzzled to extract as much coin as would pay turnpike for a walking-stick, sings with a light heart; his fingers no less light! playing administrators to the farmer's poultry, and the good housewife's sheets that whiten every hedge!

* "Cast our nabs and cares away —
This is Beggars' Holiday;
In the world look out and see
Who's so happy a king as he?
At the crowning of our king,
Thus we ever dance and sing.
Where's the nation lives so free
And so merry as do we?
Be it peace, or be it war,
Here at liberty we are.
Hang all Harmanbccks! we cry,
And the Cuffinquiers, too, by.
We enjoy our ease and rest,
To the fields we are not press'd;
When the subsidy's increas'd,
We are not a penny cost;
Nor are we called into town
To be troubled with a gown;
Nor will any go to law
With a beggar for a straw.
All which happiness he brags
He doth owe unto his rags!"
Of all the mad rascals that belong to this fraternity, the

Abraham-Man is the most fantastic. He calls himself by the name of *Poor Tom*, and, coming near to any one, cries out "Poor Tom's a-cold!" Some are exceedingly merry, and do nothing but sing songs, fashioned out of their own brains; some will dance; others will do nothing but laugh or weep; others are dogged, and so sullen, both in look and speech, that, spying but small company in a house, they boldly enter, compelling the servants, through fear, to give them what they demand, which is commonly something that will yield ready money. The "*Upright Man*" (who in ancient times was, next to the king and those "o' th' blood," in dignity,) is not a more terrible enemy to the farmer's poultry than Poor Tom.

How finely has Shakspeare spiritualized this strange

character in the part of Edgar in King Lear!
The middle aisle of old St. Paul's was a great resort for

beggars.
"In Paul's Church, by a pillar,

Sometimes ye have me stand, sir,
With a writ that shews
What care and woes
I pass by sea and land, sir.
With a seeming bursten belly,
I look like one half dead, sir,
Or else I beg With a wooden leg,
And with a night-cap on my head, sir."
Blind Beggars Song.

Wit and Drollery. Jovial Poems. 1682.

Mendicity is a monarchy; it is governed by peculiar laws, and has a language of its own. Reform
has waged war to the knife with it. The *soap-eater*, whose ingenious calling was practised in
the streets of London as far back as Henry the Eighth and Edward the Sixth, is admonished to
apply the raw material of his trade to an exterior use; * and the tatterdemalions of the Beggar's
Opera no longer enjoy the privileges that belonged to their ancestors three centuries ago, when
the Barbican, Turnmill Street, and Houndsditch, rang with their nocturnal orgies; and where
not unfrequently "an alderman hung in chains" gratified their delicate appetites; as in more
recent times,
   * Like the Dutchman, who being desired to rub his rheumatic
limb with brandy, improved upon the prescription. "I dosh
better as dat," roared Mynheer, "I drinks de prandy, and den
I rubs mine leg wit de pottle!"

the happy but bygone days of Dusty Bob and Billy Waters. * The well- known mendicants of St.
Paul's churchyard, Waithman's crossing, and Par- liament-Street have, by a sweeping act of the
   * The Sons of Carew Made a mighty ado —
The news was a terrible damper;
The blind, in their fright,
Soon recovered their sight,
And the lame thought it prudent to scamper.
They summon'd the nobs of their nation,
St. Giles's was all consternation;
The street they call Dyott
Portended a riot,
Belligerents all botheration!
Mendicity Bill,
Who for prowess and skill
Was dubb'd the bold Ajax of Drury,
With a whistle and stride
Flung his fiddle aside,
And his sky-scraper cock'd in a fury!

"While a drop's to be had to get queer-a,
I'll ne'er go a-begging for beer-a:
Our ducks and green peas
Shall the constable seize —
Our sherry, our port, and Madeira?"
But Law the bold heroes did floor, O!
On dainty fine morsels no more,
O! They merrily sup:
Dusty Bob's doubled up —
Poor Bill's occupation is o'er, O!

legislature, been compelled to brush; their brooms are laid up in ordinary, to make rods for their backs, till the very stones they once swept are ready to rise and mutiny. Well might Epicurus say, 6 Poverty, when cheerful, ceases to be poverty.'"

"Suppose, gentlemen, as the day is closing in, we each of us take our wallet and staff, trudge forth, and levy contribution! I am in a valiant humour to cry 'stand!' to a too powerfully refreshed citizen of light weight and heavy purse." And Mr. Bosky suited the action to the word.

"Sit down, soul of a grasshopper! The very ghost of his wife's tweezers would snuff out thy small courage. Thou hast slandered the beggars' craft, and, like greater rogues, shalt be condemned to live by thine own! Thou 'gibier de potence!' Thou a prigger! Why thou art only a simple prig, turned out by thy tailor! Steal if thou canst into our good graces; redeem thy turpitude by emulating at least *one* part of the beggars' calling, ballad-singing. Manifest thy deep contrition by a song."

"A bargain, Uncle Timothy. If thou wilt rake from a sly corner of that old curiosity shop, thy brain, some pageant of the ancient brethren of *Bull-Feathers-Hall*. What place more fitting for such pleasant chronicle, than the *Horns at Highgate?*"

This proposal being assented to by the middle-aged gentleman, Mr. Bosky "rosined," (swallowed a bumper) and sounded a musical flourish as a *preludio*.

"But gentlemen, you have not said what I shall sing."

"*Beggars*, Mr. Bosky, must not be choosers!"

"Something heroic?

Wonderful General Wolfe,

Uncommon brave; partic'lar!

Swam over the Persian Gulf,

And climb'd rocks perpendic'lar!

Sentimental and tender?

'The mealy potato it grows

In your garden, Miss Maddison cries;

'So I cannot walk there, for I knows,

Like love-that potatoes have *eyes!*'"

"No buffoonery, if you please, Benjamin Bosky," cried Uncle Tim.
"Or furiously funny-eh?"

My pipe at your peeper I'll light,

So pop out your jazey so curly;

A jorum of *yeast* over night,

Will make you next morning *rise* early!

Arrah I thro' your casement and blind

I'll jist sky a copper and toss one,,

If you do not, Miss Casey, look kind,

Wid your good-natured eye that's a *cross* one!"

"My good friends," sighed the middle-aged gentleman, "this unhappy nephew of mine hath as many ballads in his budget as Sancho Panza had proverbs in his belly. And yet-but he seems determined to break my heart."

Mr. Bosky appeared more bent upon cruelly cracking Uncle Timothy's sides.

"Now I bethink me of a ditty of true love, full of mirth and pastime." And Mr. Bosky began in a droll falsetto, and with mock gravity,

THE LAST OF THE PIGTAILS.=

"When I heard she was married, thinks I to myself,

I'm now an old bachelor laid on the shelf;

The last of the Pigtails that smok'd at the Sun,

My Dora has done me, and I am undone!

I call'd at her lodgings in Dean Street, Soho;

My love's gone for ever! alas! she's no go.

A nip of prime Burton shall warm my cold blood,

Since all my enjoyments are nipp'd in the bud!

The picture of famine, my frame half reduced;

I can't eat a quarter the vittles I us'd!

O dear! what can ail me? I once was so hale —

When my head's underground let this verse tell my tale.

I sought the Old Bailey, despairing and lank,

To take my last cut of boil'd buttock and flank,

To sniff my last sniff in those savoury scenes,

And sigh my last sigh over carrots and greens!

'A pot of mild porter, and take off the chill,'

A damsel came smirking, in curls, cap, and frill.

I started! she scream'd! 'twas my Dora! off flew

Flank, buttock, greens, carrots, and peas-pudding too!

'Yes, I am your true love!' she curtsey'd, and said,

'At home I'm a widow, but here I'm a maid!

My spouse kick'd the bucket last Sunday at Leeds,

And left me, a rose-bud, all cover'd with weeds.'

'For all your fine speeches, a widow, in fine,

Is an article madam, I mean to decline I

Though wedlock's a bolus to physic and fright,

A black draught —a widow! would finish me quite."

"A vile stave! Commend me to 'fonde Elderton,' * and the troop of 'metre ballad-mongers' that sleep among the dull of ancient days; but save me from that doleful doggrel of which, I shrewdly suspect, thou, Benjamin Bosky, art the perpetrator.
   * The following is a description of Elderton by a
contemporary writer in 1582. See "Reporte of the Death and
Martyr-dome of M. Campion, Jesuit, &c."
"Fonde Elderton, call in thy foolish rhime,

Thy scurill balates are to bad to sell;
Let good men rest, and mende thy self in time,
Confesse in prose thou hast not metred well;
Or if thy folly cannot chuse but fayne
Write alehotise toys, blaspheme not in thy vain."

It smells woundily of thy peculiar locality, and might have befringed the walls of Bedlam and Soho. Henceforth be the *Magnus Apollo* of thy native *Little Britain*, and divide the crown with Thomas Delony, of huck-ster-fame! Jack of Newbery, the Gentle Craft, garlands, strange histories,

    'And such small deer,

    Had been Tom's food for many a year,'
and may serve for *thine*, Benjamin; for, in poetical matters, thou hast the maw of a kite and the digestion of an ostrich."
  "A sprat to catch a herring!"
  "A tittlebat! thou triton of the minnows!"
  "But the *Bull-Feather!* Uncle Timothy, the *Bull-Feather*

    'Must not be forgotten

    Until the world's rotten.'
Let me refresh thy memory. Once upon a time — —"
  "Peace, babbler! If I must take the bull by the horns, it shall be without thy jockeyship. I will not ride double. 'Tis an idle tale, gentlemen; but there are charms in association that may render it interesting."
  Uncle Tim regaled with a fragrant pinch his satirical nose, and began

"A MIRTHFUL PAGEANT OF THE BULL-FEATHERS TO THE HORNS AT HIGHGATE.

"The ancient brethren of Bull-Feathers-Hall were a club of warm citizens; 'rich fellows enough! fellows that have had losses, with everything handsome about them.' Their place of rendezvous was the Chequer-Yard in Whitechapel, every Tuesday and Thursday at seven o'clock. The intent of their meeting was to solace themselves with harmless merriment, and promote good fellowship * among neighbours.

     * How good fellowship had declined a century before this
will be seen by the following extract from a black-letter
ballad, intituled, "A balade declaryng how neybourhed loue,
and trew dealyng is gone. Imprinted at London by Richard
Lant." (Circa 1560.)
"Where shall one fynde a man to trust,

Alwaye to stande in tyme of neede;
Thee most parte now, they are unjust,
Fayre in wordes, but false in deede:
Neybourhed nor loue is none,
True dealyng now is fled and gone."

The president, arrayed in his crimson satin gown, with his cap furred and surmounted by a pair of antlers, and seated in a chair of state beneath a canopy, commanded (by the crier of the court) every member to be covered; and in the twinkling of an eye their horns were exalted. On a velvet cushion before him lay the comuted sceptre and sword. The brethren drank out of horn-cups, and made oath upon a book of statutes bound in horn. Their revenues were derived from a toll upon all the gravel carried up Highgate Hill and Hornsey; —Cow-lane; and beyond sea, Crook-horn; Leg-horn; and Ox-mantown paying them yearly tribute! On Monday, the 2nd May, 1664, a deputation of the fraternity met at *Busby's Folly*, * near Sadler's Wells, ** Islington, from whence they marched in grand order, headed by their Captain of Pioneers, with between thirty and forty of his men, with pick-axes and spades to level the hill, and baskets to carry the gravel;

     * A print of Busbys Folly occurs in a rare volume, called
"Views of divers noted places near London, 1731," of which
Gough, the antiquary never saw hut one copy. Its site is
particularly pointed out in Ogilby's map of London to
Holyhead.
* "Sadler's Wells being lately opened, there is likely to be

a great resort of strolling damsels, half-pay officers,
peripatetic tradesmen, tars, butchers, and others, musically
inclined." —Weekly Journal, 16th March 1718.
It is curious to read at the bottom of the old bills and

advertisements of Sadler's Wells the following *alarming* announcements: —"A *horse patrol* will be sent in the New
Road that night for the *protection* of the nobility and
gentry who go from the squares and that end of the town. The
road also towards the city will be properly *guarded*."
"June 1783. *Patroles of horse and foot* are stationed from

Sadler's Wells' gate along the New Road to Tottenham Court turnpike; likewise from the City Road to Moorfields; also to St. John Street, and across the Spafields to Rosoman Row, from the hours of eight to eleven."

After which followed the standard, an enormous pair of horns mounted on a lofty pole, borne by three officers, and attended by the master of the ceremonies, the mace-bearer, the herald at-arms, the sword-bearer and the crier, their footsteps keeping time to a flourish of trumpets and horns. *

* "On Tuesday next, being Shrove Tuesday, there will be a fine *hog bar-byqu'd* whole, at the house of Peter Brett, at the Rising Sun, in Islington Road, with other diversions. — Note. It is the house where the ox was roasted whole at Christmas last." Mist's Journal, Feb. 9, 1726.
A hog barbecu'd is a West Indian term, and means a hog

roasted whole, stuffed with spice, and basted with Madeira wine. Oldfield, an eminent glutton of former days, gormandised away a fortune of fifteen hundred pounds a-year. Pope thus alludes to him —
"Oldfield, with more than harpy throat endu'd,

Cries, 'Send me, gods, a whole hog barbecu'd!'"
"On Thursday next, being 13th March 1718, the Bowling-

Greens will be opened at the Prospect House, Islington, where there will be accommodation for all gentlemen bowlers."
Bowling-greens were among the many amusements of Merrie

England. The author of "Night Thoughts" established a bowling-green in the village confided to his pastoral care, for innocent and healthful recreation.
"True piety is cheerful as the day."

"May 1757. To be bowl'd for on Monday next, at the Red Cow,

in St. George's Fields, a pair of Silver Buckles, value fourteen shillings, at five pins, each pin a yard apart. He that brings most pins at three bowls has the buckles, if the money is in; if not, the money each man has put in. Three bowls for sixpence, and a pint of beer out of it, for the good of the house,"

Arriving near the Gate-house —(gentlemen, we are within a few yards of the *very spot!*) —the viceroy of the gravel-pits went forth to meet them, presenting the horn of plenty as a token of hearty welcome; and passing through the gate, they made a circuit round the old pond, and returning to their starting-post, one of the brethren delivered a poetical oration, humorously descriptive of Bull-Feathers-Hall, and expatiating on the antiquity and dignity of horns. The speech being ended, they paraded to the dinner-table, which groaned under every luxury of the season. There they regaled themselves, amidst the sounding of trumpets and the winding of horns. Between dinner and dessert, those of the officers who had singing faces volunteered a festive chant, in which the whole company joined chorus.

> The shortest, the tallest, the foulest, the fairest,
>
> The fattest, the leanest, the commonest, rarest,
>
> When they and their cronies are merry together,
>
> Will all do their best to advance the *Bull's Feather!*

> A king and a cobbler, a lord and a loon,
>
> A prince and a pedlar, a courtier, a clown;
>
> Put all their degrees and conditions together,
>
> Are liable always to wear the *Bull's Feather.*

Any candidate desirous of being admitted a member of the fraternity was proposed by the sword-bearer; and the master of the ceremonies placing him in the adopting chair, the comptroller made three ejaculations, upon which the brethren doffed their hats. Then the master of the ceremonies exchanged his own comuted castor for a cap, and administered to his newly elected brother, on a book horned on all sides, an oath in rhyme, recapitulating a long string of duties belonging to their peculiar art and mystery, and enjoining their strict performance.

> Lastly, observe thou shalt esteem none other
>
> Equal to this our club; —so welcome brother!" *

* Bull-Feathers-Hall; or, The Antiquity and Dignity of Horns amply shown. Also a Description of the Manners, Rites, Customs, and Revenues belonging to that ingenious and

numerous society of Bull-Feathers-Hall. London: printed for the Society of Bull-Feathers-Hall. 1664. A copy of this rare tract produced at Bindley's sale five

pounds ten shillings, and at Strette's five pounds.

"Thus ends my story, gentlemen; and if you have found it tedious, visit the offence on the Lauréat of Little Britain, by enjoining him the penance of a bumper of salt and water."

But mine host of the Horns, very prim about the wig, his coat marked with his apron strings, which left a seam all round, as if he had been cut in two, and afterwards stitched together again, having been slyly telegraphed, that obedient functionary, who was as neat as his wines, entered, bearing before him what Mr. Bosky facetiously called "*a good afternoon,*" to wit, a brimming bowl, in which *whiskey* had been judiciously substituted for *salt.* Uncle Timothy rose; so did the voice of Mr. Bosky! and to such an altitude as to drown his expostulations in contumacious carolling, which, truth obliges us to add, received laughing impunity from the company.

Come merrily push round the toddy,

    The cold winter nights are set in;

To a roquelaire wrapp'd round the body

    Add a lining of lamb's-wool within!

This liquor was brew'd by my grandam,

    In a snug quiet still of her own;

'Tis fit for my Lord in his tandem,

    And royal King Will on his throne.

In the glass, see it sparkles and ripples,

    And how it runs merrily down!

The absolute monarch of tipples,

    And richly deserving a crown!

Of mirth 'tis the spring and the fountain,

    And Helicon's stream to the Muse;

The pleasantest dew of the mountain —

    So give it, good fellows, its dues.

It opens the heart of the miser,

    And conjures up truth from the knave;

It makes my Lord Bishop look wiser —

    More frisky the curate, his slave.

It makes the glad spirit still gladder,

    And moistens the splenetic vein;

When I can't see a hole through a ladder,

    It mounts on the sly to my brain.

Then push round the glasses, be cosey,

Fill bumpers to whiskey and whim;

Good luck to each man, while his nose he

Hangs pleasantly over the brim!

There's nothing remarkably odd in

A gent who to nap is inclined;

He can't want a blanket while noddin',

When he's two or three sheets in the wind.

"Sirs," exclaimed the satirical-nosed gentleman, "I alone am to blame for this audacious vivacity of my sister's son. I turned it on, and lo! it hath inundated us with buffoonery. Sirrah!" shaking the identical plant that Dr. Johnson travelled with through the Hebrides, Tom Davies's shilling's worth for the broad shoulders of Macpherson, "thou shalt find in future that I joke with my cudgel!" *

* "Hombre burlo yo con mi escopeta!" was the characteristic
saying of the celebrated Spanish bandit Josse Maria.

But it was labour in vain; the "laughing devil," so peculiar to the eye of the middle-aged gentleman, leered ludicrous defiance to his half-smiling half-sulky mouth. As a last determined effort, he shook his *head* at Mr. Bosky, whereupon Mr. Bosky shook his *hand*. The mutual grasp was electrical, and thus ended the brief farce of Uncle Timothy's furor.

"Gentlemen," said Mr. Bosky, in a subdued tone, "if I could believe that Uncle Timothy had been really in earnest, my penitential punch should be turned into bitter aloes, sweetened with assafoetida, to expiate an offence against the earliest, best, and dearest friend I ever knew! But I owed Uncle Timothy a revenge. Of late he has worn a serious brow, a mournful smile. There has been melancholy in his mirth, and sadness in his song; this, he well knows, cuts me to the quick; and it is not until he is angry-or, rather" (smiling affectionately at Uncle Tim) "until he *thinks* himself so," —(here Uncle Tim gave Mr. Bosky one of his blandest looks) "that he is 'cockered and spirited up,' and the cloud passes away. What do I not owe to my more than father?"

Uncle Timothy got enormously fidgety; he beat Lucifer's tattoo with his right leg, and began fumbling in both waistcoat pockets for his snuffbox.

"A precocious young urchin, gentlemen, in every sort of mischief!" interrupted Uncle Timothy with nervous impetuosity, "on whose birch-provoking little body as many besoms were bestowed as would set up the best chandler in Christendom!"

"An orphan too —"

"Benjamin Bosky! Benjamin Bosky! don't —*don't* be a blockhead!"

"He reared, educated, and made me what I am. And, though *sometimes* I may too far presume upon his good-nature, and foolishly, fondly fancy myself a boy again —"

"Putting hot parched peas and cherry-stones into my boots, as being good for chilblains, * and strewing the inside of my bed with horse-hair to send me to sleep, after a fortnight's dancing round my room with the toothache!"

"Three strokes from the club of Caliban would not so effectually break my head, as the reflection would break my heart that I had done aught to displease him! Now, gentlemen, the murder's out; and if for blabbing family secrets Uncle Timothy in his wrath *will* insist upon fining me-an extra glass of punch! in truth I must submit and sip."

"You see, my good friends," said Uncle Timothy, after a short pause, "that the rogue is incorrigible! But Benjamin Bosky" —(here Uncle Tim tried to look sententious, and adopted the *bowwow* style) —"I cannot but blush, deeply blush for thy morals, or rather, Benjamin Bosky, for thy no-morals, when thou canst thus blurt thy flattery in my face, because I simply did a duty that kindred imposed upon me, and the sweet consciousness of performing made light and pleasant.

* When the dreadful earthquake at Lisbon had frightened the
English people into an apprehension of the like calamity at
home, a quack advertised his pills as "being good for
earthquakes."

What I have done was at the whisper of a higher monitor than man; and from Him alone-even if I could suppose myself worthy, which I do not —I hope for reward. He who is capable of ingratitude is incapable of any virtue. But gratitude, the most dignified return we can lavish on our benefactor, is the silent aspiration of the heart, and must not, good Benjamin, be placarded on every wall, like a play-bill, a lottery puff, or thy rigmarole ballads, three yards for a penny! There is not a being, however humble his station, but may find some deserving object to awake his friendship and share his benevolence. And be assured, dear Benjamin, that a judicious and timely distribution of fortune's good gifts is the best preparation for that final moment when we must resign them altogether.

> And when life's sweet fable ends,
>
> May soul and body part like friends;
>
> No quarrels, murmurs, no delay —
>
> A kiss, a sigh, and so away."

"As Cicero said of Plato, I say of Uncle Timothy —I would rather be wrong with *him* than right with anybody else. One more volunteer from the Laureate's 'three yards for a penny,' and then my nest of nightingales —"

"Tom-tits! Benjamin Bosky, tom-tits!"

"Well, then, tom-tits! dear Uncle Timothy-shall go to roost for the night."

MR. BOSKY'S L'ENVOY,=

From childhood he rear'd me, how fondly my heart

 Forgets not, nor lets not my tongue silent be;

But whispers, while sweet tears of gratitude start,

 A blessing and pray'r for his kindness to me!

I'll breathe not his name, though its record is deep

 In my warm beating bosom, for fear he should frown,

Go read it where angels their register keep

 Of the gifted and good, for 'tis there written down.

The conversation now took a more lively turn. Mr. Bosky fired off his jokes right and left; and if there be truth in physiognomy, the animated countenance of Uncle Timothy beamed with complacency and joy. He was in full song, and showered forth his wit and eloquence in glorious profusion, beauty following upon beauty. Thus another Attic hour glided imperceptibly away. The midnight chimes at length admonished us to depart. A galaxy of stars had risen in the unclouded firmament, and a refreshing air breathed around. And as we had many times during the evening filled *our* horns, the harvest moon had filled *hers* also to light us home.

CHAPTER IV.

A merry morning, Eugenio. Did not soft slumbers and pleasant dreams follow the heart-stirring lucubrations of Uncle Timothy? I am mistaken if you rose not lighter and happier, and in more perfect peace with yourself and the world."

"My dreams were of ancient minstrelsy, Christmas gambols, May-day games, and merriments. Methought Uncle Timothy was a portly Apollo, Mr. Bosky a rosy Pan —"

"And you and I, Eugenio?"

"Foremost in the throng —"

"Of capering satyrs! Well, though our own dancing * days are over, we still retain a relish for that elegant accomplishment.

* There were rare dancing doings at The original dancing
room at the field-end of King-Street, Bloomsbury,.
in the year 1742
Hickford's great room, Panton-Street, Haymarket, 1743

Mitre Tavern, Charing-Cross,... 1743

Barber's Hall,... 1745

Richmond Assembly,... 1745

Lambeth Wells,....1747

Duke's long room, Paternoster-Row,.. 1748

Large Assembly Room at the Two Green Lamps, near Exeter

Change, (at the particular desire of Jubilee Diekey!)... in
the year 1749 The large room next door to the Hand and
Slippers, Long-Lane, West Smithfield,... 1750 Lambeth Wells,
where a Penny Wedding, in the Scotch manner, was celebrated
for the benefit of a young couple,...... 1752 Old Queen's
Head, in Cock-Lane, Lambeth,. 1755 and at Mr. Bell's, at the
sign of the Ship, in the Strand, where, in 1755, a Scotch
Wedding was kept. The bride "to be dressed without any
linen; all in ribbons, and green flowers, with Scotch masks.
There will be three bag-pipes; a band of Scotch music, &c.
&c. To begin precisely at two o'clock. Admission, two
shillings and sixpence."

As antiquaries, we have a reverence for dancing. Noah danced before the ark. The boar's head and the wine and wassail were crowned with a dance to the tune of 'The Black Almayne,' 'My Lorde Marques Galyarde,' and 'The firste Traces of due Passa.'

> 'Merrily danc'd the Quaker's wife,
>
> And merrily danc'd the Quaker!'

Why not? Orpheus charmed the four-footed family with his fiddle: shall it have less effect on the two?

"The innocent and the happy, while the dews of youth are upon them, dance to the music of their own hearts. 'See the blind beggar dance, the cripple sing!' The Irishman has his lilt; the Scotchman his reel, which he not unfrequently dances to his own *particular fiddle!* and the Englishman his country-dance.

Original

With dogs and bears, horses and geese, * game-cocks and monkeys exhibiting their caprioles, shall man be motionless and mute?

    * There is an odd print of "Vestris teaching a goose to dance." The terms, for so fashionable a professor as he was in his day, are extremely moderate; "Six guineas entrance, and one guinea a lesson." The following song is inscribed underneath.

"Of all the fine accomplishments sure dancing far the best

is,
But if a doubt with you remains, behold the Goose and
Vestris;.
And a dancing we will go, will go, &c.
Let men of learning plead and preach; their toil 'tis all in

vain,
Sure, labour of the heels and hands is better than the
brain:
And a dancing, &c.
Then talk no more, ye men of arts, 'bout keeping light and

shade,
Good understanding in the heels is better than the head:
And a dancing, &c.
Great Whigs, and eke great Tories too, both in and out will

dance,
Join hands, change sides, and figure in, now sink, and now
advance.
And a dancing, &c.
Let Oxford boast of ancient lore, and Cam of classic rules,

Noverre might lay you ten to one his heels against your
schools!
And a dancing, &c.
Old Homer sung of gods and kings in most heroic strains,

Yet scarce could get, we have been told, a dinner for his
pains.
And a dancing, &c.
Poor Milton wrote the most sublime, 'gainst Satan, Death, and

Vice,
But very few would quit a dance to purchase Paradise.
And a dancing, &c.
The soldier risks health, life, and limbs, his fortune to

advance,
While Pique and Vestris fortunes make by one night's single
dance.

And a dancing, &c.
'Tis all in vain to sigh and grieve, or idly spend our

breath,
Some millions now, and those unborn, must join the dance of
death.
And a dancing, &c.
Yet while we live let's merry be, and make of care a jest,

Since we are taught what is, is right; and what is right is
best!
And a dancing, &c.

Sweetly singeth the tea-kettle; merrily danceth the parched pea on the fire-shovel! Even grim
Death has his dance."
    "And music, Eugenio, in which I know you are an enthusiast. The Italians have a proverb,
    'Whom God loves not, that man loves not music.' The soul is said to be music.

      'But, whilst this muddy vesture of decay

      Doth grossly close it in, we cannot hear it.'

"Haydn used to say that without melody the most learned and singular combinations are but
unmeaning, empty sound. What but the simplicity and tenderness of the Scotch and Irish
airs constitutes their charm? This great composer was so extravagantly fond of Scotch, Irish,
and Welsh melodies, that he harmonised many of them, and had them hung up in frames
in his room. We remember to have heard somewhere of an officer in a Highland regiment,
who was sent with a handful of brave soldiers to a penal settlement in charge of a number
of convicts; the Highlanders grew sick at heart; the touching strains of 'Lochaber nae mair.'
heard far from home, made them so melancholy, that the officer in command forbade its being
played by the band.
    So, likewise, with the national melody, the 'Rans-des-Vaches' among the Swiss mountaineers.
When sold by their despotic chiefs, and torn from their dearest connexions, suicide and deser-
tion were so frequent when this melody was played, that orders were issued in all their regiments,
prohibiting any one from playing an air of that kind on pain of death. La maladie du pays —that
sickening after home! But Handel's music has received more lasting and general applause than
that of any other composer. By Boyce and Battishall his memory was adored; Mozart was
enthusiastic in his praise; Haydn could not listen (who can?) to his glorious Messiah * without
weeping; and Beethoven has been heard to declare, that were he ever to come to England he
should uncover his head, and kneel down at his tomb!
    * Bishop Ken says,
"Sweet music with blest poesy began,

Congenial both to angels and to Man,
Song was the native language to rehearse
The elevations of the soul in verse:
And through succeeding ages, all along,
Saints praised the Godhead in devoted song."
And he adds in plain prose, that the Garden of Eden was no

stranger to "singing and the voice of melody." Jubal was the

"father of those who handled the harp and organ." Long-
before the institution of the Jewish church, God received
praise both by the human voice and the "loud timbrel and
when that church was in her highest prosperity, King David
seems to have been the composer of her psalmody-both poetry
and music. He occupied the orchestra of the temple, and
accounted it a holy privilege "to play before the Lord" upon
"the harp with a solemn sound." Luther said, "I verily think
that, next to divinity, no art is comparable to music."
And what a glorious specimen of this divine art is his

transcendant "Hymn!" breathing the most awful grandeur, the
deepest pathos, the most majestic adoration! The Puritans —
devils and Puritans hate music-are piously economical in
their devotions, and eschew the principle "not to give unto
the Lord that which costs us nothing!" Their gift is
snuffled through the "vocal nose" —"O most sweet voices!"

"Blessings on the memory of the bard, * and 'Palms eternal flourish round his urn,' who first struck his lyre to celebrate the wooden walls of unconquered and unconquerable Merrie Eng-land! If earth hide him,

>'May angels with their silver wings o'ershade

>The ground, now sacred by his reliques made

if ocean cover him, calm be the green wave on its surface! May his spirit find rest where souls are blessed, and his body be shrined in the holiest cave of the deep and silent sea!"
  * A few old amateurs of music and mirth may possibly
remember Collins's Evening Brush, that rubbed off the rust
of dull care from the generation of 1790. His bill comprised
"Actors of the old school and actors of the new; tragedy
tailors, and butchers in heroics; bell-wethers in buskins,
wooden actors, petticoat caricatures, lullaby jinglers,
bogglers and blunderers, buffoons in blank-verse, &c. &c."
The first of the three Dibdins opened a shop of merriment at
the Sans Souci, where he introduced many of his beautiful
ballads, and sang them to his own tunes. The navy of England
owe lasting obligations to this harmonious Three. It
required not the aid of poetry and music (and how
exquisitely has Shield set the one to the other!) to
stimulate our gallant seamen; but it needed much to awaken
and keep alive enthusiasm on shore, and elevate their moral
character-for landsmen "who live at home at ease/' were
wont to consider the sailor as a mere tar-barrel, a sea-
monster. How many young bosoms have been inspired by the
lyrics of the three Dibdins! What can surpass the homely
pathos of "I thought my heart would break when I sang, Yo!
heave O!"
"The Last Whistle" and "Here, a sheer hulk, lies poor Tom

Bowling!" stirring the manly heart like the sound of a trumpet! It is wise to infuse the amorpatriæ into popular amusements; national songs work wonders among the million. In Little Russia, no sooner are the postilions mounted for a journey, than they begin to hum a patriotic air, which often continues for hours without intermission. The soldiers sing during a long and fatiguing march; the peasant lightens his labour in the same manner; and in a still evening the air vibrates with the cheerful songs of the surrounding villages.

"'Hark! the lark at Heaven's gate sings.'"

"I was not unmindful of the merry chorister! But the lark has made a pause; and I have your promise of a song. Now is the time to fill up the one, and to fulfil the other."

EUGENIO'S SONG.=

"Sweet is the breath of early morn

    That o'er yon heath refreshing blows:

And sweet the blossom on the thorn,

    The violet blue, the blushing rose.

When mounts the lark on rapid wing,

How sweet to sit and hear him sing!

No carols like the feathered choir,

Such happy, grateful thoughts inspire.

Here let the spirit, sore distress'd,

    Its vanities and wishes close:

The weary world is not the rest

    Where wounded hearts should seek repose.

But, hark! the lark his merry strain,

To heav'n high soaring, sings again.

Be hush'd, sweet songster! ev'ry voice

That warbles not like thee-Rejoice!"

"Short and sad! Eugenio. We must away from these bewitching solitudes, or thy note will belong more to the nightingale than to the lark! Let imagination carry thee back to the reign of Queen Anne, when the Spectator and Sir Roger de Coverley embarked at the Temple-Stairs on their voyage to Vauxhall. We pass over the good knight's religious horror at beholding what a few steeples rose on the west of Temple-Bar; and the waterman's wit, (a common thing in those days, *) that made him almost wish himself a Middlesex magistrate!

    * What a sledge-hammer reply was Doctor Johnson's to an aquatic wag upon a similar occasion. "Fellow! your mother, under the *pretence* (!!!) of keeping a — — — — — — is a receiver of stolen goods!"

'We were now arrived at *Spring Garden* says the Spectator, 'which is exquisitely pleasant at this time of the year. When I considered the fragrancy of the walks and bowers, with the choir of birds that sang upon the trees, and the loose tribe of people that walked under their shades, I could not but look upon the place as a kind of Mahometan paradise. Sir Roger told me it put him in mind of a little coppice by his house in the country, which his chaplain used to call an aviary of nightingales.' "And mark in what primitive fashion they concluded their walk, with a glass of Burton ale and a slice of hung-beef!

"Bonnel Thornton furnishes a ludicrous account of a stingy old citizen, loosening his purse-strings to treat his wife and family to Vauxhall; and 'Colin's * 'Description to his wife of *Green-wood Hall*, or the pleasures of *Spring Gardens*,' gives a lively picture of what this modern Arcadia was a century ago.

1 May 20, 1712.

* 'Mary! soft in feature,
I've been at dear Vauxhall;
No paradise is sweeter,
Not that they Eden call.
At night such new vagaries,
Such gay and harmless sport;
All look'd like giant fairies,
At this their monarch's court.
Methought when first I enter'd,
Such splendours round me shone,
Into a world I ventured
Where rose another sun:
Whilst music, never cloying,
As skylarks sweet I hear;
The sounds I'm still enjoying,
They 'll always soothe my ear.
Here paintings, sweetly glowing,
Where'er our glances fall,
Here colours, life bestowing,
Bedeck this green-wood hall!
The king there dubs a farmer,
There John his doxy loves;*
But my delight's the charmer
Who steals a pair of gloves!
As still amazed, I'm straying
O'er this enchanted grove;
I spy a harper playing
All in his proud alcove.
I doff my hat, desiring
He'd tune up Buxom Joan;
But what was I admiring?
Odzooks! a man of stone.
But now the tables spreading,
They all fall to with glee;
Not e'en at Squire's fine wedding
Such dainties did I see!
I long'd (poor starveling rover!)
But none heed country elves;
These folk, with lace daub'd over,
Love only dear themselves.
Thus whilst, 'mid joys abounding,
As grasshoppers they're gay;
At distance crowds surrounding

The Lady of the May.
The man i' th' moon tweer'd slily,
Soft twinkling through the trees,
As though 'twould please him highly
To taste delights like these." **

But its days are numbered. The axe shall be laid to the roots of its beautiful trees; its green
avenues turned into blind alleys;
   * Alluding to the three pictures in the Pavilions-viz. the
King and the Miller of Mansfield-Sailors in a tippling
house in Wapping-and the girl stealing a kiss from a
sleepy gentleman.
** The statue of Handel.

its variegated lamps give place to some solitary gas-burner, to light the groping inhabitants to
their dingy homes; and the melodious strains of its once celebrated vocalists be drowned in the
dismal ditty of some ballad-singing weaver, and the screeching responses of his itinerant family.
What would the gallant Mr. Lowe and his sprightly Euphrosyne, Nan Catley, say, could they
be told to what "base uses" their harmonious groves are condemned to be turned?
   * Her Royal Highness the Princess of Wales sitting under her
splendid Pavilion.

Truly their wonder would be on a par with Paganini's, should ever that musical magician encounter on the other side Styx "My Lord Skaggs and his Broomstick!" *
   * This celebrated professor played on his musical broomstick
at the Haymarket Theatre, November 1751.
"Each buck and jolly fellow has heard of Skegginello

The famous Skegginello, that grunts so pretty
Upon his broomstieado, such music he has made, O,
'Twill spoil the fiddling trade, O,
And that's a pity!
But have you heard or seen, O, his phiz so pretty,
In picture shops so grin, O,
With comic nose and chin, O,
Who'd think a man could shine so At Eh, Eh, Eh, Eh?"
There is a curious Tobacco Paper of Skaggs playing on his

broomstick in full concert with a jovial party! One of the
principal performers is a good-humoured looking gentleman
beating harmony out of the salt-box.
** Certain utilitarians affect to ridicule this ancient

civic festival, on the score of its parade, right-royally
ridiculous! and gross gluttony-as if the corporation of
London were the only gourmands who had offered sacrifices to
Apicius, and died martyrs to good living! We have been at
some pains to peep into the dining-parlours of the ancients,
and from innumerable examples of gastronomy have selected
the following, which prove that the epicures of the olden
time yielded not in taste and voracity to their brethren of

the new: —
The emperor Septimus Severus died of eating and drinking too

much. Valentinianus went off in a surfeit. Lucullus being
asked one day by his attendant, what company he had invited
to his feast, seeing so many dainties prepared, answered,
"Lucullus shall dine with Lucullus?" Vitellius Spinter was
so much given to gluttony, that at one supper he was served
with two thousand several kinds of fishes, and with seven
thousand flying fowl. Maximilian devoured, in one day, forty
pounds of solid meat, which he washed down with a hogshead
of wine. The emperor Geta continued his festival for three
days, and his dainties were introduced in alphabetical
order. Philoxenes wished he had a neck like a crane, that
the delicious morsels might be long in going down. Lucullus,
at a costly feast he gave to certain ambassadors of Asia,
among other trifles, took to his own cheek a griph (query
Griffin'!) boiled, and a fat goose in paste. Hercules and
Lepreas had a friendly contest, which could, in quickest
time, eat up a whole ox; Hercules won, and then challenged
his adversary to a drinking bout, and again beat him hollow.
If the Stoic held that the goal of life is death, and that

we live but to learn to die-if the Pythagorean believed in
the transmigration of souls, and scrupled to shoot a
woodcock lest he should dispossess the spirit of his
grandam-how much more rational was the doctrine of the
Epicurean, (after such a goodly catalogue of gormandizers!)
that there was no judgement to come.

Who has not heard of Guildhall on Lord Mayor's Day, ** and the Easter Ball at the Mansion-House? But we profane not the penetralia where even Common-Councilmen fear to tread! The City Marshals, and men in armour (*Héros malgré eux!*); the pensive-looking state-coachmen, in all the plumpness, pomp, and verdure of prime feeding, wig, and bouquet; the postilion, "a noticeable man," with velvet cap and jockey boots; the high-bred and high-fed aristocracy of the Poultry and Cheapside, and their Banquet, which might tempt Diogenes to blow himself up to such a pitch of obesity, that, instead of living in a tub, a tub might be said to live in him, are subjects too lofty for plebeian handling. Cæsar was told to beware of the Ides of March; and are not November fogs equally ominous to the London citizen? If, then, by some culinary magic, he can be induced to cram his throat rather than to cut it-to feast himself instead of the worms-to prefer a minuet in the Council Chamber to the Dance Macabre in the shades below-the gorgeous anniversaries of Gog and Magog have not been celebrated in vain. *
    * "Search all chronicles, histories, and records, in what
language or letter soever-let the inquisitive man waste
the deere treasures of his time and eye-sight —he shall
conclude his life only in this certainty, that there is no
subject upon earth received into the place of his government
with the like state and magnificence as is the Lord Maior of
the Citty of London." This was said by the author of the
"Triumphs of Truth" in 1613. The following list of City
Poets will show that the office was not an unimportant one
in the olden time: George Peele; Anthony Munday; Thomas

Dekker; Thomas Middleton; John Squire; John Webster; Thomas Heywood; John Taylor (the Water-Poet, one of Ben Jonson's adopted poetical sons, and a rare slang fellow); Edward G ay ton, and T. B. (of the latter nothing is known), both Commonwealth bards; John Tatham; Thomas Jordan; Matthew Taubman, and Elkanah Settle, the last of the poetical parsons who wedded Lord Mayors and Aldermen to immortal verse. One of the most splendid of these anniversary pageants was "London's Triumph; or, the Solemn and Magnificent reception of that Honourable Gentleman, Robert Titeliburn, Lord Maior, after his return from taking his oath at Westminster, the morrow after Simon and Jude day, being October 29, 1656. With the Speeches spoken at Foster-lane-end and Soper-lane-end." —"In the first place," (says the City Poet T. B.) "the loving members of the honourable societie exercising arms in Cripplegate Ground being drawn up together, march'd in a military order to the house of my Lord Maior, where they attended on him, and from thence march'd before him to the Three Crane Wharfe, where part of them under the red colours embarqued themselves in three severall barges; and another part took water at Stone Staires, being under green colours, as enemies to the other; and thence wafting to the other side of the water, there began an encounter between each party, which continued all the way to Westminster; a third body, consisting of pikes and musquets, march'd to Bainard's Castle, and there from the battlements of the castle gave thundering echoes to the vollies of those that pass'd along the streame. Part before and part behind went the severall barges, with drums beating, and trumpets sounding, and varietie of other musiek to take the eare, while the flags and silver pendents made a pleasant sight delectable to the beholders.

"After these came severall gentlemen-ushers adorn'd with

gold eliaines; behind them certaine rich batelielours, wearing gownes furr'd with foynes, and upon them sattin hoods; and lastly after them, followed the Worshipfull Company of Skinners itself, whereof the Lord Maior is a member. Next these, the city officers passing on before, rode the Lord Maior with the Sword, Mace, and Cap of Maintenance before him, being attended by the Recorder, and all the aldermen in scarlet gowns on horseback. (Aldermen on horseback!!) Thus attended, he rode from Bainard's Castle into Cheapside, the Companies standing on both sides of the way

as far as the upper end of the Old Jury, ready to receive him. When he was come right against the old Change, a pageant seem'd to meet him. On the pageant stood two leopards bestrid by two Moors, attir'd in the habit of their country; at the foure corners sate foure virgins arraid in cloth of silver, with their haire dishriveld, and coronets

on their heads. This seem'd to be the embleme of a city
pensive and forlorn, for want of a zealous governor: the
Moors and leopards, like evill customs tyrannizing over the
weak virginitie of undefended virtue; which made an aged
man, who sate at the fore part of the pageant, mantled in a
black garment, with a dejected countenance, seem to bewaile
the condition of his native city; but thus he remaind not
long: for at the approach of the Lord Maior, as if now he
had espy'd the safety of his country, he threw off his
mourning weeds, and with the following speech made known the
joy he had for the election of so happy and just a
magistrate.

"The speech being spoken, the first pageant past on before

the Lord Maior as far as Mercers' Chappel; a gyant being
twelve foot in height going before the pageant for the
delight of the people. Over against Soper-lane End stood
another pageant also; upon this were plac'd severall sorts
of beasts, as lyons, tygers, bears, leopards, foxes, apes,
monkeys, in a great wildernesse; at the forepart whereof
sate Pan with a pipe in his hand; in the middle was a
canopie, at the portal whereof sate Orpheus in an antique
attire, playing on his harp, while all the beasts seem'd to
dance at the sound of his melody. Under the canopie sate
four satyrs playing on pipes. The embleme of this pageant
seem'd proper to the Company out of which the Lord Maior was
elected; putting the spectators in mind how much they ought
to esteem such a calling, as clad the Judges in their
garments of honour, and Princes in their robes of majestic,
and makes the wealthy ladies covet winter, to appear clad in
their sable funs. A second signification of this emblem may
be this-that as Orpheus tam'd the wild beasts by the
alluring sound of his melody, so doth a just and upright
governor tame and govern the wild affections of men, by good
and wholesome lawes, causing a general joy and peace in the
place where he commands. Which made Orpheus, being well
experienced in this truth, to address himself to the Lord
Maior in these following lines.

"The speech being ended, the Lord Maior rode forward to his

house in Silver Street, the military bands still going
before him. When he was in this house, they saluted him with
two volleys of shot, and so marching again to their ground
in Cripple-gate Churchyard, they lodg'd their colours; and
as they began, so concluded this dayes triumph."

When the barges wherein the soldiers were, came right

against Whitehall, they saluted the Lord Protector and his
Council with several rounds of musketry, which the Lord
Protector answered with "signal testimonies of grace and
cour-tesie." And returning to Whitehall, after the Lord
Mayor had taken the oath of office before the Barons of the

Exchequer, they saluted the Lord Protector with "another volley" The City of London had been actively instrumental in the deposition and death of King Charles the First, and Cromwell could not do less than acknowledge, with some show of respect, the blank cartridges of his old friends. The furr'd gowns and gold chains, however, made the amende honorable, when they "jumped Jim Crow," and helped to restore King Charles the Second.

But Easter-Monday was not made only for the city's dancing dignitaries. It draws up the curtain of our popular merriments; and Whit-Mon-day, * not a whit less merry, trumpets forth their joyous continuation.

* June 9, 1786. On Whit-Tuesday was celebrated at Hendon in Middlesex, a burlesque imitation of the Olympic Games. One prize was a gold-laced hat, to be grinned for by six

candidates, who were placed on a platform, with horses' collars to exhibit through. Over their heads was printed in capitals,

Detur Tetriori; or

The ugliest grinner
Shall be the winner.
Each party grinned five minutes solus, and then all united

in a grand chorus of distortion. This prize was carried by a porter to a vinegar merchant, though he was accused by his competitors of foul play, for rinsing his mouth with verjuice. The whole was concluded by a hog, with his tail shaved and soaped, being let loose among nine peasants; any one of which that could seize him by the queue, and throw him across his shoulders, was to have him for a reward. This occasioned much sport: the animal, after running some miles, so tired his hunters that they gave up the chase in despair. A prodigious concourse of people attended, among whom were the Tripoline Ambassador, and several other persons of distinction.

We hail the return of these festive seasons when the busy inhabitants of Lud's town and its suburbs, in spite of hard times, tithes, and taxes, repair to the royal park of Queen Bess to divert their melancholy! We delight to contemplate the mirthful mourners in their endless variety of character and costume; to behold the forlorn holiday-makers hurrying to the jocund scene, to participate in those pleasures which the genius of wakes, kindly bounteous, prepares for her votaries. *

* On the Easter-Monday of 1840, the Regent's Park, Primrose Hill, and the adjoining fields, presented one merry mass of animated beings. At Chalk Farm there was a regular fair — with swings, roundabouts, ups-and-downs, gingerbread-stalls, theatres, donkey-races, penny chaises, and puppet-shows, representing the Islington murder, the Queen's marriage, the arrival of Prince Albert, and the departure of the Chartist rioters! Hampstead Heath, and the surrounding villages,

turned out their studs of Jerusalem ponies. Copenhagen
House, Hornsey Wood House and the White Conduit, echoed with
jollity; the holiday-makers amusing themselves with cricket,
fives, and archery. How sweetly has honest, merry Harry
Carey described the origin of "Sally in our Alley" which
touelied the heart of Addison with tender emotion, and
called forth his warmest praise. "A shoemaker's 'prentice,
making holiday with his sweetheart, treated her with a sight
of Bedlam, the puppet-shows, the flying-chairs, and all the
elegancies of Moorfields, from whence proceeding to the
Farthing Pye-house, he gave her a collation of buns,
cheese-cakes, gammon of bacon, stuffed beef, and bottled
ale; through all which scenes the author dodged them.
Charmed with the simplicity of their courtship, he drew from
what he had witnessed this little sketch of Nature."

The gods assembled on Olympus presented not a more glorious sight than the laughing divini-
ties of One-Tree-Hill!

Original

What an animated scene! Hark to the loud laugh of some youngsters that have had their roll and tumble. Yonder is a wedding party from the neighbouring village. See the jolly tar with his true blue jacket and trousers, checked shirt, radiant with a gilt brooch as big as a crown piece, yellow straw-hat, striped stockings, and pumps; and his pretty bride, with her rosy cheeks and white favours. How light are their heels and hearts! And the blythesome couples that follow in their train-noviciates in the temple of Hymen, but who ere long will be called upon to act as principals! All is congratulation, good wishes, and good humour. Scandal is dumb; envy dies for the day; disappointment gathers hope; and one wedding, like a fool, or an Irish wake, shall make many.

"O yes! O yes! O yes!

When the peripatetic pieman rings his bell

At morning, noon, or when you sit at eve;

Ladies and gentlemen, I guess

It needs no ghost to tell,

In song, recitative,

He warbles cakes and gingerbread to sell!

Tarts of gooseberry, raspberry, cranberry;

Rare bonne-bouches brought from Banbury;

Puffs and pie-ses

Of all sorts and sizes;

Ginger beer,

That won't make you queer,

Like the treble X ale of Taylor and Hanbury!"

"Here, good Christians, are five Reasons why you *shouldn't* go to a fair, published by the London Lachrymose Society for the suppression of fun."

"And here, good Christians, are five-and-fifty why you *should!* published by my Lord Chancellor Cocke Lorel, President of the High Court of Mummery, and Conscience-keeper to his merry Majesty of Queerumania, for the promotion of jollity."

One of the better order of mendicants, on whose smooth, pale brow, hung the blossoms of the grave, arrested our attention with the following madrigal which pleased us, inasmuch as it seemed to smack of the olden time.

"I love but only one

And thou art only she

That loves but only one —

Let me that only be!

Requite me with the like,

And say thou unto me

Thou lov'st but only one,

And I am only he!"

"Cold comfort this, broiling and frying under a burning hot sun!" soliloquized a blind ballad-singer. And, having two strings to his bow, and one to his fiddle, he put a favourite old tune to the rack, and enforced us to own the soft impeachment of

THE BALLAD SINGER'S APOLOGY FOR GREENWICH FAIR.=

Up hill and down hill, 'tis always the same;

Mankind ever grumbling, and fortune to blame!

To fortune, 'tis uphill, ambition and strife;

And fortune obtain'd —then the downhill of life!

We toil up the hill till we reach to the top;

But are not permitted one moment to stop!

O how much more quick we descend than we climb!

There's no locking fast the swift wheels of Old Time.

Gay Greenwich! thy happy young holiday train

Here roll down the hill, and then mount it again.

The ups and downs life has bring sorrow and care;

But frolic and mirth attend those at the fair.

My Lord May'r of London, of high city lineage,

His show makes us glad with, and why shouldn't

   Greenwich?

His gingerbread coach a crack figure it cuts!

And why shouldn't we crack our gingerbread nuts?

Of fashion and fame, ye grandiloquent powers,

Pray take your full swing-only let us take ours!

If you have grown graver and wiser, messieurs,

The grinning be ours, and the gravity yours!

To keep one bright spark of good humour alive,

Old holiday pastimes and sports we revive.

Be merry, my masters, for now is your time —

Come, who'll buy my ballads? they're reason and

rhyme."

Peckham and Blackheath fairs were celebrated places of resort in former times, and had their modicum of strange monsters.

"Geo. I. R.

"To the lovers of living curiosities. To be seen during the time of *Peckham Fair*, a Grand Collection of Living Wild Beasts and Birds, lately arrived from the remotest parts of the World.

"1. The *Pellican* that suckles her young with her heart's, blood, from Egypt.

"2. The Noble *Vultur Cock*, brought from *Archangell*, having the finest talions of any bird that seeks his prey; the fore part of his head is covered with hair, the second part resembles the wool of a Black; below that is a white ring, having a Ruff, that he cloaks his head with at night.

"3. An *Eagle of the Sun*, that takes the loftiest flight of any bird that flies. There is no bird but this that can fly to the face of the Sun with a naked eye.

"4. A curious Beast, bred from a *Lioness*, like a foreign *Wild Cat*.

"5. The He-*Panther*, from Turkey, allowed by the curious to be one of the greatest rarities ever seen in *England*, on which are thousands of spots, and not two of a likeness.

"6 & 7. The two fierce and surprising *Hyaenas*, Male and female, from the River *Gambia*. These Creatures imitate the human voice, and so decoy the Negroes out of their huts and plantations to devour them. They have a mane like a horse, and two joints in their hinder leg more than any other creature. It is remarkable that all other beasts are to be tamed, but Hyaenas they are not.

"8. An *Ethiopian Toho Savage*, having all the actions of the human species, which (when at its full growth) will be upwards of five feet high.

"Also several other surprising Creatures of different sorts. To be seen from 9 in the morning till 9 at night, till they are sold. Also, all manner of curiosities of different sorts, are bought and sold at the above place by John Bennett."

The grand focus of attraction was in the immediate vicinity of the "*Kentish Drovers*." This once merry hostelrie was a favourite suburban retreat of Dicky Suett. Cherub Dicky! who when (to use his own peculiar phrase) his "copper required cooling," mounted the steady, old-fashioned, three mile an hour Peckham stage, and journeyed hither to allay his thirst, and qualify his alcohol with a refreshing draught of Derbyshire ale. The landlord (who was quite a character) and he were old cronies; and, in the snug little parlour behind the bar, of which Dicky had the entrée, their hob-and-nobbings struck out sparks of humour that, had they exhaled before the lamps, would have set the theatre in a roar. Suett was a great frequenter of fairs. He stood treat to the conjurors, feasted the tragedy kings and queens, and many a mountebank did he make muzzy. Once in a frolic he changed clothes with a Jack Pudding, and played *Barker* and *Mr. Merriman* to a precocious giantess; when he threw her lord and master into such an ecstacy of mirth, that the fellow vowed hysterically that it was either the *devil*, or (for his fame had travelled before him) *Dicky Suett*. He was a piscator, *

* All sports that inflict pain on any living thing, without
attaining some useful end, are wanton and cowardly. Wild
boars, wolves, foxes, &c. may be hunted to extermination,
for they are public robbers; but to hunt the noble deer, for
the cruel pleasure of hunting him, is base.
With all our love of honest Izaak Walton, we feel a

shuddering when the "sentimental old savage" gives his

minute instructions to the tyro in angling how most
skilfully to transfix the writhing worm, (as though you
"loved him!") and torture a poor fish. Piscator is a
cowardly rogue to sit upon a fair bank, the sun shining
above, and the pure stream rippling beneath, with his
instruments of death, playing pang against pang, and life
against life, for his contemplative recreation. What would
he say to a hook through his own gullet? Would it mitigate
his dying agonies to hear his dirge (even the milkmaid's
song!) chanted in harmonious concert with a brother of the
angle, who had played the like sinister trick on his
companion in the waters?

and would make a huge parade of his rod, line, and green-painted tin-can, sallying forth on a
fine morning with malice prepense against the gudgeons and perch: but Dicky was a merciful
angler: he was the gudgeon, for the too cunning fishes, spying his comical figure, stole his
bait, and he hooked nothing but tin pots and old shoes. Here he sat in his accustomed chair
and corner, dreaming of future quarterns, and dealing out odd sayings that would make the
man in the moon hold his sides, and convulse the whole planet with laughter. His hypocrene
was the cream of the valley; *

* Suett had at one time a landlady who exhibited an
inordinate love for that vulgar fluid ycleped geneva; a
beverage which Dicky himself by no means held in abhorrence.
She would order her servant to procure supplies after the
following fashion: —"Betty, go and get a quartern loaf and
half a quartern of gin." Off bolted Betty-she was speedily
recalled: "Betty, make it half a quartern loaf and a
quartern of gin." But Betty had never got fairly across the
threshold, ere the voice was again heard: —"Betty, on second
thoughts, you may as well make it all gin!"

he dug his grave with his bottle, and gave up the ghost amidst a troop of spirits. Peace to his
manes! Cold is the cheerful hearth, where he familiarly stirred the embers and silent the walls
that echoed to "*Old Wigs!*" chanted by *Jeffery Dunstan* when he danced hop-scotch on a table
spread out with tumblers and tobacco-pipes! Hushed is the voice of song. At this moment, as if
to give our last assertion what Touchstone calls "the lie direct," some Corydon from Petty France,
the Apollo of a select singing party in the first floor front room, thus musically apostrophised
his Blouzellinda of Bloomsbury.

> She's all that fancy painted her, she's rosy without rouge,
>
> Her gingham gown a modest brown turned up with
>
> > bright gamboge;
>
> She learns to jar the light guitar, and plays the harpsi-
>
> > chols,
>
> Her fortune's five-and-twenty pounds in Three per Cent

Consols.

At Beulah Spa, where love is law, was my fond heart
    beguiled;
I pour'd my passion in her ear-she whisper'd, "Draw
    it mild!"
In Clerkenwell you bear the bell: what muffin-man does
    not?
And since, my Paul, you've gain'd your p'int, perhaps
    you 'll stand your pot.

The Charlie quite, I've, honour bright, sent packing for a
    cheat;
A watchman's wife, he'd whack me well when he was
    on his beat.
"Adieu!" he said, and shook his head, "my dolor be
    your dow'r;
And while you laugh, I 'll take my staff, and go and cry
    —the hour."

Last Greenwich Fair we wedded were; she's won, and
    we are one;
And Sally, since the honey-moon, has had a little son.
Of all the girls that are so smart, there's none than Sally
    smarter;
I said it 'fore I married her, and now I say it *arter*.

Geo. II. R.

"This is to give notice to all gentlemen, ladies and others, that there is to be seen from eight in the morning till nine at night, at the end of the great booth on *Blackheath*, a west of England woman 38 years of age *alive*, with *two heads*, one above the other; having no hands, fingers, nor toes; yet can she dress and undress, knit, sew, read, sing," *Query —a duet with her two mouths?* "She has had the honour to be seen by Sir Hans Sloane, and several of the Royal Society. *

"N.B. Gentlemen and ladies may see her at their own houses, if they please.

* That the caricaturist has been out-caricatured by Nature no one will deny. Wilkes was so abominably ugly that he said it always took him half an hour to talk away his face; and Mirabeau, speaking of his own countenance, said, "Fancy a tiger marked with the small-pox!" We have seen an Adonis contemplate one of Cruikshank's whimsical figures, of which his particular shanks were the bow-ideal, and rail at the artist for libelling Dame Nature! How ill-favoured were Lord Lovat, Magliabeeehi, Searron, and the wall-eyed, botde-nosed Buekhorse the Bruiser! how deformed and frightful Sir Harry Dimsdale and Sir Jeffrey Dunstan! What would have been said of the painter of imaginary Siamese twins? Yet we have "The true Description of two Monstrous Children, born in the parish of Swanburne in Buekinghamshyre, the 4th of Aprill, Anno Domini 1566; the two Children having both their belies fast joyned together, and imbracing one another with their armes: which Children were both alyve by the space of half an hower, and wer baptised, and named the one John, and the other Joan." —A similar wonder was exhibited in Queen Anne's reign, viz. "Two monstrous girls born in the Kingdom of Hungary," which were to be seen "from 8 o'clock in the morning till 8 at night, up one pair of stairs, at Mr. William Sutteliffe's, a Drugster's Shop, at the sign of the Golden Anchor, in the Strand, near Charing-Cross." The Siamese twins of our own time are fresh in every one's memory. Shakspere throws out a pleasant sarcasm at the characteristic curiosity of the English nation. Trinculo, upon first beholding Caliban, exclaims —"A strange fish! were I in England now (as I once was), and had but this fish painted, not a holiday fool there but would give a piece of silver: there would this monster make a man: when they will not give a doit to relieve a lame beggar, they will lay out ten to see a dead Indian"

This great wonder never was shown in England before this, the 13th day of March, 1741. "Vivat Rex." Peckham * and Blackheath Fairs are abolished; ——

* Peckham Fair, August 1787. —Of the four-footed race were bears, monkeys, dancing-dogs, a learned pig, &c. Mr. Flockton in his theatrical booth opposite the Kentish Drovers, exhibited the Italian fantocini; the farce of the Conjuror; and his "inimitable musical-clock." Mr. Lane, "first performer to the King," played off his "snip-snap, rip-rap, crick-crack, and thunder tricks, that the grown babies stared like worried cats." This extraordinary genius

"will drive about forty twelve-penny nails into any
gentleman's breech, place him in a loadstone chair, and draw
them out without the least pain! He is, in short, the most
wonderful of all wonderful creatures the world ever wondered
at."
Sir Jeffrey Dunstan sported his handsome figure within his

booth; outside of which was displayed a likeness of the
elegant original in his pink satin smalls. His dress,
address, and oratory, fascinated the audience; in fact,
"Jeffy was quite tonish!"
In opposition to the "Monstrous Craws" at the Royal Grove,

were shown in a barn "four wonderful human creatures,
brought three thousand miles beyond China, from the
Kickashaw Mackabee country, viz.
"A man with a chin eleven inches Ions:.

"Another with as many M'ens and warts on his face as knots

on an old thornback.
"A third with two large teeth five inches long, strutting

beyond his upper lip, as if his father had been a man-tiger!
"And the fourth with a noble large fiery head, that looked

like the red-hot urn on the top of the monument!"
"These most wonderful wild-born human beings (the Monstrous

Craws), two females and a male, are of very small stature,
being little more than four feet high; each with a monstrous
craw under his throat. Their country, language, &c. are as
yet unknown to mankind. It is supposed they started in some
canoe from their native place (a remote quarter in South
America), and being wrecked were picked up by a Spanish
vessel. At that period they were each of a dark-olive
complexion, but which has astonishingly, by degrees, changed
to the colour of that of Europeans. They are tractable and
respectful towards strangers, and of lively and merry
disposition among themselves; singing and dancing in the
most extraordinary way, at the will and pleasure of the
company."

and those of Camberwell * and Wandsworth ** are
    * A petty session (how very petty!) was held at Union Hall
on the 4th July, 1823, in order to put down Camberwell Fair,
which is as old as Domesday Book. Shakspere has truly
described these ill-conditioned, peddling, meddling
Dogberrys "You wear out a good wholesome forenoon in hearing
a cause between an orange-wife and a fosset-seller; and then
rejourn the controversy of three-pence to a second day of

audience. When you speak best to the purpose, it is not
worth the wagging of your beards, and your beards deserve
not so honourable a grave, as to stuff a botcher's cushion,
or to be entombed in an ass's pack-saddle."
** Wandsworth Fair exhibited sixty years ago Mount Vesuvius,

or the burning mountain by moonlight, rope, and hornpipe-
dancing; a forest, with the humours of lion-catching;
tumbling by the young Polander from Sadler's Wells; several
diverting comic songs; a humorous dialogue between Mr.
Swatehall and his wife; sparring matches; the Siege of
Belgrade, &c. all for three-pence!
On Whit-Monday, 1840, Messrs. Nelson and Lee sent down a

theatrical caravan to Wandsworth Fair, and were moderately
remunerated. But the "Grand Victoria Booth" was the rallying
point of attraction. Its refectory was worthy of the
ubiquitous Mr. Epps-of ham, beef, tongue, polony, portable
soup, and sheep's trotter memory!
Cold beef and ham, hot ribs of lamb, mock-turtle soup that's

portable,
Did blow, with stout, their jackets out, and made the folks

comfortable!

fast going the way of all fairs. Bow, Edmonton, * Highgate, ** Brook Green (Hammersmith,)
and
   * In the year 1820, the keeper of a menagerie at Edmonton
Fair walked into the den of a lioness, and nursed her cubs.
He then paid his respects to the husband and father, a
magnificent Barbary Lion. After the usual complimentary
greetings between them, the man somewhat roughly thrust open
the monster's jaws, and put his head into its mouth, giving
at the same time a shout that made it tremble. This he did
with impunity. But in less than two months afterwards, when
repeating the same exhibition at a fair in the provinces, he
cried, like the starling, "I can't get out! —I can't get
out!" demanding at the same time if the lion wagged its
tail? The lion, thinking the joke had been played quite
often enough, did wag its tail, and roared "Heads!" The
keeper fell a victim to his temerity.
** "July 2,1744. —This is to give notice that Highgate Fair

will be kept on Wednesday, Thursday, and Friday next, in a
pleasant shady walk in the middle of the town.
"On Wednesday a pig will be turned loose, and he that takes

it up by the tail and throws it over his head, shall have
it. To pay two-pence entrance, and no less than twelve to
enter.
"On Thursday a match will be run by two men, a hundred yards

in two sacks, for a large sum. And, to encourage the sport,
the landlord of the Mitre will give a pair of gloves, to be
run for by six men, the winner to have them.
"And on Friday a hat, value ten shillings, will be run for

by men twelve times round the Green; to pay one shilling
entrance: no less than four to start; as many as will may
enter, and the second man to have all the money above four."

West-end (Hampstead *), Fairs, with their swings, roundabouts, spiced gingerbread, penny-
trumpets, and halfpenny rattles are passed away. The showmen and Merry Andrews of Moorfields ** are

* "The Hampstead Fair Ramble; or, The World going quite Mad.
To the tune of 'Brother Soldier dost hear of the News,'
London: Printed for J. Bland, near Holbourn, 1708." A
curious broadside.

** Moorfields during the holiday seasons was an epitome of

Bartlemy Fair. Its booths and scaffolds had flags flying on
the top. A stage near the Windmill Tavern, opposite Old
Beth-lem, was famous for its grinning-matches. Moorfields
had one novel peculiarity, viz. that whilst the Merry Andrew
was practising his buffooneries and legerdemain tricks in
one quarter, the itinerant Methodist preacher was holding
forth in another. Foote makes his ranting parson exclaim,
"Near the mad mansions of Moorfields I 'll bawl,

Come fathers, mothers, brothers, sisters, all,

Shut up your shops and listen to my call!"

The Act 12 of Queen Anne aimed at the suppression of the

Moorfields' merriments. The showmen asked Justice Fuller to
license them in April, 1717, but in vain. Fuller had a
battle-royal with Messrs. Saunders and Margaret, two
Middlesex justices, who sided with the conjurors, and
forbade the execution of his warrant. Justice Fuller,
however, having declared war against Moorfields'
mountebanking, was inexorable, and committed the insurgents
to the house of correction; from whence, after three hours'
durance vile, they were released by three other magistrates.
Kennington Common was also a favourite spot for this odd

variety of sports. It was here that Mr. Mawworm encountered
the brick-bats of his congregation, and had his "pious tail"
illuminated with the squibs and crackers of the unre-
generate.

This fair commenced in the New River pipe-fields, and

continued in a direct line as far as the top of Elm Street,

where it terminated. The equestrians always made a point of
galloping their donkeys furiously past the house of
correction!

no more; the Gooseberry Fairs * of Clerkenwell and Tottenham Court Road, (the minor Newmarket and Doncaster of Donkey-racing!) are come to a brick-and-mortary end.
    * "April 9, 1748. —At the Amphitheatrical Booth at Tottenham
Court, on Monday next (being Easter Monday), Mr. French,
designing to please all, in making his Country Wake complete
by doubling the prizes given to be played for, as well as
the sports, has engaged some of the best gamesters, Country
against London, to make sides. For Cudgelling, a laced hat,
value one pound five shillings, or one guinea in gold; for
Wrestling, one guinea; Money for Boxing, besides Stage-
money. And, to crown the diversion of the day, he gives a
fine Smock to be jigged for by Northern Lasses against the
Nymphs to the westward of St. Giles's Church-to be entered
at the Royal Oak, in High Street, by Hob, Clerk of the
Revels, or his deputy. The doors will be opened at eleven
o'clock; the sport to begin at two. Cudgelling as usual
before the prizes. Best seats, Two Shillings; Pit and First
Gallery, One Shilling; Upper Gallery, Sixpence."
Mr. French advertises, May 12, 1748, at his booth at

Tottenham Court, six men sewed up in sacks to run six times
the length of the stage backwards and forwards for a prize —
a prize for wrestling and dancing to the pipe and tabor —
and the gladiator's dance. He also kept the race-course in
Tothill-Fields, August 4, 1749.
"August 8, 1730. —At Reynold's Great Theatrical Booth, in

Tottenham Court, during the time of the Fair, will be
presented a Comical, Tragical, Farcical Droll, called The
Rum Duke and the Queer Duke, or a Medley of Mirth and
Sorrow. To which will be added a celebrated Operatical
Puppet-Show, called Punch's Oratory, or the Pleasures of the
Town; containing several diverting passages, particularly a
very elegant dispute between Punch and another great Orator
(Henley?); Punch's Family Lecture, or Joan's Chimes on her
tongue to some tune. No Wires-all alive! With
entertainments of Daneing by Monsieur St. Luce, and others."

High-smoking chimneys and acres of tiles shut out the once pleasant prospect, and their Gef-
fray Gambados (now grey-headed jockeys!) sigh, amidst macadamisation and dust, for the green
sward where, in their hey-day of life, they witched the fair with noble donkeyship! —Croydon
(famous for roast-pork, and new walnuts), Harley-Bush, and Barnet fairs, are as yet unsup-
pressed; but the demons of mischief—[the English populace (their *Majesty the Many!*) are
notorious for this barbarity] —have
    * "At the London Spaw (1754), during the accustomed time of
the Welsh Fair, will be the usual entertainment of Roast
Pork, with the fam'd soft-flavor'd Spaw Ale, and every other

liquor of the neatest and best kinds, agreeable
entertainments, and inviting usage from the Publick's most
obedient servant, George Dowdell."
In the year 1795 a Dutch Fair was held at Frogmore, when a

grand fête was given by King George the Third, in
celebration of his Queen's birth-day, and the recent arrival
of the Princess of Wales. A number of dancers were dressed
as haymakers; Mr. Byrne and his company danced the Morris-
dance; and Savoyards, in character, assisted at the
merriments. Feats of horsemanship were exhibited by
professors from the Circus; and booths erected for good
eating and drinking, and the sale of toys, work-bags,
pocket-books, and fancy articles. Munden, Rock, and Incledon
diverted the company with their mirth and music; and Majesty
participated in the general joy. The Royal Dutch Fair lasted
two days, and was under the tasteful direction of the
Princess Elizabeth.

totally destroyed the magnificent oak that made Fairlop Fair * a favourite rendezvous with those
who could afford a tandem, tax-cart, or Tim-whisky. How often have we sat, and pirouetted
too, under its venerable shade.

    May Fair (which began on May-day), during the early part of the last century, was much
patronised by the nobility and gentry. It had nevertheless its Ducking Pond for the ruder class
of holiday makers. **

    * By an act passed 3rd of 2nd Victoria (not Victoria for the
Fair!) it was rendered unlawful to hold Fairlop Fair beyond
the first Friday ("Friday's a dry day!") in July. This was
the handy work of the Barking Magistrates.
"And when I walk abroad let no dog bark!"

** "June 25, 1748. —At May Fair Ducking Pond, on Monday

next, the 27th inst., Mr. Hooton's Dog Nero (ten years old,
with hardly a tooth in his head to hold a duck, but well
known for his goodness to all that have seen him hunt) hunts
six ducks for a guinea, against the bitch called the Flying
Spaniel, from the Ducking Pond on the other side of the
water, who has beat all she has hunted against, excepting
Mr. Hooton's Good-Blood. To begin at two o'clock.
"Mr. Hooton begs his customers won't take it amiss to pay

Twopence admittance at the gate, and take a ticket, which
will be allowed as Cash in their reckoning. No person
admitted without a tickct, that such as are not liked may be
kept out.
"Note. Right Lincoln Ale."

Apropos of other mirthful rendezvous.

"A new Ducking Pond to be opened on Monday next at

Lirneiouse Cause, being the 11th August, where four dogs
are to play for Four Pounds, and a lamb to be roasted whole,
to be given away to all gentlemen sportsmen. To begin at Ten
o'clock in the forenoon." —Postman, 7th August 1707.
"Erith Diversion, 24th May 1790. —This is to acquaint the

publick, that on Whit-Monday, and during the holidays, the
undermentioned diversions will take place. First, a new Hat
to be run for by men; a fine Ham to be played for at Trap-
ball; a pair of new Pumps to be jumped for in a sack; a
large Plumb-pudding to be sung for; a Guinea to be cudgelled
for-with smoking, grinning through a collar, with many
other diversions too tedious to mention.
"N.B. A Ball in the evening as usual."

But what are the hopes of man! A press-gang (this is the

freedom of the press with a vengeance! this the boasted
monarchy of the middle classes!) interrupted and put an end
to these water-side sports.
Kent has long been renowned for strong muscles and strong

stomachs!
"Bromley in Kent, July 14, 1726. —A strange eating worthy is

to perform a Tryal of Skill on St. James's Day, which is
the day of our Fair for a wager of Five Guineas-viz.: he
is to eat four pounds of bacon, a bushel of French beans,
with two pounds of butter, a quartern loaf, and to drink a
gallon of strong beer."
The old proverb of "buttering bacon" here receives

farinaceous illustration!

"In a fore one-pair room, on the west side of Sun-court," a Frenchman exhibited, during the
time of May Fair, the "astonishing strength of the 'Strong Woman,' * his wife."
    "She first let down her hair, of a length descending to her knees, which she twisted round
the projecting part of a blacksmith's anvil, and then lifted the ponderous weight from the floor.
She also put her bare feet on a red-hot salamander, without receiving the least injury." May Fair
is now become the site of aristocratical dwellings, where a strong purse is required to procure
a standing. At Horn Fair, a party of humorists of both sexes, counted in all the variety of Bull-
Feather fashion, after perambulating round Cuckold Point, startled the little quiet village of
Charlton on St. Luke's day, shouting their emulation, and blowing voluntaries on rams' horns,
in honour of their patron saint. Ned Ward gives a curious picture of this odd ceremony-and
the press of *Stonecutter Street* (the worthy successor of *Aldermary Churchyard*) has consigned it
to immortality in two Broadsides ** inspired by the Helicon of the Fleet,

    * This was probably Mrs. Alchorne, "who had exhibited as the
Strong Woman" and died in Drury Lane in 1817, at a very
advanced age. Madame also performed at Bartholomew Fair in
1752.
    ** "A New Summons to all the Merry (Wagtail) Jades to attend

at Horn Fair" —"A New Summons to Horn Fair" both without a date.

> "Around whose brink
>
> Bards rush in droves, like cart-horses to drink,
>
> Dip their dark beards among its streams so clear,
>
> And while they gulp it, wish it ale or beer,"

and illustrated by the Cruikshank of his day. Mile-end Green, in ancient times, had its popular exhibitions; —

> "Lord Pomp, let nothing that's magnificall,
>
> Or that may tend to London's graceful state,
>
> Be unperformed-as showes and solemne feastes,
>
> Watches in armour, triumphes, cresset-lightes,
>
> Bonefiers, belles, and peales of ordinance.
>
> And, Pleasure, see that plaies be published,
>
> Maie-games and maskes, with mirth and minstrelsie;
>
> Pageants and School-feastes, beares and puppit-plaies:
>
> Myselfe will muster upon Mile-end-greene,
>
> As though we saw, and feared not to be seene."

And the royal town of Windsor, * and the racecourse in Tothill-Fields ** were not without their merriments.

* "The Three Lordes and Three Ladies of London," 1590.
** "On Wednesday the 13th, at Windsor, a piece of plate is

to be fought for at cudgels by ten men on a side, from, Berkshire and Middlesex. The next day a hat and feather to be fought for by ten men on a side, from the counties aforesaid. Ten Bargemen are to eat ten quarts of hasty-pudding, well buttered, but d — —d hot! He that has done first to have a silver spoon of ten shillings value; and the second five shillings. And as they have anciently had the title of The Merry Wives of Windsor, six old women belonging to Windsor town challenge any six old women in the universe, (we need not, however, go farther than our own country) to out-scold them. The best in three heats to have a suit of head-cloths, and, (what old women generally want!) a pair of

nut-crackers." —Read's Journal, September 9, 1721.
"According to Law. September 22, 1749. —On Wednesday next,

the 27th inst., will be run for by Asses (I!) in Tothill
Fields, a purse of gold, not exceeding the value of Fifty
Pounds. The first will be entitled to the gold; the second
to two pads; the third to thirteen pence halfpenny; the last
to a halter fit for the neck of any ass in Europe. Each ass
must be subject to the following articles
"No person will be allowed to ride but Taylors and Chimney-

sweepers; the former to have a cabbage-leaf fixed in his
hat, the latter a plumage of white feathers; the one to use
nothing but his yard-wand, and the other a brush.
"No jockey-tricks will be allowed upon any consideration.

"No one to strike an ass but the rider, lest he thereby

cause a retrograde motion, under a penalty of being ducked
three times in the river.
"No ass will be allowed to start above thirty years old, or

under ten months, nor any that has won above the value of
fifty pounds.
"No ass to run that has been six months in training,

particularly above stairs, lest the same accident happen to
it that did to one nigh a town ten miles from London, and
that for reasons well known to that place.
"Each ass to pay sixpence entrance, three farthings of which

are to be given to the old clerk of the race, for his due
care and attendance.
"Every ass to carry weight for inches, if thought proper."

Then follow a variety of sports, with "an ordinary of proper

victuals, particularly for the riders, if desired."

"Run, lads, run! there is rare sport in Tothill Fields!"

CHAPTER V.

Southwark Fair ranked next to St. Bartholomew, and comprehended all the attractions for which its rival on the other side of the water was so famous. On the 13th day of September 1660, John Evelyn visited it. "I saw," said this entertaining sight-seer, "in Southwark, at St. Margaret's Faire, monkies and apes daunce, and do other feates of activity on ye high rope: they were gallantly clad *à la mode*, went upright, saluted the company, bowing and pulling off their hats; they saluted one another with as good a grace as if instructed by a daúncing-master; they turned heels over head with a basket having eggs in it, without breaking any; also with lighted candles in their hands, and on their heads, without extinguishing them, and with vessels of water, without spilling a drop. I also saw an Italian wench daunce and performe all the tricks of ye tight rope to admiration. All the Court went to see her. Likewise here was a man who tooke up a piece of iron cannon, of about 400 lbs weight, with the haire of his head onely." September 15, 1698, the curious old narrator paid it another visit. "The dreadful earthquake in Jamaica this summer" (says he) "was prophanely and ludicrously represented in a puppet-play, or some such lewd pastime in the fair of Southwark, wch caused the Queane to put downe that idle and vicious mock shew." The fair, however, revived, and outlived her Majesty many merry years. How slept the authorities some seasons ago, when Messrs. Mathews and Yates dramatised an "Earthquake" at the Adelphi!

The Bowling Green in Southwark was the high 'Change of the Fair. Mr. Fawkes, the conjuror, exhibited at his booth, over against the Crown Tavern, near St. George's Church. Dramatic representations, music and dancing, the humours of Punch and Harlequin, a glass of "good wine, and other liquors," were to be had at the several booths held at the "Golden Horse-shoe," * the "Half-Moon Inn," ** and other well-known houses of entertainment. Thither re-sorted Lee and Harper to delight the denizens of Kent Street, Guy's Hospital, and St. Thomas's, with Guy of Warwick, Robin Hood, the comical adventures of Little John and the Pindar's wife, and the Fall of Phaëton! In July 1753, the Tennis Court and booths that were on the Bowling Green, with some other buildings where the fair used to be held, were pulled down; and shortly after, that pleasant Bowling Green was converted into a potato and cabbage market!

* "Joseph Parnes's Musiek Rooms, at the sign of the Whelp and Bacon, during Southwark Fair, are at the Golden Horse-Shoe, next to the King's Bench, where you may be entertained with a variety of musick and dancing after the Scotch, Italian, and English ways. A Girl dances with sharp swords, the like not in England." —Temp. W. 3.
"There is to be seen at Mr. Hocknes, at the Maremaid, near

the King's Bench, in Southwark, during the time of the Fair, A Changeling Child, being A Living Skeleton, Taken by a Venetian Galley from a Turkish Vessel in the Archipelago. This was a fairy child, supposed to be born of Hungarian parents, but changed in the nursery; aged 9 years and more, not exceeding a foot and a half high. The legs and arms so very small, that they scarcely exceed the bigness of a man's thumb; and the face no bigger than the palm of one's hand. She is likewise a mere anatomy." —Temp. W. 3.
** "Sept. 12, 1729. —At Reynold's Great Theatrical Booth, in

the Half-Moon Inn, near the Bowling-Green, Southwark, during the Fair will be presented the Beggar's Wedding-Southwark Fair, or the Sheep-Shearing —an opera called Flora-and The Humours of Harlequin."

Southwark, or Lady Fair, has long since been suppressed. Thanks, however, to the "great painter of mankind," that we can hold it as often as we please in our own breakfast-parlours and drawing-rooms! The works of Hogarth are medicines for melancholy. If the mood be of Jacques's quality, "a most humorous sadness," it will revel in the master's whim; if of a deeper tinge, there is the dark side of the picture for mournful reflection. Though an unsparing satirist, probing vice and folly to the quick, he has compassion for human frailty and sorrow. He is no vulgar caricaturist, making merry with personal deformity; he paints wickedness in its true colours, and if the semblance be hideous, the original, not the copy, is to blame. His scenes are faithful transcripts of life, high and low. He conducts us into the splendid saloons of fashion; —we pass with him into the direst cells of want and misery. He reads a lesson to idleness, extravagance, and debauchery, such as never was read before. He is equally master of the pathetic and the ludicrous. He exhibits the terrible passions, and their consequences, with almost superhuman power. Every stroke of his pencil points a moral; every object, however insignificant, has its meaning. His detail is marvellous, and bespeaks a mind pregnant with illustration, an eye that nothing could escape. Bysshe's Art of Poetry, the well-chalked tally, the map of the gold mines, and the starved cur making off with the day's lean provision, are in perfect keeping with the distressed poet's ragged finery, his half-mended breeches, and all the exquisite minutiae of his garret. His very wig, most picturesquely awry, is a happy symbol of poetical and pecuniary perplexity. Of the same marking character are the cow's horns, rising just above the little citizen's head, in the print of "*Evening*," telling a sly tale; while the *dramatis personae* of the Strollers' Barn, the flags, paint-pots, pageants, clouds, waves, puppets, dark-lanterns, thunder, lightning, daggers, periwigs, crowns, sceptres, salt-boxes, ghosts, devils, and tragedy queens exhibit such an unique miscellany of wonders, that none but an Hogarth ever thought of bringing together. Turn, by way of contrast, to "Gin Lane," and its frightful accompaniments!

Hogarth went quite as much to see Southwark Fair and its fun (for which he had a high relish) as to transfer them to his canvass. 'Tis a holiday with the mountebanks, and he has caught them in all their grimacerie and glory. A troop of strollers, belonging to Messrs. Cibber and Bullock, attitudinising and making mouths, as a prologue to the "Fall of Bajazet," are suddenly surprised into the centre of gravity by the breaking down of their scaffold, and Kings, Queens, Turks, tumblers, monkeys, and Merry Andrews descend topsy-turvy into a china-shop below! At Lee and Harper's grand booth are the celebrated Wooden Horse of Troy, the Temptation of Adam and Eve, and Punch's Opera. A fire-eater is devouring his red-hot element, and his periwigged Jack-Pud-ding is distributing his quack nostrums. A tragedy hero has a brace of bailiffs in his train; and a prize-fighter, with his hare sconce dotted with sable patches, and a nose that might successfully bob for black-beetles against a brick wall, mounted on a blind bone-setter, perambulates the fair, challenging the wide world to mortal combat!

These, with a pretty female drummer of amazonian proportions; an equilibrist swinging on the slack rope; a juggler with his cups and balls; a pickpocket and a couple of country boobies; a bag-piper; a dancing dog; a dwarf drummer, and a music-grinder, make up a dramatis jiersono only to be equalled by the Strolling Players * and the March to Finchley.

* Pannard, a minor French poet, whom Marmontel styles the La
Fontaine of Vaudeville, has written some verses admirably
descriptive of an opera behind the scenes.
"J'ai vu le soleil et la lune

Qui tenoient des discours en l'air:
J'ai vu le terrible Neptune
Sortir tout frisé de la mer.
"J'ai vu l'aimable Cythéré
Au doux regard, au teint fleuri,
Dans un machine entourée
D'amours natifs de Chambérie."

And, after having seen a great number of other things

equally curious, he concludes with —
"J'ai vu des ombres très-palpables Se trémousser aux bords

du Styx;
J'ai vu l'enfer et tous les diables A quinze pieds du
Paradis,"
Some years ago, a strolling company at Ludlow, in

Shropshire, printed a playbill nearly as large as their
drop-scene. It announced "The Doleful History of King Lear
and his Three Daughters, with the Merry Conceits of his
Majesty's Fool, and the valorous exploits of the Duke of
Gloucester's Bastard; all written by one William
Shakespeare, a mighty great poet, who was born in
Warwickshire, and held horses for gentlemen at the sign of
the Red Bull in St. John's Street, where was just such
another playhouse as this (I!!), at which we hope the
company of all friends round the Wrekin.
"All you who would wish to cry or laugh,

Had better spend your money here than in the alehouse by
half;
And if you wish more about these things to know,
Come at six o'clock to the barn in the High Street, Ludlow,
Where, presented by live actors, the whole may be seen,
So Vivat Rex, God save the King, not forgetting the Queen."
Just as a strolling actor at Newcastle had advertised his

benefit, a remarkable stranger, no less than the Prince
Annamaboo arrived, and placarded the town that he granted
audiences at a shilling a-head. The stroller, without delay,
waited on the proprietor of the Prince, and for a good round
sum prevailed on him to command his Serene Highness to
exhibit his august person on his benefit night. The bills of
the day announced, that between the acts of the comedy
Prince Annumaboo would give a lively representation of the
scalping operation* sound the Indian war-whoop in all its
melodious tones, practise the tomahawk exercise, and dine à
la cannibal. An intelligent mob were collected to witness
these interesting exploits. At the conclusion of the third
act, his Highness marched forward flourishing his tomahawk,
and shouting, "Ha, ha! —ho, ho!" Next entered a man Avith
his face blacked, and a piece of bladder fastened to his
head with gum; the Prince, with an enormous carving-knife,
began the scalping part of the entertainment, which he
performed in a truly imperial style, holding up the piece of
bladder as a token of triumph. Next came the war-whoop, an
unearthly combination of discordant sounds; and lastly, the
banquet, consisting of raw beef-steaks, which he rolled up
into rouleaus, and devoured with right royal avidity. Having

finished his delicate repast, he wielded his tomahawk in an exulting manner, bellowed "Ha, ha! —ho, ho!" and made his exit. The beneficiare strolling through the marketplace the following day, spied the most puissant Prince Annama-boo selling pen-knives, scissors, and quills, in the character of a Jew pedlar. "What!" said the astonished Lord Townley, "my Prince, is it you? Are you not a pretty circumcised little scoundrel to impose upon us in this manner?" Moses turned round, and with an arch look, replied, "Princh be d —d! I vash no Princh; I vash acting, like you. Your troop vash Lords and Ladies last night; and to-night dey vil be Kings, Prinches, and Emperors! I vash hum pugs, you vash humpugs, all vash humpugs!"

There is a fair-an extraordinary one-the holding of which depends not on the caprice of magisterial wiggery. Jack Frost —a bold fellow! for he has taken Marlborough and Wellington by the nose-twice or thrice in a century proclaims his fair. No sooner is the joyful tidings bruited abroad, than the dutiful sons and daughters of Old Father Thames flock to his paternal bosom, which, being icy cold, they warm by roasting an ox upon it, and then transfer to its glassy surface the turmoil, traffic, and monstrosities of dry land.

Evelyn has given an interesting description of Frost Fair in 1683-4. This amusing chronicler of passing events possessed more than Athenian curiosity. He entered the penetralia of the court of King Charles the Second; and while he whispered in his closet pathetic Jeremiads over its immorality, he shocked his averted vision day after day with its impurities-still peeping! still praying! For all and sundry of the merry Monarch's "misses," and for poor *Nelly* (by far the best of them) in particular, he expressed a becoming horror in his private meditations; yet his outward bearing towards them indicated no such compunctious visitings. He was an excellent tactician. He crept into the privy councils of the regicides, and, *mirabile dictu!* retired from the enemy's camp in a whole skin; and while fortunes were being confiscated, and heads were falling on all sides, he kept his own snug in his pocket, and erect on his shoulders. Monarchy, Anarchy, High Church, Low Church, No Church, Catholicism, Anything-ism, Every-thing-ism.! plain John (he declined a baronetcy) passed over the red-hot ploughshares of political and religious persecution unsinged. And we rejoice at his good luck; for whether he treat of London's great Plague or Fire, the liaisons of his "kind master" King Charles the Second, the naughtiness of Nelly and her nymphs, or the ludicrous outbreaks of Southwark, St. Bartholomew, and Frost Fairs, he is a delightful, gentlemanly old gossiper!

On the 1st of January 1683-4, the cold was so intense, that booths (a novel spectacle) were erected on the Thames, and Jack Frost proclaimed his earliest recorded fair.

"I went crosse the Thames," says Evelyn, January 9, 1683-4, "on the ice, which now became so thick as to bear not only streetes of boothes, in which they roasted meate, and had divers shops of wares, quite acrosse as in a towne, but coaches, carts, and horses passed over. So I went from Westminster Stay res to Lambeth, and din'd with the Archbishop. I walked over the ice (after dinner) from Lambeth Stayres to the Horseferry."

"The Thames (Jany 16) was filled with people and tents, selling all sorts of wares as in a citty. The frost (Jany 24) continuing more and more severe, the Thames before London was still planned with boothes in formal streetes, all sorts of trades and shops furnished and full of commodities, even to a printing-presse, where the people and ladyes tooke a fancy to have their names printed on the Thames. This humour tooke so universally, that 'twas estimated the printer gain'd 51. a-day, for printing a line only, at sixpence a name, besides what he got by *ballads*, &c. Coaches plied from Westminster to the Temple, and from several other staires to and fro, as in the streetes, sleds, sliding with skeates, a bull-baiting, horse and coach races, puppet playes and interludes, cookes, tipling, and other lewd places, so that it seem'd to be a bacchanalian triumph, or carnival on the water."

"It began to thaw (Feb. 5), but froze againe. My coach crossed from Lambeth to the Horse-ferry at Millbank, Westminster. The booths were almost all taken downe; but there was first a map, or landskip, * cut in copper, representing all the manner of the camp, and the several actions, sports, and pastimes thereon, in memory of so signal a frost."

* These "Landskips" are interesting, and very difficult to be obtained. Thirteen, representing the Frost Fairs of 1683, —1715-16 —and 1739-40, now lie before us. "An exact and lively Mapp or Representation of Booths, and all the varieties of Showes and Humours upon the Ice on the River of Thames, by London, during that memorable Frost in the 35th yeare of the reigne of his Sacred Maty King Charles the 2d. Anno Dni 1683. With an Alphabetical Explanation of the most remarkable figures," exhibits "The Temple Staires, with people going upon the ice to Temple Street-The Duke of Yorkes Coffee House-The Tory Booth-The Booth with a Phoenix on it, and Insured as long as the Foundation Stand — The Roast Beefe Booth-The Half-way House-The Beare Garden Shire Booth-The Musiek Booth-The Printing Booth-The Lottery Booth-The Horne Tavern Booth-The Temple Garden, with Crowds of People looking over the wall-The Boat drawnc with a Hors-The Drum Boat-The Boat drawne upon vehiceles-The Bull-baiting —The Chair sliding in the Ring — The Boyes Sliding-The Nine Pinn Playing-The sliding on Scates-The Sledge drawing Coales from the other side of the Thames-The Boyes climbing up the Tree in the Temple Garden to sec ye Bull Baiting-The Toy Shoops-London Bridge." Another of these "lively Mapps" has a full-length portrait

of Erra Pater, referred to by Hudibras,
"In mathematics he was greater

Than Tycho Brahe or Erra Pater" —
prophesying in the midst of the fair.
"Old Erra Pater, or his rambling Ghost,
Prognosticating of this long strong Frost,
Some Ages past, said. yl ye Ice-bound Thames
Shou'd prove a Theatre for Sports and Games,
Her Wat'ry Green be turn'd into a Bare,
For Men a Citty seem, for Booths a Fairc;
And now this Stragling Sprite is once more come
To visit Mortalls and foretel their doom:
When Maids grow modest, ye Dissenting crew
Become all Loyal, the Falsehearted true,
Then you may probably, and not till then,
Expect in England such a Frost agen.

In 1715-16 Jack Frost paid Old Father Thames a second visit. * But whether maids had grown modest, dissenters loyal, and false-hearted men and true,

* "The best prospect of the frozen Thames with the booths on it, as taken from the Temple Stairs ye 20 day of January

1715-6, by C. Woodfield," is rich in fun, and a capital
piece of art. We owe great obligations to "Mr. Joshua Bangs"
for the following: —
"Mr. Joshua Bangs.

Printed at Holme's and Broad's Booth, at the Sign of the

Ship, against Old Swan Stairs, where is the Only Real
Printing Press on the Frozen Thames, January the 14th, 1715-
6.
"Where little Wherries once did use to ride,

And mounting Billows dash'd against their side,
Now Booths and Tents are built, whose inward Treasure
Affords to many a one Delight and Pleasure;
Wine, Beer, Cakes, hot Custards, Beef and Pies,
Upon the Thames are sold; there, on the Ice
You may have any
Thing to please the Sight,
Your Names are Printed, tho' you cannot write;
Therefore pray lose no Time, but hasten hither,
To drink a Glass with Broad and Holmes together."
'Several "Landskips" were published of this Frost Fair, in

which are shown "York Buildings Water Works —A Barge on a
Mountain of Ice —A drinking Tent on a Pile of Ice —
Theodore's Printing Booth —C.'s Piratical Song Booth-Cat in
the Basket Booth-King's Head Printing Booth-The Cap Musiek
Booth-The Hat Musick Booth-Dead Bodies floating in ye
Channel-Westminster Bridge, wh ye Works demolish'd —Skittle
Playing and other Diversions-Tradesmen hiring booths of ye
Watermen —A Number of confus'd Barges and Boats-Frost
Street from Westminster Hall to the Temple.
"This transient scene, a Universe of Glass,

Whose various forms are pictur'd as they pass,
Here future Ages may wth wonder view,
And wl they scarce could think, acknowledge true.
Printed on the River Thames in ye month of January 1740.

"Behold the liquid Thames now frozen o'er

That lately ships of mighty Burthen bore;
Here Watermen, for want to row in boats,
Make use of Bowze to get them Pence and Groats.
Frost Fair. Printed upon the Ice on the River Thames, Jan.

23, 1739-40."
"The bleak North-East, from rough Tartarian Shores,

O'er Europe's Realms its freezing Rigour pours,
Stagnates the flowing Blood in Human Veins,

And binds the silver Thames in ley Chains.
Their usual Courses Rivulets refrain,
And ev'ry Pond appears a Glassy Plain;
Streets now appear where Water was before,
And Thousands daily walk from Shore to Shore.
Frost Fair. Printed upon the River Thames when Frozen, Jan.

the 28.1739-40."
"The View of Frost Fair, Jan? 1739-40.

Scythians of old, like us remov'd,
In tents thro' various climes they rov'd;
We, bolder, on the frozen Wave,
To please your fancies toil and slave;
Here a strange group of figures rise,
Sleek beaus in furs salute your eyes;
Stout Soldiers, shiv'ring in their Bed,
Attack the Gin and Gingerbread;
Cits with their Wives, and Lawyers' Clerks,
Gamesters and Thieves, young Girls and Sparks.
This View to Future Times shall
Show The Medley Scene you Visit now."

according to old *Erra Pater's* prognostication in 1663, is a question; and in 1739-40 * he honoured him with a third, which was no less joyous than the preceding two. In 1788-9, the Thames was completely frozen over below London Bridge. Booths were erected on the ice; and puppet-shows, wild beasts, bear-baiting, turnabouts, pigs and sheep roasted, exhibited the various amusements of Bartholomew Fair multiplied and improved. From Putney Bridge down to Redriff was one continued scene of jollity during this seven weeks' saturnalia. The last Frost Fair was celebrated in the year 1814. The frost commenced on 27th December 1813, and continued to the 5th February 1814. *

* "The River Thames (4th Feby 1814) between London and
Blackfriars Bridges was yesterday about noon, a perfect
Dutch Fair. Kitchen fires and furnaces were blazing,
roasting and boiling in every direction; while animals, from
a sheep to a rabbit, and a goose to a lark, turned on
numberless spits. The inscriptions on the several booths and
lighters were variously whimsical, one of which ran thus: —
This Shop to Let. N.B. It is charged with no Land Tax or
even Ground Tient! Several lighters, lined with baize, and
decorated with gay streamers, were converted into
coffeehouses and taverns. About two o'clock a whole sheep
was roasted on the ice, and cut up, under the inviting
appellation of Lapland Mutton, at one shilling a slice!"

There was a grand walk, or mall, from Blackfriars Bridge to London Bridge, that was appropriately named *The City Road*, and lined on each side with booths of all descriptions. Several printing presses were erected, and at one of these an orange-coloured standard was hoisted, with "*Orange Boven*" printed in large characters. There were E O and Rouge et Noir tables, tee-to-tums and skittles; concerts of rough music, viz. salt-boxes and rolling-pins, gridirons and tongs, horns, and marrow-bones and cleavers. The carousing booths were filled with merry parties, some dancing to the sound of the fiddle, others sitting round blazing fires smoking and drinking. A printer's devil bawled out to the spectators, Now is your time, ladies and gentlemen-now is your time to support the freedom of the press! * Can the press enjoy greater liberty? Here you find it working in the middle of the Thames!" And calling upon his operatical powers to second his eloquence, he, with "vocal voice most vociferous," thus out-vociferated e'en sound itself—

Siste Viator! if sooner or later

You travel as far as from here to Jerusalem,

Or live to the ages of Parr or Methusalem —

On the word of old Wynkyn,

And Caxton, I'm thinking,

Tho' I don't wear a clothes —

Brush under my nose,

Or sweep my room

With my beard, like a broom,

I prophecy truly as wise Erra Pater,

You won't see again sick a wonder of Natur!"

A "Swan of Thames," too-an Irish swan! —whose abdominal regions looked as if they were stuffed with halfpenny doggrel,
    * The following is one among many specimens of Frost Fair
verse in 1813-14: —"Printed on the River Thames.
Behold the River Thames is frozen o'er,

Which lately ships of mighty burden bore;
Now different arts and pastimes here you see,

But printing claims the superiority."

entertained a half-frozen audience, who gave him shake for shake with

THE METRICAL, MUSICAL, COLD, AND COMICAL HUMOURS OF FROST FAIR.=

Open the door to me, my love,

 Prithee open the door —

Lift the latch of your h'gant thatch,

Your pleasant room, attic! or what a rheumatic

 And cold I shall catch!

And then, Miss Clark, between you and your spark

 'Twill be never a match!

I've been singing and ringing, and rapping and tapping,

And coughing and sneezing, and wheezing and freezing,

 While you have been napping,

Miss Clark, by the Clock of St. Mark,

 Twenty minutes and more!

Little Jack Frost the Thames has cross'd

In a surtout of frieze, as smart as you please! —

 There's a Bartlemy Fair and a thorough —

Slopsellers, sailors, three Tooley Street tailors,

All the élite of St. Thomas's Street,

 The Mint, and the Fleet!

The bear's at Polito's jigging his jolly toes;

Mr. Punch, with his hooked nose and hunch;

Patrick O'Brien, of giants the lion;

And Simon Paap, that sits in his lap,

The Lady that sews, and knits her hose,

And mends her clothes, and rubs her nose,

And comes and goes, without fingers and toes!

You may take a slice of roast beef on the ice;

At the Wellington Tap, and Mother Red-cap,

The stout runs down remarkably brown!

To the Thimble and Thistle, the Pig and Whistle,

Worthy Sir Felix has sent some choice relics

Of liquor, I'm told, to keep out the cold!

If you 've got a sweet tooth, there 's the gingerbread

    booth —

To the fife and the fiddle we'll dance down the middle,

Take a sup again, then dance up again!

And have our names printed off on the Thames;

Mister and Missis (all Cupids and kisses!)

Dermot O'Shinnigly, in a jig, in a glee!

And take a slide, or ha'penny ride

    From Blackfriars Bridge to the Borough!

The sun won't rise till you open your eyes —

    Then give the sly slip to the sleepers.

Don't, Miss Clark, let us be in the dark,

    But open your window and peepers.

A friend of ours who had a tumble, declared, that though he had no desire to see the city burnt down, he devoutly wished to have the streets *laid in ashes!* And another, somewhat of a penurious turn, being found in bed late in the morning, and saluted with, "What! not yet risen?" replied, "No; nor shall I till *coals fall!*"

CHAPTER VI.

And now, Eugenio, ere we cross the ferry, and mingle with the 'roaring boyes and swashbucklers' of St. Bartholomew, let us halt at the *Tabard*, and snatch a brief association with Chaucer and his Pilgrims. The localities that were once hallowed by the presence of genius we ardently seek after, and fondly trace through all their obscurities, and regard them with as true a devotion as does the pilgrim the sacred shrine to which, after his patiently-endured perils by sea and land, he offers his adoration. The humblest roof gathers glory from the bright spirit that once irradiated it; the simplest relic becomes a precious gem, when connected with the gifted and the good. We haunt as holy ground the spot where the muse inspired our favourite bard; we treasure up his hand-writing in our cabinets; we study his works as emanations from the poet; we cherish his associations as reminiscences of the man. Never can I forget your high-toned enthusiasm when you stood in the solemn chancel of Stratford-upon-Avon, pale, breathless, and fixed like marble, before the mausoleum of Shakspeare!"

"An honest and blithesome spirit was the Father of English Poetry! happy in hope, healthful in morals, lofty in imagination, and racy in humour —a bright earnest of that transcendent genius who, in an after age, shed his mighty lustre over the literature of Europe. The *Tabard!* —how the heart leaps at the sound! What would *Uncle Timothy* say if he were here?"

"All that you have said, and much more, could he say it as well." And instantly we felt the cordial pressure of a hand stretched out to us from the next box, where sat solus the middle-aged gentleman. "To have passed the Tabard, * would have been treason to those beautiful associations that make memory of the value that it is!

* "Befelle that in that seson, on a day,
In Southwerk at the Tabard as I lay,
Redy to wenden on my pilgrimage
To Canterbury, with devoute corage,
At night was eome into that hostellerie
Wei nine-and-twenty in a compagnie,
Of sondry folk, by a venture yfalle,
In felawship, and pilgrimes were they alle,
That toward Canterbury wolden ride.
The chambres and the stables weren wide,
And wel we wreren csed atte beste."

One of the most rational pleasures of the intellectual mind is to escape from the present to the past. The contemplation of antiquity is replete with melancholy interest. The eye wanders with delight over the crumbling ruins of ancient magnificence; the heart is touched with some sublime emotion; and we ask which is the' most praiseworthy-the superstition that raised these holy temples, or the piety (?) that suffers them to fall to decay? This corner is one of my periodical resting-places after a day's solitary ramble; for I have many such, in order to brush lip old recollections, and lay in fresh mental fuel for a winter evening's fireside.'Tis a miracle that this antique fabric should have escaped demolition. Look at St. Saviour's! *

* The ancient grave-yard of St. Saviour's contains the sacred dust of Massinger. All that the Parish Register records of him is, "March 20, 1639-40, buried Philip Massinger, a Stranger." John Fletcher, the eminent dramatic poet, who died of the Plague, August 19,1625, was buried in the church.

With all due respect for Uncle Timothy's opinion, we think

he is a little too hard upon the citizens, who are not the

only Vandals in matters of antiquity. The mitre has done its part in the work of demolition. Who destroyed the ancient palace of the Bishops of Ely, (where "Old John of Gaunt, time-honour'd Lancaster," breathed his last, in 1398,) with its beautiful Chapel and magnificent Gothic Hall? The site of its once pleasant garden in Holborn, from whence Richard Duke of Gloucester requested a dish of strawberries from the Bishop on the morning he sent Lord Hastings to execution, is

now a rookery of mean hovels. And the Hospital of Saint Catherine, and its Collegiate Church-where are they? Not one stone lies upon another of those unrivalled Gothic temples of piety and holiness, founded by the pious Queen Matilda. And the ancient Church of St. Bartholomew, where once reposed the ashes of Miles Coverdale, and which the Great Fire of London spared, is now razed to the ground! De Gustibusf Alderman Newman, who had scraped together out

of the grocery line six hundred thousand pounds, enjoyed no greater luxury during the last three years of his life than to repair daily to the shop, and, precisely as the clock struck two (the good old-fashioned hour of city dining), eat his mutton with his successors. The late Thomas Rippon, Chief Cashier of the Bank of England, was a similar oddity. Onee only, in a service of fifty years, did he venture to ask for a fortnight's holiday. He left town, but after a three days' unhappy ramble through beautiful green fields, he grew moping and melancholy, and prematurely returned to the blissful regions of Threadneedle Street to die at his desk!

In the contemplation of that impressive scene-amidst the everlasting freshness of nature and the decay of time —I have been taught more rightly to estimate the works of man and his Creator-the one, like himself, stately in pride and beauty, but which pass away as a shadow, and are seen no more; the other, the type of divinity, infinite, immutable, and eternal."

"But surely-may I call you Uncle Timothy?" Uncle Timothy good-humouredly nodded assent. "Surely, Uncle Timothy, the restoration of the Ladye Chapel and Crosby Hall speak something for the good taste of the citizens."

"Modestly argued, Eugenio!"

"An accident, my young friend, a mere accident, forced upon the Vandals. Talk of antiquity to a Guildhall Magnifico I * Sirs, I once mentioned the 'London Stone' to one of these blue-gown gentry, and his one idea immediately reverted to the well-known refectory of that venerable name, where he stuffs himself to repletion and scarletifies his nasal promontory, without a thought of Wat Tyler, * the Lord of the Circle! An acquaintance of mine, one Deputy Dewlap, after dining with the Patten-makers on the 9th of November, was attacked with a violent fit of indigestion.

* Small was the people's gain by the insurrection of Wat Tyler. The elements of discord, once put in motion, spread abroad with wild fury, till, with the ignoble blood of base hinds, mingled the bravest and best in the land. The people returned to their subjection wondering and dispirited. For whose advantage had all these excesses been committed? Was

their position raised? Were their grievances redressed,
their wants alleviated? Did their yoke press lighter? Were
they nearer the attainment of their (perhaps "reasonable)
wishes, by nobility and prelates cruelly slaughtered,
palaces burned down, and the learning and works of art that
humanise and soften rugged natures piled in one vast,-
indiscriminate ruin? If aught was won by these monstrous
disorders, they were not the winners. The little aristocrats
of cities, who have thrown their small weight into popular
insurrections, may have had their vanity gratified and their
maws temporarily crammed; but the masses, who do the rough
work of resistance for their more cunning masters, are
invariably the sufferers and dupes. Hard knocks and hanging
have hitherto been their reward; and when these shall grow
out of fashion, doubtless some equally agreeable substitute
will be found. "It is not an obvious way (says Wyndham) for
making the liquor more clear, to give a shake to the cask,
and to bring up as much as possible from the parts nearest
to the bottom."

His lady sent for the family doctor —a humorist, gentlemen. 'Ah!' * cried Mr. Galen, 'the
old complaint, a coagulation in the lungs. Let me feel your pulse. In a high fever! Show me
your tongue. Ay, as white as a curd. Open your mouth, wider, Mr. Deputy-you caw open it
wide enough *sometimes!* —wider still. Good heavens! what do. I see here?' —'Oh! my stars!'
screamed the Deputy's wife, 'What, my dear doctor, do you-see?' —'Why, madam, I see the
leg of a turkey, and a tureen of oyster-sauce!' 'Ha! ha! ha! —gluttons all; gluttons all!'

Mr Deputy Dewlap's Fit of Indigestion

Original

"A pise on Benjamin Bosky! the cunning Lauréat, having a visitation from sundry relatives of his cousin's wife's uncle's aunt's sister, hath enjoined me the penance, *malgré moi-même!* of playing showman to them among the Lions of London. Now I have no antipathy to poor relations-your shabby genteel-provided that, while they eat and drink at my expense, they will not fail to contradict ** me stoutly when they think I am in the wrong; but your purse-proud, half-and-half,

* When Justice Shallow invited Falstaff to dinner, he issued
the following orders: —"Some pigeons, Davy; a couple of
short-legged hens; a joint of mutton; and any pretty little
tiny kickshaws, tell William Cook." This is a modest bill of
fare. What says Massinger of City feasting in the olden
time?
"Men may talk of Country Christmasses,

Their thirty-pound butter'd eggs, their pies of carp's

tongue, Their pheasants drench'd with ambergris, the
carcases Of three fat wethers bruised for gravy, to Make
sauce for a single peacock; yet their feasts were fasts,
compared with the City's."
** A friend of Addison's borrowed a thousand pounds of him,

which finding it inconvenient to repay, he never upon any
occasion ventured to contradict him. One day the hypocrisy
became so offensively palpable, that Addison, losing all
patience, exclaimed, "For heaven's sake contradict me, sir,
or pay me my thousand pounds!"

Brummagem gentlefolks, shabby, without being-genteel! —your pettifoggers in small talk and etiquette, that know everything and nothing-listening to and retailing everybody's gossip, meddling with everybody's business-and such are the Fubsys, Muffs, and Flumgartens-are sad provocatives to my splenetic vein.

His spirits rallied when the talk was of Chaucer, whose memory we drank in a cup of sack prepared, as mine host assured us, from a recipe that had belonged to the house as an heir-loom, time out of mind, and of which Dick Tarlton had often tasted.

"Dick Tarlton, Uncle Timothy-was not he one of the types of Merrie England?"

"A mad wag! His diminished nose was a peg upon which hung many an odd jest. His 'whereabouts' were hereabouts at the Bear Garden; but the Bull in Bishopsgate Street; the Bel-Savage, without Ludgate; and his own tavern, the Tabor, in Gracious (Gracechurch) Street, came in for a share of his drolleries. Marvellous must have been the humour of this 'allowed fool, when it could 'undumpish' his royal mistress in her frequent paroxysms of concupiscence and ferocity! He was no poll-parrot retailer of other people's jokes. He had a wit's treasury of his own, upon which he drew liberally, and at sight. His nose was flat; not so his jests; and, in exchanging extemporal gibes with his audience, * he generally returned a good repartee for a bad one."

* Tarlton having to speak a prologue, and finding no
cessation to the hissing, suddenly addressed the audience in
this tetrastie: —
I lived not in the golden age,

When Jason won the fleece;
But now I am on Gotham's stage,
Where fools do hiss like geese.

On the authority of an old play, "The Three Lords and Three Ladies of London," published two years after his death, he was originally "a, water-bearer." Among England's merry crew in the olden time were Will Summers, jester to King Henry the Eighth; Patch, Cardinal Wolsey's fool; Jack Oates, fool to Sir Richard Hollis; and Archibald Armstrong, jester to King Charles the First. There was a famous jester, one Jemy Camber, "a fat foole," who enlivened the dull Court of James the Sixth of Scotland. The manner of his death, as recorded in "A Nest of Ninnies," by Robert Armin, 4to. 1608, is singular. "The Chamber-laine was sent to see him there," (at the house of a laundress in Edinburgh, whose daughter he was soliciting, and who had provided a bed of nettles for his solace,) "who when he came found him fast asleep under the bed starke naked, bathing in nettles, whose skinne when hee wakened him, was all blistered grievously. The King's Chamberlaine bid him arise and come to the King. 'I will not,' quoth he, 'I will go make my grave.' See how things chanced, he spake truer than he was awar. For the Chamberlaine going home without him, tolde the King his answere. Jemy rose, made him ready, takes his horse, and rides to the church-yard in the high towne, where he found the sexton (as the custom is there) making nine graves-three for men, three for women, and three for children; and who so dyes next, first comes, first served, * 'Lend mee thy spade,' says Jemy, and with that, digs a hole, which hole hee bids him make for his grave; and doth give him a French crowne; the man, willing to please him (more for his gold than his pleasure) did so: and the foole gets upon his horse, rides to a gentleman of the towne, and on the so-daine, within two houres after, dyed: of whom the sexton telling, hee was buried there indeed. Thus, you see, fooles have a gesse at wit sometime, and the wisest could have done no more, nor so much. But thus this fat foole fills a leane grave with his carkasse; upon which grave the King caused a stone of marble to bee put, on which poets writ these lines in remembrance of him:

'He that gard all men till jeare,

Jemy a Camber he ligges here:

Pray for his Sale, for he is geane.

And here a ligges beneath this steane.

The following poetical picture of him is exact and curious.

"This Fat Foole was a Scot borne, brought up

In Sterlin, twenty miles from Edinborough;

Who being but young, was for the King caught up,

Serv'd this King's father all his lifetime through.

A yard high and a nayle, no more his stature,

Smooth fac't, fayre spoken, yet unkynde by nature.

Two yards in compassé and a nayle I reade

102

Was he at forty yeeres, since when I heard not;

Nor of his life or death, and further heede,

Since I never read, I looke not, nor regard not,

But what at that time Jemy Camber was

As I have heard, lie write, and so let passe.

His head was small, his hayre long on the same,

One eare was bigger than the other farre:

His fore-head full, his eyes shinde like a flame,"

His nose flat, and his beard small, yet grew square;

His lips but little, and his wit was lesse,

But wide of mouth, few teeth I must confesse.

His middle thicke, as I have said before,

Indifferent thighes and knees, but very short;

His legs be square, a foot long, and no more,

Whose very presence made the King much sport.

And a pearle spoone he still wore in his cap,

To eate his meate he lov'd, and got by hap

A pretty little foote, but a big hand,

On which he ever wore rings rich and good:

Backward well made as any in that land,

Though thicke, and he did eome of gentle bloud;

But of his wisdome, ye shall quickly heare,

How this Fat Foole was made on every where."

And some capital jokes are recorded of him in this same "Nest of Ninnies." There was another fool, "leane Leonard," who belonged to "a kinde gentleman" in "the merry Forrest of Sherwood," a gluttonous fellow, of unbounded assurance and ready wit. "This leane, greedy foole, having a stomaeke, and seeing the butler out of the way, his appetite was such, as loath to tarry, he breakes open the dairy-house, eates and spoiles new cheeseeurds, cheesecakes, overthrowes creame bowles, and having filled his belly, and knew he had done evill, gets him gone to Mansfield in Sherwood, as one fearefull to be at home: the maydes came home that morning from milking, and finding such a masaker of their dairie, almost mad, thought a yeares wages could not make amends: but 'O the foole, leane Leonard,' they cryed, 'betid this mischiefe!' They complayned to their master, but to no purpose, Leonard was farre inough off; search was made for the foole, but hee was gone none new whither, and it was his pro-pertie, having done mischiefe, never to come home of himselfe, but if any one intreated him, he would easy be won.

"All this while, the foole was at Mansfield in Sherwood, and stood gaping at a shoomaker's stall; who, not knowing him, asked him what he was? 'Goe look,' says hee; 'I know not my selfe.' They asked him where he was borne? 'At my mother's backe,' says he. —'In what country?' quoth they. —'In the country,' quoth he, 'where God is a good man.' At last one of the three journeymen imagined he wras not very wise, and flouted him very merrily, asking him if he would have a stitch where there was a hole? (meaning his mouth.) 'Aye,' quoth the foole, 'if your nose may bee the needle.' The shoomaker could have found in his heart to have tooke measure on his pate with a last in steede of his foote; but let him goe as he was.

"A country plow-jogger being by, noting all this, secretly stole a piece of shoomaker's ware off the stall, and coming be-hinde him, clapt him on the head, and asked him how he did. The foole, seeing the piteh-ball, pulled to have it off, but could not but with much paine, in an envious spleene, smarting ripe, runs after him, fais at fistie cuffes with, but the fellow belaboured the foole cunningly, and got the foole's head under his arme, and bobb'd his nose. The foole remembering how his head was, strikes it up, and hits the fellowes mouth with the pitcht place, so that the haire of his head, and the haire of the clownes beard were glued together. The fellow cryed, the foole exclaimed, and could not sodanely part. In the end the people (after much laughing at the jest) let them part faire; the one went to picke his beard, the other his head. The constable came, and asked the cause of their falling out, and knowing one to be Leonard the leane foole, whom hee had a warrant for from the gentleman to search for, demaunds of the fellow how it hapned? The fellow hee could answere nothing but 4 um-um,' for his mouth was sealed up with wax, 'Dost thou scorne to speake V says hee. 41 am the King's officer, knave!' 6 Um-um,' quoth hee againe. Meaning hee would tell him all when his mouth was cleane. But the constable, thinking hee was mockt, clapt him in the stocks, where the fellow sate a long houre farming his mouth, and when hee had done, and might tell his griefe, the constable was gone to carry home Leonard to his maister; who, not at home, hee was enforced to stay supper time, where hee told the gentleman the jest, who was very merry to heare the story, contented the officer, and had him to set the fellow at liberty, who betimes in the morning was found fast asleep in the stocks. The fellow knowing himselfe faulty, put up his wrongs, quickly departed, and went to work betimes that morning with a flea in his eare."

"Jacke Oates was "a fellow of infinite jest," and took to the fullest extent the laughing licence that his coat of motley allowed him. His portrait, contained in "A Nest of Ninnies," is quite as minute and interesting as the true effigie of Leane Leonard, which follows it.

"This Foole was tall, his face small,

His beard was big and blacke,

His necke was short, inclin'd to sport

Was this our dapper Jacke.

Of nature curst, yet not the worst,

    Was nastie, given to sweare;

Toylesome ever, his endeavour

    Was delight in beere.

Goutie great, of conceit

    Apt, and full of favour;

Curst, yet kinde, and inclinde

    To spare the wise man's labour.

Knowne to many, loude of any,

    Cause his trust was truth!

Seene in toy es, apt to joy es,

    To please with tricks of youth.

Writh'd i' th' knees, yet who sees

    Faults that hidden be?

Calf great, in whose conceit

    Lay much game and glee.

Bigge i' th' small, ancle all,

    Footed broad and long,

In Motley cotes, goes Jacke Oates,

    Of whom I sing this song."

"Curled locks on idiot's heads,

    Yeallow as the amber,

Playes on thoughts, as girls with beads,

    When their masse they stamber.

Thicke of hearing, yet thin ear'd,

    Long of neck and visage,

Hookie nosde and thicke of beard,

Sullen in his usage.

Clutterfisted, long of arme,

Bodie straight and slender'd,

Boistious hipt motly warm'd,

Ever went leane Leonard.

Gouty leg'd, footed long,

Subtill in his follie,

Shewing right, but apt to wrong,

When a'pear'd most holy.

Understand him as he is,

For his marks you cannot misse."

Eugenio. —"'Tis said that he died penitent." Uncle Tim. —"I hope he did. I hope all have died penitent. I hope all will die penitent. Alas! for the self-complacent Pharisees of this world; they cannot forgive the poor player:' little reflecting of how many, not laughing but crying sins they will require to be forgiven. The breath of such hearts would wither even the flowers of Paradise."

Could we sit at the Tabard, and not remember the Globe, * with its flag floating in the air, the Boar's Head, and the Falcon!

* "Each playhouse," says W. Parkes, in his Curtain-drawer of the World, 4to. 1612, "advaneeth its flag in the air, whither, quickly, at the waving thereof, are summoned whole troops of men, women, and children." And William Rowley, in "A Search for Money, 1609," whilst enumerating the many strange characters assembled at a tavern in quest of "The Wandering Knight, Monsieur L'Argent," includes among them four or five flag-falne plaiers, poore harmlesse merrie knaves, that were now neither lords nor ladies, but honestly wore their owne clothes (if they were paid for.)
In 1698 an unsuccessful attempt was made by the puritanical

vestry of Saint Saviour's to put down the Globe Theatre, on the plea of the "enormities" practised there. But James the First, when he came to the throne, knocked their petitions on the head by granting his patent to Shakspere and others to perform plays, "as well within their usuall house called the Globe, in Surry," as elsewhere. It was what Stowe calls "a frame of timber," with, according to John Taylor, the water-poet, "a thatched hide." Its sign was an Atlas bearing a globe. It was accidentally burnt down on St. Peter's day, June 29, 1613. "And a marvaile and fair grace of God it was," says Sir Ralph Winwood in his Memorials, "that the people had so little harm, having but two little doors to get out."

Sir Henry Wootton's relation of this fire is exceedingly

interesting. "Now, to let matters of state sleep, I will
entertain you at the present with what hath happened this
week at the Banks side. The King's players had a new play,
called All is true, representing some principal pieces of
the raign of Henry 8 which was set forth with many
extraordinary circumstances of pomp and majesty, even to the
matting of the stage, the knights of the order, with their
Georges and garters, the guards with their embroidered
coats, and the like: sufficient, in truth, within a mile to
make greatness very familiar, if not ridiculous. Now King
Henry making a masque at the Cardinal Woolsey's house, and
certain canons being shot off at his entry, some of the
paper, or other stuff wherewith one of them were stopped,
did light on the thatch, where, being thought at first but
an idle smoak, and their eyes more attentive to the show, it
kindled inwardly, and ran round like a train, consuming
within less than an hour the whole house to the very ground.
"This was the fatal period of that vertuous fabrique,

wherein nothing did perish but wood and straw, and a few
forsaken cloaks; only one man had his breeches set on fire,
that would perhaps have broyled him if he had not, by the
benefit of a provident wit, put it out with bottle-ale. The
rest when we meet."—Reliquio Woottonio.

Suddenly the strings of a harp were struck. "Listen!" said Uncle Timothy, "that is no everyday
hand."

The chords were repeated; and, after a symphony that spoke in exquisite tones a variety of
passions, a voice melodious and plaintive sang—

THE OLD HARPER'S SONG.=

Sound the harp! strike the lyre! —Ah! the Minstrel is

old;

The days of his harping are very nigh told;

Yet Shakspere, * sweet Shakspere! thy name shall expire

On his cold quiv'ring lips-Sound the harp! strike the

lyre!

Its music was thine when his harp he first strung,

And thou wert the earliest song that he sung;

Now feeble and trembling his hand sweeps the wire —

Be thine its last note! —Sound the harp I strike the

lyre!

I've wander'd where riches and poverty dwell;

With all but, the sordid, thy name was a spell.

Love, pity, and joy, in each bosom beat higher;

Rage, madness, despair I —Sound the harp! strike the lyre!

The scenes of thy triumphs are pass'd as a dream;

But still flows in beauty, sweet Avon-thy stream.

Still rises majestic that heaven-pointed spire,

Thy temple and tomb! —Sound the harp! strike the

lyre!"

* The Duke of Marlborough, on being asked in the house of a
titled lady from what history of England he was quoting,
answered, "the only one I have ever read-Shakspere!"

"Gentlemen," said Uncle Timothy, and his eye glistened and his lip trembled, "the old minstrel must not depart hence without a full purse and a plentiful scrip. But first to bespeak him the best bed that this hostelrie affords, and compound a loving cup to warm his heart as he hath warmed ours. This chimney-corner shall be his harp's resting-place for the night, as perchance it hath been of many long since silent and unstrung."

The middle-aged gentleman rose to usher in the minstrel; but paused as the harp and voice were again attuned, but to a livelier measure.

"THE PEDLAR'S PACK.=

"Needles and pins! Needles and pins!

Lads and lasses, the fair begins!

Ribbons and laces

For sweet smiling faces;

Glasses for quizzers;

Bodkins and scissors;

Baubles, my dears,

For your fingers and ears;

Sneeshing for sneezers;

Toothpicks and tweezers;

Garlands so gay

For Valentine's day;

Fans for the pretty;

Jests for the witty;

Songs for the many

Three yards a penny!

I'm a jolly gay pedlar, and bear on my back,

Like my betters, my fortune through brake and

through briar;

I shuffle, I cut, and I deal out my pack;

And when I play the knave, 'tis for you to play

higher!

In default of a scrip,

In my pocket I slip

A good fat hen, lest it die of the pip!

When my cream I have sipp'd,

And my liquor I've lipp'd,

I often have been, like my syllabub-whipp'd.

But a pedlar's back is as broad as its long,

So is his conscience, and so is his song!"

"An arrant Proteus!" said Uncle Timothy, "with the harp of Urien, and the knavery of Autolicus. But we must have him in, and see what further store of ballads he hath in his budget."

And he rose a second time; but was anticipated by the Squire Minstrel, who entered, crying, "Largess! gentles, largess! for the poor harper of merry Stratford-upon-Avon."

The personage making this demand was enveloped in a large, loose camlet cloak, that had evidently passed through several generations of his craft till it descended to the shortest. His complexion was of a brickdust rosiness, through which shone dirtiness visible; his upper-lip was fortified with a huge pair of sable mustachios, and his nether curled fiercely with a bushy imperial. His eyes, peering under his broad-brimmed slouched beaver, were intelligent, and twinkled with good humour. His voice, like his figure, was round and oily; and when he doffed his hat, a shock of coal-black wiry hair fell over his face, and rendered his features still more obscure.

"Well, goodman Harper," cried Uncle Timothy, after viewing attentively this singular character, "what other Fittes, yet unsung, have you in your budget?"

"A right merry and conceited infinity!" replied the minstrel. "*Nutmegs for Nightingales!* a Balade of a priest that loste his nose for saying of masse, as I suppose; a most pleasant Ballad of patient Grissell; a merry new Song how a Brewer meant to make a Cooper cuckold, and how deere the Brewer paid for the bargaine; a merie newe Ballad intituled the pinnyng of the Basket; the Twenty-Five orders of Fooles; a Ditty delightful of Mother Watkin's ah; A warning well wayed, though counted a tale; and A prettie new Ballad, intytuled

'The crowe sits upon the wall,

Please one, and please all!

written and sung by Dick Tarlton! * Were it meet for you, most reverend and rich citizens, to bibo with a poor ballad-monger, I would crave your honours to pledge with me a cup to his merry memory."

"Meet!" quoth Uncle Timothy. "Grammercy! Dick Tarlton is meat, ay, and drink too, for the best wit in Christendom, past, present, and to come!

* Tarlton was a poet. "Tarlton's Toys" (see Thomas Nash's "Terrors of the Night," 4to. 1594,) had appeared in 1586. He had some share in the extemporal play of "The Seven Deadly Sins." In 1578, John Allde had a licence to publish "Tarlton's device upon this unlooked-for great snowe." In 1570, the same John Allde "at the long shop adjoyning unto Saint Mildred's Church in the Pultrye," published "A very Lamentable and Wofull Discours of the Fierce Fluds, which lately Flowed in Bedford Shire, in Lincoln Shire, and in many other Places, with the Great Losses of Sheep and other Cattel, the 5th of October, 1570." We are in possession of an unique black-letter ballad, written by Tarlto. It has

a woodcut of a lady dressed in the full court costume of the time, holding in her right hand a fan of feathers.
"A prettie newe Ballad, intytuled:

The crowe sits upon the wall,

Please one and please all.

To the tune of, 'Please one and please all.'

Imprinted at London for Henry Kyrkham, dwelling at the

little North doore of Paules, at. the Sygne of the blacke Boys." Tarlton's wife, Kate, was a shrew; and, if his own epigram be sooth, a quean into the bargain.
"Woe to thee, Tarjton, that ever thou were born,

Thy wife hath made thee a cuckold, and thou must wear the horn:
What, and if she hath? Am I a whit the worse?
She keeps me like a gentleman, with money in my purse."
He was not always so enduring and complaisant: for on one

occasion, in a storm, he proposed, to lighten the vessel by throwing his lady overboard!

Thy calling, vagrant though it be, shall not stand in the way of a good toast. What say you, my friends, to a loving cup with the harper, to Dick Tarlton, and Merrie England? The cup went round; and as the harper brushed his lips after the spicy draught, so did his right mustachio!

Uncle Timothy did not notice this peculiarity.

"Might I once more presume, my noble masters," said the harper. "I would humbly — —"

"Thou art Lord of Misrule for to-night," replied Uncle Timothy. "Go on presuming."

"The memory of the immortal Twenty-nine, and their patron, Holy Saint Thomas of Canterbury!"

And the minstrel bowed his head reverently, crossed his hands over his breast, and rising to his harp, struck a chord that made every bosom thrill again.

"Thy touch hath a finish, and thy voice a harmony that betoken cultivation and science."

As the middle-aged gentleman made this observation, the mustachio that had taken a downward curve, fell to the ground; its companion, (some conjuror's heir-loom,) played at follow my leader; and the solitary imperial was left alone in its glory.

The harper, to hide his confusion, hummed Lo-doiska.

Uncle Timothy, espying the phenomenon, fixed his wondering eyes full in the strange man's face, and exclaimed, "Who, and what art thou?"

"I'm a palmer come from the Holy Land." (*Singing.*)

"Doubtless!" replied Uncle Timothy. "A palmer of traveller's tales upon such ignoramuses as will believe them. Why, that mysterious budget of thine contains every black-letter rarity that Captain Cox * of Coventry rejoiced in, and bibliomaniacs sigh for. Who, and what art thou?"

* Laneham, in his Account of the Queen's Entertainment at Killingworth Castle, 1575, represents this military mason and bibliomaniac as "marching on valiantly before, clean trust, and gartered above the knee, all fresh in a velvet cap, flourishing with his ton sword and describing a

procession of the Coventry men in celebration of Hock
Tuesday, he introduces "Fyrst, Captain Cox, an od man I
promiz yoo; by profession a mason, and that right skilfull;
very cunning in fens, and hardy az Gavin; for hiz ton-sword
hangs at hiz tabbz eend; great oversight hath he in matters
of storie: for az for King Arthur z book, Huon of Burdeaus,
the foour sons of Ay mon, Bevys of Hampton, the Squyre of lo
degree, the Knight of Courtesy, the Wido Edyth, the King and
the Tanner, Robin-hood, Adam Bel, Clim of the Clough and
William of Cloudsley, the Wife lapt in a Morels Skin, the
Sakfull of Nuez, Elynor Rumming, and the Nutbrown Maid.
"What should I rehearz heer, what a bunch of Ballets and

Songs, all aunciet; and Broom broom on Hill, So Wo iz me
begon, troly lo, Over a Whinny Meg, Hey ding a ding, Bony
lass upon a green, My hony on gave me a bek, By a bank as I
lay: and a hundred more he hath fair wrapt up in parchment,
and bound with a whip cord. To stay ye no longer heerin, I
dare say he hath as fair a library for theez sciencez, and
az many goodly monuments both in prose and poetry, and at
after noonz can talk az much without book, az ony inholder
betwixt Brainford and Bagshot, what degree soever he be."

"Suppose, signors, I should be some eccentric nobleman in disguise-or odd fish of an amateur
collecting musical tribute to win a wager-or suppose-"

"Have done with thy supposes!" cried the impatient and satirical-nosed gentleman.

"Or, suppose —*Uncle Timothy!*" Here, with the adroitness of a practised mimic, the voice was
changed in an instant, the coal-black wiry wig thrown off, the bushy imperial sent to look after
the stray mustachios, the thread-bare camlet cloak and rusty beaver cast aside, and the chaffing
quaffing, loud-laughing Lauréat of Little Britain stood confessed under a stucco of red ochre!

"Was there ever such a mountebank varlet!" shouted the middle-aged gentleman, holding
fast his two sides.

"I followed close upon your skirts, and dogged you hither."

"Dogged me, puppy!"

"Mr. Moses, the old clothesman, provided my mendicant wardrobe, and mine host lent the
harp, which belongs to an itinerant musician, who charms his parlour company with sweet
sounds. I intended, dear Uncle Timothy, to surprise and please you."

"And in truth, Benjamin, thou hast done both. I am surprised and pleased!" And drawing nearer, with a suppressed voice, he added, "When sick and sorrowful, sing me that old
harper's song. When thou only art left to smooth my pillow, and close my eyes sing me that
old harper's song!

"Twill make me pass the cup of anguish by,

Mix with the blest, nor know that I had died.

"And you, Jacob Jollyboy, to plot against me with that Israelitish retailer of cast-off duds, Mr.
Moses!" continued the satirical-nosed gentleman, labouring hard to conceal his emotion under
a taking-to-task frown exceedingly imposing and ludicrous.

Mr. Jollyboy looked all confusion and cutlets.. "Where do you expect to go when you die?"

"Where Uncle Timothy goes, and '*je suis content*, 'as the Frenchman said to not half so dainty a dish of smoking-hot Scotch collops as I have the honour to set before you." And Mr. Jollyboy breathed, or rather puffed again.

The Lauréat,

"Neat, trimly drest,

Fresh as a bridegroom," and his face new wash'd,

re-entered, and with his usual urbanity did the honours of the supper-table.

The Scotch collops having been despatched with hearty good will, Uncle Timothy restricted our future libations to one single bowl. "And mind, Benjamin, only one!" This was delivered with peculiar emphasis. Mr. Bosky bowed obedience to the behest; and, as a nod is as good as a wink, he *nodded* to Mr. Jollyboy.

The bowl was brought in, brimming and beautiful; and it was five good acts of a comedy to watch the features of Uncle Timothy. He first gazed at the bowl, then at the landlord, then at the lauréat, then at us, and then at the bowl again!

"Pray, Mr. Jollyboy," he inquired, "call you this a bowl, or a caldron?"

Mr. Jollyboy solemnly deposed as to its being a real bowl; the identical bowl in which six little Jollyboys had been christened.

"Is it your intention, Mr. Jollyboy, to christen us too? Let it be tipplers, then, mine host of the Tabard!"

"As to the christening, Uncle Timothy, that would be nothing very much out of order-seeing

That some great poet says, I'll take my oath,

Man is an infant, but of larger growth.

"Besides," argued Mr. Bosky, Socratically, the *dimensions* of the bowl were not in the record; and as I thought we should be too many for a halfcrown sneaker of punch-"

"You thought you would be too many for me! And so you have been. Sit down, Mr. Jollyboy, and help us out of this dilemma. Take a drop of your own physic."

Mr. Jollyboy respectfully intimated he would rather do that than break his arm; and took his seat at the board accordingly.

"But," said Uncle Timothy, "let us have the entire *dramatis personæ* of the harper's interlude. We are minus his groom of the stole. Send our compliments over the way for Mr. Moses."

Mr. Moses was summoned, and he sidled in with a very high stock, with broad pink stripes, and a very low bow hoping "de gentlemensh vash quite veil."

"Still," cried Mr. Bosky, "we are not all mustered. The harp!" And instantly the lauréat "with flying fingers touched the" wires.

"A song from Uncle Timothy, for which the musical bells of St. Saviour's tell us there is just time." He then struck the instrument to a lively tune, and the middle-aged gentleman sang with appropriate feeling,

"THE TABARD.

"Old Tabard! those time-honour'd timbers of thine.

Saw the pilgrims ride forth to St. Thomas's shrine;

  When the good wife of Bath

  Shed a light on their path.

And the squire told his tale of Cambuscan divine.

From his harem th' alarum shrill chanticleer crew,

And uprose thy host and his company too;

  The knight rein'd his steed,

  And a f Gentles, God speed!'

The pipes of the miller right merrily blew.

There shone on that morning a halo, a ray,

Old Tabard I round thee, that shall ne'er pass away;

  When the fam'd Twenty-Nine

  At the glorified shrine

Of their martyr went forth to repent and to pray.

Though ages have roll'd since that bright April morn,

And the steps of the shrine holy palmers have worn,

  As, weary and faint,

  They kneel'd to their saint —

It still for all time shall in memory be borne.

Old Tabard! old Tabard! thy pilgrims are we!

What a beautiful shrine has the Bard made of thee I

  When a ruin's thy roof,

  And thy walls, massy proof—

The ground they adorn'd ever hallow'd shall be."

CHAPTER VII.

Methinks, Benjamin," said Uncle Timothy to the lauréat of Little Britain, as they sat *tête-à-tête* at breakfast on the morning after the adventure of the old harper —"methinks I have conceded quite enough by consenting to play Esquire Bedel to the Fubsys, Muffs, and Flumgartens. A couple of lean barn-door fowls and a loin-or, as Mrs. Flumgarten classically spells it, a lion of fat country pork at Christmas, even were I a more farinaceous feeder than I am, are hardly equivalent to my approaching purgatory. You bargained, among other sights, for Westminster Abbey. Now what possible charm can the *Poet's Corner* have for the Fubsy family, who detest poets and poetry quite as much as ever did the second George 'boedry and bainding!' Then came the British Museum. I will now take leave to have my own way. Your eloquence, persuasive though it be, shall never talk me into a new blue coat and brass buttons."

"Depend upon it, Uncle Timothy, Mrs. Flurngarten will —"

"I know it, Benjamin. That full-blown hollyhock of the aristocracy of Mammon, who has a happy knack of picking a hole in everybody's coat, will not spare mine. Let her then, for economy's sake, pick a hole in an old coat rather than a new one."

"The honour of our family is at stake," urged the lauréat. "Respect, too, for Mrs. Flumgar-ten."

Uncle Timothy whistled

"Sic a wife as Willie had,

I would na gie a button for her.

"But suppose, Benjamin, I should be so insane so stark, staring, ridiculously mad." Here Uncle Timothy paused to see what effect his budget of suppositions had upon Mr. Bosky's nerves.

But Mr. Bosky kept his nerves well strung and his countenance steady, and let Uncle Timothy go on supposing.

"Suppose I should all at once depart from the sober gravity that belongs to my years, and exhibit myself in a blue coat and brass buttons —" Uncle Timothy again paused; but he might as well have whistled jigs to a milestone. The lauréat continued immoveable and mute.

"Benjamin-Benjamin *Bosky!*" cried Uncle Timothy, nettled at his provoking imperturbability, "if, out of a mistaken civility to your country cousins, and to rid myself of these annoying importunities, I should invite the caricaturist to pillory me in the print-shops —a blue coat and brass buttons are not the journey-work of twenty minutes-for by that time I must be equipped to start: And, to swaddle myself in a ready-made fit, too long at the top, and too short at the bottom-like the Irishman's blanket! No, Benjamin Bosky! For, though of figure I have nothing to boast —" here Uncle Timothy unconsciously (?) glanced at his comely person in a mirror —"I do not intend to qualify myself for a chair on the fifth of November."

Mr. Bosky still maintained a respectful silence.

"Therefore, Benjamin, were I inclined to forego my scruples, and oblige you for this once" — as Uncle Timothy saw the apparent impossibility of obliging, he spoke more freely of his possible compliance —"the thing, you see, is absolutely impracticable."

Mr. Bosky looked anxiously at the clock, and Uncle Tim quite exulted that, while starting an insurmountable obstacle, he had dexterously-handsomely slipped out of a scrape.

At this moment a tap was heard at the door, and the old-fashioned housekeeper —a sort of animated dumb-waiter —brought in a blue bag for Uncle Timothy.

A carpet-bag is generally significant of its contents. Though now and then things not legitimately belonging to it will creep into a carpet-bag. But in a blue bag there is more room for conjecture. A very equivocal thing is a blue bag.

Uncle Timothy, after reading the direction thrice over, untied the blue bag, dived his hand in for its contents, and the first thing he fished up was a bran new blue coat, with brilliant brass buttons.

After turning the garment round and round and examining it attentively, he laid it aside, dived again and captured a rich black satin waistcoat.

The waistcoat underwent a similar scrutiny, and then took its station beside the blue coat.

A third dive brought to the surface a claret-coloured pair of continuations of a very quiet and becoming cut, to which was pinned a respectful note from Mr. Rufus Rumfit of Red Lion Square, stating that the suit had been made exactly to measure, and hoping that it would meet with Uncle Timothy's approbation.

"Pray, Benjamin," inquired the satirical-nosed gentleman, "is this Rufus Rumfit at all given to drink? He talks of having taken my measure: he had surely taken more than his own when he hazarded such an assertion. Some would-be old beau-for the habiliments, I see, are of a mature fashion-is burning to disguise his person in this harlequin suit. My life on't, Mr. Rumfit will soon discover his mistake and be back again." And' Uncle Timothy began to tumble the blue coat, black satin waistcoat, and claret-coloured continuations into the blue bag with all speed.

"The clock strikes. I have no time to lose."

During this exhumation of Mr. Rumfit's handiwork, the Lauréat of Little Britain had been coaxing a favourite parrot, with whom he generally held converse at breakfast time, to talk: but the unusual sight of so much finery had completely absorbed Poll's attention, and he remained obstinately silent, leaving Mr. Bosky to tax his ingenuity how to prevent laughing outright in Uncle Timothy's face. But the affair admitting of no longer delay, he threw himself into a theatrical posture, and exclaimed,

"'Thou wert not wont to be so dull, good Tyrrel.'"

In an instant the scales fell from the middle-aged gentleman's eyes, and he exclaimed seriously, and trying to look reproachfully, "This, Benjamin, is another of your Tomfooleries."

Mr. Bosky pleaded guilty; but urged, in mitigation, the rusty old black, and the brilliant bright blue: concluding with a glowing panegyric on the *tout ensemble*, which he declared to be the masterpiece of Mr. Rumfit's thimble and shears.

Uncle Timothy was in no humour to put himself out of one: and when, after a few minutes trying on the suit in his tiring-room, *just to see* —out of mere curiosity-if it *did* fit, he returned in full pontificalibus, a middle-aged Adonis! he seemed moderately reconciled to his new metamorphosis, and rang for the old-fashioned housekeeper.

Norah Noclack was a woman of few words. On her entrance she started, stared amazedly, and uttered the interjection, "Ah!" with the further additions of "Well, I'm sure!"

" —That with a cap and bells, a dark lantern, a pasteboard red nose, a chair, and half a score of ragged urchins to shout me an ovation, I should make an undeniable old Guy! Eh, Norah?"

The ancient housekeeper shook her antediluvian high-crowned cap and streamers in token of dissent, and Mr. Bosky was unutterably shocked at the impossible idea.

"Well," added Uncle Timothy, strutting to and fro with mock dignity,

"'Since I am crept in favour with myself,

I will maintain it with some little cost!'

"Here, Norah, run and buy me sixpenny-worth of flowers to stick in my button-hole. No dahlias, or hollyhocks."

Mr. Bosky suggested a sunflower.

The satirical-nosed gentleman looked a trifle serious, and the lauréat stood self-reproved.

Norah Noclack soon returned with a modest little bouquet, consisting of a last rose of summer, a violet or two, and, what was peculiarly appropriate, heartease.

A contest had very nearly arisen about Doctor Johnson's club, as Mr. Bosky irreverently called it, which was Uncle Timothy's constant companion. This valued relic had been *accidentally* mislaid, and there being no time to look for it, a handsome black cane, with a gold top and silk tassel, was its substitute. Mr. Bosky then dutifully tendered him a smart new beaver, intimating that the old one had that morning been converted into a nursery by his favourite pepper-and-salt puss. At this crowning specimen of the laureates ingenuity, Uncle Timothy smiled graciously, and being now gaily equipped, prepared to sally forth, when a knock of some pretension announced the presence of the august brotherin-law of Mrs. Flumgarten, one of the pleasure-taking tormentors of Uncle Timothy!

"The devil!" muttered the middle-aged gentleman. "The deuce," "the dickens," "rabbit it," "drabbit it," "boddikins," or when anything intolerably queer excited him, "od's boddikins!" were the only expletives that escaped from the lips of Uncle Timothy. But "the devil!" Even Mr. Bosky looked momentarily aghast, and the old-fashioned housekeeper, shaking her head and shrugging up her shoulders, attributed the appalling words to the supernatural influence of the blue coat and brass buttons.

"Charmin' vether this is! Fine hautum mornin's these are!" grinned Mr. Muff (his tongue too big for his mouth, and his teeth too many for his tongue,) with a consequential, self-satisfied air, that seemed to say, "Beat that if you can."

Uncle Timothy coolly remarked that the sun was just out; and Mr. Bosky, that the post was just in.

"Ven I began to dress me the vind was nor'-nor'-east, but it soon changed to sow-sow-west," was the next profound remark volunteered by Mr. Muff.

"Then," said the lauréat, "you and the wind shifted at much about the same time."

The Muffs, Fubsys, and Flumgartens, could not understand a joke, which they always took the wrong way. The intelligent master mason, nothing moved, inquired, Anything new in *Lit-tie Britain?*"

"The barber's freshly painted *pole* * over the way," replied Mr. Bosky.

"Or in *Great Britain?*" continued Mr. Muff.

"The *moon*," rejoined Uncle Timothy.

The brother-in-law of Mrs. Flumgarten was at a dead lock.

* The barber's pole, one of the popular relics of Merrie
England, is still to be seen in some of the old streets of
London and in country-towns, painted with its red, blue, and
yellow stripes, and surmounted with a gilt acorn. The lute
and violin were formerly among the furniture of a barber's
shop. He who waited to be trimmed, if of a musical turn,
played to the company. The barber himself was a nimble-
tongued, pleasant-witted fellow. William Rowley, the
dramatist, in "A Search for Money, 1609," thus describes
him: —"As wee were but asking the question, steps me from
over the way (over-listning us) a news-searcher, viz. a
barber: he, hoping to at-taine some discourse for his next
patient, left his banner of basons swinging in the ayre, and
closely eave-drops our conference. The saucie treble-tongu'd
knave would insert somewhat of his knowledge (treble-tongu'd
I call him, and thus I prove 't: hee has a reasonable
mother-tongue, his barber-sur-gions tongue; and a tongue
betweene two of his fingers, and from thence proceeds his
wit, and 'tis a snapping wit too). Well, sir, he (before he
was askt the question,) told us that the wandring knight
(Monsier L'Argent) sure was not farre off; for on Saterday-
night he was faine to watch till morning to trim some of his

followers, and its morning they went away from him betimes. Hee swore hee never clos'd his eyes till hee came to church, and then he slept all sermon-time; but certainly hee is not farre afore, and at yonder taverne (showing us the bush) I doe imagine he has tane a chamber." In ancient times the barber and the tailor, as news-mongers, divided the crown. The barber not only erected his pole as a sign, but hung his basins upon it by way of ornament.

Sounding the depths of his capacious intellect, his cogitative faculties were "in cogibundity of cogitation." He soon rallied with, "How's the generality of things in general?"

It was now Uncle Timothy's and Mr. Bosky's turn to be posed! But the interrogator relieved them by suddenly recollecting the object of his mission —"I'm come, Mister Timviddy-"

"If, sir, you mean to address me," said the satirical-nosed gentleman, "my name is not Timwiddy, but-"

"Timkins," interrupted Mr. Muff.

"Anything you please," rejoined Uncle Timothy, with the most contemptuous acquiescence. "Call me Alexander, Wat Tyler, Abelard, Joe Grimaldi, Scipio Africanus, Martin Van Butchell."

"Ve vont quarrel about Christun names, Mister Timtiffin. Plain Timvig vill do for me. The Muffs and all that's a-skin to'em is not over-purtickler about names."

Here the poll parrot, that had been listening to and scrutinizing the intruder from head to foot, struck up the old song,

"Don't you know the muffin man!

Don't you know his name?"

"A comical sort of a bird that is!" remarked the master mason. "I'm come, I say, Mister Tumvhim to fetch you to Mrs. Flumgarten; for she says it's werry mystified, but you gay-looking, dandyfied, middle-aged gentlemen, (Mrs. Flumgarten hates gay-looking, dandified, middle-aged gentlemen,) are awful loiterers by the vay. You can't see a smart bonnet or a pretty turn'd ankle, but you old galhant gay Lotharios must stop and look after'em; and that, she says, is werry low-and the Muffs, Fubsys, and Flumgartens hates vhat's low."

Uncle Timothy made a low bow.

"Mrs. Flumgarten von't go to the Museum: she could abide the stuffed birds and monkeys; but she can't a-bear old war-ses, and old bronze-eyes. She hates, too, them Algerine (Elgin?) marbles."

The middle-aged gentleman inwardly rejoiced at Mrs. Flumgarten's antipathies.

"And she von't go to the play, for Mrs. Flumgarten hates your acting nonsensical mock stuff; and she don't think she'll go to the Fancy Fair, for Mrs. Flumgarten-it's werry funny that-hates fun."

At this moment, Mr. Bosky's Louis Quatorze clock struck a musical quarter, and the parrot responded with two lines from one of the laureat's lyrics;

"Quick! quick! be off in a crack;

Cut your stick, or'twill be on your back!"

and a tag (the schoolmaster had been abroad in Little Britain!) for which my Lord Mayor-the conservator of city morals and the Thames-would have fined him five shillings.

"That Poll parrot swears like a Chrishtun!" Mr. Muff then took hold of Uncle Timothy's arm, adding, "If ye don't make haste, Mrs. Flumgarten vill look as bitter as a duck biled vith camomile-flowers."

Within my solitary bow'r

I saw a quarter of an hour

Fly heavily along!

Mr. Bosky's quarter flew by the "fast flying waggon that flies on broad wheels!"

"Ha! ha! 'no creature smarts so little as a fool.' Well said, Alexander the Little! Poll-pretty Poll!

Pretty Poll! let's you and I

Something merry and musical try,

Is my voice too high? too low?

Answer, Polly, yes or no!

Not a word, undutiful bird,

For barley-sugar and sugar-plums —fie!"

But Poll's eyes still goggled at the door through which Uncle Tim and his finery had vanished. An almond or two from that *magazin de comfitures*, Mr. Bosky's waistcoat pocket, soon revived in the abstracted bird a relish for the good things of this world. He wetted his whistle cordially with a spoonful of maraschino, and sharpening his beak against the wires of his cage, presented it for a salute. He then gave token of a song, and the lauréat led, to the tune of the *"Dandy O!"*

THE QUAKER DUET.=

O Tabitha, in truth, I'm a sober Quaker youth;

    Then Hymen's knot, the pretty girls, to spite'em, tye.

My heart is in your trap; you've crimp'd it, like your

    cap;

    And much the spurrit moves me-hum! —to —

    Poll....... Tye turn tye!

And when the knot is tyed, and you're my blushing

    bride,

    The damsels will (for leading apes must fright'em,)

    tye

The rosy bands with speed. O yes, they will, indeed!

    And the chorus at our meeting will be —

    Poll....... Tye tum tye!

I cannot hear you sigh, ah! I will not see you cry, ah!

    My constant Obadi-ah I to unite'em; tye

Our hands and hearts in one, before to-morrow's sun —

    Then take thy tender Tabitha to —

    Poll....... Tye turn tye!

CHAPTER VIII.

The Lauréat of Little Britain was now left at liberty to follow his daily avocations; but that liberty was no guarantee that he would follow them; except, as some folks follow the fashions, at a considerable distance. He read the morning papers, went upon 'Change, inquired the price of stocks, set his watch by the dial of Bow Church, returned home, turned over the leaves of his ledger, hummed, whistled, poked the fire, scribbled on the blotting-paper, and cracked a joke with his solemn clerk. Still, with all these manifestations of being mightily busy about doing nothing, it was obvious that his wits were running a wild goose chase after Uncle Timothy's new blue coat and brass buttons. But the oddest is behind. Mrs. Norah Noclack suddenly betrayed unwonted symptoms of vocality. Her first notes fell on the astonished ear of the solemn clerk, and served him as the ghost of Banquo did Macbeth-pushed him from his stool. He hurried to the stair-head, marvelling what musical coil could be going on in the still-room. He next applied his oblique eye to the key-hole, and-seeing is believing-beheld the locomotive old lass rehearsing a minuet before the mirror, to the chromatic accompaniment of her wiry falsetto. Big with the portentous discovery, he bustled to Mr. Bosky, to whom, after unpacking his budget of strange news, he proposed the instant holding of a commission of lunacy, for the due and proper administration of her few hundreds in long annuities, two large boxes, and a chest of drawers, full of old-fashioned finery, besides sundry trinkets, the spoils of three courtships.

A few days after, the carolling of Mrs. Norah surprised Uncle Timothy, who recognising the real culprit in the eccentric muse of Mr. Benjamin Bosky, he took the lauréat to task for putting his wardrobe into metre, hitching his Christian name into ludicrous rhyme, and turning the head and untuning the voice of the hitherto anti-musical Norah Noclack. Mr. Bosky exhibited deep contrition, but as Mr. Bosky's contrition bore considerable resemblance to Mr. Liston's tragedy, Uncle Timothy always dreaded to encounter it when anything serious was in the case. And so completely did the old chantress inoculate the solemn clerk with her musical mania, that one evening, when called upon for a toast and a song at the club * of the Knights of St. John of Jerusalem, held in an ancient trophied chamber over the venerable gateway of the Priory, he startled his brother knights with his unwonted enthusiasm. "Uncle Timothy! Sound trumpets! wave banners! shout voices!" This was the longest public oration that Mr. Fixture had made in his life. Certainly the only song that he was ever known to have sung was the old-fashioned housekeeper's — —

* This club consists of more than fifteen hundred members.
Their orgies are celebrated every Monday evening throughout
the year. The chair is taken at nine, and vacated at twelve.

APOTHEOSIS OF UNCLE TIM'S BRAN NEW BUTTONS AND BLUE.=

If I had my widow or maiden's whim —

I know who —I know who

It should be! Why, Uncle Tim,

In his bran new buttons and blue.

Tim's a middle ag'd gentleman sleek,

With a laughing eye and a cherry cheek!

He loves a good joke

Like other blythe folk;

A Christmas carol,

A cup from the barrel,

And a glass of old wine seven days in the week!

Hear him sing, and hear him talk,

The veriest merriest cock of the walk;

Daintily dress'd

Like a buck in his best!

Loyal and true

As his holiday blue!

With black silk stock and embroider'd vest;

In Wellingtons trim

Struts Uncle Tim!

With beaver and cane,

And smart gold chain —

Di'mond pin

Stuck under his chin —

All Little Britain

Were never so smitten!

We ne'er shall look on his like again!

Heigho! my heart is low!

Devils blue

As Tim's bran new!

Fidgets, fumes,

Mops and brooms!

Tantrums all from top to toe!

Heigho!

Such a quiz! such a beau!

Such a shape! such a make!

Would I were a lady,

As blooming as May-day;

With carriages, house, and

Twice twenty thousand;

If it only were for Uncle Timothy's sake!

CHAPTER IX.

Gentle Reader! we promised thee at the outset of our journey pleasant companions by the way, and as an earnest of that promise, we have introduced Benjamin Bosky and Uncle Tim. We would now bespeak thy courtesy for others that are soon to follow. In passing happily through life, half the battle depends upon the persons with whom we may be associated. And shall we carry spleen into the closet? —grope for that daily plague in our books, when it elbows and stares us in the face at every turn? To chronicle the "Painful Peregrinations" of Uncle Timothy through this livelong day, would exhibit him, like "Patience," not sitting "on a monument, smiling at grief," but lolling in Mr. Bosky's britschka, laughing (in his sleeve!) at the strange peculiarities of the Muffs, and listening with mild endurance to the unaccountable antipathies of Mrs. Flumgarten. Now the Fubsys might be called, *par excellence*, a prudent family.

And Prudence is a nymph we much admire,

She loves to aid the hypocrite and liar,

Helping poor rascals through the mire,

Whom filth and infamy begrime:

She's one of guilt's most useful drudges,

Her good advice she never grudges,

Gives parsons meekness, gravity to judges;

But frowns upon the man of rhyme!

Good store of prudence had the Fubsy family. Their honest scruples always prevented them from burning their fingers. They were much too wise to walk into a well. They kept on the windy side of the law. They were vastly prone to measure other people's morality by the family bushel, and had exceedingly grand notions touching their self-importance; (little minds, like little men, cannot afford to stoop!) which those who have seen a cock on a dunghill, or a crow in a gutter, may have some idea of.

Nothing pleased Mrs. Flumgarten. Mr. Bosky's equipage she politely brought into depreciating comparison with the staring yellow and blue, brass-mounted, and screw-wigged turn-out of her acquaintances the *Kickwitches*, the mushroom aristocracy of retired "Putty and Lead!" And when Mr. Muff, who was no herald, hearing something about Mr. Bosky's *arms* being painted on the panels, innocently inquired whether his *legs* were not painted too? —at which Uncle Timothy involuntarily smiled-the scarlet-liveried pride of the Fubsys rushed into her cheeks, and she bridled up, wondering what there was in Mr. Muffs question to be laughed at. Knowing the susceptibility of Mrs. Flumgarten's nervous system, Uncle Timothy desired John Tomkins to drive moderately slow. This was "scratching away at a snail's pace! a cat's gallop!"

"A little faster, John," said Uncle Timothy, mildly. This was racing along like "Sabbath-day, pleasure-taking, public-house people in a tax-cart!" Not an exhibition, prospect, person, or thing, were to her mind. The dinner, which might have satisfied Apicius, she dismissed with "faint praise," sighing a supplementary complaint, by way of errata, that there "*was no pickles!*" — and the carving-until the well-bred Mrs. Flumgarten snatched the knife and fork out of Uncle Timothy's hands-was "awful! horrid!" Then she never tastes *such* sherry as she does at her cousins' the *Shufflebothams*; and as for their black amber (Hambro'?) grapes, oh! they was fit for your perfect gentlefolks! —An inquiry from mine host, whether Uncle Timothy preferred a light or a full wine, drew forth this jocular answer, "I like a full wine, and a full bottle, Master Boniface." —"So do I," added the unguarded Mr. Muff. This was "tremendious!"

The two ladies looked at each other, and having decided on a joint scowl, it fell with annihilating blackness on the master-mason, and Mrs. Muff trod upon his toes under the table, a conjugal hint that Mr. Muff had taken enough! Mrs. Flumgarten had a momentary tiff with Mrs. Muff upon some trifling family jealousy, which brought into contest their diminutive dignities; but as the fond sisters had the good fortune to be Fubsys, and as the Fubsys enjoyed the exclusive privilege of abusing one another with impunity, the sarcastic compliments and ironical sneers they so lovingly exchanged passed for nothing after the first fire. The absence of Mr. Flumgarten, a scholar and a gentleman, who had backed out of this party of pleasure, (?) left his lady at a sad loss for one favourite subject in which she revelled, because it annoyed him; consequently there were no vulgar impertinent hits at "your clever people!" This hiatus led to some melancholy details of what she had suffered during her matrimonial pilgrimage.

"Suffered!" muttered the middle-aged gentleman, indignantly. "Yes, Madam Zantippe, you have suffered! But what? Why, your greeneyed illiterate prejudices to mar all that makes the domestic hearth intellectual and happy! Yes! you have reduced it to a cheerless desert, where you reign the restless fury of contradiction and discord!"

Master Guy Muff, the eldest born of Brutus, a youth who exhibited a capacious development of the eating and drinking organs, with a winning smile that would have made his fortune through a horse-collar, emerged from his post of honour behind the puffed sleeves and rustling skirts of "ma's," and aunt's silk gowns.

"Don't be frightened, Guy," said Mrs. Flumgarten, soothingly; "it's *only* Mr. Timwig."

"I arn't a-going to, aunt," snuffled the self-complaisant Master Guy.

John Leech

Master Guy Muff speaking his Christmas [?]

Original

"I hope, young gentleman," said uncle Timothy, (for looking at the lump of living lumber, he did not venture to suppose,) "that you learn your lessons, and are perfect in your exercises."

"What-hoop, skipping-rope, and pris'ner's base?"

"Can you parse?"

"Oh, yes? I pass my time at dumps and marloes."

"Speak your Christmas-piece to Mr. Timtiffin, do, dear Guy!" said "ma," coaxingly.

Master Guy Muff made the effort, Mr. Brutus Muff acting as prompter.

Master Guy (taking in each hand a dessert-plate).

> "Look here upon this pic-tur, and on this,
>
> The counter-counter —"

"Sink the *shop!*" whispered Uncle Timothy.

Mr. Muff. "Fit presen-ti-ment —"

"You put the boy out, Mr. Muff, as you *always* do!" snarled Mrs. Muff.

Master Muff. —

> " —Of two brothers.
>
> See what a grace was seated on that brow;
>
> Hy-Hy —"

"Isn't it something about curls and front?" said Mr. Muff.

Mrs. Muff took this as an affront to her own particular jazey, which was bushily redolent of both; she darted a fierce frown *à la* Fubsy at the interrogator, that awed him to silence.

Master Muff. —

> "A eye like Ma's to threaten and command —"

The subdued master-mason felt the full force of this line, to which his son Guy's appropriate pronunciation and personal stare gave a *new reading*. Here the juvenile spouter broke down, upon which Mrs. Flumgarten took his voice under her patronage, and having prevailed on him to try a song, the "young idea" began in an excruciating wheeze, as if a pair of bellows had been invited to sing, the following *morceau*. "More so," said Mrs. Muff, encouragingly, "because pa said it was almost good enough to be sung a Sundays after *Tabernacle*."

> There was a little bird,
>
> His cage hung in the hall;
>
> On Monday morning, May the third,
>
> He couldn't sing at all.

> And for this reason, mark,
>
> Good people, great and small,
>
> Because the pussey, for a lark,
>
> Had eat him, bones and all.

"Ah!" cried Aunt F. approvingly, "that is a song! None of your frothy comic stuff that *some folks* (!!) is so fond of."

She now entertained Uncle Timothy with an account, full of bombast and brag, of some grand weddings that had recently been celebrated in the Fubsy family-the *Candlerigs* having condescended to adulterate the patrician blood of St. Giles's in-the-Fields with the plebeian puddle of the City Gardens, the sometime suburban retreat of the Fubsys, where they farmed a magnificent chateau, which, like the great Westphalian Baron de Thunder-tan-trounck's, had a door and a window. Uncle Timothy, to change the subject, called on Mr. Brutus Muff for a song.

"I never heered Mr. Muff sing, Mr. Timwig," chimed the sisters simultaneously.

"Indeed! Then, ladies, it will be the greater novelty. Come, my good sir; but first a glass of wine with you."

"Oh, Mr. Timwiddy, you will make Mr. Muff quite top-heavy! It must only be a half a glass," said Mrs. Muff, authoritatively.

"The top half, if you please, madam," said the middle-aged gentleman; and he poured out the "regal purple stream" till it kissed, without flowing over, the brim. Mr. Muff brought the bumper to a level with his lips, and, as if half ashamed of what he was doing, put both halves out of sight!

"Is the man mad?" cried the amazed Mrs. Muff.

"Has he lost his senses?" ejaculated the bewildered Mrs. Flumgarten.

"He has found them, rather," whispered the satirical-nosed gentleman.

The bland looks and persuasive tones of Uncle Timothy, to say nothing of the last bumper, had wrought wonders on the master-mason. He looked Silenus-like and rosy, and glanced his little peering eyes across the table-Mrs. Muff having a voice too in the affair-for an assenting nod from the fierce black velvet turban of his better and bigger half. But Mrs. Muff made no sign, and he paused irresolute; when another kind word from the middle-aged gentleman encouraged him, at all hazards, to begin with,

> Doctor Pott lived up one pair,
>
> And reach'd his room by a comical stair!
>
> Like all M.D's,
>
> He pocketed fees
>
> As quick as he could,
>
> As doctors should!
>
> And rented a knocker near Bloomsbury Square.
>
> Tib his rib was not wery young,

Wery short, wery tall.,

Wery fair vithal;

But she had a tongue

Wery pat, wery glib

For a snow-white fib,

And wery veil hung!

"You shan't sing another line, that you shan't, Brutus!" vociferated Mrs. Muff. But the Cockney Roman, undaunted and vocal, went on singing,

Says Doctor Peter Pott, "As I know vhat's vhat,

My anti-nervous patent pill on Tib my rib I'll try;

If Mrs. P. vill svallow, if dissolution follow,

And she should kick the bucket, I'm sure I shan't

cry!"

"Where could he have learned such a rubbishing song? A man, too, after pa's own heart!" sighed Mrs. Muff.
Mr. Muff. —

And vel the doctor knew that a leer par les deux yeux

Mrs. Pott vithstand could not, vhen shot from Peter's

eye;

So presently plump at her he opes his organic battery,

And said the pill it vouldnt kill, no, not a little fly!

"Have you no compassion for my poor nerves?" remonstrated Mrs. Muff, pathetically.
"None vhatsumdever," replied the stoical Brutus. "Vhat compassion have you ever had for mine?"

"Besides," said he, "I svear, d'ye see,

By the goods and chattels of Doctor P.

By my vig and my cane.

Brass knocker and bell,

And the cab in vhich I cut such a svell,

That a single pill (a pill, by the by,

Is a dose!) if Mrs. Pott vill try,

Of gout and phthisic she'll newer complain,

And never vant to take physic again."

Down it slid,

And she newer did!

(The Doctor vith laughing was like to burst!)

For this wery good reason-it finish'd her first!

"I'll send," cried Mrs. Flumgarten, furiously, "for one of the L division."

"You may send to Old Nick for one of the L division!" shouted the valiant Mr. Muff, aspirating with particular emphasis the letter L.

"Here I lays, Teddy O'Blaize, (Singing)

And my body quite at its aise is;

Vith the tip of my nose and the tops of my toes

Turn'd up to the roots of the daisies!

And now, my invaluable spouse, as I carn't conwenienly sing you any more moral lessons, I'll tipple you two or three!" And Mr. Muff, with admirable coolness and precision, filled himself a bumper. "First and foremust, from this day henceforrer'd, I'm determined to be my own lord and master.

"Imprimis and secondly, I don't choose to be the hen-pecked, colly woffling, under-the-fear-of-his-vife-and-a-broomstick Jerry Sneak and Pollycoddle, that the Vhitechapel pin-maker vas! You shan't, like his loving Lizzy, currycomb my precious vig, and smuggle my last vill!"

"*Et tu Brute!*" said Uncle Timothy, in a half whisper.

"He is a brute!" sobbed Mrs. Flumgarten, "to speak so of poor dear pa!"

"Don't *purwoke* me, Mrs. Flumgarten, into 'fending and proving, or I shall let the cat out of the bag, and the kittens into the bargain! By the Lord Harry, I'll *peach*, Mrs. Muff!"

Mrs. Flumgarten's unruly member was about to pour upon the master-mason a flood of Fubsyean eloquence, when *Prudence*, the family guardian angel, took her by the tongue's tip, as St. Dunstan took a certain ebony gentleman by the nose. She telegraphed Mrs. Muff, and Mrs. Muff telegraphed the intelligent Guy. Just as Brutus was fetching breath for another ebullition, with his hand on the decanter for another bumper, he found himself half throttled in the Cornish hug of his affectionate and blubbering first-born! When a chimney caught fire, it was a custom in Merrie England to drop down it a live goose, in the quality of extinguisher! And no goose ever performed its office better than the living Guy. He opened the flood-gates of his gooseberry eyes, and played upon pa so effectually, that Mr. Muff's ire or fire was speedily put out; and when, to prevent a coroner's inquest, the obedient child was motioned by the ladies to relax his filial embrace, the mollified master-mason began to sigh and sob too. The politic sisters now proposed to cut short their day's pleasure! —Uncle Timothy, to whom it was some consolation, that while he had been sitting upon thorns, his tormentors too were a little nettled, seeing bluff John Tomkins in the stable-yard grooming *con amore* one of Mr. Bosky's pet bloods, called out, "John! I'm afraid we were too many this morning for that shying left-wheeler. Now, if he should take to kicking —"

"Kicking! Mr. Timwiddy!" screamed Mrs. Flumgarten.

"Kicking! Mr. Timwig!" echoed Mrs. Muff.

Herodotus (who practised what he preached) said, "When telling a lie will be profitable, let it be told!" —"He may lie," said Plato, "who knows *how* to do it in a suitable time." So thought John Tomkins! who hoping to frighten his unwelcome customers into an omnibus, and drive home Uncle Timothy in capital style, so aggravated the possible kickings, plungings, takings fright, and runnings away of that terrible left-wheeler, that the accommodating middle-aged gentleman was easily persuaded by the ladies to lighten the weight and diminish the danger, by returning to town by some other conveyance. And it was highly entertaining to mark the glum looks of John when he doggedly put the horses to, and how he mischievously laid his whipcord into the sensitive flanks of the "shying left-wheeler," that honoured every draft on his fetlocks, and confirmed the terrifying anticipations and multiplications of the veracious John Tomkins!

"Song sweetens toil, however rude the sound," —and John sweetened his by humming the following, in which he encored himself several times, as he drove Mrs. Flumgarten and family, to town.

Dash along! splash along! hi, gee ho!

Four-and-twenty periwigs all of a row!

Save me from a tough yarn twice over told —

Save me from a Jerry Sneak, and save me from a scold.

A horse is not a mare, and a cow is not a calf;

A woman that talks all day long has too much tongue by

half.

To the music of the fiddle I like to figure in;

But off I cut a caper from the music of the chin!

When Madam's in her tantrums, and Madam 'gins to

cry;

If you want to give her change, hold an ingun to your

eye;

But if she shakes her pretty fist, and longs to come to

blows,

You may slip through her fingers, if you only soap your

nose!

Dash along! splash along! hi, gee ho!

No horse so fast can gallop as a woman's tongue can go.

"Needs must," I've heard my granny say, "when the

devil drives."

I wish he drove, instead of *me*, this brace of scolding

wives!

CHAPTER X.

Give me a woman as old as Hecuba, or as ugly as Caifacaratadaddera, rather than Mrs. Flumgarten! Were the annoyance confined to *herself*, I should cry, 'Content,'—for she who sows nettles and thorns is entitled to reap a stinging and prickly harvest. Ill temper should ride quarantine, and have a *billet de santé*, before it is let loose upon society."

These were among the ruminations of Uncle Timothy as he sauntered homeward through the green fields. Two interesting objects lay before him: the village church and grave-yard, and a row of ancient almshouses, the pious endowment of a bountiful widow, who having been brought to feel what sorrow was, had erected them, as the last resting-place but *one*, for the aged and the poor.

There dwelt in our ancestors * a fine spirit of humanity towards the helpless and the needy. The charitable pittance was not doled out to them by the hand of insolent authority; but the wayfarer, heart-weary, and foot-sore, claimed at the gates of these pious institutions ** (a few of which still remain in their primitive simplicity) his loaf, his lodging, and his groat, which were dispensed, generally with kindness, and always with decency. Truly we may say, that what the present generation has gained in *head* (and even this admission is subject to many qualifications), it has lost in *heart!!*

* "Before the Reformation, there were no Poor's Rates. The charitable dole, given at the religious houses, and the church-ale in every parish, did the business.
"In every parish there was a Church-house, to which belonged

spits, pots, &c. for dressing provision. Here the housekeepers met, and were merry, and gave their charity. The young people came there too, and had dancing, bowling, shooting at butts, &c. Mr. A. Wood assures me, that there were few or no almshouses before the time of Henry the Eighth; that at Oxon, opposite Christchurch, was one of the most ancient in England." —Aubrey MSS.
** Was it ever intended-is it just-is it fitting, that the

Masterships of St. Cross at Winchester, and St. Katharine's, London, should be such sumptuous sinecures?

A grave had just received its "poor inhabitant the mourners had departed, and two or three busy urchins, with shovels and spades, were filling in the earth; while the sexton, a living clod, nothing loth to see his work done by proxy, looked, with open mouth and leaden eyes, carelessly on. Uncle Timothy walked slowly up the path, and pausing before the "narrow cell," enforced silence and decency by that irresistible charm that ever accompanied his presence. His pensive, thoughtful look, almost surprised the gazers into sympathy. Who was the silent tenant? None could tell. He was a stranger in the village; but their pastor must have known something of his story; for his voice faltered whilst reading the funeral service, and he was observed to weep. Uncle Timothy passed on, and continued his peregrination among the tombs. How grossly had the dead been libelled by the flattery of the living! Here was "a tender husband, a loving father, and an honest man," who certainly had never tumbled his wife out at window, kicked his children out of doors, or picked his neighbour's pocket in broad daylight on the King's highway; yet was he a hypocritical heartless old money-worshipper! There lay a "disconsolate widow," the names of whose three "lamented husbands" were chiselled on her tombstone! To the more opulent of human clay, who could afford plenty of lead and stone-perchance the emblems of their dull, cold heads and hearts-what pompous quarries were raised above ground! what fulsome inscriptions dedicated! But the poor came meanly off. Here and there a simple flower, blooming on the raised sod, and fondly cherished, told of departed friends and kindred not yet forgotten! And who that should see a rose thus affectionately planted would let it droop and wither for want of a tear?

"Ah!" thought Uncle Timothy, "may I make my last bed with the poor! —

"Let not unkind, untimely thrift

These little boons deny;

Nor those who love me while I live

Neglect me when I die!"

A monument of chaste and simple design attracted his attention. It was to the memory of a gentle spirit, whom he mourned with a brother's love. Four lines were all that had been thought essential to say; but they were sufficiently expressive.

Father! thy name we bless,

Thy providence adore.

Earth has a mortal less,

Heaven has an angel more!

The "Giver of every good and perfect gift" had taken her daughter before she knew sin or sorrow. Her epitaph ran thus: —

Oh! happy they who call'd to rest

Ere sorrow fades their bloom,

Awhile a blessing are-and bless'd —

Then sink into the tomb.

From fleeting joys and lasting woes

On youthful wing they fly —

In heaven they blossom like the rose,

The flowers that early die!

A. deep and holy calm fell upon Uncle Timothy, with a sweet assurance that a happier meeting with departed friends was not far distant. And as the guardianship of ministering angels was his firm belief and favourite theme, his secret prayer at this solemn moment was, that they might save him from the bodily and mental infirmities, the selfishness and apathy of protracted years. He read the inscriptions over again, with a full conviction of their truthfulness. *They were his own.*

At an obscure corner-and afar off—*Truth*, for a wonder, had written an epitaph upon one who loved, not his *species*, but his *specie!*

> Beneath this stone old Nicholas lies;
>
> Nobody laughs, and nobody cries.
>
> Where he's gone, and how he fares,
>
> Nobody knows, and nobody cares!

And at no great distance was a tomb entirely overgrown with rank weeds, nettles, and thorns; and there was a superstitious legend attached to it, that they all grew up in one night, and though they had been several times rooted up, still, in one night, they all grew up again! Stones had been ignominiously cast upon it; and certain ancient folks of the village gravely affirmed that, on the anniversary of the burial of the miserable crone, the *Black Sanctus* * was performed by herself and guardian spirits!

* Isaac Reed informs us (see note upon Chapman's Widow's Tears, in Dodsley's Old Plays) that "the *Black Sanctus* was a hymn to Saint Satan, written in ridicule of Monkish luxury." And Tarlton (see News out of Purgatory) quotes it in "the Tale of Pope Boniface."
"And' upon this there was a general mourning through all

Rome: the cardinals wept, the abbots howled, the monks rored, the fryers cried, the nuns puled, the curtezans lamented, the bels rang, the tapers were lighted, that such a Blacke Sanctus was not seene a long time afore in Rome.",
The Black Sanctus here said to be performed was of a

different kind. It was assuredly "a hymn to Satan," in which the crone and the most favoured of her kindred took the base; Hypocrisy leading the band, and Avarice scraping the fiddle.
"The rest God knows-perhaps the Devil"

A yew-tree stretched forth its bare branches over the tomb, which in one night also became withered and blasted!

The Poor Widow and the Village Pastor

Original

At the porch of the entre almshouse sat an aged female in awidows garb, and beside her the village pastor. From the earnestness of his address, he seemed to be exhorting her to resignation; but the tears that fell from her eyes proved how hard was the task! Though Uncle Timothy would not have done homage to the highest potentate in Christendom for all the wealth and distinction that he or she could bestow, he felt his knees tremble under him at the sacredness of humble sorrow. He walked up the neat little flower garden, and having read the grateful memorial inscribed over the ancient doorway to the charitable foundress, was about to speak, when the words, "*Blessed are they that mourn, for they shall be comforted,*" fell like the dews of heaven upon his ear! The widow looked up-she hushed every sigh-she wiped away every tear-the divine potency of the promise sustained her, and she wept no more.

Little ceremony did Uncle Timothy use towards the good pastor and his comforted mourner. His address began with a simple question, who was the brother that he had so recently consigned to the grave?

"This poor widow's only son! The story, sir, is brief and mournful. Bankruptcy and ruin hurried her husband to the grave. This asylum opened its door to receive her; and here, though reviewing the past with fond regret, she became grateful for the present, and hopeful for the future. Her son, a youth of fine intellect, submitted to the ill-paid drudgery of an office where the hands, not the head, were required; and he delighted to spare from his narrow pittance such additional comforts for his mother as were not contemplated by the pious foundress in those primitive times. He would hasten hither on beautiful summer evenings after the business of the day, to trim her little garden, surprise her with some frugal luxury, and see that she was happy. The Sabbath he never omitted passing under this roof, and he led her to my pew-for she is a gentlewoman, sir-where she sat with my family. Consumption seized his frame; and what privations did he endure, what fatigues did he brave, to conceal the first fatal symptoms from his mother! Of a melancholy temperament, endued with all the fine sensibilities of genius, death, under much less unprosperous circumstances, would have been a welcome visitor; but to die-and leave-no matter. I promised to take upon myself the solemn charge, should the dreaded moment arrive. It has arrived, and that promise, by the blessing of my God, I will faithfully redeem."

Uncle Timothy was not an envious man-he knew envy by name only. But if at this particular moment his heart could have been anatomised, O, how he envied the good pastor!

"The disease gained ground with fearful strides.

He was obliged to absent himself from business; and as his employers were no-work-no-pay philanthropists, he was left to his own slender resources, and retired here to die."

"Who sustained my lost son in his long sickness, comforted him, and received his last sigh? Ah! sir-But I dare not disobey your too strict injunction.

'Friend of the poor! the mourner feels thy aid —

She cannot pay thee, but thou wilt be paid!'

"It is not many evenings since that I accompanied my dear young friend in one of his solitary rambles. The sun was setting in golden splendour, and tinged the deep blue clouds that appeared like mountains rising above one another. 'Yon glorious orb,' he cried, with sacred fervour, 'emblem of immortality!

The setting and the rising sun

To me are themes of deep reflection —

Death, frail mortal! is the one,

The other is thy resurrection.

Oh! be that resurrection mine,

And glorious as those rays divine!

A few days after I was called to his bed-side; the hand of death had seized him; he recognised me, smiled, and gently pressed my hand. *'Every misery missed,'* he whispered, *'is a mercy!'* A faint struggle, and a short sigh succeeded, and he was gone to his rest!"

"What a poor figure would this simple record of good works, lively faith, and filial piety make in a modern obituary, where incoherent ravings are eagerly noted down by officious death-bed gossipers, and wrought into a romance, always egotistical, and too often profane! To you, madam," added Uncle Timothy, "consolation and hope have been brought by a heaven-appointed messenger. Something, however, remains to be done in a worldly sense. But I see our friend is on the eve of departure; what I was about to propose shall be submitted to him when we are alone. In the mean time, you will please to consider this humble roof but as a temporary home. It abounds in sad remembrances, which change of scene may soften down, if not entirely dispel. I have a dear, affectionate relative, who would deeply regard you, were it only for your sorrow. And as there 'is a special providence in the falling of a sparrow,' I cannot doubt that some good spirit directed me hither. God bless you! We shall very soon meet again."

And locking the kind pastor's arm in his own, he hurried down the little garden, pausing for a moment to gather a pale rose, which he placed in his bosom.

CHAPTER XI.

Railly, Master Jackimo, I'm quite ashamed on your laziness! you only gits up to lie down, and only lies down to git up! and, instead of making your bow to the ladies and gentlemen, and holding out your cap to catch the coppers, you are everlastingly a-doing o' nuffin but pulling up your shirt-collar, and cracking o' nuts. Havn't I treated you more like a relation than a monkey-giving you the best of advice? But if ever I find you at your old fun ag'in, as sure as my name's Blinking Billy, *I'll take off your goold scarlet waistcoat!*"

This was addressed by an itinerant musician, in a shocking bad hat, with a garnish of old red cotton nightcaps, to his mendicant monkey, that he had perched upon *Whittington's Stone* for the purpose of taking him more conveniently to task.

The offender was of a grave aspect, with a remarkably knowing look. He was dressed *en militaire*, with an old-fashioned scarlet waistcoat embroidered with tinsel, of which he seemed monstrously vain. He listened with becoming seriousness to the musician's expostulation, slyly reserving in the corner of his jaw a nut that he deferred to crack till opportunity should offer. But at the threat of losing his *red waistcoat*, he gibbered, chattered, and by every species of pantomimical begging and bowing, promised future amendment.

Had not the mind of Uncle Timothy been too much occupied with recent events, he would have scraped acquaintance with monkey and man, who were evidently eccentrics, and Uncle Tim was a lover of eccentricity. The moment that the monkey spied a customer, he began his work of reformation, by jumping off the stone, running the full tether of his chain, making a graceful bow, and holding out his cap for a contribution. His politeness was rewarded with sixpence from Uncle Timothy, and an approving word from his master; and the middle-aged gentleman, serenaded by a passing grind from the barrel-organ, walked slowly on.

A caravansary of exhibitors bound to Bartholomew Fair had halted at Mother Red Cap's, * an ancient hostelrie at the foot of Highgate Hill. Although weary and parched with thirst, Uncle Timothy might probably have journeyed onward, had not the "beck'ning ghost" of jovial John.

* Mother Red Cap, doubtless an emanation from Elinour Rumming, was a favourite sign during the sixteenth and seventeenth centuries, and the black Jack that she held in her hand was a symbol of good ale. Two ancient hostelries still bear her prepossessing effigy: one in the Hampstead Road, near Kentish Town; and one at Holloway. It is said that a remarkable shrew, Mother Damnable, of Kentish town, (of whom the late Mr. Bindley had an unique engraving,) gave rise to the former sign. This ill-favoured lady looks more like a witch than an ale-wife. She would have frightened her customers out of the house, and their horses out of the stable! We are inclined to give the palm of priority to the venerable red-capped mother at Holloway, who must have been moderately notorious in the time of Drunken Barnaby, when he halted to regale himself at her portal.
"Thence to Holloway, Mother Red-cap

In a troop of trulls I did hap;
Wh —s of Babylon me impalled,
And me their Adonis called;
With me toy'd they, buss'd me, cull'd me,
But being needy, out they pulled me."

Backster, * flitting in the evening grey, motioned him, in imagination, to enter.

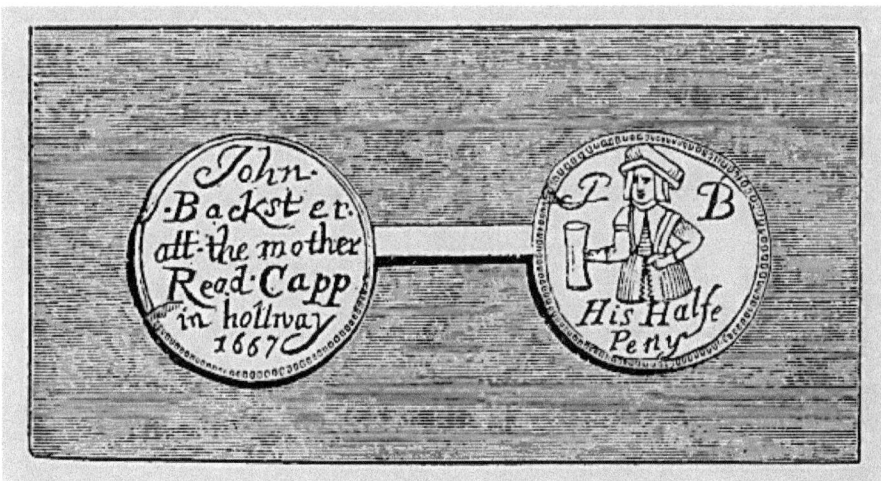

Original

He made his way to the low-roofed side parlour, where were assembled a troop of showmen and conjurors. One fellow was busily employed in shaving a baboon, ** which he intended to exhibit as a fairy; and another was rasping the rough chin of a muzzled bear, that bore the operation with exemplary patience, sitting in an arm-chair, dressed in a check waistcoat and trowsers, in his professional character of an Ethiopian savage!

* John Backster kept the Mother Red Cap at Holloway in 1667.
We are in possession of his very curious and rare Token, on
the right side of which is engraved Mother Red Cap holding a
Black Jack, with his initials of "J. B. His Half Peny:* and
on the reverse, "John Backster, att-the Mother Read-Capp in
hollway, 1667."
** The baboon and the monkey were popular drolls in ancient

times. The following lines occur in a work called "Ayres or
Phantasticke Sprites for three Voices," published by Thomas
Weelkes, "Batchelar of Musicke," 1608.
"The ape, the monkey, and baboon did meet,

And breaking of their fast in Friday Street;
Two of them sware together solemnly
In their three natures was a sympathy.
'Nay,' quoth Baboon, 'I do deny that strain,
I have more knavery in me than you twain.'
"'Why,' quoth the Ape,
'I have a horse at will
In Paris Garden, for to ride on still,
And there show tricks.' —
'Tush,' quoth the Monkey,
'I For better tricks in great men's houses lie.'
'Tush!' quoth Baboon; 'when men do know I come,
For sport from town and country they will run.'"

A conjuror was looking at a large dragon-fly through a magnifying glass, to see how it would pass off for the great high German higher-flighter; and the proprietor of an aviary was supplying a young blackbird with an artificial comb and wattles of red velvet, to find a customer for him as the great cocky, or olla bird of the desert. A showman was mending the fractured bridge of Mr. Punch's nose, while his stage-manager tried a new tail on the devil. *

* In some of the old plays the devil was dressed in a black
suit, painted with flames, and made to shine. "Let the devil
wear black for me, I'll have a suit of sables," says Hamlet.
In the mysteries and moralities of an earlier date, he was
decorated with a hairy dress, like a wild beast.

The master of the monster tea-kettle, who had recently been "up the spout," was tricking out his red-haired, strapping Dulcinea with peacocks' feathers, bits of stained glass, catskins, strips of coloured leather, and teaching her to sing some unintelligible gibberish, for the purpose of extracting from the Bartholomew Fair gulls a penny for the prodigious sight of a real wild Indian. A mermaid was in process of completion; a dog was practising a minuet, to see how his fifth leg fitted him; a learned pig * was going through his lesson in numbers and cards; a cat of extraordinary intelligence was feeding a kitten with starch, to make it stand upright; and a monkey instructing an intellectual goose how to carry a pair of miniature milkpails.

* The earliest account that we have seen of a learned pig is in an old Bartholomew Fair hill, issued by Mr. Conjuror Fawkes, which exhibits the portrait of the swinish pundit holding a paper in his mouth, with the letter Y inscribed upon it. This "most amazing pig," which had a particularly curly tail, was the pattern of docility and sagacity: the "Pig of Knowledge, Being the only one ever taught in England." He was to be visited "at a Commodious Room, at the George, West-Smithfield, During the time of the Fair and the spectators were required to "See and Believe!" Three-pence was the price of admission to behold "This astonishing animal" perform with cards, money, and watches, &c. &c. The bill concludes with the following apotheosis to the pig.
"A learned pig in George's reign,

To Æsop's brutes an equal boast;
Then let mankind again combine,
To render friendship still a toast."
Stella said that Swift could write sublimely upon a

broomstick. Who ever, as the Methodists say, better "improved" a pig? Except by roasting it! In 1732, Mr. Fawkes exhibited a "learned goose" opposite the George Inn, West-Smithfield.

A poetical licensed victualler had just painted on his board, which was emblazoned with the sign of the Griffin and
    Hoop, the following lines in capitals,

        "I, John Stubbs lyveth hear,

        Sels goode Brandy, Gin, and Bere,

        I maid mi borde a leetle whyder,

        To let you nowe I sels goode Syder:"

the lines, like the liquors, being composed by the said John Stubbs! A giant, * well padded out, was adding some inches to his stature by a pair —
    * Giants have been "At Home" not at fairs only. Og, King of Bashan, was more than twelve English feet in height. Goliah was about nine feet nine inches high-or eleven feet, according to some commentators. The Emperor Maximinus is said to have been nine feet. Turner, the naturalist, mentions having seen on the Brazil coast a race of gigantic savages, one of whom measured twelve feet! And Monsieur Thevet, in his description of America, published at Paris in 1575, declares that he saw and measured the skeleton of a South

American, which was eleven feet five inches in length. Die-
merbroeek saw at Utreeht a well-proportioned living man,
measuring eight feet six inches; and Dr. Becamus was
introduced to a youth who was nearly nine feet high; a man
almost ten feet, and a woman quite ten feet. The Patagonians
have been represented as a nation of giants. The
Philosophical Transactions of the Royal Society contain
accounts of skeletons dug up in England, measuring eight and
nine feet in length, which probably were Roman. In the
forty-first and forty-second volumes of the same work are
two engravings taken from an os front is and an os
bregmatis, the former of which is reckoned to have belonged
to a person between eleven and twelve feet high; the latter
to a giant of thirteen feet four inches. Walter Parsons,
porter to King James the First, was seven feet seven inches
in stature. The Chinese would have us believe that they
possess giants fifteen feet high. More of these prodigies
hereafter.

—of German hogloshes, with extra high heels; a fresh water sailor, with one eye, and one leg,
had a seal that exhaled an odour "most ancient and fish-like a ballad-singer was whitening his
head with chalk, * and several poor Italian boys, with tortoises, squirrels, monkeys, and white
mice, were jabbering away their *patois* in a corner with great animation.
    * Powdering the hair is supposed to have taken its rise in
modern Europe from some ballad singers at the fair of St.
Germain's in 1614, whitening their heads to make themselves
ludicrous!

One lively little fellow, the lion of the party, with brilliant black eyes, ivory teeth, and a dark
brown complexion, tinged with the bright warmth of an Italian sun, who bore on his shoulder a frolicksome marmoset * that he had been teaching to leap through a hoop, amused his
companions with a ditty that he had picked up on his journey hither from the pleasant valleys
of his father-land.

Original

* The custom of bearing an ape on the shoulder at country fairs, &c. is very ancient. Ben Jonson makes the following allusion to it in his Masque of Gypsies:
"A gypsy in his shape,

More calls the beholder,
Than the fellow with the ape,
Or the ape on his shoulder"

The person of Uncle Timothy was imposing; and the superfine broad cloth and brass buttons of Mr. Rumfit had invested it with a magisterial character that caused a sudden movement among the exhibitors when he entered their sanctorum. But the middle-aged gentleman soon convinced them that he was a man of humanity, and no magistrate; which quieted the alarms of both men and monkeys; and so gracious were his looks and demeanour, that the shaved bear, which had viewed him with scowling distrust, no longer kept aloof, but proffered his shaggy paw for a shake. At this moment the lecturing musician entered the room, and Jackimo, recognising his benefactor, jumped from the organ, ran up to him, doffed his cap, and made his best bow! Uncle Timothy and his company being now upon terms, he ordered in biscuits for the monkeys, and buns for the bears; not forgetting some nuts for his friend, who waited for the musician's nod before he cracked one of them. He then inquired of the bear-ward what his four-footed companion would like to drink? Upon which the keeper consulted his oracle, and received for reply, that a jug of homebrewed, with a toast and sugar, would be supremely acceptable! Uncle Timothy started, conceiving Bruin to have suddenly become possessed of Balaam's miraculous quality: but the mystery was soon explained; the keeper being a ventriloquist, and this one of his Bartlemy Fair tricks.

"Pray gentlemen," said Uncle Timothy, "by what means do you make these animals so apprehensive and docile? I fear there is some cruelty in the case."

"No cruelty at all, good sir," replied the lecturing musician, who was the organ of the company.

"It is your Smithfield drovers and butchers as is cruel! We don't larn our hanimals to dance on red-hot iron plates, as our aunt's sisters (ancestors?) did. Now that 'ere monkey o' mine; never was sich a wain little cove! It costes me a fortin in starch to stiffen his shirt collars; and if any on'em is in the least limp, my wig! he chatters, grins, and gies himself all the airs and graces of a fine lady. Sometimes I larn him his dooty by long lessons and short commons; sometimes I threatens-only threatens! —(but that in your honour's ear, for he's a-listening all the while!) to tip him monkey's allowance (shaking ferociously a very thin cane); but when I want to touch his feelings, I says, 'Jackimo, you're a good-for-nuffin little monster, and I'll walk off your *red waistcoat!*'"

"But the monkey and the bear, how relish they the razor?"

"Kindly, sir, kindly!" replied the Bruin shaver. "At first my old feller was summut rough and ugly; his beard turned the hedges of three oyster-knives afore I could trim him into a gentleman. But now he sees the advantage on it. *Don't you, my daisy?*"

The bear, after the fashion of the Irish echo, was made to ventriloquise in a growl, gruffly, "*I does, my tulip!*"

The several rehearsals being over, and all things put in order for their approaching campaign, the exhibitors were about to depart, when it occurred to Uncle Timothy that he had not paid his footing for being admitted behind the scenes. He addressed the real wild Indian, and begged her to call for what best pleased her palate; which call resolved itself into a rasher on the coals, a rummer of nutbrown, and a thimblefull of brandy to keep off the spasms. She was then escorted to her tea-kettle, and put under cover for the night. The bear and the monkey having been similarly disposed of, their respective shavers made merry with the rest of the show-folk. Uncle Timothy took the little Italian boys under his care, and feasted them plenteously. At this moment a *rival* tea-kettle drew up, with a caravan in the rear.

"Pray, madam," said a tragedy queen, peeping through a bit of ragged green curtain that depended before the entrance to the tea-kettle, to a dwarf in the caravan, "do you put up at Mother Red Cap's?"

* This old house, fronting the fields at Hoxton, was
formerly a noted place of resort for the Finsbury archers.
Sir William D'Avenant, in his "Long Vacation in London,"
says of the proctors and attorneys,
"Each with solemn oath agree

To meet in Fields of Finsburie;
With loynes in canvas bow-case tyde,
Where arrowes stick with mickle pride;
With hats pinn'd up, and bow in hand,
All day most fiercely there they stand,
Like ghosts of Adam Bell and Clymme,
Sol sets for fear they'll shoot at him."
A stray Toxopholite may now and then be seen at the Robin

Hood, stringing his bow, and dreaming of the 'merry days
that are past. Underneath the ancient sign is the following
inscription.
"Ye archers bold, and yeomen good,

Stop, and drink with Robin Hood;
If Robin Hood is not at home,
Stop, and drink with Little John."

"Not I, madam," responded the Lilliputian lady; "I stops at the Robin Hood * at merry Hoxton; * none but the *lower orders* stops at Mother Red Cap's!"

Original

And the caravan moved on as fast as the wall-eyed anatomy of a Rosinante could drag it.

   * Thomas Dale, Drawer at the Crown Tavern at Aldgate, kept
the Turk's Head Musiek-Booth in Smithfield-Rounds, over-
against the Greyhound Inn, during the time of Bartholomew
Fair (temp. W. 3rd), where he exhibited Scaramouch dances
and drolls, and "the Merry Cuckolds of Hogsden!" It is
stated in the Henslowe papers, deposited in the archives of
Dulwich College, that Ben Jonson killed Gabriel Spencer, a
fellow actor, in a duel fought in Hoxton Fields.

The rival tea-kettle poured out part of its contents in the person of a long, lean man, with all his
limbs rambling; no way reduceable to compass, unless you doubled him up like a pocket-rule.
His wardrobe was illustrative of Jew frippery and Rag-Fair tawdry. He was tricked out in the
relics of a ci-devant shirt; his coat was a patchwork quilt, his waistcoat and pantaloons were the
sign of the chequers, an escutcheon quartering all the colours of the rainbow.

> "In his hand
>
> A box he bore, wherein the pungent dust
>
> Of Dutch rapee, in gaudy state reclin'd.
>
> Oft would he ope the lid, and oft immerge
>
> His fingers,"

for the purpose of exciting an agreeable titillation in a very sharp nose, that blushed like a
corn-poppy.

"A glass of cold water, warm without sugar, Lady Teazle? or a strip of white satin and bitters,
my Belvidera? A pint of half-and-half in the pewter, my Calista? or a tumbler of cold without,
Mrs. Longbow?"

"D'ye think, Mr. Bigstick, I'm a rhinoscheros, a river-oss, or a crocodile? Order me a pot
of hot coffee and buttered toast; and mind, Mr. Bigstick, let it be buttered on *both* sides."

This dialogue was carried on between the long lean man and an invisible sharp-voiced personage in the tea-kettle.

"Coffee and toast for the tea-kettle," shouted the waiter.

"How many?" demanded mine host.

"Four. Lady Teaser, Belvideary, Miss Cannister, and Mrs. Longbow."

"*Mort de ma vie!*" ejaculated the long lean man. "For one! —In the Tumbletuzzy all these
characters are combined. And, *garçon*, bring me a basin of tea and a —biscuit."

The frugal refection was laid before the lean man. "Cat-lap base!" he muttered, swallowing
the scalding hot bohea, that was strongly impregnated with Sir Hugh Middleton, and champing
the dry biscuit.

"Another round of toast for Lady Teaser!"

"Buttered on *both* sides," growled the lean man, sarcastically; and he began to number with
his skinny fingers, as if counting the cost.

Uncle Timothy was the last person in the world to flout a threadbare coat, because it is
threadbare, or take a man for a sharper because he happens to be sharp-witted or sharp-set.
Your full-fed fool he thought quite as likely to have nefarious designs on his purse, as the hungry

humorist who at once lets you into the secret of his starvation. If he be deserving as well as poor, it was gratifying to Uncle Tim that he had made honest poverty forget its privations for a season; and should he prove a shirking idler on the *pavé* —, he had not been taken in at any vast expense. Reflections like these crossed his mind-and he left the room.

On his return, he found the lean man still counting with his fingers. Presently the waiter spread the table with a snow-white cloth; the clattering of knives and forks, plates and spoons, roused the lean man from his reverie; he gazed wistfully at the preparations, and looked thrice famished.

There is a story of a tyrant, who, to add to the natural torments of starvation, caused a roast chicken to be suspended every day before the prison bars of his victim, until he expired. Just such a tormentor, unwittingly, was Uncle Timothy. For the *garçon* again appeared, bearing a dish of broiled ham and poached eggs, the sight and aroma of which seared the eye-balls and tantalised the pinched nostrils of the lean man. At the same moment, "Another round for Lady Teaser!" tolled a twopenny knell in his ears.

"My friend not arrived yet?" said Uncle Timothy.

"No, sir," replied the *garçon* slyly, but respectfully.

"Let him pay, then, for his want of punctuality. I wait for nobody. Will *you*, sir," politely addressing the lean man, "do me the favour to be my guest? Though I have ordered supper for two, I cannot command appetite for two."

The lean man stared irresolutely at Uncle Timothy. Hunger and Pride were at fisticuffs; but Hunger hit pride such a blow in the stomach, that Pride gave up the contest.

And how gracefully did the middle-aged gentleman play the host! inviting his guest (though little invitation was needed) with the kindest words, and helping him to the daintiest morsels. And it was not until this supper-out of the first lustre had fully indulged his eating propensities, and cleared the board, that he found leisure to look up from his plate, and contemplate the execution he had done. But when a cauliflower-wigged tankard of stout crowned the repast, he pressed it with ecstasy to his lips, and sang joyously —

Porter! drink for noble souls!

Raise the foaming tankard high I

Water drink, you water think —

So said Johnson-so say I!

Let me take a Dutchman's draught —

Ha I —I breathe! —a glorious pull!

Malt and hops are British drops —

Froth for Frenchmen! Stout for Bull!

If you ask why Britons fight

Till they conquer or they die? —

Their stout is strong, their draughts are long —

Now you know the reason why.

"Lady Teaser is quite ready, sir," said the *garçon*, hurriedly.

"Give my respectful compliments to Lady Teazle, and tell her ladyship that I'll kiss her superlative 'pickers and stealers' in 'the twinkling of a bed-post.'"

The *garçon* made another precipitate entry, with "The tea-kettle can't wait, sir!"

"A fico for the tea-kettle! It must! —it shall! With three rounds of toast buttered on *both* sides, and coffee *à discretion*, hath the Tumbletuzzy been magnificently regaled —('Marriage is chargeable!') —and shall I not take mine ease in mine inn? Your banquet, sir, hath warmed the cockles of my heart, and made my hair curl! —

When a gentleman's stomach lacks dainty fare, (Singing)

And "Cupboard I Cupboard!" it croaks in his ear,

He rejoices, i'feggs! when bacon and eggs

' Smoke on the board, with a tankard of beer.

Without much ado, his teeth fall to,

The delicate viands vanish from view;

O'er a glass of good liquor

His heart beats the quicker,

And he drinks to his kind host, as I drink to you.

There's my card —(presenting a bill of the performances) —'Bonassus Bigstick, Esq. Bartholomew Fair.' I'll put you on our free list, which to all the world, but yourself and the public press, shall be unavoidably suspended! Ha!" —(scenting a rummer of hot punch that the *garçon* placed before him) —"'brandy for heroes!' Welcome, old friend! for a' langsyne. Yet what is punch without a song? A clerk without a Cocker; a door without a knocker; a ship without a sailor; a goose without a tailor; a rhyme without a riddle; a bow without a fiddle; a priest without a pulpit; a stage without a full pit! —As you, sir, have been instrumental to my entertainment, let me be vocal for yours! *Omnibus tulip punctum*, as we say in the classics! —I'll give you an undress rehearsal of one of my crack songs for *tomorrow* at Saint Bartlemy.

All the world's a stage, the men and women actor folks,

Very, very tragical, or very full of fun.

Nature, in a merry mood, on some has, quizzing, crack'd

her jokes;

And Mr. Dicky Dunderhead of Dunstable is one.

Ranting, tearing, stamping, staring; Whiskerandos, Domine

Now he courts the comic muse, then ogles at Melpomene;

His funny eyes, funny mouth, funny chin, and funny

nose,

So queerly tool'd, are good as goold-and Dick the worth

of money knows!

Punch's scions, see the lions! Bartlemy, come startle

me!

Ladies and gentlemen, walk in, walk in!

Shyloçk the Jew, the Brigand, and the Blackymoor,

Nigger parlous! killing Carlos on his wedding-day;

As Mother Cole, the canting soul, he drinks a drop of

Jacky more;

As Hamlet proud, he bellows loud, and scares the

ghost away!

The pit and box to sticks and stocks his acting surely

turn'em would,

When by the train to Dunsinane comes in a gallop

Birnam Wood.

"Avaunt i you fright, and quit my sight I a stool there's

not, my trump, any;

I'll thank'e, Banky, for your room! Old Nick may have

your company!"

Punch's scions, see the lions! Bartlemy, come startle

me!

Ladies and gentlemen, walk in, walk in!

With Pantaloon and Columbine he skips, trips, and frisks

along;

Round his head spins like a top as fast as it can go:

Now he twirls his magic sword, whacks the clown, and

whisks along,

Dances on his head and hands, and jumps Jim Crow.

In his jazey, crack'd and crazy, very queer in Lear he is;

And quite as queer telling Pierre how dear his Belvi-

deary is!

"A horse! my kingdom for a horse!" if legs he can but

go on two —

Another bring-twice two is four-and, like Ducrow,

I'll crow on two.

Punch's scions, see the lions! Bartlemy, come startle

me!

Ladies and gentlemen, walk in, walk in!

O, Mr. Dunderhead; is it to be wonder-ed,

Old chap, you let Miss Capulet make love to you till

dawn?

'For when you play'd at Dunstable, and overrun the

constable,

The ladies would have pledged their hearts to take you

out of pawn.

Among the stars of Smithfield bars you'll stick so fiery

off indeed,

The deuce a bit of goose you'll get, or "Nosey! off!" *

or cough, indeed;

And if in fun for number one folks think to spend a

penny fit,

They'll come and see you off a tree the bark grin, at

your benefit.

Punch's scions, see the lions! Bartlemy, come startle

me!

Ladies and gentlemen, walk in, walk in!

* About the year 1775, there was a performer on the violincello in the orchestra of Drury Lane Theatre, named
Cervetti, to whom the gods had given the appropriate
nickname of Nosey, from his enormous staysail, that helped
to carry him before the wind. "Nosey!" shouted from the
galleries, was the signal, or word of command for the
fiddlers to strike up. This man was originally an Italian
merchant of good repute; but failing in business, he came
over to England, and adopted music for a profession. He had
a notable knack of loud yawning, with which he sometimes
unluckily filled up Garrick's expressive pauses, to the
infinite annoyance of little Davy, and the laughter of the
audience. In the summer of 1777 he played at Vauxhall, at
the age of ninety-eight.
The Lauréat of Little Britain must have had just such

another Nose in his eye when he wrote the following.
That Roman Nose! that Roman Nose!

Has robb'd my bosom of repose;
For when in sleep my eyelids close,
It haunts me still, that Roman Nose!
Between two eyes as black as sloes
The bright and flaming ruby glows;
That Roman Nose! that Roman Nose!
And beats the blush of damask rose.
I walk the streets, the alleys, rows;
I look at all the Jems and Joes;
And old and young, and friends and foes,
But cannot find a Roman Nose!
Then blessed be the day I chose
That nasal beauty of my beau's;
And when at last to heaven I goes,
I hope to spy his Roman Nose!

The tea-kettle boiled over with rage, and demanded imperiously the immediate presence of the
lean man.
"Who calls on Bigstick? As the Tumbletuzzy will brook no longer delay,

'I hold it fit that we shake hands and part.'

'To-morrow, and to-morrow, and to-morrow,' you will find me at the Fair. I shall expect your promised visit.

'Adieu, adieu, adieu, remember me!'"

At this moment old blind Sally, who for more than half a century has played her way through Highgate, Holloway, and merry Islington, * tuned her hurdy-gurdy, and ground the lean man triumphantly into his tea-kettle.

* "Islington, March 20, 1698. This day here were lamentable
doings. O! in what a sad fright and consternation were the
Lick-spickets of this plaee; upon the suddain and unexpected
appearance of the ferreters of Fuddling-schools all were put
into a hurry and confusion, the men were forced to throw
down their beloved pipes of sotweed, and rudely leave their
pots without a parting kiss; the women and children too,
alas! with tears and sighs, parted with their hot cakes and
custards, before they had half stuffed their stomachs. And
the streets were filled with the mourning mob. Amongst the
rest was a fat red-faced hostess, who, with a loud and
doleful voice, said, 4 Ah! my friends, if this business
holds, I shall certainly be undone. Ah! poor Islington, thou
hast been, time out of mind, the plaee of general rendezvous
for Sunday sots. Thou hast constantly supplied the citizens'
wives and children with cakes, pies, and custards, and art
the chief plaee near the city, for breeding calves and
nursing children. Thou, I say, that hast been a place so
famous, and in such esteem, now to have the richest of thy
inhabitants utterly ruined only for profaning the Sabbath-
day. Alas! the only day we have to get money in. Who will
advise me?' —'Advise you,' said one of her sottish
customers, 'you have kept an ale-house almost thirty years,
to my knowledge, and if you have not got enough by nicking,
frothing, double-scoreing, selling coarse cakes, empty pies,
and nasty custards, to keep you now you are old, e'en go to
your old master, the devil, and let him keep you!" —"The
English Lueian, or Weekly Discoveries of the Witty
Intrigues, Comical Passages, and Remarkable Transactions in
Town and Country, &c. &c."
The above is a curious picture of an Islington ale-wife in

the olden time. The following account describes a "strange
monster" exhibited at Miles's Music-house at Islington a few
years after, with the comical interlude of the Stuffed
Alligator.
"Some time since there was brought to Miles's Music-house at

Islington, a strange sort of a monster, that does everything
like a monkey, but is not a monkey; mimics man, like a
jackanapes, but is not a jackanapes; jumps upon tables, and

into windows upon all-fours, like a cat, but is not a cat;
does all things like a beast, but is not a beast; does
nothing like a man, but is a man! He has given such
wonderful content to the Butchers of Clare Market, that the
house is every day as full as the Bear Gardens; and draws
the city wives and prentices out of London, much more than a
man hanged in chains. It happened lately upon a holiday,
when honest men walked abroad with their wives and
daughters, to the great consumption of hot buns and bottled
ale, that the fame of this mimick had drawn into the Music-
house as great a crowd of spectators as the notable
performances of Clinch of Barnet ever drew to the theatre.
The Frape being thus assembled in the lower room, and the
better sort being climbed into the gallery, a little
creature, who before walked erect, and bore the image of a
man, transformed himself into a monkey, and began to
entertain the company with such a parcel of pretty pug's
tricks, and mimical actions, that they were all as intent
upon the baboon's vagaries as if a mandrake had been
tumbling through a hoop, or a hobgoblin dancing an antick!
Whilst the eyes and ears of the assembly were thus deeply
engaged, the skin of a large alligator, stuff'd with hay,
hanging within the top of the house, and the rats having
burrowed through the ceiling, could come down at pleasure
and sport upon the back of the monster; one of the
revengeful vermin, to put a trick upon his fellows, who were
enticed by the smell of the hay to creep down the serpent's
throat, his jaws being extended, gnawed the cord in two, and
down comes the alligator with his belly full of rats, upon
the head of the monkey, and laid him sprawling; giving some
of the spectators a wipe with his tail; the rats running out
of his mouth in a wonderful hurry, like so many sailors from
between decks when a ship at midnight has struck upon a

rock!" —"A Pacquet from Will's, 1701."

CHAPTER XII.

Uncle Timothy was an excursive talker and walker. He had no set phrases; nothing ready-cut and dried (which is often *very dry*) for formal intellectual displays. When he rose in the morning, unless bound by some engagement, he hardly knew whither his footsteps would tend. He was to be seen looking into curiosity shops; rummaging old book-stalls; turning over portfolios of curious prints; stepping into an auction, a panorama, an exhibition of ancient pictures; sometimes rambling in the green fields, and not unfrequently making one of Punch's laughing audiences. It is the opinion of some would-be philosophers that their dignity is best upheld by an unbending austerity, and a supercilious contempt for whatever engaged the attention of their youth. But we tell such pretenders, that they are alike ignorant of nature and philosophy. Men of the most exalted genius have been *remarkable* for their urbanity, and even child-like simplicity of manners: and it was one of the many interesting traits in the author of *Waverley*, that, in the "sear and yellow leaf," he had nothing of age but the name; but retained all the spirit, the romance, the gaiety of his youthful days.

The world would have called Uncle Timothy idle—but

"How various his employments, whom the world

Calls idle, and who justly in return

Esteems the busy world an idler too!"

Though the world's pursuits brought more care to the heart and profit to the purse than his own, he wished they might only prove as innocent and as honest.

Uncle Timothy had just got scent of an ancient carved figure of Falstaff, that once adorned the overhanging doorway of the Boar's Head, in East-cheap; not the original scene of revelry where Prince Hal and Sir John turned night into day. That merry hostelrie, where "lean Jack" slept on benches in the afternoon, and unbuttoned himself after supper, had been replaced by another, bearing the same immortal sign, which rose on its ruins immediately after the fire of London. The Boar's Head (which we well remember) was cut in stone, and let into the brick work under the centre window of the first floor. This house had been recently pulled down, in order to make room for the new London Bridge improvements; but Uncle Timothy heard that the figure had been carefully reserved by the proprietor, as a memorial of so celebrated a site. Thither he journeyed on a voyage of discovery. The owner of the Boar's Head had departed this life; but the neighbours referred him to a nephew, dwelling in an adjoining street, who had succeeded the old gentleman in business. The worthy tradesman received him with courtesy, and proceeded to narrate what had transpired since the demolition of the tavern. The story of the figure was strictly true. His late uncle regarded it as an interesting relic, and his widow, smitten with a kindred feeling, had retired into the country, carrying with her Sir John Falstaff; and it was not at all likely that she would relinquish possession of the fat knight, until commanded by the inexorable separatist that parts the best friends. While Uncle Timothy, on his way homeward, was whistling, not for "want of thought," but the figure, he espied a new Boar's Head in the immediate vicinity of the old one; and, as the attraction was too powerful to be resisted, he walked in, and soon found himself in a spacious apartment, carved, fretted, and mullioned in the ancient style; the furniture was grotesquely ornamented and antique; the holly and mistletoe were disposed in various parts of the room; a huge fire blazed cheerfully; and round a massy oak table, black with age, sat Falstaff, Prince Henry, Sir Toby Belch, Sir Andrew Ague-cheek, Sir Hugh Evans, Justice Shallow, Poins, Peto, Touchstone, Corporal Nym, Ancient Pistol, and Lieutenant Bardolph! That "base-string of humility," Francis, waited upon the company; and the shrill tones of Hostess Quickly were heard in an angry colloquy with the "roaring girl," Doll Tearsheet. A boar's head with a lemon in his mouth adorned the centre of the table, and immediately before Sir John Falstaff was a magnificent bowl of sugared sack compounded by the dame n her very best humour, and not excelled by that memorable draught which the oily knight so cosily lapped down, when he swore to mine hostess, "upon a parcel-gilt goblet, sitting in her Dolphin Chamber at the round-table, by a sea-coal fire," that he would marry her and make her "my lady." Every guest had a horn cup silver-mounted; and black jacks of sparkling ale, and cakes in abundance, strewed the festive board. Some racy joke on Bardolph's burning nose had just been fired off, and the company were in high merriment.

"Surely," said Uncle Timothy to himself, "this is a masquerade. I am an unbidden guest; but the Enchanter's wand is over me, and I cannot either advance or retire."

Sir Andrew thrummed his viol-de-gambo; and Sir Toby, having fortified himself with a long draught out of a black jack, with true heartiness of voice and gesture struck up a glee.

Sir Toby. Because some folks are virtuous, Sir John,

    shall you and I

Forswear our wassail, cakes and ale, and sit us down

    and sigh?

The world is still a merry world, and this a merry time;

And sack is sack, Sir John, Sir Jack! though in it tastes

    the lime.

The watery eye of Sir John Falstaff twinkled with exquisite delight as he filled himself a cup of sack and responded,

There's nothing extant, Sir Toby, but cant.

A plague of all cowards! Here, Bardolph, my Trigon!

    You and I will repent,

    And keep a lean Lent.

    Presuming it long,

    Let us first have a song,

    And dismally troll

    It over a bowl,

To honesty, manhood, good fellowship bygone.

Pistol, my Ancient!

Pistol. I'll ne'er prove a stopper,

    By my sword, that's true steel!

Bardolph. By nose, that's true copper!

Falstaff. Corporal Nym —

Nym.. In sack let me swim!

Falstaff. Gadshill and Peto —

Gadshill & Peto. Sweet wag! take our veto.

Falstaff. Motley too —

Clown. My cockscomb to you!

Falstaff. Good Justice Shallow —

Shallow. I'm true to you, "Tallow!"

Falstaff. Sir Andrew, Sir Hugh —

Sir Andrew & Sir Hugh. We'll drink as you brew!

Falstaff. Poins joins! Hal shall!

  Dame Partlet the hen! Doll! Francis! —Francis. Anon! —

All. We're all your liege subjects, right glorious

  Sir John!

   Chorus.

The lawyer's head, and the shark's head,

The puritan parson's, and clerk's head,

  Are all very well

  For a shot or a shell;

  Exceedingly fit

  To fill up a pit!

But the head that was rear'd

When Christmas cheer'd

In the rollicking, frolicking days of yore,

 When the Lord of Misrule,

  The Friar and Fool,

With Robin and Marian, led the brawl,

And the hobby-horse frisk'd in the old-fashion'd hall,

 Was the wassailing Head of the bristly Boar!

We are minions of the moon,

Doughty heroes, hot for fight!

May a cloud her brightness shroud,

   And help us to a purse to-night.

Buckram'd varlets! coward knaves!

   Angels, watches, rings unfob! —

Prince and Poins. Up with staves, and down with

   braves —

We true men the robbers rob!

Touchstone. Mistress Audrey, in the dance,

With your love-lorn swain advance.

Though our carpet *s not so sheen

As shady Arden's forest green,

And the lamps are not so bright

As chaste Luna's silver light,

Nor our company so gay

As when trips the sprightly fay,

I will dance, and I will sing,

Mingling in the laughing ring.

Chorus.

Shout for the Head of the bristly Boar!

   Jovial spirits, as we are now,

Did merrily bound while the cup went round

   Under the holly and mistletoe bough.

Sing O the green holly! sing O the green holly!

Nothing's so sweet as divine melancholy.

Ingratitude blighting true friendships of old,

No bleak winter wind is so bitter and cold.

The room now seemed to extend in width and in length; the sounds of revelry ceased, and other characters appeared upon the scene. Lady Macbeth, her eyes bending on vacancy, her lips moving convulsively, her voice audible, but in fearful whispers, slept her last sleep of darkness, guilt, and terror. The Weird Sisters danced round their magic caldron, hideous, anomalous, and immortal! The noble Moor ended "life's fitful season," remorseful and heartbroken. The "Majesty of buried Denmark" revisited "the pale glimpses of the moon." Ariel, dismissed by Pros-pero, warbled his valedictory strain, and flew to his bright dwelling, "under the blossom that hangs on the bough." The chiefs and sages of imperial Rome swept along in silent majesty. Lear, on his knees, bareheaded, with heavenward eye, quivering lip, and hands clasped together in agony, pronounced the terrible curse, and in his death realised all that can be imagined of human woe. Shylock, the representative of a once-despised and persecuted race, pleaded his cause before the senate, and lost it by a quibble. Obe-ron, Puck, and the ethereal essences of a Midsummer Night's Dream flitted in the moonbeams. Benedick and Beatrice had their wars of wit and combats of the tongue. The Lady Constance, alternately reproachful, despairing, and frenzied, exhibited a matchless picture of maternal tenderness. Juliet breathed forth her sighs to the chaste stars. Isabella read a lesson to haughty authority, when she asks her brother's forfeited life at the hands of the Duke, worthy of holy seer or sage *; and Ophelia, in her distraction, was simple, touching, and sublime.

   * An eminent dignitary of the Church of England was once discoursing with the author on the morality of Shakspere. He regretted that the Bard had not spoken on that most glorious of all subjects, Man's Redemption, beyond a few lines (exquisitely beautiful) in the first seene of Hamlet. The author immediately pointed out the following terse, but transcendant passage from "Measure for Measure."
"Why, all the souls that were, were forfeit once;

And HE that might the 'vantage best have took,

Found out the remedy."

It would pass the bounds of the most exalted eulogy to

record the prelate's answer, and how deeply affected he was whilst making it.

Though these soul-stirring scenes were perfectly familiar to Uncle Timothy, and from youth to age had been his morning study and his nightly dream, they had never been invested with such an absorbing reality before, and he stood transfixed, a wondering spectator of the glorious vision-for such to his aching sight it seemed to be. At this moment, the embroidered arras that hung before the oriel window of the tapestried chamber was slowly drawn aside, and the *figure of Shakspere,* his eyes beaming with immortality, and his lofty brow discoursing of all things past, present, and to come, stood revealed to view! "Flowers of all hues, and without thorn the rose," sprung up spontaneously beneath his feet.

And as he walk'd along th' enamell'd bed

Of flow'rs, disposed in many a fairy ring,

Celestial music answer d to his tread,

As if his feet had touch'd some hidden spring

Of harmony-so soft the airs did breathe

In the charmed ear-around-above-beneath?

He spoke-But his voice was of "no sound that the earth knows."

The sensations of Uncle Timothy grew intensely painful-amounting almost to agony. He made a sudden effort to rush forward, and in making it, *awoke!* when he found himself seated snugly in an arm-chair before a bright "sea-coal fire," at the Mother Red Cap, where he had fallen asleep after the exit of the Bartholomew Fair troop, in their progress to the *"Rounds."* And thus ended Uncle Timothy's *Vision of the Boar's Head!*

CHAPTER XIII.

Gentlemen, on this anniversary of St. Bartholomew, let us not forget that we owe his Fair to a priest and jester."

"A priest and a jester, Mr. Merripall? —ha! ha! ho!"

"In sooth, Brother Stiflegig," replied the comical coffin-maker to his inquiring mute, whose hollow laugh sounded like a double knock; "and the merry monk is no more to be blamed for the disorders that, fungus-like, have grown out of it, than is Sir Christopher Wren for the cobwebs and dust that deface the dome of St. Paul's. Right is not always the *reverse* of wrong. Brush away the cobwebs and the dust, but spare the dome. Don't cut off a man's head to cure his toothach, or lop off his leg to banish his gout *in toto!*"

The latter clause of this remark was much applauded by a sensitive member, who had evinced great anxiety to protect his physiognomy from the cutting draught of the door; and by another, who was equally careful to keep his ten toes from being trod upon. But the sexton and the two mutes exchanged significant glances, that plainly hinted their non-approval of this anti-professional, ultraliberality on the part of the comical coffin-maker.

"Gentlemen," resumed Mr. Merripall, rising —

THE JOVIAL PRIOR OF ST. BARTHOLOMEW!=

> Sons of the fair, to Father Rahère
>
> Chant a stave in a hollow mew;
>
> Hosier Lane shout back the strain
>
> Through the cloisters of holy Bartholomew.
>
> Saunders, Gyngell, merrily mingle;
>
> Richardson join in the choir:
>
> Two-legg'd dancers, four-legg'd prancers,
>
> You can't cry nay (neigh?) to the Prior.

Now fire away in full chorus! —

> Peace to the soul of the bald-pated droll!
>
> Sound him a larry-cum-twang!
>
> Toss off a toast to his good-humour'd ghost,
>
> And let it come off with a bang!"

We were passing by those ancient houses in Duke Street, Smithfield, undecided whether or not to drop in upon the little Drysalter, when our attention was arrested by this chorus of mirth proceeding from one of the many obscure hostelries with which these ancient turnings and windings abound. We had stumbled on the Pig and Tinder-box, near Bartholomew Close. The chair was on his legs-an exceedingly long pair, in black stockings-leading a loud cheer. Mr. Merripall, the comical coffin-maker, was president of the Antiqueeruns. On each side of him sat his two mutes, Messrs. Hatband and Stiflegig; the sexton, Mr. Shovelton, by virtue of his office, was vice; the rest were tradesmen in the neighbourhood, to whom porter, pipes, punch, purl, pigtail, and politics were a pleasing solace after the business of the day; and a warlike character was given to the club by the infusion of some of the Honourable the Artillery Company, and the "angel visits" of a city-marshal. Its name, though implying the reverse of a jest, had its origin in a joke, arising from the mispronunciation of a member, to whom a little learning had proved a dangerous thing. This intelligent brother, at the christening of the club, moved that it be called the "*Antiqueeruns,*" from the antiquity of their quarter and quality, which was carried, as he triumphantly announced, "*my ninny contra decency!*" (nemine contradicenti?) A palpable misnomer-for the quorum consisted of the queerest fellows imaginable, and their president, Mr. Merripall, was a host in fun.

Our entrance had not been noticed during their upstanding jollity; but now, when every member was seated, we became "the observed of all observers."

"Spies in the camp!" growled a priggish person of punchy proportions, with a little round dumpling head, and short legs, whose pompous peculiarities had been sorely quizzed by some prying penny-a-liner. "I move, Mr. Cheer, that our fifteenth rule be read by the vice."

"Spies in the camp, Mr. Allgag! —pooh! Yet what signifies, if there's no treason in it? The gentlemen have only mistaken a private room for a public one."

"It's all very well, Mr. President, for you to say there was no malice aforethought to broil us on their penny gridiron, when these people popped in upon us whipsy dicksy (ipse dixit?) and un-awars. But" (rapping the table) "we live in an age of spies and spinnage!" (espionage?)

"*Gammon* and spinnage!" chuckled the comical coffin-maker.

"Order! order!" from several voices.

"The Cheer is out of order! A gentleman don't oughtn't to be interrupted will he nil he, vie et harness (vi et armis?). Who seconds my motion?"

"I," winked the sexton.

"Then we'll put it to the vote. As many of you as are of this opinion hold up your hands."

Mr. Allgag, though an oyster in intellect, was the small oracle of an insignificant, captious, factious section of the Antiqueeruns. A few hands were held up, and the fulminating fifteenth rule was read aloud, which imposed a fine of five shillings on each intruder, and a forcible ejection from the room.

"I blush for these pitiful proceedings," exclaimed the comical coffin-maker; "and rather than become a party to them, I will vacate the chair."

"Well and good! I'll be your locum trimmings," (tenens?) rejoined the Holborn Hill Demosthenes; and he half strutted, half waddled from his seat, as if to take possession. The mutes looked grave; even the rebellious vice was panic-struck at the prodigious boldness of Mr. Allgag. "I'll take the cheer. As for the turning out part of the story —"

"Who talks of turning out?" cried the Lauréat of Little Britain, bursting suddenly into the room. "Is it you?" addressing the affrighted sexton, who shook his head ruefully in the negative; "or you?" advancing to the terrified mutes, who shook in their shoes. "Not you! good Master Merri-pall," giving the comical coffin-maker a hearty shake by the hand. "Or is it you, sir?" placing himself in a provokingly pugnacious attitude before the Holborn Hill Demosthenes. "What a bluster about an unintentional intrusion! If, gentlemen, my friends must be fined, I will be their guarantee."

So saying, he ejected us with gentle violence from the room, and in a few minutes after we found ourselves in his elegant little library, where everything was as neat and prim as himself-not" a bust, bijou, or book out of its place.

"A heavy retribution had well nigh fallen upon you, my good friends, for passing my door without looking in. It matters not what chance medley brought me to your rescue; but I'm a merciful man, and the only fine I impose is, that you sit down, be comfortable, and stay till I turn you out."

The fine seemed so very moderate, that we were glad to compromise.

"Everything around you-books, plate, pictures-ay, my old-fashioned housekeeper into the bargain-are the selection of Uncle Tim."

"And by this beeswing, Mr. Bosky, we guess Uncle Timothy is butler too."

"Most profoundly opined! Yonder," pointing to an antique painted glass door, "is his cabinet —

'There Caxton sleeps, with Wynkyn at his side,

One clasp'd in wood, and one in strong cow-hide.'

"An odd thought strikes me. What say you to a dish of conjurors, with a garnish of monsters and mountebanks, served up by mine host of St. Bartlemy, Uncle Tim?" And Mr. Bosky disappeared through the glass door, but returned in an instant, bearing in his hand a smartly-bound volume. "Shall I unclasp the *Merry Mysteries of Bartlemy Fair?* You may go farther and fare worse."

"We want no whetters or provocatives, Mr. Bosky."

"Well, seeing that, like Justice Greedy, you long to give thanks and fall to, my musical grace shall not be a tedious one.

> Our host, Uncle Tim, does the banquet prepare,
>
> An Olla Podrida of Bartlemy Fair!
>
> Ye lovers of mirth, eccentricity, whim,
>
> Fill a glass to the health of our host, Uncle Tim.
>
> And when you have fill'd, O! dismiss from your
>
>> mind
>
> Whatever is selfish, ungrateful, unkind;
>
> Let gentle humanity rise to the brim,
>
> And then, if you please, you may toast Uncle Tim!
>
> You need not be told that the wine must be old,
>
> As sparkling and bright as his wit and his whim;
>
> Of clear rosy hue, and generous too,
>
> Like the cheek and the heart of our friend, Uncle
>
>> Tim!
>
> So now stir the fire, let business retire,
>
> The door shut on Mammon, we'll have none of him!
>
> But tell the sly fox, when he quietly knocks,
>
> We are only at home to thy Tome, Uncle Tim!

Mr. Bosky trimmed the lamp, drew the curtains, wheeled round the sofa, opened the morocco-bound manuscript, and began. But Mr. Bosky's beginning must stand at the head of our next chapter.

CHAPTER XIV.

Garrick never introduced a hero upon the scene without a flourish of trumpets-nor shall we.

> "Bid Harlequino decorate the stage
>
> With all magnificence of decoration —
>
> Giants and giantesses, dwarfs and pigmies,
>
> Songs, dances, music, in their amplest order.
>
> Mimes, pantomimes, and all the mimic motion
>
> Of scene deceptiovisive and sublime!"

For St. Bartholomew makes his first bow in *The Ancient Records of the Rounds*.

The learned need not be told that a fair was originally a market for the purchase and sale of all sorts of commodities; and what care the unlearned for its derivation? For them it suffices that 'tis a market for fun. Our merry Prior of St. Bartholomew knowing the truth of the old proverb, that, "all work and no play makes Jack a dull boy," mingled pastime with business, and put Momus into partnership with Mammon. For many years they jogged on together, somewhat doggedly, to be sure, for Momus was a fellow of uproarious merriment; and while Mammon, with furred gown and gold chain, was weighing atoms and splitting straws, Momus split the sides of his customers, and so entirely won them over to his jocular way of doing business, that Mammon was drummed out of the firm and the fair. But Mammon has had his revenge, by causing Momus to be confined to such narrow bounds, that his lions and tigers lack space to roar in, and his giants are pinched for elbow room. * Moreover, he and his sly bottle-holder, Mr. Cupidity Cant (who from the time of Prynne to the present has been a bitter foe to good fellowship), threaten to drive poor Momus out of house and home. Out upon the ungracious varlets! let them sand their own sugar, ** not ours! and leave Punch alone.

* The American giant refuses to come over to England this
summer, because the twenty-first of June is not long enough
for him to stand upright in! And the Kentucky dwarf is so
short that he has not paid his debts these five years!
** "Have you sanded the sugar, good Sandy,

And water'd the treacle with care?
Have you smuggled the element into the brandy?"
"Yes, master." —"Then come in to prayer!"

Let them be content to rant in their rostrums, and peep over their particular timber, lest we pillory the rogues, and make them peep through it!

Father Rahére founded the Priory, Hospital, and Church of St. Bartholomew in Smithfield, at the instigation ('tis said) of the saint himself, who appeared to him in Rome, whither he had repaired on a pilgrimage. We learn from the Cottonian MSS. that he "of te hawnted the Kyng's palice, and amo'ge the noysefull presse of that tumultuous courte, enforsed hymselfe with jolite and carnal suavité: ther yn spectaclis, yn metys, yn playes, and other courtely mokkys and trifyllis, intruding he lede forth the besynesse of alle the daye." He was a "pleasant witted gentleman," and filled the post of minstrel to King Henry the First, which comprehended musician, improvisatore, jester, &c.; and Henry the Second granted to the monastery of St. Bartholomew (of which Rahére was the first prior) the privilege of a three days' fair for the drapers and clothiers: hence Cloth Fair. His ashes rest under a magnificent tomb in the church of St. Bartholomew the Great. This beautiful shrine is still carefully preserved. How different has been the fate of the desecrated sepulchre of the "moral Gower," which the Beetian Borough brawlers would have pounded, with their Ladye Chapel, to macadamise the road!

"It is worthy of observation," (says Paul Hentzer, 1598,) "that every year when the Fair is held, it is usual for the Mayor to ride into Smithfield, dressed in his scarlet gown, and about his neck is a golden chain, besides that particular ornament that distinguishes the staple of the kingdom. He is followed by the Aldermen in scarlet gowns, and a mace and a cap are borne before him. Where the yearly fair is proclaimed a tent is placed, and after the ceremony is over the mob begin to wrestle before them, two at a time, and conquerors are rewarded by them by money thrown from the tent. After this, a parcel of live rabbits are turned loose among the crowd, and hunted by a number of boys, with great noise, &c. Before this time, also, there was an old custom for the *Scholars of London* to meet at this festival, at the *Priory of St. Bartholomew*, to dispute in logic and grammar, and upon a *bank, under a tree, (!)* the best of them were rewarded with *bows and silver arrows?* Bartholomew Fair, until about 1743, was held a fortnight; and the spacious area of Smithfield was filled with booths for drolls and interludes, in which many popular comedians of the time performed, from the merry reign of Mat Coppinger to the laughing days of Ned Shuter. Sir Samuel Fludyer, in 1762, and Mr. Alderman Bull, (*not John Bull!*) in 1774, enforced some stringent regulations that amounted almost to an abolition."

And now, my merry masters! let us take a stroll into the ancient fair of St. Bartholomew, *vulgo* Bartlemy, with John Littlewit, the uxorious proctor; Win-the-fight Littlewit, his fanciful wife; Dame Purecraft, a painful sister: Zeal-of-the-land Busy, the puritan Banbury man; and our illustrious cicerone, rare Ben Jonson.

In the year 1614, and long before, one of the most delicious city dainties was a Bartholomew *roast pig.* * A cold turkey-pie and a glass of rich malmsey were "creature comforts" not to be despised even by such devout sons of self-denial as Mr. Zeal-of-the-land Busy, who always popped in at pudding-time. ** But Bartholomew pig, "a meat that is nourishing, and may be longed for," that may be eaten, "very exceeding well eaten," but not in a fair, was the *ne plus ultra* of savoury morsels: therefore Win-the-fight Little wit, with a strawberry breath, cherry lips, and apricot cheeks, the better half (not in folly!) of one of "the pretty wits of Paul's," shams Abram, and pretends to long for it, in order to overcome the scruples and qualms of Dame Purecraft and the Banbury man, who, but for such longing, would have never consented to her visiting the fair.

* "Now London's Mayor, on saddle new,
Rides to the Fair of Bartlemew;
He twirls his chain, and looketh big,
As if to fright the head of pig,
That gaping lies on every stall." —Davenant. Shakspere, in

the First Part of King Henry the Fourth, speaks of an ox
being roasted at Bartholomew Fair.
** "I ne'er saw a parson without a good nose —

But the devil's as welcome wherever he goes." —Swift.

The Rabbi being called upon by the dame to legalise roast pig, proposes that it shall be eaten with a reformed mouth, and not after the profane fashion of feeding; and, that the weak may be comforted, himself will accompany them to the fair, and eat exceedingly, and prophesy!

Among the minor delicacies of Ursula's * cuisine-Ursula, "uglye of clieare," the pig-woman and priestess of St. Bartlemy, "all fire and fat!" —are tobacco, colt's-foot, bottled-ale, and tripes;

and a curious picture of Smithfield manners is given in her instructions to Mooncalf to froth the cans well, jog the bottles o' the buttock, shink out the first glass ever, and drink with all companies.

* "Her face all bowsy,
Comclye crinkled,
Wonderously wrinkled
Like a roste pigges eare,
Brystled Avith here.
Her nose some dele hoked,
And camouslye eroked,
Her skin lose and slacke,
Grained like a saeke
With a croked backe." —Skelton.

We have an irruption of other popular characters into the fair, all in high keeping with the time and place: —a costard-monger; a gilt gingerbread woman; a mountebank; a corn-cutter; a wrestler; a cut-purse (a babe of booty, or child of the horn-thumb!); a gamester; a ballad-singer; an "ostler, trade-fallen a roarer (a swash-buckler, in later times a mohock); puppet-show keepers and watchmen; Bartholomew Cokes, a natural born fool and squire; Waspe, his shrewder serving-man; Overdo, a bacchanalian justice; a gang of gypsies, and their hedge-priest, patriarch of the cut-purses, or Patrico to the A bram men and their prickers and prancers; and lastly, Mr. Lanthorn Leatherhead, a supposed caricature of Inigo Jones, with whom Ben Jonson was associated in some of his magnificent court masques. All these characters exhibit their humours, and present a living picture of what Bartholomew Fair was in 1614. We have the exact dress of the flaunting City Madam —a huge velvet custard, or three-cornered bonnet; for these pretenders to sanctity not only adorned their outward woman with the garments of vanity, but were the principal dealers in feathers (another fashionable part of female dress in the days of Elizabeth and James I.) in the Blackfriars. All the merchandise of Babylon (i.e. the fair!) is spread out to our view; Jews-trumps, rattles, mousetraps, penny ballads, * purses, pin-cases, Tobie's dogs, "comfortable bread," (spiced gingerbread,) hobbyhorses, drums, lions, bears, Bartholomew whistling birds, (wooden toys,) dolls, ** and Orpheus and his fiddle in gin-work! We have its cant phrases, mendacious tricks, and practical jokes; and are invited into "a sweet delicate booth," with boughs, to eat roast pig with the fire o' juniper and rosemary branches; and "it were great obstinacy, high and horrible obstinacy, to decline or resist the good titillation of the famelic sense," and not enter the gates of the unclean for once, with the liquorish Rabbi.

* Gifford says, "In Jonson's time, scarcely any ballad was
printed without a woodcut illustrative of its subject. If it
was a ballad of 'pure love,' or of 'good life/ which
afforded no scope for the graphic talents of the Grub Street
Apelles, the portrait of 'good Queen Elizabeth,'
magnificently adorned, with the globe and sceptre, formed no
unwelcome substitute for her loving subjects."
** The following was the costume of a Bartlemy Fair doll, or

baby: —
"Her petticoat of sattin,

Her gown of crimson tabby,
Laced up before, and spangled o'er,
Just like a Barthol'mew Baby"
The Comedian's Tales; or, Jests, Songs, and Pleasant

Adventures of several Famous Players. 1729.

The sound beating of Justice Overdo, Waspe's elevation of Cokes on pick-back, and the final confutation of Zeal-of-the-land Busy, complete the humours of, and give the last finish-ing-touches to this authentic and curious picture of ancient Bartholomew Fair.

Bravo, Ben Jonson! Not the surly, envious, malignant Ben, but the rare, *chère* Bartlemy Fair Ben! the prince of poets! the king of good fellows! the learned oracle of the Mermaid and the Devil; * the chosen companion of the gallant Raleigh; the poetical father of many worthy adopted sons; and, to sum up emphatically thy various excellencies, the friend, "fellow" and elegiast of Shakspere!

 * In the Apollo Room in the Devil Tavern (on the site of which stands the Banking-house of Messrs. Child,) Ben Jonson occupied the President's chair, surrounded by the "Erudit i, urbani, hilares, honesti" of that glorious age. Take his picture as drawn by Shakerley Marmion, a contemporary dramatist of some note, and (as Anthony Wood styles him) a "goodly proper gentleman."
"The boon Delphic god

Drinks sack, and keeps his Bacchanalia,
And has his incense, and his altars smoking,
And speaks in sparkling prophesies"
His Leges Conviviales were engraved in black marble over the

chimney; and over the door were inscribed the following
verses by the same master-hand.
"Welcome all who lead or follow

To the oracle of Apollo:
Here he speaks out of his pottle,
Or the tripos, his tower bottle;
All his answers are divine,
Truth itself doth flow in wine.
Hang up all the poor hop-drinkers,
Cries old Sim, the king of shinkers;
He the half of life abuses,
That sits watering with the Muses.
Those dull girls no good ean mean us;
Wine-it is the milk of Venus,
And the poet's horse accounted:
Ply it, and you all are mounted.
'Tis the true Phobian liquor,
Cheers the brains, makes wit the quieker;
Pays all debts, cures all diseases,
And at once three senses pleases.
Welcome all who lead or follow
To the oracle of Apollo!"
Such an association of intellectual minds, where worldly

distinctions are unknown, where rank lays down its state,
and genius forgets the inequalities of fortune, is the
highest degree of felicity that human nature can arrive at.

Yes, thou didst behold him face to face! Great and glorious privilege! Thou his detractor! What a beauteous garland hast thou thrown upon his tomb! O for the solemn spirit of thy majestic monody, ("Sidney's sister, Pembroke's mother") the imagination of thy green "Underwoods," to sing of thee, as thou hast sung of him!

The death of James I. (for Jamie was much addicted to sports, and loved the Puritans, as the Puritans and Lucifer love holy water!) was "a heavy blow, and a great discouragement" to the nation's jollity: and the troubles and treasons of the succeeding unhappy reign indisposed men's hearts to merriment, and turned fair England into a howling wilderness. Bartholomew Fair in 1641 * exhibits a sorry shadow of its joyous predecessor—'Tis Fat Jack, mountain of mirth! dwindled into the lean and slipper'd pantaloon! Zeal-of-the-land Busy had become rampant; and Dame Ursula, if the old lady yet lived, was most probably a reformed sister, and purveyor of roast pig to the Rabbi at home!

* "Bartholomew Faire;
Or,

Variety of fancies, where you may find A faire of wares, and

all to please your mind.
With the severall enormityes and misdemeanours which are

there seene and acted. London: Printed for Richard Harper, at the Bible and Harpe, in Smithfield. 1641."

As a picture, it wants the vivid colouring of the former great painter. It seems to have been limned by a wet, or parcel puritan, a dead wall between pantile and puppet-show! Our first move is into Christ Church cloisters, "which are hung so full of pictures, that you would take that place, or rather mistake it, for St. Peter's in Rome. And now, being arrived through the long walke, to Saint Bartholomew's hospitall," he draws a ludicrous picture of a "handsome wench" bartering her good name for "a moiety of bone-lace; a slight silver bodkin; a hoop-ring, or the like toye." Proceeding into the heart of the fair, it becomes necessary that while one eye is watching the motion of the puppets, the other should look sharp to the pockets. "Here's a knave in a foole's coat, with a trumpet sounding, or on a drumme beating, invites you, and would faine persuade you to see his puppets; there is a rogue like a wild woodman, or in an antick-ship, like an incubus, desires your company to view his motion. On the other side, Hocus Pocus, with three yards of tape, or ribbon in's hand, shews his legerdemaine * to the admiration and astonishment of a company of cock-oloaches.

* "Legerdemain is an art whereby one may seem to work wonderful, impossible, and incredible things, by agility, nimbleness, and slight of hand.
"An adept must be one of an audacious spirit, w'ith a nimble

conveyance, and a vocabulary of cabalistic phrases to astonish the beholder-as Hey! Fortuna! Furia! Nunquam credo I Saturnus, Jupiter, Mars, Venus, &c. &c.
"He must throw himself into such odd gestures as may divert

the eyes of the spectators from a too strict observation of his manner of conveyance."
Then follow certain rules for concealing balls and money in

the hand, and other secrets worth knowing to students in the

art and mystery of conjuration. From "The Merry Companion;
or, Delights for the Ingenious. By Richard Neve" (whose
jocular physiognomy, with the exhibition of one of his hocus
pocus tricks, graces the title). 1721.

Amongst these you shall see a grey goose-cap (as wise as the rest) with a 'what do ye lacke?' in his mouth, stand in his boothe, shaking a rattle, or scraping on a fiddle, with which children are so taken that they presently cry out for these fopperies. And all these together make such a distracted noise that you would think Babel was not comparable to it. Here there are also your gamesters in action; some turning off a whimsey, others throwing for pewter, who can quickly dissolve a round shilling into a three-halfpenny saucer. Long Lane at this time looks very faire,-and puts on her best cloaths with the wrong side outward, so turn'd for their better turning off; and Cloth Faire is now in great request; well fare the ale-houses therein; yet better may a man fare (but at a dearer rate) in the Pig-market, alias Pasty-nooke, or Pye-corner, where pigges are al houres of the day on the stalls, piping hot, and would cry (if they could speak) 'come eat me.'" The chronicler calls over the coals a "fat greasie hostesse" for demanding an additional shilling for a pig's head when a lady's longing is in the case; inveighs against the unconscionable exactions, and excessive inflammations of reckonings, and concludes with a re-iterated and rhyming caution: —

> "Now farewell to the Faire; you who are wise,
>
> Preserve your purses, whilst you please your eyes." *

The restoration of King Charles II. threw England into a transport of joy. Falstaff had not more his bellyfull of Ford, than had the nation of Jack Presbyter. **

* The historian has forgot to describe the wonderful
performances of Francis Battalia, the Stone-Eater.
** "Presbyter is but Jack Priest writ large." —Milton.

In "The Lord Henry Cromwell's speech to the House, 1658," he

is made to say: 44 Methinks I hear 'em (the Players) already
crying, thirty years hence at Bartholomew Fair, 'Step in,
and see the Life and Death of brave Cromwell. Methinks I see
him with a velvet eragg about his shoulders, and a little
pasteboard hat on his head, riding a tittup, a tittup to his
Parliament House, and a man with a bay leaf in his mouth,
crying in his behalf, 'By the living G—I will dissolve
you!' which makes the porters cry, 4 O, brave Englishman!'
Then the devil carries him away in a tempest, which makes
the nurses squeak, and the children cry,"

Merry bells, roasted rumps, the roar of cannon, the crackling of bonfires, and the long-continued shouts of popular ecstacy proclaimed his downfall; the Maypole was crowned with the garlands of spring; in the temples devoted to Thalia and Melpomene * were again heard the divine inspirations of the dramatic muse; the light fantastic toe tripped it nimbly to the sound of the pipe and tabor, and St. Bartholomew, his—

* The Hamlet, Macbeth, Othello, and Sir John Falstaff of
Betterton. The character of this great master of the

histrionic art is thus drawn by an eminent contemporary
author: —

"Roscius, a sincere friend and a man of strict honor: grown

old in the arms and approbation of his audience: not to be
corrupted even by the way of living and manners of those
whom he hourly conversed with.

"Roscius born for everything that he thinks fit to

undertake, has wit and morality, fire and judgment, sound
sense and good nature. Roscius, who would have still been
eminent in any station of life he had been called to, only
unhappy to the world, in that it is not possible for him to
bid time stand still, and permit him to endure for ever, the
ornament of the stage, the delight of his friends, and the
regret of all, who shall one day have the misfortune to lose
him."

—rope-dancers, and trumpeters, * were all alive and merry at the fair.

The austere reign of the cold and selfish William of Nassau diminished nothing of its jollity.
Thomas Cotterell "from the King's Arm's Tavern, Little Lincoln's Fields," kept the King's Arms
Music Booth in Smithfield; and one Martin transferred his sign of "The Star" from Moor-fields,
to the Rounds. At this time flourished a triumvirate of Bartlemy heroes too remarkable to be
passed lightly over, Mat Coppinger, Joe Haynes, and Thomas Dogget.

The pranks, cheats, and conceits of Coppinger are recorded in an unique tract ** of considerable freedom and fun.

* In the Loyal Protestant, Sept. 8, 1682, is an
advertisement forbidding all keepers of shows, &c. to make
use of drums, trumpets, &c. without license from the
Serjeant and Comptroller of His Majesty's trumpets. And
there is a notice in the London Gazette, Dee. 7, 1685,
commanding all "Rope Dancers, Prize Players, Strollers, and
other persons shewing motions and other sights," to have
licenses from Charles Killigrew, Esq. Master of the Revels.

** "An Account of the Life, Conversation, Birth, Education,

Pranks, Projects, Exploits, and Merry Conceits of the

Famously Notorious Mat. Coppinger, once a Player in
Bartholomew Fair, and since turned bully of the town; who,
receiving sentence of death at the Old Bailey on the 23rd of
February, was executed at Tyburn on the 27th, 1695. London,
Printed for T. Hobs, 1695."

His famous part was the cook-maid in "*Whittington*," Bartholomew Fair droll. The last September of his life he acted a Judge there, little dreaming that in the ensuing February he should
be brought before one, (for stealing a watch and seven pounds in money,) and sent on a pilgrimage to Tyburn-tree! He was a poet, and wrote a volume * of adulatory verses, calculated
for the meridian of the times in which he lived. The following is the comical trick he put upon
a countryman in Bartholomew Fair.

The company (i.e. strolling players) finding the country too warm for them, came with our spark to town, in expectation of recruiting their finances by the folly of such as should resort to Bartholomew Fair.

* Poems, Songs, and Love-Verses upon several subjects. By
Matthew Coppinger, Gent. 1682. Dedicated to the Duchess of
Portsmouth; of whom, amongst an hundred extravagant things,
he says,
"You are the darling of my King, his pleasure,

His Indies of incomparable treasure!"

Upon the credit of which they took a lodging in Smithfield, and made shift to get up a small booth to shew juggling tricks in, the art of hocus pocus, and pouder-le-pimp. The score being deep on all hands, the people clamouring for money, and customers coming but slowly in, they consulted how to rub off, and give their creditors the bag to hold. To this Coppinger dissented, saying he would find out the way to mend this dulness of trading; and he soon effected it by a lucky chance. A country fellow, on his return from Newgate-market on horseback, resolving to have a gape at Jack Pudding, sat gazing, with his mouth at half-cock; and, so intent was he, that his senses seemed to be gone wool-gathering. Coppinger, whispering some of his companions, they stept to "Tom Noddies" horse, one of them ungirthing him, and taking off the bridle, the reins of which the fellow held in his hand, they bore him on the pack-saddle on each side, and led the horse sheer from under him; whilst another with counterfeit horns, and a vizard, put his head out of the head-stall, and kept nodding forwards, so that "Ninny" verily supposed, by the tugging of the reins, that he was still on "cock-horse!" The signal being given, they let him squash to the ground, pack-saddle and all; when, terrified at the sight of the supposed devil he had got in a string, and concluding Hocus Pocus had conjured his horse into that antic figure, he scrambled up, and betaking him to his heels back into the country, frightened his neighbours with dismal stories that Dr. Faustus and Friar Bacon were alive again, and transforming horses into devils in Bartholomew Fair! The tale, gathering as it spread, caused the booth to be thronged; which piece of good-luck was solely attributable to Coppinger's ingenuity.

Original

Plain Joe Haynes, * the learned Doctor Haynes, or the dignified Count Haynes-for by these several titles he was honourably distinguished-was the hero of a variety of vagabondical adventures both at home and abroad.

* Wood's Athenæ Oxon. ii. p. 976. "Joseph Haynes, or Heynes,
matriculated as a servitor of Queen's College, 3d May, 1689.
Mr. Ja. Tirrel saith he is a great actor and maker of plays;
but I find him not either in Langbaine or Term Cat/' Old
Anthony, like "good old Homer," sometimes nods. Haynes had
been upon the stage many years before, and was too
profligate to be admitted of the university at that period.
In the memoir of Joe Haynes, in the Lives of the Gamesters,

he is said to have died in the beginning of the year 1700,
aged 53. This is a mistake.
He was married, as appears from the following lines in the

Prologue to "The Injured Lovers."
"Joe Haynes's fate is now become my share,

For I'm a poet, marrÿd, and a player."

Downes says he was one of those "who came not into the

company until after they had begun in Drury Lane." Drury
Lane first opened on 8th April, 1663.
He wrote and spoke a variety of prologues and epilogues,

particularly the epilogue to the "Unhappy Kindness, or
Fruitless Revenge," in the habit of a horse-offieer, mounted
on an ass, in 1697. In after times his example was imitated
by Shuter, Liston, and Wilkinson (not Tate).
His principal characters were, Syringe, in the Relapse;

Roger, in Æsop; Sparkish, in the Country Wife; Lord
Plausible, in the Plain Dealer; Pamphlet and Rigadoon, in
Love and a Bottle; Tom Errand, in the Constant Couple; Mad
Parson, in the Pilgrim; Benito, in the Assignation; Noll
Bluff, in the Old Bachelor; Rumour, in A Plot and No Plot,
(to which, in 1697, he spoke the prologue); and Jamy, in
Sawney the Scot.

He is the first comedian who rode an ass upon the stage. He acted the mountebank, Waltho Van Clutterbank, High German, chemical, wonder-working doctor and dentifricator, and spoke his famous "Horse-doctor's harangue" to the mob. He challenged a celebrated quack called "The Unborn Doctor," at the town of Hertford, on a market-day, to have a trial of skill with him. Being both mounted on the public stage, and surrounded by a numerous auditory eager to hear this learned dispute, Joe desired that each might stand upon a joint stool. "Gentlemen," said Joe, "I thank you for your good company, and hope soon to prove how grossly you have been deceived by this arch-impostor. I come hither neither to get a name, nor an estate: the first, by many miraculous cures performed in Italy, Spain, Holland, France, and England, *per* *totum terrarium, orbem*, has long been established. As to the latter, those Emperors, Kings, and foreign potentates, whom I have snatched from the gaping jaws of death, whose image I have the honour to wear (showing several medals), have sufficiently rewarded me. Besides, I am the seventh son of a seventh son; so were my father and grandfather. To convince you, therefore, that what I affirm is truth, I prognosticate some heavy judgment will fall on the head of that impudent quack. May the charlatan tumble ingloriously, while the true doctor remains unhurt!" At which words, Haynes's Merry-Andrew, who was underneath the stage, with a cord fast to B — — —'s stool, just as B-was going to stutter out a reply, pulled the stool from under him, and down he came; which, passing for a miracle, Joe was borne home to his lodging in triumph, and B — — —hooted out of the town. *

Some of Doctor Haynes's miraculous mock cures, were the Duchess of Boromolpho of a cramp in her tongue; the Count de Rodomontado of a bilious passion, after a surfeit of buttered parsnips; and Duke Philorix of a dropsy-of which he died! He invites his patients to the "Sign of the Prancers," in vico vulgo dicto, Rattlecliffero, something south-east of Templum Danicum in the Square of Profound-Close, not far from "Titter-Tatter Fair!" He was a good-looking fellow, of singular accomplishments, and in great request among the ladies. "With the agreeableness of my mien, ** the gaiety of my conversation, and the gallantry of my dancing, I charmed the fair sex wherever I came.

* "The Life of the late Famous Comedian, Jo. Hayns.
Containing his comical exploits and adventures, both at home
and abroad. London. Printed for J. Nutt, near Stationer's-
Hall, 1701."
** "The Reasons of Mr. Joseph Hains, the Player's,

Conversion and Reconversion. Being the Third and Last Part to
the Dialogue of Mr. Bays. London: Printed for Richard
Baldwin, near the Black Bull in the Old Baily, 1690." This
tract is intended as a skit upon Dryden, whose easy
"conversion and reconversion" are satirised in a very
laughable manner. In 1689, Haynes spoke his "Recantation
Prologue upon his first appearance on the stage after his
return from Rome," in the character of a theatrical
penitent!
John Davies ridicules the coxcombs of his day, that it

engrossed the whole of their meal-times in talk of plays,
and censuring of players.
"As good play as work for nought, some say,

But players get much good by nought but play."

'Signor Giusippe,'" (he was now Count Haynes!) "says one, 'when will you help me to string my lute? Signor Giusippe,' says another, 'shall we see you at night in the grotto behind the Duke's palace?' 'Signor Giusippe,' says a third, 'when will you teach me the last new song you made for the Prince of Tuscany?' and so, i' faith they Giusipped me, till I had sworn at least to a dozen assignations."

His waggery was amusing to all who were not the butts of it. He once kept a merchant that had a laced-band which reached from shoulder to shoulder, two good hours in a coffee-house near the Exchange, while he explained the meaning of chevaux de frize; telling him there were horses in Frize-land that were bullet-proof! At another time he parleyed with a grocer a full quarter of an hour in the street, inquiring which was the near est way from Fleet Street to the Sun Tavern in Piccadilly; whether down the Strand, and so by Charing Cross; or through Lincoln's Inn Fields and Covent-Garden? though the simpleton declared his spouse sent him post-haste for a doctor, and-for all that Joe knew-made him lose an heir-apparent to "some dozen pounds of raisins, as many silver apostle spoons, Stow's London, and Speed's Chronicle."

His astonished father-confessor, while listening to his sham catalogue of frightful enormities, looked as death-like as a frolicsome party of indigo porters in a dark cellar, by the melancholy light of burnt brandy! "For," said the penitent wag, "last Wednesday I stole a consecrated bell from one of St. Anthony's holy pigs, and coined it into copper farthings! Such a day I pinned a fox's tail on a monk's cowl; and passing by an old gentlewoman sitting in her elbow-chair by the door, reading 'The Spiritual Carduus-posset for a Sinner's Belly-Ache," (this, saving our noble comedian's presence, is more after the fashion of Rabbi Busy, than Friar Peter!) "I abstracted her spectacles from off her venerable purple nose, and converted them to the profane use of lighting my tobacco by the sunshine."

"Hark!" said Mr. Bosky, as a voice of cock-crowing cacchination sounded under his window, "there is my St. Bartlemy-tide chorister. For twenty years has Nestor Nightingale proclaimed the joyous anniversary with a new song." And having thrown up the sash, he threw down his accustomed gratuity, and was rewarded with

THE INQUISITIVE FARMER, OR HARLEQUIN HANGMAN.=

Harlequin, taking a journey to Bath,

Put up at an inn with his dagger of lath.

He supp'd like a lord-on a pillow of down

He slept like a king, and he snored like a clown.

Boniface said, as he popp'd in his head,

"In that little crib by the side of your bed,

As honest a farmer as e'er stood in shoes,

(My chambers are full) would be glad of a snooze."

The farmer began, as in clover he lay,

To talk of his clover, his corn-rigs, and hay,

His bullocks, his heifers, his pigs, and his wife;

Not a wink could our Harlequin get for his life.

He reckon'd his herds, and his flocks, and his fleece,

And drove twice to market his ducks and his geese;

He babbled of training, and draining, and scythes,

And hoeing, and sowing, and taxes, and tithes.

"To the fair do you carry a pack, or a hunch?

Are you mountebank doctor, or pedlar, or Punch?

What is your calling? and what is your name?

Are you single, or married-or coward, or game?"

Poor Harlequin, fretting, lay silent and still,

While the farmer's glib tongue went as fast as a mill.

"Where are you going? and whence do you come?

How long do you tarry? —the deuce! are you dumb?"

"I'm the hangman" said Harlequin, sir, of the town;

I cut in the morning a highwayman down;

And fix in the market-place up, for a flag,

To-morrow his head, which I bear in my bag!"

The talkative farmer jump'd up in a fright —

("If you look for the bag, friend, it lies on your right!")

Ran out of the chamber, and roar'd for the host,

Shrieking, and shaking, and pale as a ghost!

Boniface listen'd, bolt upright in bed,

To the cock-and-bull story of hangman and head;

And then caught the mountebank, snug on his back,

Holding his sides, which were ready to crack!

Loud laugh'd the landlord at Harlequin's trick.

"As soon," cry'd the farmer, "I'd sup with Old Nick,

As sleep in this room with that gibbetting wag,

With a head on his shoulders, and one in his bag!"

"Bravo, Nestor!" said the Lauréat of Little Britain; "Norah Noclack (as the taciturn old lady has grown musical) will draw thee a cup of ale for thy ditty, and make thee free of the buttery."

END OF THE FIRST VOLUME.

VOLUME 2

Table of Contents

CHAPTER I.

My friends," —continued Mr. Bosky, after an approving smack of the lips, and "*Thanks*, my kind mistress! many happy returns of St. Bartlemy!" had testified the ballad-singer's hearty relish and gratitude for the refreshing draught over which he had just suspended his well-seasoned nose, * —"never may the mouths be stopped —

> * "Thom: Brewer, my Mus: Servant, through his proneness to
> good fellowshippe, having attained to a very rich and
> rubicund nose, being reproved by a friend for his too
> frequent use of strong drinkes and sacke, as very pernicious
> to that distemper and inflammation in his nose. 'Nay,
> faith,' says he, 'if it will not endure sacke, it is *no*
> *nose* for me.'" —L' Estrange, No. 578. Mr. Jenkins.

—(except with a cup of good liquor) of these musical itinerants, from whose doggrel a curious history of men and manners might be gleaned, to humour the anti-social disciples of those pious publicans who substituted their nasal twang for the solemn harmony of cathedral music; who altered St. Peter's phrase, 'the Bishop of your souls,' into 'the Elder (‼) of your souls;' for 'thy kingdom come,' brayed 'thy Commonwealth come!' and smuggled the water into their rum-puncheons, which they called *wrestling with the spirit*, and making the *enemy weaker!* 'Show me the popular ballads of the time, and I will show you the temper and taste of the people.' *

> * "Robin Consciencean ancient ballad, (suggested by
> Lydgate's "London Lackpenny,") first printed at Edinburgh in
> 1683, gives a curious picture of London tradesmen, &c. Robin
> goes to Court, but receives cold welcome; thence to
> Westminster Hall. "It were no great matter," quoth the
> lawyers, "if Conscience quite were knock'd on the head." He
> visits Smithfield, and discovers how the "horse-cowrsers'
> artfully coerce their "lame jades" to "run and kick." Then
> Long Lane, where the brokers hold conscience to be "but
> nonsense." The butter-women of Newgate-market claw him, and
> the bakers brawl at him. At Pye Corner, a cook, glancing at
> him "as the Devil did look o'er Lincoln," threatens to spit
> him.
> The salesmen of Snow Hill would have stoned him; the

> "fishwives" of Turn-again Lane rail at him; the London
> Prentices of Fleet Street, with their "What lack you,
> countryman?" seamper away from him. The "haberdashers, that
> sell hats I the mercers and silk-men, that live in
> Paternoster Row," all set upon him. He receives no better
> treatment in Cheapside —A cheesemonger in Bread Street; "the
> lads that wish Lent were all the year," in Fish Street; a
> merchant on the Exchange; the "gallant girls," whose "brave
> shops of ware" were "up stairs and the drapers and
> poulterers of Graccchurch Street, to whom conscience was
> "Dutch or Spanish," flout and jeer him. A trip to Southwark,
> the King's Bench, and to the Blackman Street demireps,
> proves that "conscience is nothing." In St. George's Fields,
> "rooking rascals," playing at "nine pins," tell him to prate
> on till he is hoarse." Espying a windmill hard by, he hies
> to the miller, whose excuse for not dealing with him was,

that he must steal out of every bushel "a peek, if not three
gallons." Conscience then trudges on "to try what would
befall i' the country," whither we will not follow him.

I delight in a Fiddler's Fling, and revel in the exhilarating perfume of those odoriferous garlands * gathered on sunshiny holidays and star-twinkling nights, bewailing how disappointed
lovers go to sea, and how romantic young lasses follow them in blue jackets and trousers!
　* "When I travelled," said the Spectator, "I took a
particular delight in hearing the songs and fables that are
come from father to son, and are most in vogue among the
common people of the countries through which I passed; for
it is impossible that anything should be universally tasted
and approved by a multitude (though they are only the rabble
of a nation), which hath not in it some peculiar aptness to
please and gratify the mind of man."
Old tales, old songs, and an old jest,

Our stomachs easiliest digest.
"Listen to me, my lovly shepherd's joye,
And thou shalt heare, with mirth and muckle glee,
Some pretie tales, which, when I was a boye,
My toothless grandame oft hath told to mee.

Nay, rather than the tuneful race should be extinct, expect to see me some night, with my paper
lantern and cracked spectacles, singing you woeful tragedies to love-lorn maids and cobblers'
apprentices." *
　* Love in a Tub, a comedy, by Sir George Etherege.

And, carried away by his enthusiasm to the days of jolly Queen Bess, the Lauréat of Little
Britain, with a countenance bubbling with hilarity, warbled *con spirito*, as a probationary ballad
for the *Itinerant ship*, (!)

THE KNIGHTING OF THE SIRLOIN.

Elizabeth Tudor her breakfast would make

On a pot of strong beer and a pound of beefsteak,

Ere six in the morning was toll'd by the chimes —

O the days of Queen Bess they were merry old times!

From hawking and hunting she rode back to town,

In time just to knock an ambassador down;

Toy'd, trifled, coquetted, then lopp'd off a head;

And at threescore and ten danced a hornpipe to bed.

With Nicholas Bacon,1 her councillor chief,

One day she was dining on English roast beef;

That very same day when her Majesty's Grace *

Had given Lord Essex a slap on the face.

* When Queen Elizabeth came to visit Sir Nicholas Bacon,
Lord Keeper, at his new house at Redgrave, she observed,
alluding to his corpulency, that he had built his house too
little for him. "Not so, madam," answered he; "but your
Highness has made me too big for my house!"
The term "your Grace' was addressed to the English Sovereign

during the earlier Tudor reigns. In her latter years
Elizabeth assumed the appellation of "Majesty" The following
anecdote comprehends both titles. "As Queen Elizabeth passed
the streets in state, one in the crowde cried first, 'God
blesse your Royall Majestie!' and then, 'God blesse your
Noble Grace!' 'Why, how now,' sayes the Queene, 'am I tenne
groates worse than I was e'en now?'" The value of the old
"Ryal," or "Royall," was 10s., that of the "Noble" 6s. Sd.
The Emperor Charles the Fifth was the first crowned head
that assumed the title of "Majesty."

My Lord Keeper stared, as the wine-cup she kiss'd,

At his sovereign lady's superlative twist,

And thought, thinking truly his larder would squeak,

He'd much rather keep her a day than a week.

"What call you this dainty, my very good lord?" —

"The Loin," —bowing low till his nose touch'd the

   board —

"And-breath of our nostrils, and light of our eyes! *

Saving your presence., the ox was a prize."

  * Queen Elizabeth issued an edict commanding every artist
who should paint the royal portrait to place her "in a
garden with a full light upon her, and the painter to put
any shadow in her face at his peril!" Oliver Cromwell's
injunctions to Sir Peter Lely were somewhat different. The
knight was desired to transfer to his canvass all the
blotches and carbuncles that blossomed in the Protector's
rocky physiognomy. Sir Joshua Reynolds, (— — — — with
fingers so lissom, Girls start from his canvass, and ask us
to kiss 'em!) having taken the liberty of mitigating the
utter stupidity of one of his "Pot-boilers," i.e. stupid
faces, and receiving from the sitter's family the reverse of
approbation, exclaimed, "I have thrown a glimpse of meaning
into this fool's phiz, and now none of his friends know
him!" At another time, having painted too true a likeness,
it was threatened to be thrown upon his hands, when a polite
note from the artist, stating that, with the additional
appendage of a tail, it would do admirably for a monkey, for
which he had a commission, and requesting to know if the
portrait was to be sent home or not, produced the desired
effect. The picture was paid for, and put into the fire!

   "Unsheath me, mine host, thy Toledo so bright.

   Delicious Sir Loin! I do dub thee a knight.

   Be thine at our banquets of honour the post;

   While the Queen rules the realm, let *Sir Loin* rule the

      roast!

   And'tis, my Lord Keeper, our royal belief,

   The Spaniard had beat, had it not been for *beef*!

Let him come if he dare! he shall sink! he shall quake!

With a duck-ing, Sir Francis shall give him a Drake.

Thus, Don Whiskerandos, I throw thee my glove!

And now, merry minstrel, strike up 'highly Love,'

Come, pursey Sir Nicholas, caper thy best —

Dick Tarlton shall finish our sports with a jest."

The virginals sounded, Sir Nicholas puff'd,

And led forth her Highness, high-heel'd and be-ruff'd —

Automaton dancers to musical chimes!

O the days of Queen Bess, they were merry old times!

"And now, leaving Nestor Nightingale to propitiate Uncle Timothy for this interpolation to his Merrie Mysteries, let us return and pay our respects, not to the dignified Count Haynes, the learned Doctor Haynes, but to plain Joe Haynes, the practical-joking Droll-Player of Bartholomew Fair: *
  * Antony, vulgo Tony Aston, a famous player, and one of
Joe's contemporaries. The only portrait (a sorry one) of
Tony extant, is a small oval in the frontispiece to the
Fool's Opera, to which his comical harum-scarum
autobiography is prefixed.

In the first year of King James the Second, * our hero set up a booth in Smithfield Rounds, where he acted a new droll, called the Whore of Babylon, or the *Devil and the Pope*. Joe being sent for by Judge Pollixfen, and soundly rated for presuming to put the pontiff into such bad company, replied, that he did it out of respect to his Holiness; for whereas many ignorant people believed the Pope to be a blatant beast, with seven heads, ten horns, and a long tail, like the Dragon of Wantley's, according to the description of the Scotch Parsons! he proved him to be a comely old gentleman, in snow-white canonicals, and a cork-screw wig. The next morning two bailiffs arrested him for twenty pounds, just as the *Bishop of Ely* was riding by in his coach. Quoth Joe to the bailiffs, "Gentlemen, here is my cousin, the Bishop of Ely; let me but speak a word to him, and he will pay the debt and charges."
  * Catholicism, though it enjoined penance and mortification,
was no enemy, at appointed seasons, to mirth. Hers were
merry saints, for they always brought with them a holiday. A
right jovial prelate was the Pope who first invented the
Carnival! On that joyful festival racks and thumbscrews,
fire and faggots, were put by; whips and hair-shirts
exchanged for lutes and dominos; and music inspired equally
their diversions and devotions.

The Bishop ordered his carriage to stop, whilst Joe (close to his ear) whispered, "My Lord, here are a couple of poor waverers who have such terrible *scruples of conscience*, that I fear they'll hang themselves." —"Very well," said the Bishop. So calling to the bailiffs, he said, "You two men, come to me to-morrow, and I'll satisfy you." The bailiffs bowed, and went their way; Joe (tickled in the midriff, and hugging himself with his device) went his way too. In the morning the bailiffs repaired to the Bishop's house. "Well, my good men," said his reverence, "what are your scruples of conscience?" —"Scruples!" replied the bailiffs, "we have no scruples, We are bailiffs, my Lord, who yesterday arrested *your cousin Joe Haynes* for twenty pounds. Your Lordship promised to *satisfy* us to-day, and we hope you will be as good as your word." The Bishop, to prevent any further scandal to his name, immediately paid the debt and charges.

The following theatrical adventure occurred during his pilgrimage to the well-known shrine,

"Which at Loretto dwelt in wax, stone, wood.

And in a fair white wig look'd wondrous fine."

It was St. John's day, and the people of the parish had built a stage in the body of the church, for the representation of a tragedy called the *Decollation of the Baptist*. * Joe had the good luck to enter just as the actors were leaving off their "damnable faces," and going to begin.

* The Chester Mysteries, written by Randle or Ralph Hig-den, a Benedictine of St. Werburg's Abbey in that city, were first performed during the mayoralty of John Arneway, who filled that office from 1268 to 1276, at the cost and charges of the different trading companies therein. They were acted in English ("made into partes and pagiantes") instead of in Latin, and played on Monday, Tuesday, and Wednesday in Whitsun week. The companies began at the abbey gates, and when the first pageant was concluded, the moveable stage ("a high scaffolde with two rowmes; a higher and a lower, upon four wheeles") was wheeled to the High Cross before the Mayor, and then onward to every street, so that each street had its pageant. "The Harrowing of Hell" is one of the most ancient Miracle Plays in our language. It is as old as the reign of Edward the Third, if not older. The Prologue and Epilogue were delivered in his own person by the actor who had the part of the Saviour. In 1378, the Scholars of St. Paul's presented a petition to Richard the Second, praying him to prohibit some "inexpert people" from representing the History of the Old Testament, to the serious prejudice of their clergy, who had been at great expense in order to represent it at Christmas. On the 18th July, 1390, the Parish Clerks of London played Religious Interludes at the Skinners' Well, in Clerkenwell, which lasted three days. In 1409, they performed The Creation of the World, which continued eight days. On one side of the lowest platform of these primitive stages was a dark pitchy cavern, whence issued fire and flames, and the howlings of souls tormented by demons. The latter occasionally showed their grinning faces through the mouth of the cavern, to the terrible delight of the spectators! The Passion of Our Saviour was the first dramatic spectacle acted in Sweden, in the reign of King John the Second. The actor's name was Lengis who was to pierce the side of the person on the

cross. Heated by the enthusiasm of the scene, he plunged his lance into that person's body, and killed him. The King, shocked at the brutality of Lengis, slew him with his scimetar; when the audience, enraged at the death of their favourite actor, wound up this true tragedy by cutting off his Majesty's head!

They had pitched upon an ill-looking surly butcher for *King Herod*, upon whose chuckle-head a gilt pasteboard crown glittered gloriously by the candlelight; and, as soon as he had seated himself in a rickety old wicker chair, radiant with faded finery, that served him for a throne, the orchestra (three fifes and a fiddle) struck up a merry tune, and a young damsel began so to shake, her heels, that with the help of a little imagination, our noble comedian might have fancied himself in his old quarters at St. Bartholomew, or Sturbridge Fair. *

* Stourbridge, or Sturbridge Fair, originated in a grant from King John to the hospital of lepers at that place. By a charter in the thirtieth year of Henry the Eighth, the fair was granted to the magistrates and corporation of Cambridge. In 1613 it became so popular, that hackney coaches attended it from London; and in after times not less than sixty coaches plied there. In 1766 and 1767, the "Lord of the Tap," dressed in a red livery, with a string over his shoulders, from whence depended spigots and fossetts, entered all the booths where ale was sold, to determine whether it was fit beverage for the visitors. In 1788, Flockton exhibited at Sturbridge Fair. The following lines were printed on his bills: —
"To raise the soul by means of wood and wire,

To screw the fancy up a few pegs higher;
In miniature to show the world at large,
As folks conceive a ship who 've seen a barge.
This is the scope of all our actors' play,
Who hope their wooden aims will not be thrown away!"

The dance over, King Herod, with a vast profusion of barn-door majesty, marched towards the damsel, and in "very choice Italian" (which the parson of the parish composed for the occasion, and we have translated) thus complimented her:

"Bewitching maiden I dancing sprite!

I like thy graceful motion:

Ask any boon, and, honour bright!

It is at thy devotion."

The *danseuse*, after whispering to a saffron-complexioned crone, who played *Herodias*, fell down upon both knees, and pointing to the *Baptist*, a grave old farmer! exclaimed,

"If, sir, intending what you say,

192

Your Majesty don't flatter — —

I would the Baptist's head to-day

Were brought me in a platter."

The bluff butcher looked about him as sternly as one of Elkanah's * blustering heroes, and, after taking a fierce stride or two across the stage to vent his royal choler, vouchsafed this reply,
        * Elkanah Settle, the City Lauréat, after the Revolution, kept a booth at Bartholomew Fair, where, in a droll, called St. George for England, he acted in a dragon of green leather of his own invention. In reference to the sweet singer of "annual trophies" and "monthly wars" hissing in his own dragon, Pope utters this charitable wish regarding Colley,
"Avert it, heaven, that thou, my Cibber, e'er Shouldst wag a

serpent-tail in Smithfield Fair!"

"Fair cruel maid, recall thy wish,

O pray think better of it!

I'd rather abdicate, than dish

The cranium of my *prophet*."

Miss still continued pertinacious and positive.

"Your royal word's not worth a fig,

If thus in flams you glory;

I claim your promise for my jig,

The *Baptist's* upper story."

This satirical sally put the imperial butcher upon his mettle; he bit his thumbs, scratched his carrotty poll, paused; and, thinking he had lighted on a loop-hole, grumbled out with stiff-necked profundity,

" A wicked oath, like sixpence crack'd,

Or pie-crust, may be broken."

The *damsel*, however, was "down upon him" before he could articulate "Jack Robinson," with

"But not the promise of a King,

Which is a *royal token.*"

This polished off the rough edges of his Majesty's misgivings, and the decollation of John the Baptist followed; but the good people, resolving to make their martyr some small amends, permitted his representative to receive absolution from a *portly priest* who stood as a spectator at one corner of the stage; while the two soldiers who had decapitated him in effigy, with looks full of contrition, threw themselves into the confessional, and implored the ghostly father to assign them a stiff penance to expiate their guilt. Thus ended this tragedy of tragedies, which, with all due deference to Joe's veracity, we suspect to have had its origin in *Bartholomew Fair.*

Joe Haynes shuffled off his comical coil on Friday, the 4th of April 1701. The Smithfield muses mourned his death in an elegy, * a rare broadside, with a black border, "printed for J. B. near the Strand, 1701."

* "An Elegy on the Death of Mr. Joseph Haines, the late
Famous Actor in the King's Play-House," &c. &c.
"Lament, you beaus and players every one,

The only champion of your cause is gone:
The stars are surly, and the fates unkind,
Joe Haines is dead, and left his Ass behind!
Ah, cruel fate! our patience thus to try,
Must Haines depart, while asses multiply?
If nothing but a player down would go,
There's choice enough besides great Haines the beau!
In potent glasses, when the wine was clear,
Thy very looks declared thy mind was there.
Awful, majestic, on the stage at sight,
To play (not work) was all thy chief delight:
Instead of danger and of hateful bullets,
Roast beef and goose, with harmless legs of pullets!
Here lies the Famous Actor, Joseph Haines,
Who, while alive, in playing took great pains,
Performing all his acts with curious art,
Till Death appear'd, and smote him with his dart."

Thomas Dogget, the last of our triumvirate, was "a little lively sprat man." He dressed neat, and something fine, in a plain cloth coat and a brocaded waistcoat. He sang in company very agreeably, and in public very comically. He was the *Will Kempe* of his day. He danced the Cheshire Round full as well as the famous *Captain George*, but with more nature and nimbleness. *

* Dogget had a sable rival. "In Bartholomew Fair, at the
Coach-House on the Pav'd Stones at Hosier-Lane-End, you
shall see a Black that dances the Cheshire Rounds, to the
admiration of all spectators." Temp. William Third.
Here, too, is Dogget's own bill! "At Parker's and Dogget's

Booth, near Hosier-Lane-End, during the time of Bartholomew
Fair, will be presented a New Droll, called Fryar Bacon, or
the Country Justice; with the Humours of Tollfree the
Miller, and his son Ralph, Acted by Mr. Dogget. With variety
of Scenes, Machines, Songs, and Dances. Vivat Rex, 1691."

A writer in the Secret Mercury of September 9, 1702, says, "At last, all the childish parade shrunk off the stage by matter and motion, and enter a hobbledehoy of a dance, and Dogget, in old woman's petticoats and red waistcoat, as like Progue Cock as ever man saw. It would have made a stoic split his lungs if he had seen the temporary harlot sing and weep both at once; a true emblem of a woman's tears!" He was a faithful, pleasant actor. He never deceived his audience; because, while they gazed at him, he was working up the joke, which broke out suddenly into involuntary acclamations and laughter. He was a capital face-player and gesticulator, and a thorough master of the several dialects, except the Scotch; but was, for all that, an excellent Sawney.

Original

His great parts were Fondlewife, in the Old Bachelor; Ben, in Love for Love; Hob, in the Country Wake, &c. Colley Cibber's account of him is one glowing panegyric. Colley played Fondle wife so completely after the manner of Dogget, copying his voice, person, and dress with such scrupulous exactness, that the audience, mistaking him for the original, applauded vociferously. Of this Dogget himself was a witness, for he sat in the pit..

"Whoever would see him pictured, * may view him in the character of Sawney, at the Duke's Head in Lynn-Regis, Norfolk." Will the jovial spirit of Tony Aston point out where this interesting memento hides its head? "Go on, I'll follow thee." He died at Eltham in Kent, 22nd September 1721.

* The only portrait of Dogget known is a small print,
representing him dancing the Cheshire Round, with the motto
"Ne sut or ultra crepidam
** Baddeley, the comedian, bequeathed a yearly sum for ever,

to be laid out in the purchase of a Twelfth-cake and wine,
for the entertainment of the ladies and gentlemen of Drury
Lane Theatre.

How small an act of kindness will embalm a man's memory! Baddeley's Twelfth Cake ** shall be eaten, and Dogget's coat and badge * rowed for,
    While Christmas frolics, and while Thames shall flow.
"And shall not," said Mr. Bosky, "a bumper flow, in spite of the *'Sin of drinking healths?*" ** to

Three merry men, three merry men,

    Three merry men they be!

Two went dead, like sluggards, in bed;

One in his shoes died of a noose

    That he got at Tyburn-Tree!

Three merry men, three merry men,

    Three merry men are we!

Push round the rummer in winter and summer,

By a sea-coal fire, or when birds make a choir

    Under the green-wood tree!

The sea-coal burns, and the spring returns,

    And the flowers are fair to see;

But man fades fast when his summer is past,

Winter snows on his cheeks blanch the rose —

No second spring has he!

Let the world still wag as it will,

Three merry wags are we!

A bumper shall flow to Mat, Thomas, and Joe

A sad pity that they had not for poor Mat

Hang'd dear at Tyburn-Tree.

* "This day the Coat and Badge given by Mr. Dogget, will
be rowed for by six young watermen, out of their
apprenticeship this year, from the Old Swan at Chelsea." —
Daily Advertiser, July 31, 1753.
** The companion books to the "Sin of Drinking healths,"

were the "Loathsomness of Long Haire," and the "Unlove-
liness of Love Locks," by Messrs. Praise-God-Barebones and

Fear-the-Lord Barbottle.

CHAPTER II.

It would require a poetical imagination to paint the times when a gallant train of England's chivalry rode from the Tower Royal through Knight-rider Street and Giltspur Street (how significant are the names of these interesting localities, bearing record of their former glory!) to their splendid tournaments in Smithfield-or proceeding down Long Lane, crossing the Barbican (the Specula or Watch-tower of Romanum Londinium), and skirting that far-famed street * where, in ancient times, dwelt the Fletchers and Bowyers, but which has since become synonymous with poetry —

* In Grub Street resided John Fox, the Martyrologist, and Henry Welby, the English hermit, who, instigated by the ingratitude of a younger brother, shut himself up in his house for forty-four years, without being seen by any human being. Though an unsociable recluse, he was a man of the most exemplary charity.

—and poverty-ambled gaily through daisy-dappled meads to Finsbury Fields, * to enjoy a more extended space for their martial exercises.

* In the days of Fitzstephen, Finsbury or Fensbury was one vast lake, and the citizens practised every variety of amusement on the ice. "Some will make a large cake of ice, and, seating one of their companions upon it, they take hold of one's hand, and draw him along. Others place the leg-bones of animals under the soles of their feet, by tying them round their ancles, and then, taking a pole shod with iron into their hands, they push themselves forward with a velocity equal to a bolt discharged from a crossbow." We learn from an old ballad called "The Life and Death of

the Two Ladies of Finsbury that gave Moorfields to the city, for the maidens of London to dry their cloaths," that Sir John Fines, "a noble gallant knight," went to Jerusalem to "hunt the Saracen through fire and flood," but before his departure, he charged his two daughters "unmarried to remain," till he returned from "blessed Palestine." The eldest of the two built a "holy cross at 'Bedlam-gate, adjoining to Moorfield and the younger "framed a pleasant well," where wives and maidens daily came to wash. Old Sir John Fines was slain; but his heart was brought over to England from the Holy Land, and, after "a lamentation of three hundred days," solemnly buried in the place to which they gave the name of Finesbury. When the maidens died "they gave those pleasant fields unto the London citizens, "Where lovingly both man and wife May take the evening air;

And London dames to dry their cloaths May hither still

repair!"

Then was Osier Lane (the Smithfield end of which is immortalised in *Bartholomew Fair* annals) a long narrow slip of greensward, watered on both sides by a tributary streamlet from the river

Fleet, on the margin of which grew a line of *osiers*, that hung gracefully over its banks. Smith-field, once "a place for honourable justs and triumphs," became, in after times, a rendezvous for bravoes, and obtained the title of "*Ruffians' Hall*" Centuries have brought no improvement to it. The modern jockeys and chaunters are not a whit less rogues than the ancient "horse-coursers," and the many odd traits of character that marked its former heroes, the swash-bucklers, * are deplorably wanting in the present race of irregulars, who are monotonous bullies, without one redeeming dash of eccentricity or humour. The stream of time, that is continually washing away the impurities of other murky neighbourhoods, passes, without irrigating, Smithfield's blind alleys and the squalid faces of their inhabitants.

* In ancient times a serving-man carried a buckler, or
shield, at his back, which hung by the hilt or pommel of his
sword hanging before him. A "swash-buckler" was so called
from the noise he made with his sword and buckler to
frighten an antagonist.

Yet was it *Merryland* in the olden time-and, forgetting the days, when an unpaved and miry slough, the scene of *autos da fé* for both Catholics and Protestants, as the fury of the dominant party rode religiously rampant, as *such* let us consider it. Pleasant is the remembrance of the sports that are past, which

> To all are delightful, except to the spiteful!
>
> To none offensive, except to the pensive;

yet if the pensiveness be allied to, "a most humorous sadness," the offence will be but small.

At the "Old Elephant Ground over against Osier Lane, in Smithfield, during the time of the fair," in 1682, were to be seen "the Famous Indian Water-works, with masquerades, songs, and dances," —and at the Plough-Musick Booth (a red flag being hung out as a sign) the fair folks were entertained with antic-dances, jigs, and sarabands; an Indian dance by four blacks; a quarter-staff dance; the merry shoemakers; a chair-dance; a dance by three milkmaids, with the comical capers of *Kit the Cowherd*; the Irish trot; the humours of *Jack Tars* and *Scaramouches*; together with good wine, cider, mead, music, and mum.

Cross we over from "Osier Lane-end" (the modern H is an interpolation,) to the King's Head and Mitre Music Booth, "over against Long Lane-end." Beshrew me, Michael Root, thou hast an enticing bill of fare —a dish of all sorts-and how gravely looketh that apathetic Magnifico William, by any grace, but his own, "Sovereign Lord" at the head and front of thy Scaramouches and Tumblers! To thy merry memory, honest Michael! and may St. Bartlemy, root and branch, flourish for ever!

"Michael Root, from the King's-head at Ratcliff-cross, and Elnathan Root, from the Mitre in Wapping, now keep the King's-head and Mitre Musick-Booth in Smithfield Rounds, where will be exhibited A dance between four Tinkers in their proper working habits, with a song in character; Four Satyrs in their Savage Habits present you with a dance; Two Tumblers tumble to admiration; A new Song, called A hearty Welcome to Bartholomew Fair; Four Indians dance with Castinets; A Girl dances with naked rapiers at her throat, eyes, and mouth; a Spaniard dances a saraband incomparably well; a country-man and a country-woman dance Billy and Joan; & young lad dances the Cheshire rounds to admiration; a dance between two Scaramouches and two Irishmen; a woman dances with sixteen glasses on the backs and palms of her hands, turning round several thousand times; an entry, saraband, jig, and hornpipe; an Italian posture-dance; two Tartarians dance in their furious habits; three antick dances and a Roman dance; with another excellent new song, never before performed at any musical entertainment."

John Sleep, or Sleepe, was a wide-awake man in "mirth and pastime famous for his mum-meries and mum; of a locomotive turn, and emulated the zodiac in the number of his signs.

He kept the Gun, in Salisbury Court, and the King William and Queen Mary in Bartholomew Fair; the Rose, in Turnmill Street (the scene, under the rose! of Falstaff's early gallantries); and the Whelp and Bacon in Smithfield Rounds. That he was a formidable rival to the Messrs. Root; a "positive" fellow, and a polite one; teaching his Scaramouches civility, (one, it seems, had made a hole in his manners!) and selling "good wines, &C." let his comically descriptive advertisement to "all gentlemen and ladies" pleasantly testify.

"John Sleepe keepeth the sign of the King William and Queen Mary, in Smithfield Rounds, where all gentlemen and ladies will be accommodated with good wines, &c. and a variety of musick, vocal and instrumental; besides all other mirth and pastime that wit and ingenuity can produce.

"A little boy dances the Cheshire rounds; a young gentlewoman dances the saraband and jigg extraordinary fine, with French dances, that are now in fashion; a Scotch dance, composed by four Italian dancing-masters, for three men and a woman; a young gentlewoman dances with six naked rapiers, so fast, that it would amaze all beholders; a young lad dances an antick dance extraordinary finely; another Scotch dance by two men and one woman, with a Scotch song by the woman, so very droll and diverting, that I am positive did people know the comick humour of it, they would forsake all other booths for the sight of them."

In the following bill Mr. Sleep becomes still more *wonderful and extraordinary* —

"John Sleep now keeps the Whelp and Bacon in Smithfield Rounds, where are to be seen, a young lad that dances a Cheshire round to the admiration of all people, The Silent Comedy, a dance representing the love and jealousy of rural swains, after the manner of the Great Turk's mimick dances performed by his mutes; a lad that tumbles to the admiration of all beholders; a young woman that dances with six naked rapiers, to the wonderful divertisement of all spectators; & young man that dances after the Morocco fashion, to the wonderful applause of all beholders; a nurse-dance, by a woman and two drunkards, wonderful diverting to all people; a young man that dances a hornpipe the Lancaster way, extraordinary finely; a lad that dances a Punch, extraordinary pleasant and diverting; a grotesque dance, called the Speak-ing Movement, shewing in words and gestures the humours of a musick booth, after the manner of the Venetian Carnival; and a new Scaramouch, more civil than the former, and after a far more ingenious and divertinger way!"

Excellent well, somniferous John! worthy disciple of St. Bartlemy.

Green, at the "Nag's Head and Pide Bull," advertises eight "comical and diverting" exhibitions; hinting that he hath "that within which passeth shew but declines publishing his "other ingenious pastimes in so small a bill." Yet he contrives to get into this "small bill" as much puff as his contemporaries. His pretensions are as superlative as his Scaramouches, and quite as diverting. "A young man dances with twelve naked swords," and "a young woman with six naked rapiers, after a more pleasant and far inge-niuser fashion than had been danced before."

These Bartholomew Fair showmen are sadly deficient in gallantry. With them the "gentlemen" always take precedence of the "ladies." The Smithfield muses should have taught them better manners.

Manager Crosse * "at the Signe of the George," advertises a genuine Jim Crow, "a black lately from the Indies, who dances antic dances after the Indian manner." In those days the grinning and sprawling of an ebony buffoon were confined to the congenial timbers of Bartlemy fair!

* Managers Crosse, Powell, Luffingham, &c. Temp. Queen Anne and George I.

Was the "young gentlewoman with six naked rapiers" ubiquitous, or had she rivals in the Rounds? But another lady, no less attractive, "invites our steps, and points to yonder" booth-where, "By His Majesty's permission, next door to the King's Head in Smithfield, is to be seen a woman-dwarf, * but three foot and one inch ** high, born in Somersetshire, and in the fortieth year of her age."

And, as if we had not seen enough of "strange creatures alive? mark the following "advertise-ment": —

"Next door to the Golden Hart, in Smithfield, is to be seen a live Turkey ram. Part of him is covered with black hair, and part with white wool. He hath horns as big as a bull's; and his tail weighs sixty pounds! Here is also to be seen alive the famous civet cat, and one of the holy lambs curiously spotted all over like a leopard, that us'd to be offered by the Jews for a sacrifice. Vivat Rex."

This Turkey ram's tail is a tough tale, * even for the ad libitum of Smithfield Rounds. Such a tail wagged before such a master must have exhibited the two greatest wags in the fair.

The Roots were under ground, or planted in a cool arbour, quaffing-not Bartlemy "good wines," (doctors never take their own physic!) —but genuine nutbrown. Their dancing-days were over; for "Root's booth" (temp. Geo.I.) was now tenanted by Powell, the puppet-showman, and one Luf-fingham, who, fired with the laudable ambition of maintaining the laughing honours of their predecessors, issued a bill, at which we cry "What next?" as the sailor did when the conjuror blew his own head off.

"At Root's booth, Powell from Russell Court, and Luffingham from the Cyder Cellar, in Covent-Garden, now keep the King Charles's Head, and Man and Woman fighting for the Breeches, in Bartholomew Fair, near Long Lane: where two figures dance a Scaramouch after a new grotesque fashion; a little boy, five years old, vaults from a table twelve foot high on his head, and drinks the King's health standing on his head, with two swords at his throat; a Scotch dance by three men and a woman; an Irishwoman dances the Irish trot; Roger of Coventry is danced by one in a countryman's habit; a cradle dance, being a comical fancy between a woman and her drunken husband fighting for the breeches; a woman dances with fourteen glasses on the back of her hands full of wine. Also several entries, as Almands Pavans, Galliads, Gavots, English Jiggs, and the Sabbotiers dance, so mightily admired at the King's Playhouse. The company will be entertained with vocal and instrumental musick, as performed at the late happy Congress at Reswick, in the presence of several princes and ambassadors."

Here will I pause. For the present, we have supped full with Scaramouches. "Six naked rapiers" at my throat all night would be a sorry substitute for the knife and fork I hope to play anon, after a "more pleasant and far ingeniuser" fashion, with some plump roast partridges.

A select coterie of Uncle Timothy's brother antiquaries have requested to be enlightened on Bartlemy fair lore. Will you, my friend Eugenio, during the Saint's saturnalia, join us in the ancient "Cloth quarter"? On, brave spirit! on. Rope-dancers invite thee; conjurors conjure thee; *Punch* squeaks thee a screeching welcome; mountebanks and posture-masters, * with every variety of physiognomical and physical contortion, lure thee to their dislocations.

   * "From the Duke of Marlborough's Head in Fleet Street, during the fair, is to be seen the famous posture-master, who far exceeds Clarke and Higgins. He twists his body into all deformed shapes, makes his hip and shoulder-bones meet together, lays his head upon the ground, and turns his body round twice or thrice without stirring his face from the place." —1711.

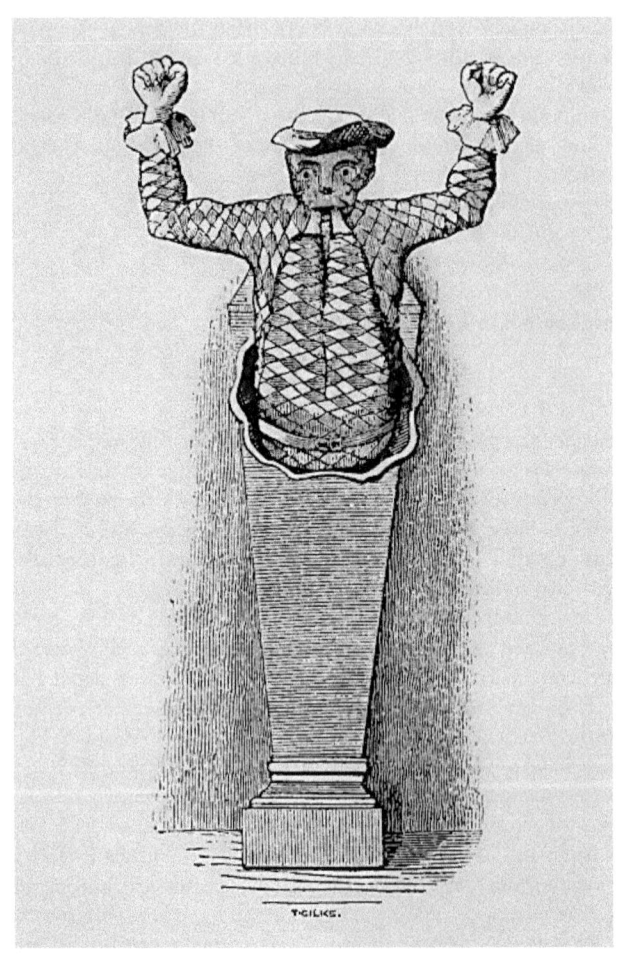

Original

Fawkes's dexterity of hand; the moving pictures; Pinchbeck's musical clock; Solomon's Temple; the waxwork, all alive! the Corsican fairy; * the dwarf that jumps down his —

    * "The Corsican Fairy, only thirty-four inches high, and weighing but twenty-six pounds, well-proportioned and a perfect beauty. She is to be seen at the corner of Cow-Lane, during Bartholomew Fair." —1743.

—own throat! * the High German Artist, born without hands or feet; ** the cow with Jive legs; the —

    * "Lately arrived from Italy Signor Capitello Jumpedo, a surprising dwarf, not taller than a common tobacco-pipe. He will twist his body into ten thousand shapes, and then open wide his mouth, and jump down his own throat! He is to be spoke with at the Black Tavern, Golden Lane." January 18, 1749. This is the renowned "Bottle Conjuror." Some such deception was practised either by himself, or an imitator, at Bartholomew Fair.

** "Mr. Mathew Buchinger, twenty-nine inches high, born

without hands or feet, June 2, 1674, in Germany, near Nuremburgh. He has been married four times, and has eleven children. He plays on the hautboy and flute; and is no less eminent for writing and drawing coats of arms and pictures, to the life, with a pen. He plays at cards, dice, and ninepins, and performs tricks with cups, balls, and live birds." Every Jack has his Jill; and as a partner, not in a connubial sense, my little Plenipo! we couple thee with "The High German Woman, born without hands or feet, that threads her needle, sews, cuts out gloves, writes, spins fine thread, and charges and discharges a pistol. She is now to be seen at the corner of Hosier Lane, during the time of the fair." —Temp. Geo. II.

Apropos of dwarfs-William Evans, porter to King Charles the

First, who was two yards and a half in height, "dancing in an antimask at court, drew little Jeffrey the dwarf out of his pocket, first to the wonder, then to the laughter of the beholders." Little Jeffrey's height was only three feet nine inches. But even the gigantic William Evans, and George the Fourth's tall porter whom we remember to have seen peep over the gates of Carlton House, were nothing to the modern American, who is so tall as to be obliged to go up a ladder to shave himself!

—hare that beats a drum; * the Savoyard's puppet-shew; the mummeries of Moorfields, *** urge thee forward on thy ramble of two centuries through Bartholomew Fair, which, like

    'Th' adventure of the Bear and Fiddle

    Is sung-but breaks off in the middle.'"

* Ben Jonson, in his play of Bartholomew Fair, mentions this singular exhibition having taken place in his time; and Strutt gives a pictorial description of it, copied from a drawing in the Harleian collection (6563) said to be upwards of four centuries old.
** Moorfields, spite of its "melancholy Moor Ditch" was

formerly famous for,
"Hills and holes, and shops for brokers,

Open sinners, canting soakers;
Preachers, doctors, raving, puffing,
Praying, swearing, solving, huffing,
Singing hymns, and sausage frying,
Apple roasting, orange shying;
Blind men begging, fiddlers drawling,
Raree-shows and children bawling —
Gingerbread! and see Gibraltar!
Humstrums grinding tunes that falter;
Maim'd and halt aloft are staging,
Bills and speeches mobs engaging;
'Good people, sure de ground you tread on,
Me did put dis voman's head on!'"
"The Flying Horse, a noted victualling house in Moor-fields,

next to that of the late Astrologer Trotter, has been molested for several nights past, stones, and glass bottles being thrown into the house, to the great annoyment and terror of the family and guests." —News Letter of Feb. 25, 1716.

As the Lauréat closed his manuscript, the door opened, and who should enter but Uncle Timothy.

"Ha! my good friends, what happy chance has brought you to the business abode and town Tusculum of the Boskys for half-a-dozen generations of Drysalters?"

"Something short of assault and battery, fine and imprisonment."

And Mr. Bosky, after helping Uncle Timothy off with his great coat, warming his slippers, wheeling round his arm-chair to the chimney-corner, and seeing him comfortably seated, gave a detail of our late encounter at the Pig and Tinder-Box.

The old-fashioned housekeeper delivered a note to Mr. Bosky, sealed with a large black seal.

"An ominous looking affair!" remarked the middle-aged gentleman.

"A death's head and cross-bones!" replied the Lauréat of Little Britain. "'Ods, rifles and triggers! if it should be a challenge from the Holborn Hill Demosthenes."

"A challenge! a fiddlestick!" retorted Uncle

Tim, "he's only a tame cheater!' Every bullet that he fires I 'll swallow for a forced-meat ball."
Mr. Bosky having broken the black seal, read out as follows: —

"Mr. Merripall presents his respectful services to Benjamin Bosky, Esq. and begs the favour of his company to dine with the High Cockolorum Club * of associated Undertakers at the Death's Door, Battersea Rise, to-morrow, at four. If Mr. Bosky can prevail upon his two friends, who received such scurvy treatment from a fraction of the Antiqueeruns, to accompany him, it will afford Mr. M. additional pleasure."

* It may be curious to note down some of the odd clubs that existed in 1745, viz. The Virtuoso's Club; the Knights of the Golden Fleece; the Surly Club; the Ugly Club; the Split-Farthing Club; the Mock Heroes Club; the Beau's Club; the Quack's Club; the Weekly Dancing Club; the Bird-Fancier's Club; the Chatter-wit Club; the Small-coal Man's Music Club; the Kit-cat Club; the Beefsteak Club; all of which and many more, are broadly enough described in "A Humorous Account of all the Remarkable Clubs in London and Westminster." In 1790, among the most remarkable clubs were, The Odd Fellows; the Humbugs, (held at the Blue Posts, Russell Street, Covent Garden,) the Samsonic Society; the Society of Bucks; the Purl-Drinkers; the Society of Pilgrims (held at the Woolpack, Kingsland Road); the Thespian Club; the Great Bottle Club; the Je ne sçai quoi Club (held at the Star and Garter, Pall Mall, and of which the Prince of Wales, and the Dukes of York, Clarence, Orleans (Philip Egalité), Norfolk, Bedford, &c. &c. were members); the Sons of the Thames Society (meeting to celebrate the annual contest for Dogget's Coat and Badge); the Blue Stocking Club; and the No pay, no liquor Club, held at the Queen and Artichoke, Hampstead Road, where the newly-admitted member, having paid his fee of one shilling, was invested with the inaugural honours, viz. a hat fashioned in the form of a quart pot, and a gilt goblet of humming ale, out of which he drank the healths of the brethren. In the present day, the Author of Virginius has conferred classical celebrity on a club called "The Social Villagers" held at the Bedford Arms, a merry hostelrie at Camden Town.

It was at one of these festivous meetings that Uncle Timothy

produced the following Lyric of his own.
Fill, fill a bumper! no twilight, no, no!

Let hearts, now or never, and goblets o'erflow!
Apollo commands that we drink, and the Nine,
A generous spirit in generous wine.
The bard, in a bumper; behold, to the brim
They rise, the gay spirits of poesy-whim!
Around ev'ry glass they a garland entwine
Of sprigs from the laurel, and leaves from the vine.
A bumper! the bard who, in eloquence bold,
Of two noble fathers the story has told;
What pangs heave the bosom, what tears dim the eyes,
When the dagger is sped, and the arrow it flies.
The bard, in a bumper! Is fancy his theme?
'Tis sportive and light as a fairy-land dream;
Does love tune his harp? 'tis devoted and pure;
Or friendship? 'tis that which shall always endure.
Ye tramplers on liberty, tremble at him;
His song is your knell, and the slave's morning hymn!
His frolicksome humour is buxom and bland,

And bright as the goblet I hold in my hand.
The bard! brim your glasses; a bumper! a cheer!
Long may he live in good fellowship here.
Shame to thee, Britain, if ever he roam,
To seek with the stranger a friend and a home!
Fate in his cup ev'ry blessing infuse,
Cherish his fortune, and smile on his muse;
Warm be his hearth, and prosperity cheer
Those he is dear to, and those he holds dear.
Blythe be his autumn as summer hath been; —
Frosty, but kindly, and sweetly serene
Green be his winter, with snow on his brow;
Green as the wreath that encircles it now!
To dear Paddy Knowles, then, a bumper we fill,
And toast his good health as he trots down the hill;
In genius he 5s left all behind him by goles!
But he won't leave behind him another Pat Knowles!

"An unique invitation!" quoth Uncle Tim. "Gentlemen, you must indulge the High Coclcoorums, and go by all means."

Mr. Bosky promised to rise with the lark, and be ready for one on the morrow; and, anticipating a good day's sport, we consented to accompany him.

Supper was announced, and we sat down to that social meal. In a day-dream of fancy, Uncle Timothy re-peopled the once convivial chambers of the *Falcon* and the *Mermaid*, with those glorious intelligences that made the reigns of Elizabeth and James I. the Augustan age of England. We listened to the wisdom, and the wit, and the loud laugh, as Shakspere and "rare Ben," * in the full confidence of friendship, exchanged "thoughts that breathe, and words that burn," so beautifully described by Beaumont in his letter to Jonson.

* "Shakespeare was god-father to one of Ben Jonson's
children, and after the christening, being in a deepe study,
Jonson came to cheere him up, and ask't him why he was so
melancholy? 'No, faith, Ben, (says he,) not I, but I have
been considering a great while what should be the fittest
gift for me to bestow upon my god-child, and I have resolv'd
at last.' —'I pr'y thee, what' says he —'F faith, Ben, I'le
e'en give him a douzen good Lattin spoones, and thou shalt
translate them.'" —L'Estrange, No. 11. Mr. Dun. —Latten was
a name formerly used to signify a mixed metal resembling
brass. Hence Shakspere's appropriate pun, with reference to
the learning of Ben Jonson.
Many good jests are told of "rare Ben." When he went to

Basingstoke, he used to put up his horse at the "Angel,"
which was kept by Mrs. Hope, and her daughter, Prudence.
Journeying there one day, and finding strange people in the
house, and the sign changed, he wrote as follows: —
"When Hope and Prudence kept this house, the Angel kept the

door;
Now Hope is dead, the Angel fled, and Prudence turn'd a w — —!"
At another time he designed to pass through the Half Moon in

Aldersgate Street, but the door being shut, he was denied entrance; so he went to the Sun Tavern at the Long Lane end, and made these verses: —
"Since the Half Moon is so unkind,

To make me go about;
The Sun my money now shall have,
And the Moon shall go without."
That he was often in pecuniary difficulties the following

extracts from Henslowe's papers painfully demonstrate. "Lent un to Bengemen Johnson, player, the 28 of July, 1597, in Redy money, the some of fower powndes, to be payed agayne when so ever ether I, or any for me, shall demande yt — Witness E. Alleyn and John Synger." —"Lent Bengemyne Johnson, the 5 of Janeway, 1597-8, in redy money, the some of Vs."

"What things have we seen

Done at the Mermaid! heard words that have been

So nimble, and so full of subtle flame,

As if that every one from whom they came,

Had meant to put his whole wit in a jest!"

Travelling by the swift power of imagination, we looked in at *Wills and Buttons*; beheld the honoured chair that was set apart for the use of Dryden; and watched Pope, then a boy, lisping in numbers, regarding his great master with filial reverence, as he delivered his critical aphorisms to the assembled wits. Nor did we miss the Birch-Rod that "the bard whom pilfer'd pastoral renown" hung up at Buttons to chastise "tuneful Alexis of the Thames' fair side," his own back smarting from some satirical twigs that little Alexis had liberally laid on! We saw St. Patrick's Dean "steal" to his pint of wine with the accomplished Addison; and heard Gay, Arbuthnot, and Boling-broke, in witty conclave, compare lyrical notes for the Beggar's Opera-not forgetting the joyous cheer that welcomed "King Colley" to his midnight troop of titled revellers, after the curtain had dropped on Fondle wife and Foppington. And, hey presto! snugly seated at the Mitre, we found Doctor Johnson, lemon in hand, demanding of Goldsmith, * —
    * If ever an author, whether considered as a poet, a critic,
an historian, or a dramatist, deserved the name of a
classic, it was Oliver Goldsmith. His two great ethic poems,
"The Traveller," and "The Deserted Village," for sublimity
of thought, truth of reasoning, and poetical beauty, fairly
place him by the side of Pope. The simile of the bird
teaching its young to fly, and that beginning with "As some
tall cliffy" have rarely been equalled, and never surpassed.
For exquisite humour and enchanting simplicity of style, his
essays may compare with the happiest effusions of Addison;
and his "Vicar of Wakefield," though a novel, has advanced

the cause of religion and virtue, and may be read with as
much profit as the most orthodox sermon that was ever
penned. As a dramatist, he excelled all his contemporaries
in originality, character, and humour. As long as a true
taste for literature shall prevail, Goldsmith will rank as
one of its brightest ornaments: for while he delighted the
imagination, and alternately moved the heart to joy or
sorrow, he "gave ardour to virtue and confidence to truth."
A tale of woe was a certain passport to his compassion; and

he has given his last guinea to an indigent suppliant.
To Goldsmith has been imputed a vain ambition to shine in

company; it is also said that he regarded with envy all
literary fame but his own. Of the first charge he is
certainly guilty; the second is entirely false; unless a
transient feeling of bitterness at seeing preferred merit
inferior to his own, may be construed into envy. A great
genius seldom keeps up his character in conversation: his
best thoughts, clothed in the choicest terms, he commits to
paper; and with these his colloquial powers are unjustly
compared. Goldsmith well knew his station in the literary
world; and his desire to maintain it hi every society, often
involved him in ridiculous perplexities. He would fain have
been an admirable Crichton. His ambition to rival a
celebrated posture-master had once very nearly cost him his
shins. These eccentricities, attached to so great a man,
were magnified into importance; and he amply paid the tax to
which genius is subject, by being envied and abused by the
dunces of his day. Yet he wanted not spirit to resent an
insult; and a recreant bookseller who had published an
impudent libel upon him, he chastised in his own shop. How
delightful to contemplate such a character! If ever there
was a heart that beat with more than ordinary affection for
mankind, it was Goldsmith's.

—Garrick, * Boswell, and Reynolds, "Who's for *poonch?*" — —
  * Garrick was born to illustrate what Shakspere wrote; —to
him Nature had unlocked all her springs, and opened all her
stores. His success was instantaneous, brilliant, and
complete. Colley Cibber was constrained to yield him
unwilling praise; and Quin, the pupil of Betterton and
Booth, openly declared, "That if the young fellow was right,
he, and the rest of the players, had been all wrong." The
unaffected and familiar style of Garrick presented a
singular contrast to the stately air, the solemn march, the
monotonous and measured declamation of his predecessors. To
the lofty grandeur of tragedy, he was unequal; but its
pathos, truth, and tenderness were all his own. In comedy,
he might be said to act too much; he played no less to the
eye than to the ear-he indeed acted every word. Macklin
blames him for his greediness of praise; for his ambition to

engross all attention to himself, and disconcerting his brother actors by "pawing and pulling them about." This censure is levelled at his later efforts, when he adopted the vice of stage-trick; but nothing could exceed the ease and gaiety of his early performances. He was the delight of every eye, the theme of every tongue, the admiration and wonder of foreign nations; and Baron, Le Kain, and Clairon, the ornaments of the French Stage, bowed to the superior genius of their illustrious friend and contemporary. In private life he was hospitable and splendid: he entertained princes, prelates, and peers-all that were eminent in art and science. If his wit set the table in a roar, his urbanity and good-breeding forbade any thing like offence. Dr. Johnson, who would suffer no one to abuse Davy but himself, bears ample testimony to the peculiar charm of his manners; and, what is infinitely better, to his liberality, pity, and melting charity. By him was the Drury Lane Theatrical Fund for decayed actors founded, endowed, and incorporated. He cherished its infancy by his munificence and zeal; strengthened its maturer growth by appropriating to it a yearly benefit, on which he acted himself; and his last will proves that its prosperity lay near his heart, when contemplating his final exit from the scene of life. In the bright sun of his reputation there were, doubtless, spots: transient feelings of jealousy at merit that interfered with his own; arts that it might be almost necessary to practise in his daily commerce with dull importunate playwrights, and in the government of that most discordant of all bodies, a company of actors. His grand mistakes were his rejection of Douglass and The Good Na-tured Man; and his patronage of the Stay-maker, and the school of sentiment. As an author, he is entitled to favourable mention: his dramas abound in wit and character; his prologues and epilogues display endless variety and whim; and his epigrams, for which he had a peculiar turn, are pointed and bitter. Some things he wrote that do not add to his fame; and among them are The Fribbleriad, and The Sick Monkey. One of the most favourite amusements of his leisure was in collecting every thing rare and curious that related to the early drama; hence his matchless collection of old plays, which, with Roubilliac's statue of Shakspere, he bequeathed to the British Museum: a noble gift! worthy of himself and of his country!

The 10th of June, 1776, was marked by Garrick's retirement

from the stage. With his powers unimpaired, he wisely resolved (theatrically speaking) to die as he had lived, with all his glory and with all his fame. He might have, indeed, been influenced by a more solemn feeling —
"Higher duties crave

Some space between the theatre and grave;

That, like the Roman in the Capitol,
I may adjust my mantle, ere I fall,"
The part he selected upon this memorable occasion was Don

Felix, in the Wonder. We could have wished that, like
Kemble, he had retired with Shakspere upon his lips; that
the glories of the Immortal had hallowed his closing scene.
His address was simple and appropriate-he felt that he was
no longer an actor; and when he spoke of the kindness and
favours that he had received, his voice faltered, and he
burst into a flood of tears. The most profound silence, the
most intense anxiety prevailed, to catch every word, look,
and action, knowing they were to be his last; and the public
parted from their idol with tears for his love, joy for his
fortune, admiration for his vast and unconfined powers, and
regret that that night had closed upon them for ever.
Garrick had long been afflicted with a painful disorder. In

the Christmas of 1778, being on a visit with Mrs. Garrick at
the country seat of Earl Spencer, he had a recurrence of it,
which, after his return to London, increased with such
violence, that Dr. Cadogan, conceiving him to be in imminent
danger, advised him, if he had any worldly affairs to
settle, to lose no time in dispatching them. Mr. Garrick
replied, "that nothing of that sort lay on his mind, and
that he was not afraid to die." And why should he fear? His
authority had ever been directed to the reformation, the
good order, and propriety of the Stage; his example had
incontestibly proved that the profession of a player is not
incompatible with the exercise of every Christian and moral
duty, and his well-earned riches had been rendered the mean
of extensive public and private benevolence. He therefore
beheld the approach of death, not with that reckless
indifference which some men call philosophy, but with
resignation and hope. He died on Wednesday, January 20th,
1779, in the sixty-second year of his age.
"Sure his last end was peace, how calm his exit!

Night dews fall not more gently to the ground,
Nor weary worn-out winds expire so soft."
On Monday, February 1st, his body was interred with great

funeral pomp in Westminster Abbey, under the monument of the
divine Shakspere.

——"And Sir John Hawkins," exclaimed Uncle Timothy, with unwonted asperity, "whose ideas
of virtue never rose above a decent exterior and regular hours! calling the author of the *Traveller*
an Idiot' It shakes the sides of splenetic disdain to hear this Grub Street chronicler * of fiddling
and fly-fishing libelling the beautiful intellect of Oliver Goldsmith! Gentle spirit! thou wert
beloved, admired, and mourned by that illustrious cornerstone of religion and morality, Samuel
Johnson, who delighted to sound forth thy praises while living, and when the voice of fame
could no longer soothe 'thy dull cold ear,' inscribed thy tomb with an imperishable record!

Deserted is the village; the hermit and the traveller have laid them down to rest; the vicar has performed his last sad office; the good-natured man is no more-He stoops but to conquer!"

 * The negative qualities of this sober Knight long puzzled
his acquaintances (friends we never heard that he had any!)
to devise an epitaph for him. At last they succeeded —
"Here lies Sir John Hawkins,

Without his shoes and stockings!"

The Lauréat, well comprehending an expressive look from his Mentor, rose to the pianoforte, and accompanied him slowly and mournfully in

THE POET'S REQUIEM.

Ah! yes, to the poet a hope there is given

In poverty, sorrow, unkindness, neglect,

That though his frail bark on the rocks may be driven,

And founder-not all shall entirely be wreck'd;

But the bright, noble thoughts, that made solitude sweet,

His world! while he linger'd unwillingly here,

Shall bid future bosoms with sympathy beat,

And call forth the smile and awaken the tear.

If, man, thy pursuit is but riches and fame;

If pleasure alluring entice to her bower;

The Muse waits to kindle a holier flame,

And woos thee aside for a classical hour.

And then, by the margin of Helicon's stream,

Th' enchantress shall lead thee, and thou from afar

Shalt see, what was once in life's feverish dream,

A poor broken spirit, * a bright shining star! — —

Hail and farewell! to the Spirits of Light,

Whose minds shot a ray through this darkness of ours —

The world, but for them, had been chaos and night,

A desert of thorns, not a garden of flowers!

* Plautus turned a mill; Terenee was a slave; Boethius died
in a jail; Tasso was often distressed for a shilling; Benti-
voglio was refused admission into an hospital he had himself
founded; Cervantes died (almost) of hunger; Camoens ended
his days in an almshouse; Vaugelas sold his body to the
surgeons to support life; Burns died penniless,
disappointed, and heart-broken; and Massinger, Lee, and
Otway, were "steeped in poverty to the very lips." Yet how
consoling are John Taylor the Water Poet's lines! Addressing

his friend, Wm. Fennor, he exclaims,
"Thou say'st that poetry descended is From poverty: thou

tak'st thy mark amiss —
In spite of weal or woe, or want of pelf,

It is a kingdom of content itself,!"
To the above unhappy list may be added Thomas Dekker the

Dramatist. "Lent unto the Company the 'of February, 1598, to
discharge Mr. Dicker out of the Counter in the Poultry, the
some of Fortie Shillinges." In another place Mr. Henslowe
redeems Dekker out of the Clinke.

This was a subject that awakened all Uncle Timothy's enthusiasm!

> "Age could not wither it, nor custom stale
>
> Its infinite variety."

But it produced fits of abstraction and melancholy; and Mr. Bosky knowing this, would inter-
pose a merry tale or song. Upon the present occasion he made a bold dash from the sublime
to the ridiculous, and striking up a comical voluntary, played us out of Little Britain. —

> When I behold the setting sun,
>
> And shop is shut, and work is done,
>
> I strike my flag, and mount my tile,
>
> And through the city strut in style;
>
> While pensively I muse along,
>
> Listening to some minstrel's song,
>
> With tuneful wife, and children three —
>
> O then, my love! I think on thee.
>
> In Sunday suit, to see my fair
>
> I take a round to Russell Square;
>
> She slyly beckons while I peep.
>
> And whispers, "down the area creep!"
>
> What ecstacies my soul await;
>
> It sinks with rapture-on my plate!

When cutlets smoke at half-past three —

And then, my love! I think on thee.

But, see the hour-glass, moments fly —

The sand runs out-and so must I!

Parting is so sweet a sorrow,

I could manger till to-morrow!

One embrace, ere I again

Homeward hie to Huggin Lane;

And sure as goose begins with G,

I then, my love! shall think on thee.

Mr. William Shakspere says

In one of his old-fashion'd plays,

That true love runs not smooth as oil —

Last Friday week we had a broil.

Genteel apartments I have got,

The first floor down the chimney-pot;

Mount Pleasant! for my love and me —

And soon one pair shall walk up three!

"Gentlemen," said Uncle Timothy, as he bade us good night, "the rogue, I fear, will be the spoil of you, as he hath been of me!"

CHAPTER III.

With the fullest intention to rise early the next morning, without deliberating for a mortal half-hour whether or not to turn round and take t' other nap, we retired to a tranquil pillow.

> But what are all our good intentions?
>
> Vexations, vanities, inventions!
>
> Macadamizing what? —a certain spot,
>
> To ears polite" politeness never mentions —
>
> Tattoos, t' amuse, from empty drums.
>
> Ah! who time's spectacles shall borrow?
>
> And say, be gay to-day —to-morrow —
>
> When query if to-morrow comes.

To-morrow came; so did to-morrow's bright sun; and so did Mr. Bosky's brisk knock. Good report always preceded Mr. Bosky, like the bounce with which champagne sends its cork out of the bottle! But (there are two sides of the question to be considered-the *inside* of the bed and the *out!*) they found us in much such a brown study as we have just described. Leaving the Lauréat to enjoy his triumph of punctuality, (an "alderman's virtue!") we lost no time in equipping ourselves, and were soon seated with him at breakfast. He was in the happiest spirits. "'Tis your birthday, Eugenio! Wear this ring for my sake; let it be friendship's * talisman to unite our hearts in one. Here," presenting some tablets beautifully wrought, "is Uncle Timothy's offering. Mark," pointing to the following inscription engraved on the cover, "by what poetical alchemy he hath transmuted the silver into gold!"

* Bonaparte did not believe in friendship: "Friendship is
but a word. I love no one-no, not even my brothers; Joseph,
perhaps, a little. Still, if I do love him, it is from
habit, because he is the eldest of us. Duroc! Yes, Mm I
certainly love: but why? His character suits me: he is cold,
severe, unfeeling; and then, Duroc never weeps!" Bonaparte
counted his fortunate days by his victories, Titus by his
good actions.
"Friendship, peculiar boon of Heaven,

The noble mind's delight and pride,
To men and angels only given,
To all the lower world denied." —Dr. Johnson.

> Life is short, the wings of time
>
> Bear away our early prime,
>
> Swift with them our spirits fly,

The heart grows chill, and dim the eye. — —

Seize the moment I snatch the treasure!

Sober haste is wisdom's leisure.

Summer blossoms soon decay;

"Gather the rose-buds while you may!"

Barter not for sordid store

Health and peace; nor covet more

Than may serve for frugal fare

With some chosen friend to share!

Not for others toil and heap,

But yourself the harvest reap;

Nature smiling, seems to say,

"Gather the rose-buds while you may!"

Learning, science, truth sublime,

Fairy fancies, lofty rhyme,

Flowers of exquisite perfume!

Blossoms of immortal bloom!

With the gentle virtues twin'd,

In a beauteous garland bind

For your youthful brow to-day —

"Gather the rose-buds while you may!"

Life is short-but not to those

Who early, wisely pluck the rose.

Time he flies-to us 'tis given

On his wings to fly to Heaven.

Ah! to reach those realms of light,

Nothing must impede our flight;

Cast we all but Hope away!

"Gather the rose-buds while we may!"

Now a sail up or down the river has always been pleasant to us in proportion as it has proved barren of adventure. A collision with a coal-barge or steam-packet —a squall off Chelsea Reach, may do vastly well to relieve its monotony: but we had rather be dull than be ducked. We were therefore glad to find the water smooth, the wind and tide in our favour, and no particular disposition on the part of the larger vessels to run us down. Mr. Bosky, thinking that at some former period of our lives we might have beheld the masts and sails of a ship, the steeple of a church, the smoke of a patent shot manufactory, the coal-whippers weighing out their black diamonds, a palace, and a penitentiary, forbore to expatiate on the picturesque objects that presented themselves to our passing view; and, presuming that our vision had extended beyond some score or two of garden-pots "all a-growing, all a-blow-ing," and as much sky as would cover half-a-crown, he was not over profuse of vernal description. But, knowing that there are as many kinds of minds as moss, he opened his inquisitorial battery upon the waterman. At first Barney Binnacle, though a pundit among the wet wags of Wapping Old Stairs, fought shy; but there is a freemasonry in fun; and by degrees he ran through all the changes from the simple leer to the broad grin and horse-laugh, as Mr. Bosky "poked" his droll sayings into him. He had his predilections and prejudices. The former were for potations drawn from a case-bottle presented to him by Mr. Bosky, that made his large blue lips smack, and his eyes wink again; the latter were against steamers, the projectors of which he would have placed at the disposal of their boilers! His tirade against the Thames Tunnel was hardly less severe; but he reserved the magnums of his wrath for the Greenwich railroad. What in some degree reconciled us to Barney's anathemas, were his wife and children, to whom his wherry gave their daily bread: and though these gigantic monopolies might feather the nests of wealthy proprietors, they would not let poor Barney Binnacle feather either his nest or his oar.

"There's truth in what you say, Master Barney," observed the Lauréat; "the stones went merrily into the pond, but the foolish frogs could not fish out the fun. I am no advocate for the philosophy of expediency."

"Surely, Mr. Bosky, you would never think of putting a stop to *improvement!*"

"My good friends, I would not have man become the victim of his ingenuity —a mechanical suicide! Where brass and iron, hot water and cold, can be made to mitigate the wear and tear of his thews and sinews, let them be adopted as auxiliaries, not as principals. I am no political economist. I despise the muddle-headed dreamers, and their unfeeling crudities. But for them the heart of England would have remained uncorrupted and sound. * Trifle not with suffering. Impunity has its limit. A flint will show fire when you strike it.

* We quite agree with Mr. Bosky. Cant and utilitarianism have produced an insipid uniformity of character, a money-grubbing, care-worn monotony, that cry aloof to eccentricity and whim. Men are thinking of "stratagems and wars," the inevitable consequence of lots of logic, lack of amusement, and lean diet. No man is a traitor over turtle, or hatches plots with good store of capon and claret in his stomach. Had Cassius been a better feeder he had never conspired against Cæsar. Three meals a day, and supper at night, are four substantial reasons for not being disloyal, lank, or lachrymose.

"In this world ninety-nine persons out of one hundred must toil for their bread before they eat it; *ask leave* to toil-some philanthropists say, even before they hunger for it. I have therefore yet to learn how that which makes human labour a drug in the market can be called, an *improvement*. The stewardships of this world are vilely performed. What blessings would be conferred, what wrongs prevented, were it not for the neglect of opportunities and the prostitution of means. Is it our own merit that we have more? our neighbour's delinquency that he has less? The infant is born to luxury; —calculate his claims! Virtue draws its last sigh in a dungeon; Vice receives its tardy summons on a bed of down! The titled and the rich, the purse-proud nobodies, the noble nothings, occupy their vantage ground, not from any merit of their own; but from that lucky or unlucky chance which might have brought them into this breathing world with two heads on their shoulders instead of one! I believe in the theoretical benevolence, and practical malignity of man."

We never knew Mr. Bosky so eloquent before; the boat became lop-sided under the fervent thump that he gave as a clencher to his oration. Barney Binnacle stared; but with no vacant expression.

His rugged features softened into a look of grateful approval, mingled with surprise.

"God bless your honour!"

"Thank you, Barney Some people's celestial blessings save their earthly breeches-pockets. But a poor mans blessing is a treasure of which Heaven keeps the register and the key."

Barney Binnacle bent on Mr. Bosky another inquiring look, that seemed to say, "Mayhap I've got a *bishop* on board."

"If every gentleman was like your honour," replied Barney, "we should have better times; and a poor fellow wouldn't pull up and down this blessed river sometimes for days together, without yarning a copper to carry home to his hungry wife and children." And he dropped his oar, and drew the sleeve of his threadbare blue jacket across his weather-beaten cheek.

This was a result that Mr. Bosky had not anticipated.

"How biting," he remarked, "is the breeze! Egad, my teeth feel an inclination to be so too!" The fresh air gave him the wind in his stomach; a sufficient apology for the introduction of a cold pigeon-pie, and some piquant etceteras that he had provided as a whet to the entertainment in agreeable perspective at Battersea Rise. Opining that the undulation of the boat was likely to prevent "good digestion," which-though everybody here helped himself-should "wait on appetite," he ordered Barney to moor it in some convenient creek; and as Barney, not having been polished in the Chesterfield school, seemed mightily at a loss how to dispose of his hands, Mr. Bosky, who was well-bred, and eschewed idleness, found them suitable employment, by inviting their owner to fall to. And what a merry party were we! Barney Binnacle made no more bones of a pigeon than he would of a lark; swallowed the forced-meat balls as if they had been not bigger than Morrison's pills; demolished the tender rump-steak and flaky pie-crust with a relish as sweet as the satisfaction that glowed in Mr. Bosky's benevolent heart and countenance, and buzzed the pale brandy (of which he could drink any given quantity) like sugared cream! The Lauréat was magnificently jolly. He proposed the good healths of Mrs. Binnacle and the Binnacles major and minor; toasted old Father Thames and his Tributaries; and made the welkin ring with

MRS. GRADY'S SAINT MONDAY VOYAGE TO BATTERSEA.

Six-foot Timothy Glover,

 Son of the brandy-nos'd bugleman,

He was a general lover,

 Though he was only a fugleman;

Ogling Misses and Ma'ams,

 Listing, drilling, drumming'em —

Quick they shoulder'd his arms —

 Argumentum ad humming'em!

Mrs. Grady, in bonnet and scarf,

 Gave Thady the slip on Saint Monday,

With Timothy tripp'd to Hore's wharf,

 Which is close to the Glasgow and Dundee.

The river look'd swelling and rough,

 A waterman plump did invite her;

"One heavy swell is enough;

 I'm up to your craft-bring a lighter!"

They bargain'd for skipper and skiff,

 Cry'd Timothy, "This is a windy go!"

It soon blew a hurricane stiff,

 And blue look'd their noses as indigo!

"Lack-a-daisy! we're in for a souse!

 The fish won't to-day see a rummer set;

Land us at Somerset House,

Or else we shall both have a summerset!"

They through the bridge Waterloo whirl'd

    To Lambeth, a finer and fatter see!

Their shoulder-of-mutton sail furl'd,

    For a shoulder of mutton at Battersea.

Tim then rang for coffee and tea,

    Two Sally Luns and a crumpet.

"I don't like *brown* sugar," said he.

    "If you don't," thought the lad, "you may *lump* it."

To crown this delightful regale,

    Waiter! your stumps, jolly boy, stir;

A crown's worth of oysters and ale,

    Ere we give the sail homeward a hoister!"

"Of ale in a boiling-hot vat,

    My dear daddy dropp'd, and was, Ah! boil'd."

"A drop I can't relish of that

    In which your papa, boy, was parboil'd."

Fresh was the breeze, so was Tim:

    How pleasant the life of a Midge is;

King Neptune, my service to him!

    But I'll shoot Father Thames and his bridges!

His levee's a frosty-faced fair,

    When Jack freezes him and his flounders;

His river-horse is but a may'r,

And his Tritons are cockney ten-pounders!

"Tim Glover, my tale is a trite'un;

    I owe you a very small matter, see;

The shot I'll discharge, my polite'un,

    You paid for the wherry to Battersea.

"With powder I've just fill'd my horn;

    See this pocket-pistol! enough is it?

You'll twig, if a gentleman born,

    And say, f Mr. Grady, quant. sujfficit.'"

Mrs. Grady, as other wives do,

    Before my Lord May'r in his glory,

Brought Thady and Timothy too.

    Cry'd Hobler, "O what a lame story!

"You cruel Teague, lest there accrue ill,

    We'll just bind you over, Sir Thady,

To keep the peace." —"Keep the peace, jewel

    Not that piece of work, Mrs. Grady!"

His Lordship he gaped with surprise,

    And gave the go-by to his gravity;

His cheeks swallow'd up his two eyes,

    And lost in a laugh their concavity.

Then Grady gave Glover his fist,

    With, f 1{ Truce to the shindy between us I"

Each lad, when the ladies had kiss'd,

Cut off with his hatchet-faced Venus!

Ogling misses and ma'ams,

Listing, drilling, drumming'em —

Quick they shoulder'd his arms —

Argumentum ad humming 'em.

The concluding chorus found us at the end of our excursion. Barney Binnacle was liberally rewarded by Mr. Bosky; to each of his children he was made the bearer of some little friendly token; and with a heart lighter than it had been for many a weary day, he plied his oars homeward, contented and grateful.

"Talk of brimming measure," cried the Lauréat exultingly, "I go to a better market. The overflowings of an honest heart for *my* money!"

In former days undertakers would hire sundry pairs of skulls, and row to Death's Door * for a day's pleasure.

* "The Search after Claret, or a Visitation of the Vintners"
4to. 1691, names the principal London Taverns and their
Signs, as they then existed. But the most curious account is
contained in an old ballad called "London's Ordinary: or
every Man in his Humour" printed before 1600. There is not
only a humorous list of the taverns but of the persons who
frequented them. In those days the gentry patronised the
King's Head (in July 1664, Pepys dined at the "Ordinary"
there, when he went to Hyde Park to see the cavaliers of
Charles
II. in grand review); the nobles, the Crown: the knights,

the Golden Fleece; the clergy, the Mitre; the vintners, the
Three Tuns; the usurers, the Devil; the friars, the Nuns;
the ladies, the Feathers; the huntsmen, the Greyhound; the
citizens, the Horn; the cooks, the Holy Lamb; the drunkards,
the Man in the Moon; the cuckolds, the Ram; the watermen,
the Old Swan; the mariners, the Ship; the beggars, the Egg-
Shell and Whip; the butchers, the Bull; the fishmongers, the
Dolphin; the bakers, the Cheat Loaf; the tailors, the
Shears; the shoemakers, the Boot; the hosiers, the Leg; the
fletchers, the Robin Hood; the spendthrift, the Beggar's
Bush; the Goldsmiths, the Three Cups; the papists, the
Cross; the porters, the Labour in vain; the horse-coursers,
the White Nag. He that had no money might dine at the sign
of the Mouth; while
"The cheater will dine at the Checquer;

The pickpocket at the Blind Alehouse;
'Till taken and try'd, up Holborn they ride,
And make their end at the gallows."

222

Then it was not thought infra dig. (in for a dig?) to invite the grave-digger: the mutes were the noisiest of the party; nothing palled on the senses; and to rehearse the good things that were said and sung would add some pungent pages to the variorum editions of Joe Miller. But undertakers are grown gentlemanlike and unjolly, and Death's Door exhibits but a skeleton of what it was in the merry old times.

We were cordially received by their president, the comical coffin-maker, who, attired in his "Entertaining Gown" (a mourning cloak), introduced us to Mr. Crape, of Blackwall; Mr. Sable, of Blackman-street; Mr. Furnish of Blackfriars; and Mr. Blue-mould, of Blackheath: four truant teetotallers, who had obtained a furlough from their head-quarters, the Tea-Kettle and Toast-Rack at Aldgate pump. Messrs. Hatband and Stiflegig, and Mr. Shovelton, hailed us with a friendly grin, as if desirous of burying in oblivion the recent émeute at the Pig and Tinder-Box. The club were dressed in black (from Blackwell Hall), with white neckcloths and high shirt-collars; their clothes, from a peculiar and professional cut, seemed all to have been turned out by the same tailor; they marched with a measured step, and looked exceedingly grave and venerable. Dinner being announced, we were placed in the vicinity of the chair. On the table were black game and black currant-jelly; the blackstrap was brought up in the black bottle; the knives and forks had black handles; and Mr. Rasp, the shroud-raaker, who acted as vice, recommended, from his end of the festive board, some black pudding, or polony in mourning. The desert included black grapes and blackberries; the rules of the club were printed in black-letter; the toasts were written in black and white; the pictures that hung round the room were in black frames; a well-thummed Sir Richard Blackmore and Blackwood's Magazine lay on the mantel; the stove was radiant with black-lead; the old clock-case was ebony; and among the after-dinner chants "Black-ey'd Susan" was not forgotten. The host, Mr. Robert Death, had black whiskers, and the hostess some pretty black ringlets; the surly cook looked black because the dinner had been kept waiting; the waiter was a nigger; and the barmaid had given boots (a ci-devant blackleg at a billiard-table) a black eye. A black cat purred before the fire; a black-thorn grew opposite the door; the creaking old sign was blackened by the weather; and to complete the sable picture, three little blackguards spent their half-holiday in pelting at it! The banquet came off pleasantly. Mr. Merripall, whose humour was rich as crusted port, and lively as champagne, did the honours with his usual suaviter in modo, and was admirably supported by his two mutes from Turnagain-lane; by Mr. Catchpenny Crambo, the bard of Bleeding-Hart-Yard, who supplied "the trade" with epitaphs at the shortest notice; Mr. Sexton Shovelton, and Professor Nogo, F.R.S., F.S.A., M.R.S.L., LL.B., a learned lecturer on Egyptian mummies.

"Our duty," whispered Mr. Bosky, "is to

Hear, see, and say nothing.

Eat, drink, and pay nothing!"

After the usual round of loyal and patriotic toasts, Mr. Merripall called the attention of the brethren to the standing toast of the day.

"High Cockolorums and gentlemen! 'Tis easy to say 'live and let live;' but if everybody were to live we must die. Life is short. I wish-present company always excepted-it was as short as my speech! ——The grim tyrant!"

Verbum sat.; and there rose a cheer loud enough to have made Death demand what meant those noisy doings at his door.

"Silence, gentlemen, for a duet from brothers Hatband and Stiflegig."

Had toast-master Toole * bespoke the attention of the Guildhall grandees for the like musical treat from Gog and Magog, we should hardly have been more surprised. Mr. Bosky looked the incarnation of incredulity.

* This eminent professor, whose sobriquet is "Lungs" having
to shout the health of "the three present Consuls," at my
Lord Mayor's feast, proclaimed the health of the "Three per
Cent. Consols,"

After a few preliminary openings and shuttings of the eyes and mouth, similar to those of
a wooden Scaramouch when we pull the wires, Brothers Hatband and Stiflegig began (chro-
matique),

Hatband. When poor mutes and sextons have nothing

    to do,

        What should we do, brother?

Stiflegig. Look very blue I

Hatband. Gravediggers too?

Stiflegig. Sigh "malheureux!"

Hatband. Funerals few?

Stiflegig. Put on the screw!

Hatband. But when fevers flourish of bright scarlet

    hue,

        What should we do, brother?

Stiflegig. Dance fillalloo!= — —

Both. Winter to us is a jolly trump card, fine hot May makes a fat churchyard!

Stiflegig. Should all the world die, what the deuce

    should we do?

Hatband. I'll bury you, brother!

Stiflegig. I'll bury you!

Hatband. I'll lay you out.

Stiflegig. No doubt! no doubt!

Hatband. I'll make your shroud.

Stiflegig. You do me proud!

Hatband. I'll turn the screw.

Stiflegig. The same to you!

Hatband. When you're past ailing,

I'll knock a nail in!

Last of the quorum,

Ultimus Cockolorum!

When you're all dead and buried, zooks! what

shall I do?

Cockolorums in full chorus.

Sing High Cockolorum, and dance fillalloo!

"Gentlemen," said Mr. Merripall, again rising, "all charged? *Mulligrum's Pill!*"

Doctor Dose, a disciple of that art which is founded in conjecture and improved by murder, returned thanks on the part of Messrs. Mulligrum, Thorogonimble and Co. It was a proud day for the pill; which through good report and evil report had worked its way, and fulfilled his predictions that it would take and be taken. He would not ask the Cockolorums to swallow one. —Here the mutes made horribly wry faces, and shook their heads, as much as to say it would be of very little use if he did. —It was sufficient that the pill bore the stamp of their approbation, and the government three-halfpenny one; and he begged to add, that all pills without the latter, and the initials of Mulligrum, Thorogonimble, and Dose, were counterfeits.

The table sparkled with wit. Mr. Merripall cracked his walnuts and jokes, and was furiously facetious on Mr. Rasp, a rough diamond, who stood, or rather sat his horse-play raillery with dignified composure. But Lumber Troopers * are men, and Ralph Rasp was a past Colonel of that ancient and honourable corps. He grew more rosy about the gills, and discharged sundry short coughs and hysterical chuckles, that betokened a speedy ebullition. His preliminary re-mark merely hinted that no gentleman would think of firing off Joe Millers at the Lumber Troop: —Ergo, Mr. Merripall was no gentleman. The comical coffin-maker quietly responded that the troop was a nut which everybody was at liberty to crack for the sake of the *kernel*!

* This club was originally held at the Gentleman and Porter, New-street Square, and the Eagle and Child, Shoe Lane. The members were an awkward squad to the redoubtable City Trained Bands. It being found double hazardous to trust any one of them with a pinch of powder in his cartouch-box, and the points of their bayonets not unfrequently coming in sanguinary contact with each other's noses and eyes, their muskets were prudently changed for tobacco pipes, and their cartouches for papers of right Virginia. The privileges of the Lumber Trooper are great and manifold. He may sleep on any bulk not already occupied; he may knock down any watchman, provided the watchman does not knock him down first; and he is not obliged to walk home straight, if he be tipsy. The troop are supported by Bacchus and Ceres; their crest is an Owl; the shield is charged with a Punch Bowl

between a moon, a star, and a lantern. The punch is to
drink, and the moon and star are to light them home, or for
lack of either, the lantern. Their motto is, In Node
Lcetamur.

A quip that induced on the part of Mr. Hatband a loud laugh, while the more sombre features of
brother Stiflegig volunteered convulsions, as if they had been acted upon by a galvanic battery.
Mr. Rasp coolly reminded Mr. Merripall that the grapes were sour, Brother Pledge having
black-balled him. This drew forth a retort courteous, delivered with provoking serenity, that
the fiction of the ball came most opportunely from a gentleman who had always three blue
ones at everybody's service! The furnace that glowed in Mr. Rasp's two eyes, and the hearings
of his bosom discovered the volcano that burned beneath his black velvet vest. His waistband
seemed ready to burst. Never before did he look so belicose! Now, Mr. Bosky, who loved
fun much, but harmony more, thinking the joke had been carried quite far enough, threw in
a conciliatory word by way of soothing angry feelings, which so won the Lumber Trooper's
naturally kind heart, that he rose from his seat.

"Brother Merripall, you are a chartered libertine, and enjoy the privilege of saying what you
will. But-you were a little too hard upon the troop-indeed you were! My grandfather was a
Lumber Trooper-my father, too-you knew my father, Marmaduke Merripall."

"And I knew a right honourable man! And I know another right honourable man, my very
good friend, his son! And-but — — —"

'Tis an old saying and a true one, that adversity tries friends. So does a momentary quarrel, or
what is more germane to our present purpose, a mischievous badinage, in which great wits and
small ones too, will occasionally indulge. Mr. Merripall had been wront-good naturedly! —to
make Mr. Rasp his butt; who, though he was quite big enough for one, sometimes felt the
sharp arrows of the comical coffin-maker's wit a thorn in his "too-too solid flesh." The troop
was his tender point.

"And who has not his tender point?" said Mr. Bosky, "except the man that caught cold of
his own heart, and died of it!"

The hand of Mr. Rasp was instantly stretched forth, and met more than half way by that
of Mr. Merripall.

"Brother," said the president, "let me make amends to the troop by requesting you will propose me as a member. Only," and he shot a sly glance from his eye, "save me from the balls,
black and blue, of that Presbyterian pawnbroker, Posthumus Pledge of Pye-corner."

Mr. Rasp promised to comply, and moreover to set forth his friend's military prowess to
the best advantage.

"I think," said he, "your division stormed the Press-yard, and captured the whipping-post,
during the Aldersgate Street Volunteer campaigning in 1805."

"Right, brother Ralph, and when the Finsbury awkward squad routed your left wing in the
City Road, and you all ran helter-skelter into the boiled buttock of beef shop in the Old Bailey,
we valiant sharp-shooters protected your flank, and covered your inglorious retreat!" And he
entertained the company with this appropriate recitation: —

> When all were in alarms,
>
> (Boney threat'ning to invade us,)
>
> And ("See the Conquering Hero comes!")
>
> General Wheeler, general dealer
>
> In coffee, treacle, tea, tobacco, plums,

Snuff, sugar, spices, at wholesale prices,

And figs —(which, 's life!

　　At Fife

　　He sold in drums!) —

Would up and down parade us,

And cry, "Present!" and "Shoulder arms!"

When pert apprentices, God bless us!

And tailors did address and dress us,

With "Stand at ease!" (up to your knees

In mud and mire) "Make ready! Fire!"

Singeing the curls of Moses Muggs, Esquire —

A Briton, hot for fight and fame,

　　Burning to give the foes of Bull

　　Their belly-full,

Limp'd forth-but no admission! —he was lame.

"Lame!" cried the Briton; "zounds! I say,

I came to fight, and not to run away!"

"The red-coat," continued Mr. Merripall, "has no vision beyond '*eyes right*' He would march till doomsday, unless commanded to halt, and everlastingly maintain the same poker-like position, if the word were not given him to stand at ease. He goes forth to kill at a great rate," (Dr. Dose pricked up his ears,) "and be killed at a small one per diem (the mutes looked glum,) "carrying into battle a heart of oak, and out of it a timber toe!"

"Our visitors," was the next toast.

"Gentlemen," said the president, "we cannot afford the expensive luxury of drinking your healths; but we sincerely join in 'my service to you.'"

Here Dr. Dose passed over to us his box-not for a pinch, but a pill! which pill, though we might drink, we declined to swallow. Mr. Rasp was in high feather, and plied the four teetotallers very liberally with wine. Seeing the comical coffin-maker in committee with his two mutes, he chirruped joyously,

Mr. Chairman, I'll thank you not

Thus to keep the wine in the pound;

Better by half a cannon shot

Stop than the bottle! —so push it round.

Summer is past, and the chilling blast

Of winter fades the red red rose;

But wine sheds perfume, and its purple bloom

All the year round like the ruby glows!

Fill what you like, but drink what you fill,

Though it must be a bumper, a bumper, or nil.

Water congeals in frost and snows,

But summer and winter the red wine flows!

Now, my Cockolorums, for a volley in platoons!

Chorus.

The blossoms fall, and the leaves are sear,

And merry merry Christmas will soon be here;

I wish you, gentles, a happy new year,

A pocket full of money, and a barrel full of beer!

A messenger arrived with a despatch for Mr. Merripall, announcing the demise of Alderman Callipash. There was an immediate movement on the part of the mutes.

"Gentlemen," said the president, "no such violent hurry; the alderman will wait for us. Our parting toast first —*The Dance of Death!* Come, brother Crape, strike up the tune, and lead the carant."

Original

Mr. Crape practised an introductory caper, in the process of which he kicked the shins of one Cockolorum, trod upon the gouty toe of another, and then led off, the club keeping the figure with becoming gravity, and chanting in full chorus:

Undertakers, hand in hand,

Are a jovial merry band;

Tho' their looks are lamentable,

And their outward man is sable,

Who on this side Charon's ferry

Are so blythe as those that bury?

Hark! hark! the Parish Clerk

Tunes his pitch-pipe for a lark!

As we gaily trip along

Booms the bell's deep, dull ding-dong!

Freaking, screaking, out of breath,

Thus we dance the *Dance of Death!*

The cricket cries, the owl it hoots,

Music meet for dancing mutes!

When burns brightly blue the taper,

Sextons, 'tis your time to caper.

Now our song and dance are done,

Home we hasten every one.

Messrs. Crape, Crambo, Sable, Shovelton, Hatband, and Stiflegig, joined a pleasant party outside of a hearse that had been doing duty in the neighbourhood; and an empty mourning-coach accommodated Mr. Rasp, Mr. Bluemould, Dr. Dose, and Professor Nogo. Mr. Furnish, and a few, heated with wine, took water; but as the moon had just emerged from behind a black cloud, and shone with mild lustre, we preferred walking, particularly with the jocular companionship of Mr. Bosky and Mr. Merripall. And Death's door was closed for the night.

CHAPTER IV.

Had we been inclined to superstition, what a supernatural treat had been the discourse of Mr. Merripall! His tales of "goblins damned" were terrible enough to have bristled up our hair till it lifted our very hats off our very heads. His reminiscences of resurrection men * were extensive and curious; he knew their "whereabouts" for ten miles round London.

 * Two resurrection men stumbling over a fellow dead drunk in the kennel, bagged, and bore him away to a certain anatomist. The private bell gave a low tinkle, the side-door down a dark court opened noiselessly, the sack was emptied of its contents into the cellar, and the fee paid down. In an hour or two after, the same ceremony (the subject being really defunct) was repeated. The bell sounded a third time, and the anatomical charnel-house received another inmate. The tippler, having now slept off his liquor, began to grope about, and finding all dark, and himself he knew not where, bellowed lustily. This was just as the door was closing on the resurrection men, who being asked what should be done with the noisy fellow, answered coolly, "Keep him till you want him!"

We mean not to insinuate that Mr. Merripall had any share in bringing his departed customers to light again. He was a virtuoso, and his cabinet comprised a choice collection of the veritable cords on which the most notorious criminals had made their transit from this world to the next. He was rich in mendacious caligraphy. Malefactors of liberal education obligingly favoured him with autograph confessions, and affectionate epistles full of penitence and piety; while the less learned condescendingly affixed their contrite crosses to any document that autographmania might suggest. The lion of his library was an illustrated copy of the Newgate Calendar, or New Drop Miscellany, and round his study its principal heroes hung-in frames! He boasted of having shaken by the hand-an honour of which Old Bailey amateurs are proudly emulous-all the successful candidates for the Debtors' Door for these last twenty years; and when Mr. Bosky declared that he had never saluted a dying felon with "My dear sir!" coveted his acquaintance, and craved his autograph, he sighed deeply for the Laureat's want of taste, grew pensive for about a second, and then, as if suddenly recollecting himself, exclaimed,

"Gentlemen, we are but a stone's throw from the *Owl and Ivy Bush*, where a society called 'The Blinkers' hold their nightly revels: it will well repay your curiosity to step in and take a peep at them. Their president has one eye permanently shut, and the other partially open; the vice has two open eyes, blinking 'like winkin' all the members are more or less somniferous; and though none of them are allowed to fall fast asleep at the club, it is contrary to etiquette to be wide awake. Their conversation is confined to monosyllables, their talk, like their tobacco, being short-cut. Their three cheers are three yawns; they sit round the table with their eyes shut, and their mouths open, the gape, or gap, being filled up with their pipes, from which rise clouds of smoke that make their red noses look like lighted lamps in a fog. To the Reverend Nehemiah Nosebags, their chaplain, I owe the honour of becoming a member; for happening to sit under his proboscis and pulpit, my jaws went through such a gaping exercise at his soporific word of command, that he proposed me as a highly promising probationer, and my election was carried amidst an unanimous chorus of yawns."

"Here" exclaimed Mr. Bosky, "is the Owl and Ivy Bush."

"No," rejoined Mr. Merripall, "'tis the Three Jolly Trumpeters. On the opposite side of the way is the Owl and Ivy Bush."

Mr. Bosky gazed at the sign, and then, with no small degree of wonderment, at Mr. Merripall. The Lauréat of Little Britain looked signs and wonders!

"I'll take my affidavit to the Owl!" raising his eye-glass to the solemn bird that winked wickedly beneath a newly-varnished cauliflower-wig of white paint; "and though the Ivy Bush looks much more like a birch broom, it looks still less like a Jolly Trumpeter."

"Egad, you're right!" said the comical coffin-maker; "though, to my vision, it seems as if both houses had changed places since I last saw them."

The contents of a brace of black bottles flowing under Mr. Merripall's satin waistcoat, and their fumes ascending to what lay within the circumference of his best beaver, might possibly account for this phenomenon.

"Hollo!'" cried the comical coffin-maker, as an uproarious cheer and the knocking of knuckles upon the tables proclaimed merry doings at the Owl and Ivy Bush, "the Blinkers were not wont to be so boisterous. What a riotsome rattle! —hark!"

And the following chorus resounded through the Owl and Ivy Bush: —

We're jovial, happy, and gay, boys!

We rise with the moon, which is surely full soon,

Sing with the owl, our tutelar fowl,

Laugh and joke at your go-to-bed folk,

Never think-but what we shall drink,

Never care-but on what we shall fare —

Turning the night into day, boys!

"What think you of that, Mr. Merripall?" said the Lauréat of Little Britain.

We entered the room, and a company more completely wide awake it was never our good fortune to behold.

"Surely," whispered Mr. Bosky, "that vociferous gentleman in the chair can never be your one-eye-shut-and-the-other-half-open president; nor he at the bottom of the table, with his organs of vision fixed, like the wooden Highlander's that stands entry over 'Snuff and Tobacco,' your blinking vice."

Mr. Merripall looked *incredulus odi*, and would have made a capital study for Tam O'Shanter.

"Have the kindness to introduce me to the Rev. Nehemiah Nosebags," said Mr. Bosky, again addressing his mute and mystified companion.

"Why not ask me to trot out the Pope?" replied the somewhat crotchety and comical coffin-maker.

A peal of laughter and huzzas echoed from the twin tavern over the way, and at the same moment mine host, who was very like a China joss, puffed up stairs, looking as wild as "a wilderness of monkeys," with the astounding news that a trick had been played upon himself and brother publican by Lord Larkinton, Sir Frederick Fitz-fun, and the Honourable Colonel Frolick, who had taken the liberty of transposing their respective signs. Hence a straggling party of the *Peep o' day Boys*, whose proper location was the Three Jolly Trumpeters, had intruded into the taciturnity and tobacco of the Owl and Ivy Bush. This unravelled the cross purposes that at one time seemed to call in question the "*mens sana in corpore sano*" of Mr. Merripall.

"Many men," addressing Mr. Bosky, as they jogged out of the Three Jolly Trumpeters, "like to enjoy a reputation which they do not deserve; but" —here Mr. Merripall looked serious, and in right earnest —"to be thought tipsy, my good friend, without having had the gratification of getting so, is,

> 'Say what men will, a pill
>
> Bitter to swallow, and hard of digestion.'"

And the Lauréat of Little Britain fully agreed with the axiom so pertinaciously and poetically laid down by the comical coffin-maker.

The three practical jokers now emerged from their ambush to take a more active part in the sports. With the Peep of day Boys they would have stood no chance, for each member carried in his hand an executive fist, to which the noble tricksters were loth to cotton, for fear of being worsted. Lord Larkinton led the van up the stairs of the Owl and Ivy Bush, and dashing among the Blinkers, selected their president for his partner; Colonel Frolick patronized the vice; and Sir Frederick Fitzfun made choice of the Rev. Nehemiah Nosebags. The rest of the club were arranged to dance in pairs—a very stout member with a very lean one, and a very short one with a very tall one-so that there was variety, without being charming. Each danced with his pipe in his mouth. It was no pipe no dance.

They led off in full puff, dancing about, upon, and on all-fours under the tables. The fire-irons were confided to a musical brother, with instructions to imitate the triangles; and as the company danced round the room-the room, returning the compliment, danced round them.

The club having been capered within an inch of their lives, Lord Larkinton begged Mr. Bo-peep to favour them with Jim Crow, consenting to waive the *jump obligato*, in consideration of his previous exertions. But he must sing it in character; and in the absence of lamp-black and charcoal, the corks were burnt, to enable Sir Frederick Fitzfun and Colonel Fro lick (my Lord holding his partner's physiognomy between his palms like a vice-the vice and Mr. Nosebags looking ruefully on) to transform Mr. Bopeep into a negro chorister. His sable toilet being completed, the president opened with "*Jim Crow*;" but his memory failing, he got into "*Sich a gittin' up stairs.*" At fault again, he introduced the "Last rose of summer," then "The boaty rows" "Four-and-twenty fiddlers all of a row" "Old Rose and burn the bellows" "Blow high, blow low" "Three Tooley Street Tailors" "By the deep nine"

"I know a bank" and "You must not sham Abraham Newland" —all of which he sang to the same tune, "Jim Crow" being the musical bed of torture to which he elongated or curtailed them. As an accompaniment to this odd medley, the decanters and tumblers flew about in all directions, some escaping out at window, others irradiating the floor with their glittering particles. Colonel Frolick, brandishing a poker, stood before the last half inch of a once re-splendent mirror contemplating his handiwork and mustaches, and ready to begin upon the gold frame. Every square of crown glass having been beaten out, and every hat's crown beaten in, Lord Larkinton politely asked the Rev. Nehemiah Nosebags to crown all with a song. The chaplain, looking as melancholy as the last bumper in a bottle before it's buzzed, snuffled, in a Tabernacle twang,

"The-e bir-ird that si-ings in yo-on-der ca-age."

"Make your bird sing a little more lively," shouted my Lord, "or we shan't get out of the cage to-night!"

Many a true word spoken in jest; for mine host, thinking his Lordship's next joke might be to unroof, batter down, or set fire to the Owl and Ivy Bush, rushed into the room marshalling a posse of the police, when a battle royal ensued, and sconces and truncheons, scraping ac-quaintance with each other, made "a ghostly rattle." Disappointed of Mr. Nosebags' stave, and having no relish for those of the constables, we stole away, leaving Colonel Frolick beating a tattoo on some dozen of oil-skin hats; Lord Larkinton and Sir Frederick Fitzfun pushing forward the affrighted

Bopeep and his brethren to bear the brunt of the fray; an intolerable din of screaming, shouting servants, ostlers and helpers; and the barking of a kennel of curs, as if "the dogs of three parishes" had been congregated and let loose to swell the turmoil.

"The sons of care are always sons of night." Those to whom the world's beauteous garden is a cheerless desert hide their sorrows in its friendly obscurity. If in one quarter the shout of revelry is heard, as the sensualist reels from his bacchanalian banquet-in another, the low moan of destitution and misery startles night's deep silence, as they retire to some bulk or doorway to seek that repose which seldom lights but "on lids unsullied with a tear." We had parted with our merry companions, and were hastening homeward, when, passing by one of those unsightly pauper prison-houses that shame and deface our land, we beheld a solitary light flickering before a high narrow casement, the grated bars of which told a mournful tale, that the following melody, sang with heart-searching pathos, too truly confirmed: —

A wand'rer, tho' houseless and friendless I roam,

Ah! stranger, I once knew the sweets of a home;

The world promised fair, and its prospects were bright,

My pillow was peace, and I woke to delight.

Do you know what it is from loved kindred to part?

The sting of the scorpion to feel in your heart?

To hear the deep groan of an agonised sire?

To see, broken-hearted, a mother expire?

To hear bitter mockings an answer to prayer?

Scorn pointing behind, and before you despair! —

To hunger a prey, and to passion a slave —

No home but the outcast's, no rest but the grave!

To feel your brain wander, as reason's faint beam

Illumines the dark, frenzied, sorrowful dream;

The present and past! —See! the moon she rides higher

In mild tranquil beauty, and shoots sparks of fire!

The music ceased, the pauper-prison door opened, and a gentle voice, addressing another, was heard to say, "Tend her kindly-my purse shall be yours, and, what is of far higher import, though less valued here, God's holiest blessing. Every inmate of these gloomy walls has a claim upon your sympathy; but this hapless being demands the most watchful solicitude. She is a bruised reed bowed down by the tempest —a heart betrayed and bleeding —a brow scathed by the lightning of heaven! I entered upon this irksome duty but to mitigate the cruel hardships that insolent authority imposes upon the desolate and oppressed. With my associates in office I wage an unequal warfare; but my humble efforts, aided by yours, may do much to alleviate sufferings that we cannot entirely remove. She has lucid intervals, when the dreadful truth flashes upon her mind. Smooth, then, the pillow for her burning brow, bind up her broken heart, and the gracious Power that inflicts this just, but awful retribution will welcome you as an angel of mercy, when mercy, and mercy only, shall be your passport to his presence! Good night."

The door closed, and the speaker-unseeing, but not unseen-hurried away. It was Uncle Timothy!

Bulky as a walrus, and as brutal, out-frogging the frog in the fable, an over-fed, stolid, pudding-crammed libel upon humanity, sailing behind his double chin, and with difficulty preserving his equilibrium, though propped up by the brawny arm of Catspaw Crushem, Mr. Poor Law Guardian Pinch —a hiccup anticipating an oath-commanded us to "move on."

Addressing his relieving officer, he stammered out, *en passant*, "Hark'e, Catspaw, don't forget to report that crazy wagrant to the Board tomorrow. We'll try whether cold water, a dark crib, and a straight jacket won't spoil her caterwauling. The cretur grows quite obstroperous upon our gruel" (!!!)

      O England! merrie England!

      Once nurse of thriving men;

      I've learn'd to look on many things,

      With other eyes since then!

CHAPTER V.

In the narrowest part of the narrow precincts of Cloth Fair there once stood a long, rambling, low-roofed, gable-fronted hostelrie, with carved monsters frightfully deformed, and of hideous obesity, grinning down upon the passengers from every side. Its exterior colour was a dingy yellow; it had little antique casements, casting "a dim," if not a "religious light," within; the entrance was by a low porch, with seats on each side, where, on summer days, when leaves are green, the citizen in the olden time might breathe the fresh air of the surrounding meadows, and rest and regale himself. The parlour was panelled with oak, and round it hung The March to Finchley, the Strolling Players, and Southwark Fair, half obscured by dust, in narrow black frames, with a tarnished gold beading. An ancient clock ticked (like some of the customers!) in a dark corner; on the high grotesquely carved mantelpiece piped full-dressed shepherds and shepherdesses, in flowery arbours of Chelsea china; from the capacious ingle projected two wooden arms, on which the elbows of a long race of privileged old codgers had successively rested for more than three centuries; the egg* of an ostrich tattooed by the flies, and a silent aviary of stuffed birds, (monsters of fowls Î) which had been a roost for some hundreds of generations of spiders, depended from a massy beam that divided the ceiling; a high-backed venerable arm-chair, with Robin Hood and his merry men in rude effigy, kept its state under an old-fashioned canopy of faded red arras; a large fire blazed cheerfully, the candles burned bright, and a jovial party, many of whose noses burned blue, were assembled to celebrate for the last time their nocturnal merriments under the old roof, that on the morrow (for *improvement* had stalked into the Fair!) was to be levelled to the ground.

"Gentlemen," said the President, who was a rosy evergreen, with "fair round belly," and a jolly aspect, "a man and boy, for forty years, have I been a member of the *Robin Hood*, and fanned down my punch in this room! What want we with mahogany, French-polished, and fine chim-ney-glasses? Cannot every brother see his good-looking face in a glass of his own? Or a gas-lamp before the door, with a dozen brass burners? Surely our 'everlasting bonfire lights' will show us the way in! This profanation is enough to make our jovial predecessors, the heroes of the Tennis Court, the Mohocks, and Man-hunters of Lincoln's Inn Fields tremble in their tombs! —But I don't see Mr. Bosky."

It would have been odd if the President had seen Mr. Bosky; for he sat wedged betwixt two corporation members, whose protuberances, broad shoulders, and dewlaps effectually obscured him from view.

"Here am I, Mr. President."

"But where is Uncle Timothy?"

"That," replied the Lauréat, "can my cousin's wife's uncle's aunt's sister best say. Three hours ago I left him on the top of St. Paul's; by this time he may be at the bottom of the Thames Tunnel, or at Madame Tussaud's, *tête-à-tête* with Oliver Cromwell, Napoleon, and Young Oxford." A murmur of disappointment rose from the brethren, with a benediction on distant relations that did not keep a hundred miles off.

"Gentlemen," resumed the President, "'if sack and sugar be a sin, God help the wicked!' Since we cannot have Uncle Timothy's good company, we will have his good health. Uncle Timothy, with three!"

A heartfelt cheer made the old hostelrie ring again.

Uprose the Lauréat-but a twinkle from the eye of the President to a covey of intelligent cronies, on whom the scarlet rays of his countenance more intensely fell, produced a supplementary cheer that shook the Cloth-quarter.

Mr. Bosky was thrown a little off his balance. He paused-flushed-but his heart having left his mouth, he replenished the vacuum with a bumper, assuring the company that they might as soon expect from him a long face as a long speech. For their kind wishes to Uncle Timothy he thanked them from the bottom of his soul-and glass!

"Gentlemen, when the money-grub retires, no regrets follow him to his unsociable crib; nothing misses him but the everlasting counter, to which cupidity has so long nailed his bird-limed fingers. How different with a generous spirit! with whom are associated the remembrance of happy hours snatched from the dull realities of life! This day terminates the mercantile career of our worthy President. May he be blest in his retirement! Gentlemen, the health of Mr. Deputy Doublechin —(no skylights, Brother Blizzard!) —upstanding, with all the honours!"

The two corporation members having taken "their whack," were not to be roused without a smart thump on the shoulder. The deputy returned thanks in a pleasant vein.

"My friends," he added, "short reckonings-you know the old adage —I am a song in your debt, and as the one I now volunteer will be the last of the many I have sung in this cosey corner, my vocal Vale shall be our tutelary freebooter."

And with "full-throated ease" this jovial impersonation of John Bull chanted —

ROBIN HOOD.

Robin Hood! Robin Hood I a lawgiver good.

Kept his High Court of Justice in merry Sherwood.

No furr'd gown, or fee, wig, or bauble had he;

But his bench was a verdant bank under a tree!

And there sat my Lord of his own good accord,

With his Peers of the forest to keep watch and ward;

To arbitrate sure between rich and poor,

The lowly oppress'd and the proud evil doer.

His nobles they are without riband or star,

No 'scutcheon have they with a sinister bar;

But Flora with leaves them a coronet weaves,

And their music is-hark! when the horn winds afar.

The chaplain to shrive this frolicsome hive

Is a fat curtail Friar, the merriest alive!

His quarter-staff, whack! greets a crown with a crack!

And, 'stead of rough sackcloth, his penance is sack!

The peerless in beauty receives their fond duty,

Her throne is the greensward, her canopy flowers!

What huntress so gay as the Lady of May?

The Queen of the Woodlands, King Robin's, and ours!

His subjects are we, and'tis centuries three

Since his name first re-echo'd beneath this roof-tree!

With Robin our King let the old rafters ring!

They have heard their last shout! they have seen their

last spring!

And though we may sigh for blythe moments gone by,

Yet why should we sorrow, bold foresters, why?

Since those who come after their full share of laughter

Shall have, when death's sables have veil'd you and I.

As the club was literary as well as convivial, such of the members as the gods had made poetical, critical, or historical, favoured the company at these appointed meetings with their lucubrations. Uncle Timothy's had been antiquarian and critical, Mr. Bosky's facetious and vocal: —

A merry song is better far

Than sharp lampoon or witty libel.

One brother, Mr. Boreum, who had got the scientific bee in his bonnet, was never so happy as when he could detect a *faux pas* in the sun's march, discover a new mountain in the moon, or add another stick to the bundle that has been so long burthensome to the back of the man in it! and Mr. Pigtail Paddlebox, a civil engineer, maintained, by knock-me-down-proof-positive, that Noah's Ark was an antediluvian steamer of some five hundred horse-power! The evening's contribution was Uncle Timothy's, The Second Part of the *Merrie Mysteries of Bartlemy Fair*, which Mr. Bosky having promised to read with good emphasis and discretion, the President's hammer commanded silence, and he proceeded with his task.

CHAPTER VI.

The world is a stage; men and women are the players; chance composes the piece; Fortune (blind jade!) distributes the parts; the fools shift the scenery; the philosophers are the spectators; the rich occupy the boxes; the powerful, the pit; and the poor, the gallery. The forsaken of Lady Fortune snuff the candles-Folly makes the concert-and Time drops the curtain!

In a half sportive, half melancholy mood, we record this description of the tragi-comedy of human life. To weep, like Heraclitus, might exalt us to philanthropists; to make the distresses of mankind a theme of derision would brand us as buffoons. Though inclining to the example of Democritus-for life is too short seriously to grapple with the thousand absurdities that daily demand refutation-we take the middle course.

Far be from us the reproach of having no regard for our fellow-men, or pity for their errors!

Every one views a subject according to his particular taste and disposition. * Some happy fancies can find

"Tongues in trees, books in the running brooks,

Sermons in stones, and good in every thing."

   * To view Niagara's Falls one day
A Priest and Tailor took their way;
The Parson cried, while wrapt in wonder,
And listening to the cataract's thunder,
"Lord! how thy works amaze our eyes,
And fill our hearts with vast surprise!"
The Tailor merely made this note: —
"Lord! what a place to sponge a coat!"

Such would draw a truth from a tumbler, and a moral from a mountebank!

"Look through my glass," says the philosopher, "Through mine" says the metaphysician. "Will your honour please to take a peep through my glass?" inquires the penny showman. The penny showman's glass for our money!

We are not to be hoodwinked by high-sounding authorities, who, like Tom Thumb, manufacture the giants they take the credit of killing! Bernier tells us, that whenever the Great Mogul made a remark, no matter how commonplace, the Omrahs lifted up their hands and cried "Wonder! wonder! wonder!" And their proverb saith, If the King exclaims at noon-day, "It is night" you are to rejoin, "Behold the moon and stars!"

Curious reader, picture to yourself a town-bred bachelor, with flowing wig, brocaded waistcoat, rolled silk stockings, and clouded cane, marching forth to take a survey of Bartholomew Fair, in the year 1701. Fancy the prim gentleman describing what he saw to some inquiring country kinsman in the following laconic epistle, and you will have a lively contemporary sketch of Smithfield Rounds.

Cousin Corydon,

Having no business of my own, * nor any desire to meddle with other people's, no wife to chin-music me, no brats to torment me, I dispelled the megrims by a visit to St. Bartholomew.

   * "A Walk to Smith-field; or, a True Description of the
Humours of Bartholomew Fair. 1701."

The fair resembled a camp; only, instead of standing rank and file, the spectators were shuffled together like little boxes in a sharper's Luck-in-a-Bag. With much ado I reached Pye-Corner, where our English Sampson exhibited. Having paid for a seat three stories high in this wooden tent of iniquity, I beheld the renowned Man of Kent, * equipped like an Artillery Ground champion at the mock storming of a castle, lift a number of weights, which hung round him like bandaliers about a Dutch soldier.

"He fired a cannon, and with his own strength

Lifted it up, although 'twas of great length;

He broke a rope which did restrain two horses,

They could not break it with their two joint forces!'

* "The English Sampson, William Joy, aged twenty-four years, was horn in the Isle of Thanet, in Kent. He is a man of prodigious strength, of which he hath given proofs before his Majesty King William the Third, at Kensington, their Royal Highnesses the Prince and Princess of Denmark, and most of the nobility, at the Theatre Royal in Dorset Garden. AD. 1699."
"James Miles, from Sadler's Wells in Islington, now keeps

the Gun Musick Booth in Smithfield Rounds where the Famous Indian Woman lifts six hundred weight with the hair of her head, and walks about the booth with it."
Topham, the Strong Man, lifted three hogsheads of water,

weighing 183 lbs. the 28th of May 1741, in honour of Admiral Vernon, before thousands of people, in Bath Street, Cold-Bath-Fields. In his early years he exhibited at Bartholomew Fair. He united the strength of twelve men. The ostler of the Virgin's Inn having offended him, he took one of the spits from the kitchen and bent it round his neck like a handkerchief; but as he did not choose to tuck the ends in the ostler's bosom, the iron cravat excited the laughter of the company, till he condescended to untie it. He died by his own hand, on the 10th August 1749, the victim of his wife's infidelity.
"The Wonderful Strong and Surprising Persian Dwarf, three

feet six inches high. He is fifty-six years old, speaks eighteen languages, sings Italian songs, dances to admiration, and with ropes tied to his hair, when put over his shoulders, lifts the great stone A." This "great stone" is half as big as the little Sampson himself!

I then jostled to a booth, in which was only a puppet-show, * where, for twopence, I saw Jepthas rash Vow; or, The Virgins Sacrifice. In I went, almost headlong, to Pinkethmans Medley, ** to see the Vaulting of the horse, and the famous wooden puppets dance a minuet and a ballet.
* Only a Puppet-show! —Marry-come-up! Goodman Chronicler, doth not the mechanist, a very Prometheus, give life,

spirit, and motion to what was a mopstick or the leg of
ajoint-stool?

** "At Pinkethman, Mills, and Bullock's booth, over-against

the Hospital Gate, will be presented The Siege of Barcelona,
or the Soldier's Fortune; containing the comical exploits of
Captain Blunderbuss and his man Squib; his adventures with
the Conjuror, and a surprising scene where he and Squib are
enchanted. Also the Diverting Humours of Corporal Scare-
Devil. To which will be added, The wonderful Performance of
Mr. Simpson, the vaulter, lately arrived from Italy. The
musick, songs, and dances are by the best performers, whom
Mr. Pinkethman has entertained at extraordinary charge,
purely to please the town."

At the Dutch Womans booth, * the Wheelbarrow dance, by a little Flemish girl ten years old,
was in truth a miracle! A bill having been thrust into my hand, of a man and woman lighting
for the breeches. **

    * "You will see the famous Dutchwoman's side-capers,
upright-capers, cross-capers, and back-capers on the tight
rope. She walks, too, on the slack rope, which no woman but
herself can do." —"Oh, what a charming sight it was to see
Madam What-d'ye-call-her swim it along the stage between her
two gipsy daughters! You might have sworn they were of right
Dutch extraction." —A Comparison between the Two Stages,
1702.
Dancing on the rope was forbidden by an order of Parliament,

July 17, 1647. The most celebrated rope-dancer on record is
Jacob Hall, who lived in the reign of King Charles the
Second. His feats of agility and strength, and the
comeliness of his person, gained him universal patronage,
and charmed, in particular, that imperious wanton, the
Duchess of Cleveland. Henry the Eighth, in one of his
"Progresses" through the city of London, "did spye a man
upon the uppermost parte of St. Powle's Church: the man did
gambol and balance himself upon his head, much to the fright
and dismay of the multitude that he might breake his necke.
On coming down, he did throw himselfe before the King
beseechingly, as if for some reward for the exployt;
whereupon the King's highness, much to his surprise, ordered
him to prison as a roge and sturdy vagabonde." —Black-
Letter Chronicle, Printed in 1565.
** Our facetious friends, Messrs. Powell and Luffingham, at

"Root's Booth"

I had the curiosity to look at this family picture, which turned out to be the Devil and Doctor
Faustus, * the wife representing the Devil, and the husband the Doctor!

Original

The tent of the English rope-dancers ** the rabble took by storm; —
    * In a Bartlemy Fair bill, temp. James II. after the
representation of "St. George for England," wherein is shown
how the valiant "saint slew the venomous Dragon," the public
were treated with "the Life and Death of Doctor Foster,
(Faustus?) with such curiosity, that his very intrails turns
into snakes and sarpints!"
** On the top of the following bill is a woodcut of the

"Ladder Dance," and the "two Famous High German children"
vaulting on the tight rope. "At Mr. Barnes's Booth, between
the Croton Tavern and the Hospital Gate, with the English
Flag flying on the top, you will see Mr. Barnes dancing with
a child standing upon his shoulders; also tumbling through
hoops, over halberds, over sixteen men's heads, and over a
horse with a man on his back, and two boys standing upright
upon each arm! With the merry conceits of Pickle Herring and
his son Punch."

—but myself and a few heroes stood the brunt of the fray, and saw the Ladder Dance, and
excellent vaulting on the slack and tight rope, by Mr. Barnes and the Lady Mary; I had a
month's mind to a musick booth; but the reformation of manners having suppressed them all
but one, I declined going thither, for fear of being thought an immoral person, and paid my
penny to take a peep at the Creation of the World. Then

> "To the Cloisters ** I went, where the gallants resort,
>
> And all sorts and sizes come in for their sport,
>
> Whose saucy behaviour and impudent air
>
> Proclaim'd them the subjects of Bartlemy Fair!
>
> There strutted the sharper and braggart, (a brace!)
>
> And there peep'd a goddess with mask on her face!= — —
>
> I view'd all the shops where the gamblers did raffle,
>
> And saw the young ladies their gentlemen baffle;
>
> For though the fine sparks might sometimes have good
>
>   fate,
>
> The shop had the money, the lass had the plate."

* The Lady Mary, the daughter of a noble Italian family, was
born in Florence, and immured in a nunnery, but eloped with
a Merry Andrew, who taught her his professional tricks. She
danced with great dexterity on the rope, from which (when
urged by the avarice of her inhuman partner to exhibit
during a period of bodily weakness) she fell, and died
instantaneously.
** "The Cloister in Bartholomew Fair, a poem, London.

Thus ends the ramble, Cousin Corydon! of (Thine, as thy spouse's own,) Ingleberry Griskin.

Thanks! worthy chronicler of ancient St. Bartlemy.

Will Pinkethman was a first-rate comedian. The biographer of his contemporary, Spiller, says, "the managers of the Haymarket and Drury Lane always received too much profit from Pinkey's phiz, to encourage anybody to put that out of countenance!" And Pope refers to one popular qualification that he possessed, viz. eating on the stage (as did Dicky Suett, in after days, Dicky Gossip, to wit!) with great comic effect.

> "And idle Cibber, how he breaks the laws,
>
> To make poor Pinkey eat with vast applause!"

He was celebrated for speaking prologues and epilogues. * He realised a good fortune by his Puppet-show, and kept a booth at Bartholomew Fair. Two volumes of "Jests" * bear his name. Many of them are as broad as they are long. His love-letter to Tabitha, the fair Quakeress, signed "Yea and Nay, from thy brother in the light," is wickedly jocose.

Thus Bartholomew Fair, in 1701, boasted its full complement of mimes, mountebanks, vaulters, costermongers, *** gingerbread women, ("ladies of the basket!") puppet-shows, **** physiognoscopography —

* Particularly "The New Comical Epilogue of Some-Body and
No-Body, spoken by way of Dialogue between Mr. Pink-ethman
and Jubilee Dicky" (Norris, so christened from his playing
Beau Clincher in Farquhar's Trip to the Jubilee.)
** "Pinkethman's Jests, or Wit Refin'd, being a new year's

gift for young gentlemen and ladies, 1721, First and Second
Parts.'7 A fine mezzotinto portrait of Pinkethman,
represents him in a laced coat and a flowing wig, holding in
his hand a scroll, on which is inscribed, "Ridentibus
arrident Vultus
*** Archdeacon Nares defines a costard-monger, or coster-

mon-ger, to be "a seller of apples, one who generally kept a
stall,"
**** "Here are the rarities of the whole Fair,

Pimperle-Pimp, and the wise Dancing Mare;
Here's Vienna besieg'd, a rare thing,
And here's Punchinello, shewn thrice to the King.
Ladies mask'd to the Cloisters repair,
But there will be no raffling, a pise on the May'r!"
From Playford's Musical Companion, 1701.

—Punches, and Roast Pig. * But its Drama was in abeyance. ** The elite of Pye-Corner, Gilt-spur Street, and the Cloth-quarter, preferred Pinkethman's Medley and Mr. Barnes's Rope-dancers, to "The Old Creation of the World New Revived," with the intrigues of Lucifer in the Garden of Eden —

* "A Catch-Mr. Henry Purcell —
Here's that will challenge all the Fair:

Come buy my nuts and damsons, my Burgamy Pear. Here's the

Whore of Babylon, the Devil and the Pope: The girl is just
going on the rope.
Here's Dives and Lazarus, and the World's Creation: Here's

the Dutch Woman, the like's not in the nation. Here is the
booth where the tall Dutch Maid is,
Here are the bears that dance like any ladies.

Tota, tota, tot goes the little penny trumpet,
'Here's your Jacob Hall, that can jump it, jump it.
Sound trumpet: a silver spoon and fork;
Come, here's your dainty Pig and Pork"
** "The old Droll Players' Lamentation, being very pleasant

and diverting. 1701."
"Oh! mourn with us all you that live by play,

The Reformation took our gains away:
We are as good as dead now money's gone,
No Droll is suffer'd, not a single one!
Jack Pudding now our grandeur doth exceed,
And grinning granny is by fates decreed
To laugh at us, and to our place succeed.
But after all, these times would make us rave,
That won't let's play the Fool as well as Knave!"

—and Adam and Eve driven out of Paradise," —"Judith and Holofernes," * —"Dives and Pauper," —the "Humours of Noah's Ark, or the Drolleries of the Deluge," —"Jeptha's Rash Vow," —and "The Pleasant Conceited History of Abraham and Isaac!" These Mysteries ** were only endured when tacked to "a Comick Dance of gigantic automatons the "merriments of Sir John Spendall and Punchinello; Pickle-Herring and Punch." Of the multifarious and ludicrous literature of the "Rounds" little remains. The serious portion consisted, as we have shown, of such representations taken from Bible History, after the manner of the Chester and Coventry Monks, and the ancient Parish Clerks of Clerkenwell, as were most likely to beget an awful attention in the audience; and the comic, of detached scenes of low humour from Shakspere, and Beaumont and Fletcher, like "The Wits ***

* "To be sold in the Booth of Lee and Harper, and only
printed for, and by G. Lee, in Blue Maid Alley, Southwark."
** Spence, in his anecdotes, describes a Mystery he saw at

Turin, "where a damned female soul, in a gown of flame-
coloured satin, intreats, as a favor, to be handed over to

the fires of purgatory, for only as many years as there are drops of water in the ocean!"
*** "The Wits, or Sport upon Sport: being a curious

collection of several Drolls and Farces, as they have been sundry times acted at Bartholomew and other Fairs, in halls and taverns, on mountebanks' stages at Charing Cross, Lincoln's Inn Fields, and other places, by Strolling Flayers, Fools, Fiddlers, and Zanies, with loud laughter and applause. Now newly collected by your old friend, Francis Kirkman, 1673." The author says, in his preface to the Second Part, "I have seen the Red Bull Playhouse, which was a large one, so full, that as many went back for want of room as had entered; and as meanly as you may think of these Drolls, they were acted by the best comedians then, and now in being. I once saw a piece at a country inn, called 'King Pharaoh, with Moses, Aaron, and some others; to explain which figures was added this piece of poetry,
Here Pharaoh, with his goggle eyes, does stare on

The High Priest Moses, with the Prophet Aaron.
Why, what a rascal
Was he that would not let the people go to eat the Pascal!
I believe he who pictured King Pharaoh had never seen a king

in his life; for all the majesty he was represented with was goggle eyes, that his picture might be answerable to the verse."

—or Sport upon Sport" and "The Stroller's Pacquet Open'd —except when a Smithfield bard, "bemus'd in beer," ventured upon originality, and added "Robin Hood, * an Opera," and "The Quaker's Opera," ** to the classical press of Bartholomew Fair.
    * "Robin Hood, an opera, as it is performed at Lee and Harper's Great Theatrical Booth in Bartholomew Fair, 1730."
** "The Quaker's Opera, as it is performed at Lee and

Harper's Great Theatrical Booth in Bartholomew Fair, 1728."
This is the story of Jack Sheppard dramatised and set to

rough music! It may be gratifying to the curious to see how the adventures of this house and prison-breaker were "improved" (‼) by a Methodist Preacher under the Piazza of Covent Garden. "Now, my beloved, we have a remarkable instance of man's care for his tabernacle of clay in the notorious malefactor Jack Sheppard! How dexterously did he, with a nail, pick the padlock of his chain! how manfully burst his fetters; climb up the chimney; wrench out an iron bar; break his way through a stone wall, till he reached the leads of the prison! and then fixing a blanket through the wall with a spike, he stole out of the chapel! How intrepidly did he descend from the top of the Turner's house! and how cautiously pass down the stairs, and make his escape at the street-door! Oh, that ye were all like Jack Sheppard! Let me exhort ye, then, to open the locks of your hearts with the nail of repentance; to burst asunder the fetters of your beloved desires; to mount the chimney of hope; take from thence the bar of good resolution; break through the stone wall of despair; raise yourselves to the leads of divine meditation; fix the blanket of faith with the spike of the conventicle; let yourselves down the Turner's house of resignation, and descend the stairs of humility; so shall you come to the door of deliverance, from the prison of iniquity, and escape the clutches of that old executioner, the devil."

Good company has occasionally visited the "Rounds." Evelyn * went there, but it was to gape and grumble.

 * 1648. 28 Aug: Saw ye celebrated follies of Bartholomew
Fair, which follies were more harmless, in those days, than
the solemn and sinister mummery of a Brownist's conventicle,
a Presbyterian Synod, and a Quakers' meeting.

In the year 1670 (see "Some Account of Rachel Lady Russell,") Lady Russell, with her sister, Lady Northumberland, and Lady Shafts-bury, returned from Bartholomew Fair loaded with fairings for herself and children! Sept. 1, 1730, the "Four Indian Kings" visited Pink-ethman and Giffard's booth, and saw Wat Tyler and Jack Straw. Sir Robert Walpole, * when Prime Minister, starred and gartered, graced the fair with his presence. Frederick Prince of Wales, in 1740, attended by a party of the Yeomen of the Guard with lighted flambeaux, contemplated its pantomimical wonders, with Manager Rich for his cicerone; as, in after times, did David Garrick and his lady, marshalled by the bill-sticker of Old Drury! On tendering his tester at the Droll Booth, the cashier, recognising the fine expressive features and far-beaming eye of Roscius, with a patronising look and bow, refused the proffered fee, politely remarking, "Sir, we never take money from one another."

 * A coloured print of Bartholomew Fair in 1721, copied from
a painting on an old fan mount, represents Sir" Robert
Walpole as one of the spectators.

Pinkethman's "Pantheon, or Temple of the Heathen Gods, consisting of five curious pictures, and above one hundred figures that move their heads, legs, and fingers, in character," long continued the lion of Bartholomew and Southwark fairs. * On the 19th August, 1720, great preparations were made against the approaching festival. Stables were transmogrified into palaces for copper kings, lords, knights, and ladies! and cock-lofts and laystalls into enchanted castles and Elysium bowers! The ostlers beguiled the interval by exercising their pampered steeds, and levying contribution on such as happened to be enjoying the pure air of Hounslow Heath and Finchley Common! Mob quality in hackney coaches, and South-Sea squires in their own, resorted to Pinkethman's booth to divert themselves with his "comical phiz, and newly-imported French dancing dogs!" The mountebanks were all alive and merry, and a golden harvest was reaped in the Rounds.

 * Sept. 13, 1717. Several constables visited Pinkethman's
booth in Southwark Fair, and apprehended Pinkethman, with
others of his company, just as they had concluded a play, in
the presence of near 150 noblemen and gentlemen seated on

the stage. They were soon liberated, on making it appear that they were the King's Servants. The Prince visited the booth.

Other exhibitions has the saint had beside his own. Exhibitions, as a nuisance, * from that *corpus sine pectore*, the London common council! *"Do thou amend thy face!"* was the reply of Falstaff to Bardolph, when the owner of the "fiery trigon" inflicted a homily on that "sweet creature of bombast."' How much more needful, sons of repletion! is reform to you, than the showman, who seldom sees any punch but his own; the Jack-Pudding, who grins wofully for a slice of his namesake; and the "strong man," who gets little else between his teeth but his table! Why not be merry your own way, and let mountebanks be merry theirs? Are license and excess to be entirely on the side of "robes and furrd gowns?"

> * In "A Pacquet from Wills, 1701," an actress of "the
> Playhouse," writing to "a Stroller in the Country," says,
> "My dear Harlequin, I hoped, according to custom, at the
> grand revels of St. Bartholomew to have solaced ourselves
> with roast pig and a bottle. But the master of that great
> bee-hive, the city, to please the canting, zealous horn-
> heads, has buzzed about an order there shall be no fair! The
> chief cause, say the reformers, is the profane drolls (
> Whittington to wit) that ridicule the city's majesty, by
> hiring a paunch-bellied porter at half-a-crown a day, to
> represent an Alderman in a scarlet gown! when a lean-ribbed
> scoundrel in a blue jacket, for mimicking a fool, shall have
> forty shillings!" In 1743, 1750, 1760, 1798, 1825, and 1840,
> further attempts were made to put down the fair. In 1760 one
> Birch, (for whom St. Bartholomew had a rod in pickle!)
> bearing the grandiloquent title of Deputy City Marshal (‼)
> lost his life in a fray that broke out between the
> suppressing authorities and the fair folk.

The amendment of Bardolph's face (nose!) per se, was not a crying case of necessity; a burning shame to be extinguished with a zeal hot as the "fire o' juniper." It only became so in conjunction with the reformation of Falstaff's morals! *

> * If every man attended to his own affairs, he would find
> little time to pry into those of others. An idle head is the
> devil's garret. Your intermeddler is one who has either
> nothing to do, or having it to do, leaves it undone. It is
> good to reform others; 'tis better to begin with ourselves.
> He who censures most severely the faults of his neighbour is
> generally very merciful to his own. "One day judgeth
> another," says old Stow, "and the last judgeth all."
> We laugh at the hypocrite when caught in his own snare-when

> guilty of the suppressio veri, he is openly detected in the
> suggestio falsi, and made to pay the penalty of his
> duplicity. An ancient beau, bounding with all the vigour and
> alacrity that age, gout, and rheumatism usually inspire,
> cuts not a more ridiculous figure!
> Hermes, or Mercury, was a thief, and the god of thieves;

> Venus, a gay lady; Bacchus, a wine-bibber; and Juno, a

scold. And what apology offers sweet Jack Falstaff, kind
Jack Falstaff, true Jack Falstaff, valiant Jack Falstaff,
for his infirmities! He lets judgment go by default! "Dost
thou hear, Hal? thou knowest, in the state of innocency,
Adam fell; and what should poor Jack Falstaff do, in these
days of villany?"
This is truth as deep as the centre. Whoever shall cast a

pebble at old Jack after this, must have his conscience
Macadamised!

Be your grace * short, and your meals long. Abate not one slice of venison, one spoonful of
turtle. Be the fat, white and green, all your own! ** But war not with *Punch* —
    "Let the poor devil *eat*; allow him *that!*"
    "Curtail not our holiday Septembrisers of their fair proportion of fun."
    "To those sentiments," exclaimed Deputy Doublechin, "I most heartily respond!"
    * The Rev. R. C. Dillon (Lord Mayor's chaplain in 1826)
published in 1830 a "Sermon on the evil of fairs in general,
and Bartholomew Fair in particular." Who would have thought
that this pious functionary had been so great a foe to the
fair?
The following odd combinations occur in the title of a

sermon published in 1734. "The deformity of sin cured; a
sermon preached at St. Michael's Crooked Lane, before the
Prince of Orange, (the Prince was not quite straight!) by
the Rev. J. Crookshanks. Sold by Matthew Denton at the
Crooked Billet, near Cripplegate.
** A physician once observed that he could tell of what

country a man was by his complaint. If it laid in the head,
he was a Scotchman; if in the heart, he was an Irishman; if
in the stomach, he was an Englishman.

And as the worshipful deputy's responses, six days out of the seven, were *wet* ones, the punch
and a glee went merrily round.

                Punchinello's a jolly good fellow!

        Making us merry, and making us mellow.

        In the bowl, in the fair too, a cure for dull care too;

        All ills that we find flesh or skin and bone heir to!

        Verily he is the spirit of glee,

        So in him drink to him with three times three!

        Hip! hip! once, twice, thrice, and away!

        Punchinello, *mon ami! a votre santé.*

CHAPTER VII.

And so, Mr. M'Sneeshing, you never heard of the ingenious *ruse* played off by Monsieur Scaramouch?" said the Lauréat, as he refreshed his nostrils with a parsimonious pinch from the mull of sandy-poled Geordie, conchologist and confectioner, from the land o' cakes. And while Deputy Doublechin was busy admiring a grotesque illumination in Uncle Timothy's *Merrie Mysteries*, Mr. Bosky favoured the company with

THE UP-TO-SNUFF FRENCH SCARAMOUCH.

Monsieur Scaramouch, sharp-set enough,

At a Paris dépôt for tobacco and snuff,

Accosted the customers every day

With *"Pardonnez moi, du Tabac, s'il vous plâit!"*

He look'd such a gentleman every inch,

The Parisians all condescended a pinch;

Which, taken from Bobadils, barbers, and beaux,

Went into his *pocket* —instead of his *nose!*

Scaramouch sold, with a merry ha I ha!

Ev'ry pinch to his friend, *le marchand de tabac*:

Then buyer and seller the price of a franc

To the *noses* of all their contributors drank!

From boxes supplies came abundant enough,

He breakfasted, dined, and drank tea upon snuff!

It found him in fuel, and lodging, and cloaths —

He pamper'd the palate by pinching the nose!

An ell he would take if you gave him an inch,

In the shape of a very exorbitant pinch —

The proverb, All's fish to the net that shall come,

Duly directed his finger and thumb.

One day a dragoon *en botine*, and three crosses,

With a pungent *bonne bouche* came to treat his proboscis;

Our Scaramouch, sporting his lowest *congee*,

Smil'd, *"Pardonnez moi, du Tabac s'il vousplâit!"*

"Volontiers and his box, which, containing a pound,

A reg'ment of noses might titillate round,

Mars offer'd to Scaramouch quick, with a bounce;

Whose pinch very soon made it minus an ounce!

"Coquin!" and a cane, that he kept for the nonce,

Of Scaramouch threaten'd the perriwigg'd sconce;

Who, fearing a crack, while 'twas flourishing quick,

Cut in a crack the dragoon and his stick!

"Had the vay-gabond served me the like o' that" droned Mr. M'Sneeshing, suddenly rapping down the lid of his mull, and looking suspiciously about him, to see if there was a Scaramouch among the party! "I'd ha' crack'd his croon!"

Mr. Bosky's reply all but tripped off his tongue.

'Twas caviare to the Scotchman, so he suppressed it, and proceeded with the *Merrie Mysteries.*

St. Bartholomew was not to be driven from his "Rounds" by the meddling citizens. He kept, on a succession of brilliant anniversaries from 1700 to 1760, his state at his fair. The Smithfield drama had revived under the judicious management of popular actors; * the art of legerdemain had reached perfection in the "surprising performances" of Mr. Fawkes; ** wrestling *** fencing —

* "There is one great playhouse erected in the middle of
Smithfield for the King's Players. The booth is the largest
that was ever built." —Dawkes's News-letter, 1715.
** "Feb. 15. 1731. The Algerine Ambassadors went to see

Fawkes, who showed them a prospect of Algiers, and raised up
an apple-tree which bore ripe apples in less than a minute's
time, of which the company tasted." —Gentlemans Mag. Fawkes
died May 25, 1731, worth ten thousand pounds. John White,
author of "Arts Treasury, and Hocus Pocus; or a Rich Cabinet
of Legerdemain Curiosities," was a noted conjuror
contemporary with Fawkes.
*** Stow, lamenting the decline of wrestling, that used to

be the pride and glory of Skinners-Well and Finsbury Fields,
says, "But now of late yeeres, the wrestling is only
practised on Bartholomew-day in the afternoone."

—and single-stick, fought their way thither from Stokes's * amphitheatre in Islington Road, and Figg's ** academy for full-grown gentlemen in Oxford Street, then "Marybone Fields!" Powel's puppet-show still gloried in its automaton wonders; Pinchbecks musical clock struck all beholders with admiration; and Tiddy Doll *** with his gingerbread cocked hat garnished with Dutch gold, the prime oddity of the fair, made the "Rounds" ring with his buffooneries.

* "At Mr. Stokes's amphitheatre, Islington Road, on Monday, 24th June, 1733, I John Seale, Citizen of London, give this invitation to the celebrated Hibernian Hero, Mr. Robert Barker, to exert his utmost abilities with me: And I Robert Barker accept this invitation; and if my antagonist's courage equal his menaces, glorious will be my conquest! Attendance at two; the Masters mount at five. Vivat Rex et Regina."

"This is to give notice, that to-morrow, for a day's

diversion (‼) at Mr. Stokes's Amphitheatre, a mad bull, dressed up with fireworks, will be baited; also cudgel-playing for a silver cup, and wrestling for a pair of buckskin breeches. Sept. 3rd, 1729. Gallery seats, 2s. 6d., 2s., 1s. 6d. and 1s."

** Messrs. Figg and Sutton fought the "two first and most

profound" fencers in the kingdom, Messrs. Holmes and Mac-quire: Holmes coming off with a cut on his metacarpus from the sword of Mr. Figg. On the 3rd Dec. 1731, a prize was fought for at the French Theatre in the Haymarket, between Figg and Sparks, at which the Duke of Lorraine and Count Kinsi were present; the Duke was much pleased, and ordered them a liberal gratuity.

*** A vendor of gingerbread cakes at Bartholomew and May

Fairs. His song of "Tiddy doll loi loi!" procured him his popular sobriquet.

Original

Among the galaxy of Bartholomew Fair stars that illumined this flourishing period was The Right Comical Lord Chief Joker, James Spiller, the Mat o' the Mint of the Beggar's Opera, the airs of which he sang in a "truly sweet and harmonious tone." His convivial powers were the delight of the merry butchers of Clare-Market, the landlord of whose house of call, a quondam gaoler, but a humane man, deposed the original sign of the "Bull and Butcher," and substituted the head of Spiller. His *vis comica*, leering at a brimming bowl, is prefixed to his Life and Jests, printed in 1729. A droll story is told of his stealing the part of the *Cobbler of Preston* (written by Charles Johnson,) out of Pinkethman's pocket, after a hard bout over the bottle, and carrying it to Christopher Bullock, who instantly fell to work, and concocted a farce with the same title a fortnight before the rival author and theatre could produce theirs! The dissolute Duke of Wharton, one night, in a frolic, obliged each person in the company to disrobe himself of a garment at every health that was drank. Spiller parted with peruke, waistcoat, and coat, very philosophically; but when his shirt was to be relinquished, he confessed, with many blushes, that he had forgot to put it on! He was a careless, wild-witted companion, often a tenant of the Marshalsea; till his own "Head" afforded him in his latter days a safe garrison from the harpies of the law. He died Feb. 7, 1729, aged 37. A poetical butcher of Clare-Market * would not let him descend to the grave "without the meed of one melodious tear."

Other luminaries shed a radiance on the "Rounds." Bullock (who, in a merry epilogue, tripped up Pinkethman by the heels, and bestrode him in triumph, Pinkey returning the compliment by throwing him over his head). Mills (familiarly called "honest Billy Mills!" from his kind disposition).

* "Down with your marrow-bones and cleavers all,
And on your marrow-bones ye butchers fall!
For prayers from you, who never pray'd before,
Perhaps poor Jemmy may to life restore.
What have we done? the wretched bailiffs cry,
That th' only man by whom we liv'd, should die!
Enrag'd, they gnaw their wax, and tear their writs,
While butchers' wives fall in hysteric fits;
For sure as they're alive, poor Spiller's dead;
But, thanks to Jack Legar! we've got his head.
He was an inoffensive, merry fellow,
When sober, hipp'd; blythe as a bird, when mellow."
For Spiller's benefit ticket, engraved by Hogarth, twelve

guineas have been given! There is another, of more dramatic
interest, with portraits of himself and his wife in the
Cobbler of Preston.

Harper (a lusty fat man, with a countenance expressive of mirth and jollity, the rival of Quin in Falstaff, and the admirable Job-son to Kitty Clive's inimitable Nell). Hippisley (whose first appearance the audience always greeted with loud laughter and applause). Chapman (the Pistol and Touchstone of his day). Joe Miller * (whose name is become synonymous with good and bad jokes; a joke having ironically been christened a Joe Miller, to mark the wide contrast between joking and Joe!).

* This reputed wit was, after all, a moderately dull fellow.
His book of Jests is a joke not by him, but upon him: a joke
by Joe being considered la chose impossible. As an actor, he
never rose to particular eminence. His principal parts were
Sir Joseph Wittol and Teague. There are two portraits of

him. One, in the former character, prefixed to some editions of his Jests; and a mezzotinto, in the latter, an admirable likeness, full of force and expression. The first and second editions of "Joe Miller's Jests" appeared in 1739. They are so scarce that four guineas have been given for a copy at book auctions. From a slim pamphlet they have increased to a bulky octavo! He died August 15, 1738, at the age of 54, and was buried on the east side of the churchyard of St. Clement Danes. We learn from the inscription on his tombstone (now illegible) that he was "a tender husband, a sincere friend, & facetious companion, and an excellent comedian." Stephen Duck, the favourite bard of "good Queen Caroline." wrote his epitaph.

Hallam * (whom Macklin accidentally killed in a quarrel about a stage wig).

Original

Woodward, Yates, Shuter, ** —
   * A very rare portrait of Hallam represents him standing
before the stage-lights, holding in one hand a wig, and
pointing with the other to "An infallible recipe to make a
wicked manager of a theatre" (a merciless satire on
Macklin,) dated 'Chester, 20, 1750." A stick is thrust into
his left eye by one behind the scenes. For this accident,
which caused his death, Macklin was tried at the Old Bailey
in May, 1735, and found guilty of manslaughter.
** When actors intend to abridge a piece they say, "We will

John Audley it!" It originated thus. In the year 1749,
Shuter played drolls at Bartholomew Fair, and was wont to
lengthen the exhibition until a sufficient number of people
were collected at the door to fill his booth. The event was
signified by a Merry Andrew crying out from the gallery,
"John Audley!" as if in the act of inquiry after such a
person, though his intention was to inform Shuter there was
a fresh audience in high expectation below! In consequence
of this hint, the droll was cut short, and the booth cleared
for the new crop of impatient expectants! Shuter
occasionally spent his evenings at a certain "Mendicants'
convivial club," held at the Welch's Head, Dyott Street, St.
Giles's; which, in 1638, kept its quarters at the Three
Crowns in the Vintry.

—and very early in life, little Quick. * Ned had a sincere regard for Mr. Whitfield, and often
attended his ministry at Tottenham Court Chapel.
   * During one of Quick's provincial excursions the stage-
coach was stopped by a highwayman. His only fellow
traveller, a taciturn old gentleman, had fallen fast asleep.
"Your money" exclaimed Turpin's first cousin. Quick,
assuming the dialect and manner of a raw country lad,
replied with stupid astonishment, "Mooney, zur! uncle there
(pointing to the sleeping beauty,) pays for I, twinpikes and
all!" The highwayman woke the dozer with a slap on the face,
and (in classical phrase) cleaned him out, leaving our
little comedian in quiet possession of the golden receipts
of a bumper.
Upon one occasion he played Richard III. for his benefit.

His original intention was to have acted it with becoming
seriousness; but the public, who had anticipated a
travestie, would listen to nothing else; and Quick (with the
best tragic intentions!) was reluctantly obliged to humour
them. When he came to the scene where the crook-back'd
tyrant exclaims,
"A horse! a horse! my kingdom for a horse!"

Quick treated his friends with a hard hit, and by way of

putting a finishing stroke to the fun, added, with a voice, look, and gesture perfectly irresistible,
"And if you can't get a horse, bring a jackass?"

One Sunday morning he was seated in a pew opposite the pulpit, and while that pious, eloquent, but eccentric preacher, was earnestly exhorting sinners to return to the fold, he fixed his eyes full upon Shuter, adding to what he had previously said, "And thou, poor Ramble, (Ramble was one of Ned's popular parts,) who hast so long rambled, come you also! O! end your ramblings and return." Shuter was panic-struck, and said to Mr. Whitfield after the sermon was over, "I thought I should have fainted! How could you use me so?"

Cow-Lane and Hosier-Lane "Ends" were great monster marts. At the first dwelt an Irish giant, Mr. Cornelius McGrath, who, if he "lives three years longer, will peep into garret windows from the pavement:" and the "Amazing" Corsican Fairy. "Hosier-Land End" contributed "a tall English youth, eight feet high;" two rattle-snakes, "one of which rattles so loud that you may hear it a quarter of a mile off;" and "a large piece of water made with white flint glass," containing a coffee-house and a brandy-shop, running, at the word of command, hot and cold fountains of strong liquor and strong tea! The proprietor Mr. Charles Butcher's poetical invitation ran thus: —

> "Come, and welcome, my friends, and taste ere you pass,
>
> 'Tis but sixpence to see it, and two-pence each glass."

The "German Woman that danced over-against the Swan Tavern by Hosier Lane," having "run away from her mistress," diminished the novelties of that prolific quarter. But the White Hart, in Pye-Corner, had "A little fairy woman from Italy, two feet two inches high;" and Joe Miller, "over-against the Cross-Daggers," enacted "A new droll called the Tempest, or the Distressed Lovers; with the Comical Humours of the Inchanted Scotchman; or Jockey and the three witches!"

Hark to yonder scarlet beefeater, who hath cracked his voice, not with "hallooing and singing of anthems," but with attuning its dulcet notes to the deep-sounding gong! And that burly trumpeter, whose convex cheeks and distended pupils look as if, like Æolus, he had stopped his breath for a time, to be the better able to discharge a hurricane! Listen to their music, and you shall hear that Will Pinkethman hath good store of merriments for his laughing friends at "Hall and Oates's Booth next Pye-Corner," where, Sept. 2, 1729, will be presented The Merchant's Daughter of Bristol; "a diverting" Opera, called The Country Wedding; and the Comical Humours of Roger. —The Great Turk by Mr. Giffard, and Roger by Mr. Pinkethman.

Ha! "lean Jack," jolly-fac'd comedian, Harper, thou body of a porpoise, and heart of a tittle-bat! that didst die of a round-house fever; * and Zee, ** rosy St. Anthony! thy rival trumpeter, with his rubicund physiognomy screened beneath the umbrage of a magnificent bowsprit, proclaim at the Hospital Gate "The Siege of Berthulia; with the Comical Humours, of Rustego and his man Terrible."

* Harper, being an exceedingly timid man, was selected for prosecution by Highmore, the Patentee of Drury Lane, for joining the revolters at the Haymarket. He was imprisoned, but though soon after released by the Court of King's Bench, he died in 1742, of a fever on his spirits.
** Anthony Lee, or Leigh, (famous for his performance of

Gomez, in Dryden's play of the Spanish Friar,) and Cave

Underhill, diverting themselves in Moorfields, agreed to get up a sham quarrel. They drew their swords, and with fierce countenances advanced to attack each other. Cave (a very lean man) retreated over the rails, followed by Lee (a very fat man); and after a slight skirmish, retired to the middle of the field. Tony puffed away after him; a second encounter took place; and, when each had paused for awhile to take breath, a third; at the end of which, there being a saw-pit, near them, they both jumped into it! The mob, to prevent murder, scampered to the pit, when to their great surprise they found the redoubtable heroes hand in hand in a truly comical posture of reconciliation, which occasioned much laughter to some, while others (having been made fools of!) were too angry to relish the joke. The mock combatants then retired to a neighbouring tavern to refresh themselves, and get rid of a troublesome tumult. —The Comedian's Tales, 1729.

Original

What an odd-favoured mountebank! "a threadbare juggler, and a fortune-teller, a needy, hollow-ey'd, sharp-looking wretch," with a nose crooked as the walls of Troy, and a chin like a shoeing horn; those two features having become more intimately acquainted, because his teeth had fallen out! Behold him jabbering, gesticulating, and with auricular grin, distributing this Bartholomew Fair bill.

"Sept. 3, 1729. At Bullock's Great Theatrical Booth will be acted a Droll, called Dorastus and Faunia, or the Royal Shepherdess; Flora, an opera; with Toilet's Rounds; the Fingalian Dance, and a Scottish Dance, by Mrs. Bullock."

Thine, Hallam, is a tempting bill of fare. "The Comical Humours of Squire Softhead and his man Bullcalf, and the Whimsical Distresses of Mother Catterwall!" With a harmonious concert of "violins, hautboys, bassoons, kettle-drums, trumpets, and French horns!" Thine, too, Hippisley, immortal Scapin! transferring the arch fourberies of thy hero to Smithfield Rounds. At the George Inn, where, with Chapman, thou keepest thy court, we are presented with "Harlequin Scapin, or the Old One caught in a sack; and the tricks, cheats, and shifts of Scapin's two companions, Trim the Barber, and Bounce-about the Bully." The part of Scapin by thy comical self.

At this moment a voice, to which the neigh of Bucephalus was but a whisper, announced that the unfortunate owner had lost a leg and an arm in his country's service, winding up the catalogue with some minor dilapidations, all of which are more or less peculiar to those patriots who during life find their reward in hard blows and poverty, and in death receive a polite invitation to join a water party down the pool of oblivion! The Lauréat paused.

Mr. M'Sneeshing. "Lost his leg in battle! —ha! ha! ha! —a gude joke! He means in a man-trap! I should be glad to know what business a pauper body like this has blathering abroad? Are there not almshouses, and workhouses, and hospitals, for beggars and cripples? Though I perfectly agree wi' Sandy M'Grab, Professor * of Humanity, that sic like receptacles, and the anti-Presbyterian abomination of alms-giving are only so many premiums for roguery and vay-gabondism. Let every one put his shoulder to the wheel, his nose to the grindstone, and make hay while the sun shines."

* At Oxford and Cambridge they write L.L.D. —in Scotland,
L.S.D. viz. 35s. 3d. for the diploma!

Mr. Bosky. But are there not many on whom the sun of prosperity never shone?

Mr. M'Sneeshing. Their unthriftiness and lack of foresight alone are to blame!

Mr. Bosky. Is to want a shilling, to want every virtue? Men think highly of those who rapidly rise in the world; whereas nothing rises quicker than dust, straw, and feathers! Would you provide no asylum for adversity, sickness, and old age?

Mr. M'Sneeshing. Hard labour and sobriety (tossing off his heeltap of toddy) will ward off the two first, and old age and idleness (yawning and stretching himself in his chair) deserve to — —

Mr. Bosky. Starve?

Mr. M'Sneeshing. To have just as much-and *nae mair!* —as will keep body and soul together! Would you not *revile*, rather than *relieve*, the lazy and the improvident?

Mr. Bosky. Not if they were hungry and poor! *

Mr. M'Sneeshing. Nor cast them a single word of reproach?

* "In the daily eating this was his custom. (Archbishop
Parker's, temp. Elizabeth.) The steward, with the servants
that were gentleman of the better rank, sat down at the
tables in the hall on the right hand; and the almoner, with
the clergy, &c., sat on the other side, where there was
plenty of all sorts of provision. The daily fragments

thereof did suffice to fill the bellies of a great number of
poor hungry people that waited at the gate. And moreover it
was the Archbishop's command to his servants, that all
strangers should be receive and treated with all manner of
civility and respect."
The poor and hungry fed and treated with "civility and

respect!" What a poser and pill for Geordie M'Sneeshing and
Professor M'Grab!

Mr. Bosky. I would see that they were fed first, and then, if I reproved, my reproof should
be no pharisaical diatribes. The bitterest reproaches fall short of that pain which a wounded
spirit suffers in reflecting on its own errors; a lash given to the soul will provoke more than
the body's most cruel torture.

Mr. M'Sneeshing. Vera romantic, and in the true speerit of — —

Mr. Bosky. *Charity*, I hope.

Mr. M'Sneeshing. Chay-ri-ty? (putting his hand into his coat-pocket.)

Mr. Bosky. Don't fumble; the word is not in M'Culloch!

Mr. M'Sneeshing. Peradventure, Mr. Bosky, you would build a Union poor-house (sarcastically).

Mr. Bosky. I would not.

Mr. M'Sneeshing. An Hospital? (with a sardonic grin!)

Mr. Bosky. I would!

Mr. M'Sneeshing. Where?

Mr. Bosky. In the *Human Heart!* You may not know of such a place, Mr. M'Sneeshing.
Your hospital would be where some countrymen of yours build castles, in Sky and Ayr!

And the Lauréat abruptly quitted the room, leaving Mr. M'Sneeshing in that embarrassing
predicament, "*Between the de'il and the deep sea!*"

But his mission was soon apparent. "Three cheers for the kind young gentleman!" resounded
from the holiday folks, and a broadside of blessings from the veteran tar! This obfuscated
concholo-gist Geordie, and he was about to launch a *Brutum fulmen*, a speech *de omnibus rebus
et quibusdam aliis*, as the magging mouthpiece of Professor

M'Grab; when, to the great joy of Deputy Doublechin, the miserable drone-pipe of this
leatherbrained, leaden-hearted, blue-nosed, frost-bitten, starved nibbler of a Scotch kail-yard,
was quickly drowned in the sonorous double-bass of our saltwater Belisarius.

My foes were my country's, my messmates the brave.

My home was the deck, and my path the green wave;

My musick, loud winds, when the tempest rose high —

I sail'd with bold Nelson, and heard his last sigh!

His spirit had fled-we gaz'd on the dead —

The sternest of hearts bow'd with sorrow, and bled.

As o'er the deep waters mov'd slowly his bier,

What victory, thought we, was ever so dear?

Far Egypt's hot sands have long since quench'd my

sight —

To these rolling orbs what is sunshine or night?

But the full blaze of glory that beam'd on thy bay,

Trafalgar I still pours on their darkness the day.

An ominous tap at the window-the "White Serjeant's!" invited Geordie to a tête-à-tête with a singed sheep's head, and the additional treat of a curtain-lecture, not on political but domestic economy, illustrated with sharp etchings by Mrs. M'Sneeshing's nails, of which his physiognomy had occasionally exhibited proof impressions! To his modern Athenian (!) broad brogue, raised in defiance of the applauding populace outside, responded the polite inquiry, "*Does your mother know you're out?*" * and other classical interrogatories. The return of Mr. Bosky was a signal for cheerfulness, mingled with deeper feelings; during which were not forgotten, "Old England's wooden walls?" and "Peace to the souls of the heroes!"

"Hail! all hail I the warriors grave,

Valour's venerable bed —

Hail! the memory of the Brave!

Hail! the Spirits of the Dead!

* Certain cant phrases strike by their odd sound and
apposite allusion.
"No mistake!"

"Who are you?"

"Cut my lucky!"

"Does your mother know you're out I"

"Hookey!" &c. &c. are terms that metaphorically imply

something comical Yet oblivion, following in the march of
time, shall cast its shadows over their mysterious meanings.
On "Hookey!" the bewildered scholiast of future ages will
hang every possible interpretation but the right one; with
"Blow me tight!" he will give a loose to conjecture; and
oft to Heaven will he roll his queer eye, the query to

answer, "Who are you?"

CHAPTER VIII.

And hail to the living," exclaimed Lieutenant O'Larry, the Trim of the Cloth Quarter —"To them give we a trophy, time enough for a tomb!" And having knocked out the ashes of his pipe, he tuned it, and (beating time with his wooden leg) woke our enthusiasm with

WATERLOO.

And was it not the proudest day in Britain's annals

    bright?

And was he not a gallant chief who fought the gallant

    fight?

Who broke the neck of tyranny, and left no more to do? —

That chief was Arthur Wellington! that fight was

    Waterloo!

O, when on bleak Corunna s heights he rear'd his ban

    ner high,

Britannia wept her gallant Moore; her scatter'd armies

    fly —

To raise her glory to the stars, and kindle hearts of

    flame,

The mighty victor gave the word, the master-spirit

    came.

Poor Soult, like Pistol with his leek! he soon compell'd

    to yield;

And then a glorious wreath he gain'd on Talaveras field.

See! quick as lightning, flash by flash! another deed

    is done —

And Marmont has a battle lost, and Salamanca's won.

The shout was next "Vittoria!" —all Europe join'd the

    strain.

Ne'er such a fight was fought before, and ne'er will be

    again!

Quoth Arthur, "With 'th' Invincibles' another bout

I'll try;

And show you when f the Captain * comes a better by

and by!"

But lest his sword should rusty grow for want of daily

use,

He gave the twice-drubb'd Soult again a settler at

Toulouse.

His Marshals having beaten all, and laid upon the shelf,

He waits to see the Captain" come, and take a turn

himself.

Now Arthur is a gentleman, and always keeps his word;

And on the eighteenth day of June the cannons loud

were heard;

The flow'r of England's chivalry their conquror rallied

round;

A sturdy staff to cudgel well "the Captain" off the

ground!

"Come on, ye fighting vagabonds!" amidst a show'r

of balls,

A shout is heard; the voice obey'd —the noble Picton

falls!

On valour's crimson bed behold the bleeding Howard

lies —

Oh! the heart beats the muffled drum when such a

hero dies!

The cuirassiers they gallop forth in polish'd coats of

    mail:

"Up, Guards, and at'em!" and the shot comes rattling

    on like hail!

A furious charge both man and horse soon prostrates and

    repels,

And all the cuirassiers are cracked like lobsters in their

    shells!

Where hottest is the fearful fight, and fire and flame

    illume

The darkest cloud, the dunnest smoke, there dances

    Arthur s plume!

That living wall of British hearts, that hollow square,

    in vain

You mow it down-see! Frenchmen, see! the phalanx

    forms again.

The meteor-plume in majesty still floats along the

    plain —

Brave, bonny Scots! ye fight the field of Bannockburn

    again!

The Gallic lines send forth a cheer; its feeble echoes

    die —

The British squadrons rend the air-and "Victory!"

    is their cry.

'T was helter-skelter, devil take the hindmost, sauve

    qui peut,

With "Captain" and " Invincibles" that day at Wa

    terloo!

O how the Beiges show'd their backs! but not a Briton

    stirr'd —

His warriors kept the battle-field, and Arthur kept his

    word.

    "Hurrah! hurrah! hurrah!"

    When the cheering had subsided,

"Good morning (bowed Mr. Bosky) to your conjuring cap, Wizard of St. Bartlemy! Namesake of Guido, in tatterdemalion dialect, 'Old Guy!' who, had he possessed your necromantic art, would have transformed his dark lantern into a magic one, and ignited his powder without lucifer or match; yourself and art being a match for Lucifer! What says that mysterious scroll adorned with 'lively sculptures' of Mr. Punch's scaramouches, (formerly Mrs. Charke's *) and illuminated with your picture in a preternatural (pretty natural?) wig, every curl of which was woven by the fairy fingers of Queen Mab!"

Original

"Mr. *Fawkes*, at his booth over-against the King's Head, exhibits his incomparable dexterity of hand, and Pinchbeck's musical clock, that plays several fine tunes, imitates the notes of different birds, and shews ships sailing in the river. You will also be entertained with a surprising tumbler just arrived from Holland, and a Lilliputian posture-master, only five years old, who performs such wonderful turns of body, the like of which was never clone by a child of his age and bigness before." —1730.

* The deserted daughter of Colley Cibber, of whose erratic
life some passages are recorded in her autobiography. 1750.

At the Hospital Gate, ("all the scenes and decorations entirely new,") Joe Miller, * "honest Billy Mills" and Oates, invite us to see a new opera, called The Banished General, or the Distressed Lovers; the English Maggot, a comic dance; two harlequins; a trumpet and kettledrum concert and chorus; and the comical humours of Nicodemus Hobble-Wollop, Esq. and his Man Gudgeon! Squire Nicodemus by the facetious Joe. And at the booth of Fawkes, Pinchbeck and Terwin, "distinguished from the rest by bearing English colours," will be performed Britons Strike Home;. ** As if to redeem the habitual dulness of Joe Miller, one solitary joke of his stands on respectable authority. Joe, sitting at the window of the Sun Tavern in Clare Street, while a fish-woman was crying, "Buy my soles! Buy my maids!" exclaimed, "Ah! you wicked old creature; you are not content to sell your own soul, but you must sell your maid's too!"

** The commander of the General Ernouf (French sloop of war)
hailed the Reynard sloop, Captain Coglilan, in English, to
strike. "Strike!" replied the Briton, "that I will, and very
hard!" He struck so very hard, that in thirty-five minutes
his shot set the enemy on fire, and in ten minutes more she
blew up! Captain Coghlan now displayed equal energy in
endeavouring to rescue his vanquished foe; and, by great
exertions, fifty-five out of a crew of one hundred were
saved.

"Don Superbo Hispaniola Pistole by Mr. C —b —r, and Donna Americana by Mrs. Cl-ve, the favourite of the town!" Dare Conjuror Fawkes insinuate that Cibber, if he did not actually "wag a serpent-tail in Smithfield fair," still put on the livery of St. Bartholomew, in the Brummagem Don Pistole? That *Kitty Clive*, the termagant of Twickenham! with whom the fastidious and finical Horace Walpole was happy "to touch a card," bedizened in horrible old frippery, rioted it in the "Rounds?" If true, what a standing joke for David Garrick, in their "combats of the tongue!" If false, "surprising and incomparable" must have been thy "dexterity of hand," base wizard! which shielded that bold front of thine from the cabalistic retribution of her nails!

Leverigo the Quack, and his Jack Pudding Pinkanello, have mounted their stage; and, hark! the Doctor (Leveridge, famous for his "O the Roast Beef of Old England!") tunes his manly pipes, accompanied by that squeaking Vice! for the *Mountebank's song*. *

273

Original

* "Here are people and sports of all sizes and sorts,
Cook-maid and squire, and mob in the mire;
Tarpaulins, Frugmalions, Lords, Ladies, Sows, Babies,
And Loobies in scores:
Some howling, some bawling, some leering, some fleering;
While Punch kicks his wife out of doors!
To a tavern some go, and some to a show,
See poppets, for moppets; Jack-Puddings for Cuddens; Rope-

dancing, mares prancing; boats flying, quacks lying; Pick-
pockets, Pick-plackets, Beasts, Butchers, and Beaux; Fops
prattling, Dice rattling, Punks painted, Masks fainted, In
Tally-man's furbelow'd cloaths!"

Original

In another quarter, Jemmy Laroch * warbles his raree-show ditty; while Old Harry persuades the gaping juveniles—

* Here's de English and French to each other most civil,

Shake hands and be friends, and hug like de devil!

O Raree-show, &c.

Here be de Great Turk, and the great King of no land,

A galloping bravely for Hungary and Poland.

O Raree-show, &c.

Here's de brave English Beau for the Packet Boat tarries,

To go his campaign vid his tailor to Paris.

O Raree-shoiv, &c.

Here be de English ships bringing plenty and riches,

And dere de French caper a-mending his breeches!

O Raree-show, &c.

—to take a peep at his gallant show. * Duncan Macdonald ** "of the Shire of Caithness, Gent.," tells, how having taken part in the Rebellion of 1745, he fled to France, where, being a good dancer, he hoped to get a living by his heels.

* "Old Harry with his Raree-show." A print by Sutton
Nicholls, with the following lines.
"Reader, behold the Efigie of one

Wrinkled by age, decrepit and forlorne,
His tinkling bell doth you together call
To see his Raree-show, spectators all,
That will be pleas'd before you by him pass,
To put a farthing, and look through his glass.
'Tis so long since he did himself betake
To show the louse, the flea, and spangled snake.
His Nippotate, which on raw flesh fed,
He living shew'd, and does the same now's dead.
The bells that he when living always wore,
He wears about his neck as heretofore.
Then buy Old Harry, stick him up, that he
May be remember'd to posterity."
** "With a pair of French post boots, under the soles of

which are fastened quart-bottles, with their necks
downwards, Mr. Macdonald exhibits several feats of activity
on the slack wire; after this he poises a wheel on his right

toe, on the top of which is placed a spike, whereon is
balanced by the edge a pewter-plate; on that a board with
sixteen wine-glasses; and on the summit a glass globe, with
a wheaten straw erect on the same. He then fixes a sharp-
pointed sword on the tip of his nose, on the pommel of which
he balances a tobacco-pipe, and on its bowl two eggs erect!
With his left forefinger he sustains a chair with a dog
sitting in it, and two feathers standing erect on the nobs;
and to shew the strength of his wrist, there are two weights
of l00 lbs. each fastened to the legs of the chair!" &c. &c.

Original

But his empty quart bottles, with "their necks downwards," produced him not the price of a full one; his glass globe Louis Ragout valued not the straw that stood erect upon it; and his nose, sustaining on its tip a sharp-pointed sword, put not a morsel into his mouth; so that, finding his wire and trade equally slack, and that he could balance everything but his accounts, he took his French boots and French leave; left his board for his lodging, and his chair for his cheer, hoping to experience better luck at Bartholomew Fair! Posture-master Phillips, * pupil of Joseph Clarke, ** exercises his crooked calling, and becomes hunch-backed, pot-bellied, sharpbreasted, and crippled disjointing arms, shoulders, and legs, and twisting his supple limbs into bows and double knots!

* "August 23, 1749, a gallery in Phillips's booth broke down. F our persons were killed and several wounded."
** Clarke, who lived in the reigns of King James II. and

King William, was a terrible torment to his tailors; for
when one came to measure him, he contrived to have an
enormous hump on his left shoulder, and when the coat was
tried on, it had shifted to his right I The tailor
apologized for his blunder, took home the garment, altered
it, returned, and again attempted to make it fit, when, to
his astonishment and dismay, he found his queer customer as
straight as an arrow! A legion of tailors came to Adonize
him, but he puzzled them all.

Hans Buling * displays his monkey's humours, and his own. The Auctioneer of Moorfields ** transfers his book-stall to the cloisters. "Poor Will Ellis" offers for sale his simple "effigie." ***

* A well-known charlatan, who advertised his nostrums, attended by a monkey.
** This grave-looking, spectacled personage, in a rare print

by Sutton Nieholls, stands at his book-stall in Moorfields,
puffing the contents of his sale catalogue, among which are
"The History of Theves;" "English Rogue;" "Aristotle's
Masterpiece and "Poems by Rochester
"Come, sirs, and view this famous library,

'Tis pity learning shou'd discouraged be.
Here's bookes (that is, if they were but well sold)
I will maintain't are worth their weight in gold.
Then bid apace, and break me out of hand;
Ne'er cry you don't the subject understand:
For this, I'll say, howe'er the case may hit,
Whoever buys of me —I teach'em wit."
*** Sitting on the railings in Moorfields. Beneath are some

lines, giving an account how "Bedlam became his sad portion
and lot for the love of Dear Betty." Coming to his senses,
he turned poet: —
"Now innocent poetry 's all my delight;

And I hope that you'll all be so kind as to buy't:

That poor Will Ellis, when laid in his tomb,
May be stuck in your closet, or hung in your room."

Original

The "Dwarf Man and the Black" give us a chance of meeting our love at — —first sight. *
* "Sept. 8, 1757. Daily Advertiser. If the lady who stood
near a young gentleman to see the Dwarf Man and the Black in
Bartholomew Fair, on Wednesday evening, is single and will
inform the gentleman (who means the strictest honour) where
he may once more have the happiness of meeting her, she will
be waited on by a person of fortune. The lady wore a black
satin hat, puffed inside and out, a black cardinal, and a
genteel sprigged gown."

The Midas-eared Musician scrapes on his violincello a teeth-setting-an-edge voluntary. John Coan, * the Norfolk Pigmy, motions us to his booth; and Hale the Piper ** dancing his "horn-pipe," bagpipes us a welcome to the fair!

"What," exclaimed the Lauréat, "has become of this century of mountebanks? Ha! not one moving-still as the grave!"

Mr. Bosky was not often pathetic; but, being suddenly surprised into sentimentality, it is impossible to say what melancholy reflections might have resulted from the Merrie Mysteries, had not the landlord interrupted him by ushering into the room Uncle Timothy.

* This celebrated dwarf exhibited at Bartholomew Fair, Aug.
17, 1752.
** Under an engraving of Hale the Piper, by Sutton Nieholls,

are the music to his hornpipe, and the following lines.
"Before three monarchs I my skill did prove,

Of many lords and knights I had the love;
There's no musician e'er did know the peer
Of Hale the Piper in fair Darby Shire.
The consequence in part you here may know,
Pray look upon his hornpipe here below."
Hail! modest piper, and farewell!

"Welcome, illustrious brother!" shouted Deputy Doublechin. "Better late than never!"

Uncle Timothy greeted the President, nodded to all around, and shook hands with some old stagers nearest the chair.

"Gentlemen," continued the enthusiastic deputy, brimming Uncle Tim's glass, "our noble Vice drinks to all your good healths. Bravo! this looks like the merry old times! We have not a moment to lose. To-morrow prostrates this ancient roof-tree! Shall it be sawed asunder unsung? No, Uncle Timothy-no! rather let it tumble to a dying fall!"

The satirical-nosed gentleman would as soon have been suspected of picking a pocket as eschewing a pun.

"Your eloquence, Mr. Deputy, is irresistible —"Man anticipates Time in the busy march of destruction. His own mortal frame, broken by intemperance, becomes a premature ruin; he fells the stately oak in the towering majesty of its verdure and beauty; he razes the glorious temple hallowed by Time! and the ploughshare passes over the sacred spot it once dignified and adorned!

Man is ever quarrelling with Time. Time flies too swiftly; or creeps too slowly. His distempered vision conjures up a dwarf or a giant; hence Time is too short, or Time is too long! Now Time hangs heavy on his hands; yet for most things he cannot find Time! Though fame-serving, he makes a lackey of Time; asking Time to pay his debts; Time to eat his dinner; Time for all things! He abuses those, that never gave him a hard word; and, in a fit of ennui, to get rid of himself he kills Time; which is never recovered, but lost in Eternity!" And Uncle Timothy, keeping time and the tune, sang his retrospective song of

OLD TIME.

From boyhood to manhood, in fair and rough weather.

Old Time! you and I we have jogg'd on together;

Your touch has been gentle, endearing, and bland;

A fond father leading his son by the hand!

In the morning of life, ah! how tottering my tread —

(True symbol of age ere its journey is sped!)

But Time gave me courage, and fearless I ran —

I held up my head, and I march'd like a man!

Old Time brought me friendship, and swift flew the
        hours;

Life seem'd an Elysium of sunshine and flowers!

The flowers, but in memory, bear odour and bloom;

And the sun set on friendship, laid low in the tomb!

Yet, Time, shall I blame thee, tho' youth's happy glow

Is fled from my cheeks, that my locks are grey? —No!

What more can I wish (not abusing my prime)

To pilot me home, than a friend like Old Time?

Quite *at home*" is a comfortable phrase! A man may be in his own house, and "not at home" or a hundred miles away from it, and yet "quite at home." Quite at home" denotes absence of restraint (save that which good breeding imposes), ostentatious display, affected style, and the petty annoyances of your small gentry, who clumsily ape their betters. Good entertainment, congenial company, pleasant discourse, the whole seasoned with becoming mirth, and tempered with elegance and refinement, make a man "Quite at home"

"Not at home" is when Mister mimics Captain Grand, and Madam is in her tantrums; when our reception is freezing, and the guests are as sour as the wine; when no part or interest is taken in our pursuits and amusements; when frowns and discouragements darken our threshold; when the respect that is paid us by others is coldly received, or wilfully perverted by those whose duty it is to welcome to our hearth the grateful tribute; and when we are compelled to fly from home in order to be at home. "Quite at home" is quite the contrary! Then are affection, cheerfulness, mutual confidence, and sympathy, our household gods: every wish is anticipated, every sorrow soothed, and every pleasure shared!

Mr. Bosky, in his snug dining-parlour, entertaining a small party, was "Quite at home!" There were present, Mr. Merripall, Deputy Doublechin, Mr. Crambo the Werter-faced young gentleman, who looked (as the comical coffin-maker hinted) "in prime twig to take a journey down a pump!" Mr. Titlepage of Type Crescent; Mr. Flumgarten (who had left his "Hollyhock" to "waste her sweetness" on Pa, ilia, and Master Guy Muff!); and Borax Bumps, Esq. the craniologist.'Tis an easy thing to collect diners-out. High-feeding; the pleasure of criticising the taste of our host; quizzing his cuisine, and reckoning to a shade the expence of taking "the shine" out of him when we have our revenge! never fail to attract a numerous gathering. "Seeing company," in the fashionable sense of the word, is a series of attempts to eclipse those who are civil or silly enough to entertain us. Extremes belong to man only. There are some niggards who shut out all society; fasting themselves and making their doors fast!

Plentiful cheer, good humour, and a hearty welcome enlivened Mr. Bosky's table, the shape of which was after the fashion of King Arthur s, and the beef (this Mr. Bosky called having a round with his friends!) was after the fashion of the table. The party would have been a round dozen, but for the temporary absence of Messrs. Hatband and Stiflegig, who stood sentinel at a couple of door-posts round the corner, and were not expected to be off guard until a few glasses had gone round. The conversation was various and animated. Deputy Doublechin, who had a great genius for victuals, declaimed with civic eloquence upon the on-and-off-the-river champagne, white bait, venison and turtle treats, for which Gog and Magog, and the City Chamber "stood Sam the comical coffin-maker rambled on a pleasant excursion to the cemeteries; Mr. Titlepage discoursed fluently upon waste demy; Mr. Bumps examined the craniums of the company, commencing with the "destructive" "adhesive" acquisitive," "imaginative" and "philoprogenitive" developments of Deputy Doublechin; Mr. Flumgarten, who was "Quite at home!" proved himself a master of every subject, and was most facetious and entertaining; and the Bard of Bleeding Hart Yard, after reciting a couplet of his epitaph upon an heroic young gentleman who was hung in chains,

"My uncle's son lies here below,

And rests at peace-when the wind don't blow!"

sang, *moderato con anima,* his

LEGEND OF KING'S-CROSS.

Those blythe Bow bells! those blythe Bow bells! a merry

    peal they ring,

And see a band of beaux and belles as jocund as the

    spring;

But who is she with gipsy hat and smart pink satin

    shoes?

The lily fair of Jockey s Fields, the darling of the mews.

But where is Jimmy Ostler John, whom folks call "stable

    Jack"?

Alas! he cannot dance the hey, his heart is on the rack.

The Corp'ral's cut him to the core, who marries Betsy

    Brown;

The winter of his discontent he spends at Somers' Town.

A pot of porter off he toss'd, then gave his head a toss,

And look'd cross-buttocks when he met nis rival at King's

    Cross;

The Corp'ral held right gallantly to widows, maids, and

    wives,

A bunch of roses in his fist, and Jack his bunch of fives.

Cry'd Betsy Brown, "All Troy I'll to a tizzy bet, 'tis

    he!

I never thought to see you more, methought you went

    to sea:

That you, the crew, and all your togs, (a mouthful for a

shark!)

Good for nothing, graceless dogs! had perish'd in a bark."

"I'm him as was your lover true, O perjur'd Betsy

    Brown!

Your spark from Dublin up, I'll soon be doubling up in

    town!

If, Pat, you would divine the cause, behold this nymph

    divine;

You 've won the hand of Betsy Brown, now try a taste

    of mine!"

The Corp'ral laid a bet he'd beat, but Betsy held her rib —

"Be aisy, daisy I —Lying lout! we'll see which best can

    fib!

A trick worth two I'll shew you, by St. Patrick, merry

    saint!"

Poor Betsy fainted in his arms-the Corp'ral made a

    feint.

Jack ey'd the pump, and thither hied, and filled a bucket

    quick,

And chuck'd it o'er his chuck, for fear she should the

    bucket kick;

Then gave a tender look, and join'd a tender in the

    river —

What afterwards became of him we never could diskiver.

"The City of London and the trade thereof," and other standing toasts, having been drunk with the accustomed honours, Uncle Timothy addressed Mr. Bosky,

"Thy *Epilogue*, Benjamin. Drop we the curtain on this mountebank drama, and cry quittance to conjurors."

Mr. Bosky. But what is an *Epilogue* without a dress coat, a *chapeau bras*, black velvets and paste buckles? *Nous verrons!*

And the Lauréat rose, put on a stage face, stood tea-pot fashion, and poured out his soul.

> Mr. Bosky. Knights of the Table Round! in verse
>
> sublime,
>
> I fain would tell how once upon a time,
>
> When George the Second, royally interr'd,
>
> Resign'd his sceptre to King George the
>
> Third-
>
>
> Uncle Tim. Bosky, dismounting Pegasus, suppose
>
> You sit, and speak your epilogue in prose,
>
> Not in falsetto flat, and thro' the nose,
>
> Like those
>
> Who warble "knives to grind," and cry
>
> "old clothes!"

Mr. Bosky (resuming his seat and natural voice). The monarch, glorying in the name of Briton, assumed the imperial diadem amidst the acclamations of his loyal subjects; the mime, though not Briton born, but naturalized, had done nothing to alienate his right comical peers, or diminish his authority in the High Court and Kingdom of Queerummania. But *Punch* had fallen on evil times and tongues. A few sticks of the rotten edifice of *utilitarianism* had been thrown together; men began to prefer the dry, prickly husks of disagreeable truths, to the whipt-syllabubs of pleasant fiction; all recreations were resolving themselves in "*Irishman's Holiday (change of work!)* the vivacity of small beer, and the strength of workhouse gruel! an unjolly spirit had again come over the nation; and people thought that by making this world a hell upon earth, they were nearer on their road to heaven! The contemporaries of *Punch*, too, had declined in respectability. A race of inferior conjurors succeeded to the cups and balls of Mr. Fawkes; the equilibrists and vaulters * danced more like a pea on a tobacco-pipe, than artists on the wire; and a troop of barn-door fowls profaned the classic boards on which Dogget, Pinkethman, and Spiller, once crowed so triumphantly.

* "Mr. Maddox balances on his chin seven pipes in one another; a chair, topsy-turvy, and a coach-wheel. Also a sword on the edge of a wine-glass; several glasses brim full of liquor; two pipes, cross-ways, on a hoop; a hat on his nose; and stands on his head while the wire is in full

swing, without touching it with his hands." These
performances he exhibited at Sadler's Wells, the Haymarket
Theatre, &c. from 1753 to 1770.
"At the New Theatre Royal in the Haymarket this day, the

24th October, 1747, will be performed by a native Turk,
Mahommed Caratha, the most surprising équilibrés on the
slack-rope, without a balance.
"Perhaps where Lear has rav'd, and Hamlet died,

On flying cars new sorcerers may ride;
Perhaps (for who can guess th' effects of chance?)
Here Hunt may box, or Mahomet may dance."

Dame Nature, whose freaks in former times had contributed much to the amusement of the fair, turned spiteful-for children were born perversely well-proportioned; so that a dwarf ("*Homunculi quanti sunt cum recogito!*") became a great rarity in the monster market; giants, like ground in the city, fetched three guineas a foot; humps rose, and the woods and forests were hunted for wild men. The same contradictory spirit ruled the animal creation. Cows had heretofore been born with a plurality of heads; and calves without tails were frequently retailed in the market. The pig, whose aptitude for polite learning had long been proverbial, sulked over his ABC, and determined to be a dunce; the dog * refused to be —

* In the year 1753, "Mrs. Midnight's company" played at the
Little Theatre in the Haymarket. A monkey acted the part of
a waiter; and three dogs, as Harlequin, Pierrot, and
Columbine, rivalled their two-legged competitors; a town was
besieged by dogs, and defended by monkeys, the latter
tumbling their assailants over the battlements. The dogs and
monkeys performed a grand ballet; and a couple of dogs,
booted and spurred, mounted a brace of monkeys, and gal-
lopped off in Newmarket style. We are not quite certain
whether Mrs. Midnight and her comedians travelled so far
east as Smithfield Rounds.

—taught to dance; and the monkey, * at all times a trump-card, forswore spades and diamonds. There was a mortality among the old dwarfs and Merry Andrews and the glory of Bar-tlemy Fair, *Roast Pig*, had departed!

Original

* Spinacuta's monkey amused the French King and Court by
dancing and tumbling on the slack and tight rope; balancing
a chandelier, a hoop, and a tobacco-pipe, on the tip of his
nose and chin, and making a melodramatic exit in a shower of
fireworks. He afterwards exhibited at Sadler's Wells and
Bartholomew Fair.
** "August 31, 1768. Died Jonathan Gray, aged nearly one

hundred years, the famous Merry Andrew, who formerly
exhibited at the fairs about London, and gained great
applause by his acting at Covent Garden Theatre, in the
entertainment called Bartholomew Fair"
"October 3, 1777. Yesterday, died in St. Bartholomew's

Hospital, Thomas Carter, the dwarf who was exhibited at last
Bartholomew Fair. He was about 25 years of age, measuring

only three feet four inches high. It is supposed that over
drinking at the fair caused his death."

That crackling dainty, which would make a man *manger son propre père!* gave place to horrible
fried sausages, from which even the mongrels and tabbies of Smithfield instinctively turned
aside with anti-cannibal misgivings! Unsavoury links! fizzing, fuming, bubbling, and squeaking
in their own abominable black broth! "An ounce of civet, good apothecary, to sweeten mine
imagination!" Your Bartlemy Fair kitchen is not the spice islands.
  In 1661, one of Dame Ursula's particular orders to Mooncalf was to froth the cans well.
In 1655,

  "For a penny you may see a fine puppet play,

  And for two-pence a rare piece of art;

  And a penny a can, I dare swear a man

  May put six (!) of 'em into a quart?

Only six! Mark to what immeasurable enormity these subdivisions of cans had risen fifty years
after. Well might *Roger in Amaze* * exclaim —
  * "Roger in Amaze; or the Countryman's Ramble through
Bartholomew Fair. To the tune of the Dutch Woman's Jigg.
1701."

  "They brought me cans which cost a penny a piece,

  adsheart,

  I'm zure twelve (!!) ne'er could fill our country quart"

288

"Remember twelve!" Yet these were days of comparative honesty —"a ragged virtue," which, as better clothes came in fashion, was cast off by the drawers, and an indescribable liquid succeeded, not in a great measure, but "small by degrees and beautifully less," to the transcendant tipple of *Michael Roots*. From the wry faces and twinges of modern drinkers (it seems impossible to stand *upright* in the presence of a Bar-tlemy Fair brewing!) we guess the tap has not materially improved. The advance of prices on the "fine puppet play" * and the two-penny *rare piece of art*" were not resisted; the O.P.'s were made to mind their P's and Q's by the terrors of the Pied Poudre.

* "Let me never live to look so high as the two-penny room
again," says Ben Jonson, in his prologue to Every Man out of
his Humour, acted at the Globe, in 1599. The price of the
"best rooms" or boxes, was one shilling; of the lower places
two-pence, and of some places only a penny. The two-penny
room was the gallery. Thus Decker, "Pay your two-pence to a
player, and you may sit in the gallery-Bellman's Night
Walk. And Middleton, "One of them is a nip, I took him once
into the two-penny gallery at the Fortune." In Every Man out
of his Humour there is also mention of "the lords' room over
the stage." The "lords' room" answered to the present stage-
boxes. The price of them was originally one shilling. Thus
Decker, in his Gull's Hornbook, 1609, "At a new play you
take up the twelve-penny room next the stage, because the
lords and you may seem to be hail fellow, well met."

For many dismal seasons the fair dragged on from hand to mouth, hardly allowing its exhibitors (in the way of refection) to put the one to the other. And though my Lord Mayor * and the keeper of Newgate might take it cool, (in a tankard!) it was no laughing matter to the hungry mountebank, who could grin nobody into his booth; to the thirsty musician (who had swallowed many a butt!) grinding on his barrel; and the starved balladmonger (corn has ears, but not for music!) singing for his bread. We hasten to more prosperous times. "Another glass, and then." Yet, ere the sand of the present shall have run out, good night to St. Bartholomew! We cannot say with Mr. Mawworm, "We likes to be despised!" nor are we emulous of "crackers," unless they appertain unto wine and walnuts.

* On the morning the fair is proclaimed, according to
ancient custom, his Magnificence the Mayor drinks "a cool
tankard" (not of aqua pura,) with that retentive knight, the
keeper of Newgate.

But, sooner than our grotesque friends shall want a chronicler, we will apostrophise the learned pig, the pig-faced lady, and the most delicate monster that smokes his link for a cigar, picks his teeth with a hay-fork, and takes his snuff with a fire-shovel. Not that we love Sir Andrew less, but that we love St. Bartle-my more.

Higman Palatine * in 1763 delighted the court at Richmond Palace, and the commonalty at the "Rounds," with his "surprising deceptions;" and, gibing his heel, followed the toe of Mr. Breslaw. **

* "Mr. Palatine exhibits with pigeons, wigs, oranges,
cards, handkerchiefs, and pocket-pieces; and swallows
knives, forks, punch-ladles, and candle-snuffers."
** In 1775, Breslaw performed at Cockspur Street, Hay-

market, and in after years at Hughes's Riding School and

Bartholomew Fair. Being at Canterbury with his troop, he met
with such bad success that they were almost starved. He
repaired to the churchwardens, and promised to give the
profits of a night's conjuration to the poor, if the parish
would pay for hiring a room, &c. The charitable bait took,
the benefit proved a bumper, and next morning the
churchwardens waited upon the wizard to touch the receipts.
"I have already disposed of dem," said Breslaw —"de profits
were for de poor.
I have kept my promise, and given de money to my own people,

who are de poorest in dis parish "Sir!" exclaimed the
churchwardens, "this is a trick!" —"I know it," replied
Hocus Pocus —"I live by my tricks!"

In after years there fell on Mr. Lane * ('tis a long lane that has never a turning!) a remnant of
Fawkes's mantle. But was not our conjuror ("you must borrow me the mouth of Gargantua!")
and his *Enchanted Sciatoricon*," little too much in advance of the age? The march of intellect **
had not set in with a very strong current. The three R's (reading, 'riting, and 'rithmetic!) comprehended the classical attainments of a "City Solon and a Tooley Street Socrates."
    * "Grand Exhibition by Mr. Lane, first' performer to the
King, opposite the Hospital Gate. His Enchanted Sciatoricon
will discover to the company the exact time of the day by
any watch, though the watch may be in the pocket of a person
five miles off. The Operation Palingenesia: any spectator
sending for a couple of eggs, may take the choice of them,
and the egg, being broke, produces a living bird of the
species desired, which in half a minute receives its full
plumage, and flies away. The other egg will, at the request
of the company, leap from one hat to another, to the number
of twenty." Then follow "His Unparalleled Sympathetic
Figures,"
"Magical Tea Caddie" and above one hundred other astonishing

tricks for the same money.
** This is the age of progression. Intellect and steam are

on the quick march and full gallop. Butchers' boys, puffing
cigars, and lapping well-diluted caldrons of "Hunt's
Roasted," illuminate with penny lore the hitherto unclassic
shambles of Whitechapel and Leadenhall. The mechanic, far
advanced in intelligence and gin, roars "animal parliaments,
universal suffering, and vote by bullet." And the Sunday
School Solomon, on being asked by meo magister, "Who was
Jesse?" lisps "the Flower of Dumblain!" —"When was Rome
built, my little intelligence?" —"In the night, sir." —"Eh!
How?" —
"Because I've heerd grandmother say, Rome warn't built in a

day!" —"Avez vous du mal, monsieur?" was the question put to
a young Englishman, after a turn over in the French

diligence. —"Non" replied the six-lessons linguist, "Je riai
qu'un portmanteau!"

But we have since advanced to the learning of Mr. Lane; like the lady, who complained to
the limner that her portrait looked too ancient for her, and received from Mr. Brush this
pertinent reply, "Madam, you will grow more and more like it every day!" *Ingleby*, * "emperor
of conjurors," (who let his magic cat out of the bag in a printed book of legerdemain,) and
Gyngell played, only with *new variations*, the same old sleight-of-hand tricks over again. The
wizard's art is down among the dead men.

* "Theurgicomination! or New Magical Wonders, by Sieur
Ingleby. He plays all sorts of tricks upon cards; exhibits
his Pixidees Metallurgy, or tricks upon medals; and
Operation in
Popysomance, being the art of discovering people's thoughts.

Any gentleman may cut off a cock's head, and at the Sieur's
bidding it shall leap back to its old quarters, chanticleer
giving three crows for its recovery!"

As "dead men" died on the Laureat's lips, the joyous presence was announced of Mr. Hercules
Hatband and Mr. Stanislaus Stiflegig. Uncle Timothy proposed a glass round; and to make up
for lost time (in a libation to mountebanks), tumblers for the mutes.

"Our nephew is fat, and scant of breath we will give him a few minutes to recruit. Marmaduke Merripall, I call upon you for a song."

"An excellent call! Uncle Timothy," shouted Deputy Doublechin.

Up jumped Borax Bumps, Esq. and running his shoulder of mutton palms with scientific velocity over the curly-wigged cranium of the comical coffin-maker, he emphatically pronounced
the "organ of tune" to exhibit a musical Pelion among its intellectual nodosities.

"I should take your father, sir, to have been a parish clerk, from this mountainous develope-
ment of Sternhold and Hopkins."

"My song shall be a toast" said the comical coffin-maker:

"TOASTED CHEESE!"

Taffy ap-Tudor he couldn't be worse —

The Leech having bled him in person and purse.

His cane at his nose, and his fee in his fob,

Bow'd off, winking Crape to look out for a job.

"Hur Taffy will never awake from his nap!

Ap-Tudor! ap-Jones! oh!" cried nurse Jenny-ap-

Shenkin ap-Jenkin ap-Morgan ap-Rice —

But Taffy turn'd round, and call'd out in a trice,

"Jenny ap-Rice, hur could eat something nice,

A dainty Welch rabbit-go toast hur a slice

Of cheese, if you please, which better agrees

With the tooth of poor Taffy than physic and fees."

A pound Jenny got, and brought to his cot

The prime double Glo'ster, all hot! piping hot!

Which being a bunny without any bones,

Was custard with mustard to Taffy ap-Jones.

"Buy some leeks, Jenny, and brew hur some caudle —

No more black doses from Doctor McDawdle!"

Jenny stew'd down a bunch into porridge, (Welch

    punch!)

And Taffy, Cot pless him! he wash'd down his lunch.

On the back of his hack next mom Doctor Mac

Came to see Jenny preparing her black!

Ap answer'd his rap in a white cotton cap,

With another Welch rabbit just caught in his trap!

"A gobbling? you ghost Î" the Leech bellow'd loud,

"Does your mother know, Taffy, you're out of your
    shroud?"

"Hur physic'd a week-at hur very last squeak,

Hur try'd toasted cheese and decoction of leek."

"I'm pocketting fees for the self-same disease

From the dustman next door —I'll prescribe toasted
    cheese

And leek punch for lunch!" But the remedy fails —

What kills Pat from Kilmore, cures Taffy from Wales.

CHAPTER X.

In the year 1776," continued the Lauréat, "Mr. Philip Astley * transferred his equestrian troop to the 'Rounds.' To him succeeded Saunders, ** who brought forward into the 'circle' that 'wonderful child of promise,' his son, accompanied by the tailor riding to Brentford! To thee, Billy Button! and thy 'Buffo Caricatto,' Thompson, the tumbler, we owe some of the heartiest laughs of our youthful days. Ods 'wriggling, giggling, galloping, galloway,' we have made merry in St. Bartlemy!"

   * In the early part of his career Mr. Astley paraded the streets of London, and dealt out his hand-bills to the servants and apprentices whom his trumpet and drum attracted to the doors as he passed along.
** Master Saunders, only seven years old, jumps through a

hoop, and brings it over his head, and dances a hornpipe on the saddle, his horse going three-quarters speed round the circle! The Tailor riding to Brentford, by Mr. Belcher. — Bartholomew Fair, 1796."

There were grand doings at the fair in 1786, 87 and 88. Palmer, "at the Greyhound," placarded Harlequin Proteus, and the Tailor done over. At the George Inn, Mr. Flockton exhibited the Italian Fantoccini, and the Tinker in a bustle. Mr. Jobson * put his puppets in motion; Mrs. Garmaris caravan, with the classical motto, *Hoc tempus et non aliter*, advertised vaulting by the juvenile imp. "Walk in, ladies and gentlemen," cried Mr. Smith, near the Swan Livery Stables; "and be enchanted among the rocks, fountains, and waterfalls of art!" Patrick O'Brien (o'ertopping Henry Blacker,** the seven feet four inches giant of 1761,) arrived in his teakettle. A goose, instructed by a poll parrot, sang several popular songs.

   * Mr. Jobson added the following* verses to his bill:
"Prithee come, my lads and lasses,

Jobson's oddities let's see;
Where there's mirth and smiling faces,
And good store of fun and glee!
Pleasant lads and pretty lasses,
All to Jobson s haste away;
Point your toes, and brim your glasses!
And enjoy a cheerful day."
** "Mr. O'Brien measures eight feet four inches in height,

but lives in hopes of attaining nine feet," the family altitude!

Three turkeys danced cotillons and minuets. The military ox went through his manual exercise; and the monkey taught the cow her horn-book. Ive's company of comedians played "The Wife well managed," to twenty-eight different audiences in one day! The automaton Lady; the infant musical phenomenon without arms, and another phenomenon, equally infantine and musical, without legs; a three-legged heifer, with four nostrils; a hen webfooted, and a duck with a cock's head, put forth their several attractions. Messrs. White, at the Lock and Key, sold capital punch; savoury sausages (out-frying every other fry in the fair,) fizzed at "the Grunter's Ordinary or Relish-Warehouse, in Hosier Lane; and Pie-Corner" rang with the screeching drollery of Mr. Mountebank Merry Andrew Macphinondraughanarmonbolinbrough!

The "wonderful antipodean," Sieur Sanches, who walked against the ceiling with his head downwards, and a flag in his hand; Louis Porte *

* Louis Porte was an inoffensive giant. Not so our English
monsters. On the 10th of Sept. 1787, a Bartlemy Fair
Giant was brought before Sir William Plomer at Guildhall,

for knocking out two of his manager's fore-teeth, for which
the magistrate fined him two guineas per tooth! In March
1841, a giantess, six feet nine inches high, from Modern
Athens and Bartholomew Fair, killed her husband in a booth
at Glasgow; and in the same year, at Barnard-Castle Easter
Fair, a giant stole a change of linen from a hedge, for
which he was sent to prison for three months.
On the 26th May, 1555, (see Strype's Memorials,) there was a

May-game at St. Martin's in the Fields, with giants and
hobby-horses, drums, guns, morris-dancers, and minstrels.

("*Hercule du Roi!*") a French equilibrist; Pietro Bologna, a dancer on the slack-wire; Signor Placida ("the Little Devil!"); "La Belle Espagnole" (on the tight-rope); the "real wild man of the woods;" * the dancing-dogs of Sieur Scaglioni; ** General Jacko, *** and Pidcock's **** menagerie, (to which succeeded those of Polito and Wombwell,) one and all drove a roaring trade at Bartholomew Fair.

* "This Ethiopian savage has a black face, with a large
white circle round it. He sits in a chair in a very pleasing
and majestic attitude; eats his food like a Christian, and
is extremely affable and polite."
** These dogs danced an allemand, mimicked a lady spinning,

and a deserter going to execution, attended by a chaplain,
(a dressed-up puppy!) in canonicals.
*** "June 17, 1785, at Astley's, General Jacko performs the

broad-sword exercise; dances on the tight-rope; balances a i
pyramid of lights; and lights his master home with a link."
In the following September the General opened his campaign

at Bartholomew Fair.
**** Were you to range the mighty globe all o'er,

From east to west, from north to southern shore;
Under the line of torrid zone to go —
No deserts, woods, groves, mountains, more can shew
To you, than Pidcock in his forest small —
Here, at one view, you have a sight of all."

We chronicle not the gods, emperors, dark bottle-green demons, and indigo-blue nondescripts that have since strutted their hour upon the boards of "Richardson's Grand Theatrical Booth." * They, like every dog, have had their day; and comical dogs were most of them!

Of the modern minstrelsy of the "Rounds," the lyrics of Mr. Johannot, Joe Grimaldi, and the very merry hey down derry, "Neighbour Prig" song of Charles Mathews, ** are amusing specimens.

* In Sept. 1806, Mr. and Mrs. Carey (the reputed father and mother of Edmund Kean, the tragedian,) played at Richardson's Theatre, Bartholomew Fair, the Baron Montaldi and his daughter, in a gallimaufry of love, murder, brimstone, and blue fire, called "The Monk and Murderer, or the Skeleton Spectre!"
** Mathews was the Hogarth of the stage; his characters are

as finely discriminated, as vigorously drawn, as highly finished, and as true to nature, as those of the great painter of mankind. His perception of the eccentric and outré was intuitive; —his range of observation comprehended human nature in all its varieties; he caught not only the manner, but the matter of his originals; and while he hit off with admirable exactness the peculiarities of individuals, their very turn of thought and modes of expression were given with equal truth. In this respect he surpassed Foote, whose mimicry seldom went beyond personal deformities and physical defects —a blinking eye, a lame leg, or a stutter. He was a satirist of the first class, without being a caricaturist; exhibiting folly in all its Protean shapes, and laughing it out of countenance —a histrionic Democritus! His gallery of faces was immense. He had as many physiognomies as Argus had eyes. The extraordinary and the odd, the shrewd expression of knavish impudence, the rosy contentedness of repletion, the vulgar stare of boorish ignorance, and the blank fatuity of idiocy, he called up with a flexibility that had not been witnessed since the days of Garrick. Many of his most admired portraits were creations of his own: the old Scotchwoman, the Idiot playing with a Fly, Major Longbow, &c. &c. The designs for his "At Homes" were from the same source; meaner artists filled in the back-ground, but the figures stood forth in full relief, the handiwork of their unrivalled impersonator. Who but remembers his narration of the story of the Gamester, his Monsieur Mallét, and particular parts of Monsieur Morbleu? —Nothing could be more delightful than his representation of the "pauvre barbiere had the air, the bienséance of the Chevalier, who had danced a minuet at the "Cour de Versailles" His petit chanson, "C'est V Amour!" and his accompanying capers, were exquisitely French. His transitions from gaiety to sadness-from restlessness to civility-his patient and impatient shrugs, were admirably given.
In legitimate comedy, his old men and intriguing valets were

excellent; while Lingo, Quotem, Nipperkin, Midas Sharp, Wiggins, &c. &c. in farce, have seldom met with

merrier representatives. His broken English was superb; his
country boobies were unsophisticated nature; and his Paddies
the richest distillation of whisky and praties. He was the
finest burletta singer of his day, and in his patter songs,
his rapidity of utterance and distinctness of enunciation
were truly wonderful.

His Dicky Suett in pawn for the cheesecakes and raspberry

tarts at the pastry-cook's, in St. Martin's Court, was no
less faithful than convulsing; Tate Wilkinson, Cooke, Jack
Bannister, and Bensley, were absolute resurgams; and if he
was not the identical Charles Incledon, "there's no purchase
in money."

He was the first actor that introduced Jonathan into

England, for the entertainment of his laughter-loving
brothers and sisters. The vraisemblance was unquestionable,
and the effect prodigious.

A kindred taste for pictures, prints, and theatrical relics,

often brought the writer into his company. At his pleasant
Thatched Cottage at Kentish Town, rising in the midst of
green lawns, flower-beds, and trellis-work, fancifully
wreathed and overgrown with jasmine and honey-suckles! was
collected a more interesting museum of dramatic curiosities
than had ever been brought together by the industry of one
man. Garrick medals in copper, silver, and bronze; a lock of
his hair; the garter worn by him in Richard the Third; his
Abel Drug-ger shoes; his Lear wig; his walking-stick; the
managerial chair in which he kept his state in the green-
room of Old Drury; the far-famed Casket (now in the
possession of the writer) carved out of the mulberry-tree
planted by Shakspere; the sandals worn by John Kemble in
Coriolanus on the last night of that great actor's
performance, and presented by him to his ardent admirer on
that memorable occasion, were all regarded by Mathews as
precious relics. He was glad of his sandals, he wittily
remarked, since he never could hope to stand in his shoes!
The Penruddock stick, and Hamlet wig were also carefully
preserved. So devoted was he to his art, and so just and
liberal in his estimation of its gifted professors, that he
lost no opportunity of adding to his interesting store some
visible tokens by which he might remember them.

He was the friendliest of men. The facetious companion never

lost sight of the gentleman; he scorned to be the buffoon —
the professional lion of a party, however exalted by rank.
It was one of his boasts —a noble and a proud one too! —that
the hero of a hundred fights, the conqueror of France, the
Prince of Waterloo! received him at his table, not as Punch,
but as a private gentleman. He had none of the low vanity
that delights to attract the pointed finger. He was content

with his supremacy on the stage-an universal imitator,
himself inimitable!

In the summer of 1830, we accompanied him to pay the veteran

Quick a visit at his snug retreat at Islington. Tony Lumpkin
(then in his seventy-fifth year), with little round body,
flaring eye, fierce strut, turkey-cock gait, rosy gills,
flaxen wig, blue coat, shining buttons, white vest, black
silk stockings and smalls, bright polished shoes, silver
buckles, and (summer and winter) blooming and fragrant
bouquet! received us at the door, with his comic treble! The
meeting was cordial and welcome. No man than Quick was a
greater enthusiast in his art, or more inquisitive of what
was doing in the theatrical world. Of Ned Shuter he spoke in
terms of unqualified admiration, as an actor of the broadest
humour the stage had ever seen; and of Edwin, as a
surpassing Droll, with a vis comica of extraordinary power.
He considered Tom Weston, though in many respects a glorious
actor, too rough a transcript of nature, and Dodd (except in
Sir Andrew Ague-cheek, which he pronounced a master-piece of
fatuity,) too studied and artificial. He could never account
for Garrick's extreme partiality for Woodward, (David
delighted to act with him,) whose style was dry and hard;
his fine gentleman had none of the fire, spirit, and
fascination of Lewis; it was pert, snappish, and not a
little ill-bred; but his Bobadil and Pa-rolles were
inimitable. He declared the Sir Fretful Plagiary of his
guest equal to the best thing that Parsons ever did; yet
Parson's Old Doiley was for ever on his lips, and "Don't go
for to put me in a passion, Betty!" was his favourite tag,
when mine hostess of the King's Head, Islington, put too
much lime in his punch. He thought King the best prologue-
speaker of his time. In characters of bluff assurance and
quaint humour-Brass, Trappanti, Touchstone, &c. —he had no
superior. Garrick was his idol! His sitting-room was hung
round with engravings of him in Drugger, Richard, Sir John
Brute, Kitely, cheek-by-jowl with himself in Sancho, Tony
Lumpkin, "Cunning Isaac," Spado, &c. The time too swiftly
passed in these joyous reminiscences. Quick promised to
return the visit, but increasing infirmities forbade the
pleasant pilgrimage; and soon after he became the Quick and
the dead!

Our last visit to Mr. Mathews at Kentish Town was in March,

1833. "'Tis agony point with me just now," he writes. "I
have been scribbling from morning till night for three
weeks.

I am hurried with my entertainment: my fingers are cramped

with writing; and on my return, I find twenty-five letters,
at least, to answer. I shall be at home Tuesday and
Wednesday; can you come up? Do. Very sincerely yours, in a

gallop, Charles Mathews. —P.S. It will be your last chance
of seeing my gallery here" We accepted the invitation, and
spent a delightful day.

What more than a hasty glance can we afford the Wild Indian Warriors; the Enchanted Skeleton; Comical Joe on his Piggy-Wiggy; the Canadian Giantess; Toby, the sapient pig; the
learned goose; * Doncaster Dick, the great; Mr. Paap, ** Sieur Borawliski, Thomas Allen,
and Lady Morgan the little; the wonderful child (in spirits) with two heads, three legs, and
four arms ("no white leather, but all real flesh"); the Bonassus, "whose fascinating powers are
most wonderful." the Chinese Swinish Philosopher (a rival of Toby!).
    * "It tells us the time of day; the day of the month; the
month of the year; takes a hand at whist; and (the
profundity of this goose's intellects!) counts the number of
ladies and gentleman in the room."
** Mr. Simon Paap was the most diminutive of dwarfs, not

excepting Jeffery Hudson, and the "Little Welchman" who, in
1752, advertised his thirty inches at sixpence a-head. Simon
measured but twenty-eight inches, and weighed only twenty-
seven pounds. Count Borawliski was three feet three inches
high; so was Thomas Allen. Lady Morgan, the "Windsor Fairy,"
was a yard high. Her Ladyship and Allen were thus be-rhymed
by some Bartlemy Fair bard:
"The lady like a fairy queen,

The gentleman of equal stature;
O how curious these dear creatures!
Little bodies! little features!
Hands, feet, and all alike so small,
How wondrous are the works of nature!"

Mrs. Samwell's voltigeurs on the slack-wire, and Tyrolesian stilts; the Spotted Negro Boy;
Hokee Pokee; the learned dog near-sighted, and in spectacles; the Red Barn Tragedy, and
Corder's * execution "done to the life!" the Indian Jugglers; the Reform Banquet; Mr. Haynes,
the fire-eater; ** the Chinese Conjuror, who swallows fifty needles, which, after remaining
some time in his throat, are pulled out threaded; the chattering, locomotive, laughing, lissom,
light-heeled Flying Pieman; and the diverting humours of Richardson's clown, Rumfungus
Hook-umsnoolcumwalkrisky? This ark of oddities *** must

        "Come like shadows, so depart."

  * A countryman from Hertford, being in the gallery of Covent
Garden Theatre, at the tragedy of Macbeth, and hearing
Duncan demand of Malcolm,
"Is execution done on Cawdor?" exclaimed, "Yes, your honour?

he was hanged this morning."
** June 7, 1821 at the White Conduit House, Islington, Mons.

Chabert, after a luncheon of phosphorus, arsenic, oxalic

acid, boiling oil, and molten lead, walked into a hot oven, preceded by a leg of lamb and a rumpsteak. On the two last, when properly baked, the spectators dined with him. An ordinary most extraordinary! Some wags insinuated that, if the Salamander was not "done brown," his gulls were!
*** The following account of Bartlemy Fair receipts, in

1828, may be relied on: —Wombwell's Menagerie, 1700L.; Atkins' ditto, 1000L.; and Richardson's Theatre, 1200L.; the price of admission to each being sixpence. Morgan's Menagerie, 150L.; admission threepence. Balls, 80L.; Ballard, 89L.; Keyes, 20L.; Frazer, 26L.; Pikey 40L.; Pig-faced Lady, 150L.; Corder s Head, 100L.; Chinese Jugglers, 50L.; Fat
Boy and Girl, 140L.; Salamander, 30L.; Diorama Navarin,

60L.; Scotch Giant, 201. The admission to the last twelve shows varied from twopence to one halfpenny.

Mr. Titlepage. With a little love, murder, larceny, and lunacy, Mr. Bosky, your monsters with two heads would cut capital figures on double crow

Mr. Crambo. If I had their drilling and dovetailing, a pretty episode should they make to my forthcoming Historical Romance of Mother Brown-rigg! I've always a brace of plots at work, an upper and an under one, like two men at a saw-pit! Indeed, so horribly puzzled was I how to get decently over the starvation part of my story, till I hit upon the notable expedient of joining Mrs. B. in holy matrimony to a New Poor Law Commissioner, that it was a toss-up whether I hanged myself or my heroine! That union happily solemnised, and a few liberal drafts upon Philosophical Necessity, by way of floating capital, my plots, like Johnny Gilpin's wine-bottles, hung on each side of my Pegasus, and preserved my equipoise as I galloped over the course!

By suspending the good lady's suspension till the end of vol. three (I don't cut her down to a single one), the interest is never suffered to drop till it reaches the New one. Or, as I'm doing the Newgate Calendar, (I like to have two strings to my bow!) what say you, gents? if, in my fashionable novel of Miss Blandy (the Oxford lass, who popped off in her pumps for dosing —"poison in jest!"—her doting old dad,) St. Bartlemy and his conjurors were made to play first fiddle! D' ye think, friend Merripall, you could rake me up from your rarities a sketch of Mother Brownrigg coercing her apprentices? (There I am fearfully graphic! You may count every string in the lash, and every knot in the string!) A print of her execution? (There I melt Jack Ketch, and dissolve the turnkeys.) Or, an inch of the identical twine (duly attested by the Ordinary!) that compressed the jugular of Miss Mary?

Mr. Merripall. I promise you all three, Mr. Crambo. Let the flogging and the finishing scene be engraved in mezzotinto, and the rope in line.

Uncle Timothy. Many years since I accompanied my old friend, Charles Lamb, to Bartholomew Fair. It was his pet notion to explore the droll-booths; perchance to regale in the "pens:" indeed, had roast pig ("a Chinese and a female," dredged at the critical moment, and done till it crackled delicately,) continued one of its tit-bits, he had bargained for an ear! "In spirit a lion, in figure a lamb," the game of jostling went on merrily; and when the nimble fingers of a chevalier dindustrie found their way into his pocket, he remarked that the poor rogue only wanted "change." As little heeded he the penny rattles scraped down his back, and their frightful harmony dinned in his ears. Of a black magician, who was marvellously adroit with his daggers and gilt balls, he said, "That fellow is not only a Negro man, sir, but a necromancer!" He introduced himself to Saunders, whose fiery visage and scarlet surtout looked like Monmouth Street in a blaze! and the showman suspended a threatened blast from his speaking-trumpet to bid him welcome. A painted show-cloth announced in colossal capitals that a twoheaded cow was to be seen at sixpence a head.

Elia inquired if it meant at per our heads or the cow's? On another was chalked "Ladies and gentlemen, two-pence; servants, one penny.11 Elia subscribed us the exhibitors "most obedient servants," posted our plebeian pence, and passed in. We peeped into the puppet-shows; paid our respects to the wild animals; visited Gyngell and Richardson; patronised ("nobly daring!") a puff of the Flying Pieman's; and, such was his wild humour, all but ventured into a swing! This was a perilous joke! His fragile form canted out, and his neck broken! Then the unclassical evidence of the Bartlemy Fair folk at the "Crowner's quest." What a serio-comic chapter for a posthumous edition of Elia's Last Essays! Three little sweeps luxuriating over a dish of fried sausages caught his eye. This time he would have his way! We entered the "parlour" and on a dingy table-cloth, embroidered with mustard and gravy, were quickly spread before us, "hissing hot," some of "the best in the fair." His olfactory organs hinted that the "odeur des graillons" which invaded them was not that of Monsieur Ude; still he inhaled it heroically, observing that, not to argue dogmatically, yet categorically speaking, it reminded him of curry. "Lunch time with us," quoth Elia, "is past, and dinner-time not yet come," and he passed over the steaming dish to our companions at the *table d'hote*, with a kind welcome, and a winning smile. They stared, grinned, and all three fell to. We left them to their enjoyments; but not before Elia had slipped a silver piece into their little ebony palms. A copious libation to "rare Ben Jonson" concluded the day's sports. I never beheld him happier, more full of antique reminiscences, and gracious humanity.

"The peace of heaven,

The fellowship of all good souls go with him!"

Uncle Timothy rose to retire.

"One moment, sir," said the Lauréat; "we have not yet had Mr. Flumgarten's song."?

"My singing days, Cousin Bosky, are over," replied the ill-matched hubby of the "Hollyhock;" "but, if it please the company, I will tell them a tale."

CHAPTER XI.

Mr. Merripall, having gathered that the tale was of a ghostly character, would not suffer the candles to be snuffed, but requested his mutes to sprinkle over them a pinch or two of salt, that they might burn appropriately blue. He would have given his gold repeater for a death-watch; and when a coffin bounced out to him from the fire (howbeit it might be carrying coals to Newcastle!) he hailed it as a pleasant omen. Messrs. Hatband and Stiflegig, catching the jocular infection, brightened up amazingly.

THREE CHURCHES IN A ROW

I.=

If you journey westward-ho,

Three churches all of a row,

Ever since the days of the Friars,

Have lifted to Heaven their ancient spires.

The bells of the third are heard to toll —

    For Pauper, Dives?

    Pastor, Cives?

For a rich or a poor man's soul?

Winding round the sandy mound

    Coaches and four, feathers and pall,

    Startle the simple villagers all!

    Sable mutes, death's recruits!

Marshall the hearse to the holy ground.

Eight stout men the coffin bear —

What a creak is here! what a groan is there!

As the marching corps toil through the church door —

For the rich dead must be buried in lead;

Their pamper'd forms are too good for the worms!

They cheat in dust, as they cheated before.

Mumbles the parson, and mumbles the clerk,

    Prayer, response,

    All for the nonce!

Who shall shrive the soul of a shark?

Slides the coffin deep in the ground;

Earth knocks the lid with a hollow sound!

It lies in state, and the silver'd plate

Glares in the ghastly sepulchre round!

Death has his dole!

At last, at last the body's nail'd fast!

But who has the soul?

See a mourner slowly retire,

With a conscience ill at ease

For opening graves and burial fees,

He hath yet to pay his debt —

Tho' Heaven delays, can Heaven forget?

Forget? As soon as the sun at noon.

That gilds yon spire,

Shall cease to roll-or that mourner's soul

Itself expire!

Swift the arrow, eagle's flight,

Thought, sensation, sound, and light!

But swift indeed is the spirit's speed

To the glory of day, or the darkness of night!

Who knocks at the brazen gate? A fare

By the ferryman row'd to the gulf of despair!

With hissing snakes twisted into a thong,

    ("I drove you on earth, I drive you below,

    Gee up! gee up! old Judas, gee ho!")

A furious crone whipp'd a spirit along! —

    Her blood-shot sight

    Caught the ferryman's sprite;

"Welcome! welcome!" she shriek'd with delight —

"Thy father is here for his gifts to me,

    And here am I, his torment to be" —

    (And the cruel crone

    Lash'd out a groan!

    A deep-drawn breath

    From the ribs of death,

Where the undying worm gnaw'd the marrowless bone!)

"For what I have given thy brethren and thee!

Gold was to keep up our family name!'

    Spirit

    A penny-wise fame!

It has kept it up! for 'tis written in shame

On earth: and, behold! in that bright shining flame!

Old Man.

Death so soon to knock at thy door I

And send thee hither at forty and four.

Spirit.

My sire! my sire! unholy desire,

The hypocrite's guile,

Mask'd under a smile I

And avarice made me a pillow of fire;

The ill-gotten purse has carried its curse

Old Man.

Hath Jacob done better?

Spirit.

Nor better nor worse!

Losses and crosses, and sorrow and care

Have furrowed his cheeks and whitened his hair.

Betray'd in turn by the heart he betray'd,

Exalting his horn

To the finger of scorn,

He lies in the bed that his meanness has made.

Old Man. —Crone.

Our gold! our gold! ten thousand times told!

Thus to fly from the family fold.

Spirit.

Father! mother! my spirit is wrung:

Water! water! for parch'd is my tongue.

Is this fiery lake ne'er to be cross'd?

Are those wild sounds the shrieks of the lost?

And that stern angel sitting alone,

Lucifer crown'd, on his burning throne?

Old Man.

But how fares Jonathan, modest and meek?

My Meeting-House walking-stick thrice in the week!

    Ere wife and cough

    Carried me off—

Instead of heathenish Latin and Greek,

I early taught him my maxims true —

Do unto all as you'd have others do

To yourself, good Jonathan? Certainly not!

But learning never will boil the pot; —

A penny sav'd is a penny got; —

A groat per year is per day a pin; —

Let those (the lucky ones!) laugh that win; —

Keep your shop, and your shop will keep you!

    Grasps his clutch little or much?

    Has his good round sum rolled into a plum?

A voice spake in thunder —"His time is not come!"

There is an eye that compasses all,

Good and ill in this earthly ball;

That pierces the dunnest, loneliest cell,

Where wickedness hides, and marks it well!

Years have wheeled their circles round,

And the ancient sexton re-opens the ground;

A weary man at the end of his span —

Again the bell tolls a funeral sound,

And the nodding plumes pass down the hill —

'Tis the time of the year when the buds appear,

  And the blackbird pipes his music shrill;

On the breeze there is balm, and a holy calm,

  Whispers the troubled heart, "Be still! "

Ah! how chang'd since we saw him last,

That mourner of twenty long winters past!

He halts and bends as he slowly wends —

Bereft! bereft! what hath he done?

That death should smite his only son!

  Fix'd to the sod,

Bitter tears his cheeks bedew;

His broken heart is buried too!

With gentle hand, and accents bland,

  The man of God

Leads him forth —'tis silence deep —

And fathers, mothers, children weep.

For what man gives the world, he learns

Too late, how little it returns!

Nor counts he, till the funeral pall

Has made a shipwreck of his all,

His pleasures, pains; his losses, gains;

And finds that, bankrupt! naught remains.

In the watches of the night

E'en our very thoughts affright —

And see! before the mourner's sight

    A dark and shadowy form appears;

    Hark! a voice salutes his ears,

    " Hush thy sorrow, dry thy tears!

Father! 'twas to save thy son

    From av'rice, cunning, passion, pride,

    That he hath left the path untried,

The crooked path that worldlings run,

    And, happy spirit! early died.

If thou couldst know who dwell below

In deep unutterable woe;

Or wing with me thy journey far

Above, where shines the morning star;

And hear the bright angelic choirs

    (Casting their crowns before His feet,)

    In choral hymns His praise repeat,

And strike their golden lyres —

Another sun would never rise,

And gild the azure vault of heaven,

Ere thy petition reach'd the skies

    To be forgiven."

Was it a dream? —The mournful man

Next morn his alter'd course began.

To his kindred he restor'd

What unjustly swelled his hoard.

With a meek, contented mind,

He liv'd in peace with all mankind;

And thus would gratefully prolong

To heaven his morn and evening song; —

I have no time to pray, to plead

For all the blessings that I need;

For what I have, a patriarch's days

Would only give me time to praise! —

He died in hope. Yon narrow cell

Guards his sleeping ashes well.

The rest can holy angels tell!...

"This will I carry with me to my pillow," said Uncle Timothy. "My friends, good night."

CHAPTER XII.

Achubby young gentleman, a "little *Jack Horner* eating his Christmas pie," abutting from "*The Fortune of War*," at Pie-Corner, marks the memorable spot where the Great Fire of London concluded its ravages. The sin of *gluttony*, * to which, in the original inscription (now effaced,) the fire was attributed, is still rife; a considerable trade in eatables and drinkables being driven, and corks innumerable drawn, in defiance, under the chubby young gentleman's bottle nose.

* "There was excessive spending of venison, as well as other
victuals, in the halls. Nay, and a great consumption of
venison there was frequently at taverns and cooks' shops,
insomuch that the Court was much offended with it.
Whereupon, anno 1573, that the City might not continue to
give the Queen and nobility offence, the Lord Mayor, Sir
Lionel Ducket, and Aldermen, had by act of Common Council
forbidden such feasts hereafter to be made; and restrained
the same only to necessary meetings, in which, also, no
venison (‼) was permitted." —Stow.
Venison was also prohibited in the taverns and cooks' shops.

Our modern civic gourmands and gourmets, wiser grown! have
propitiated the Court by occasional invitations to take part
in their gluttony.

A Bartlemy Fair shower of rain overtook us while we were contemplating the dilapidated mansion of the Cock Lane Ghost; and, as it never rains in Bartle-my Fair, but it pours, we scudded along to the parlour of The Fortune of War, as our nearest shelter; where we beheld Mr. Bosky, though he beheld not us, bombarding his little body with cutlets and bottled beer, in company with a tragedy queen; a motion-master; and a brace of conjurors, Mr. Rumfiz and Mr. Glumfiz. Mr. Rumfiz was a merry fellow, who had fattened on blue fire, which he hung out for a sign upon his torrid nose; with Mr. Glumfiz dolor seemed to wait on drinking, and melancholy on mastication; for he looked as if he had been regaling on fishhooks and castor-oil, instead of Mr. Bosky's bountiful cheer.

"'Tis hard to bid good-b'ye to an old friend that we may never see again! Heigho! I'm sorry and sick; as cross and as queer as the hatband of Dick! Good-b'ye to St. Bartholomew."

This was sighed forth by the lean conjuror, who, as he emitted a cloud of tobacco-smoke, seemed ready to pipe his eye, and responded to by the tragedy queen with a look ultra tragical!

"Bah!" chuckled the corpulent conjuror, "à bas the blue devils! If ruin must come, good luck send that it may be blue. Though poor in purse, let me be rich in nose! Saint Bartlemy in a consumption-ha! ha! Pinched for standing-room, the comical old grig laughs and lies down! and, so droll he looks in dissolution, that I must have my lark out, though one of his boa-con-strictors should threaten to suck me down in a lump. He dies full of years and fun, the patriarch of posture-masters and puppet-showmen! Merry be his memory! and Scaramouches eternal caper round his sarcophagus! Shall we cry him a canting canticle? Rather let us chant a rattling roundelay!"

> Major Domo's a comical homo I
>
> Sic transit gloria mundi;
>
> Highty-tighty I frolicksome,, flighty I
>
> Soon will Bartlemy Fair and fun die.

Coat of motley, cap and bells,

O'er his bier shall dolefully jingle;

Conjurors all shall bear his pall,

And mountebanks follow it, married and single!

Giants, dwarfs in sable scarfs.

Merry mourners! will not tarry one;

Humps, bumps shall stir their stumps!

And toes of timber dot and carry one!

Harlequin droll the bell shall toll,

Mister Punch shall shrive and bury him;

Tumblers grin while they shovel him in,

And Charon send Joe Grim to ferry him!

B'ye, b'ye! we all must die;

Ev'ry day with death's a dun day;

Monday, Tuesday, Wednesday, Thursday,

Friday, Saturday, Sunday!

Nothing could resist the hilarity of Mr. Rumfiz. The tragedy queen gave a lop-sided smile from under the ruins of a straw-bonnet; the motion-master grinned approbation; Mr. Glumfiz was tumultuously tickled. At this moment an infantine tumbler, dressed in a tinselled scarlet jacket dirty-white muslin-fringed trousers, and yellow leather pumps, made a professional entry on his head and hands, to summon the two conjurors from their cups to their balls.

"Keep the blue fire hot till I come, Mr. Glumfiz!" said the Lauréat.

"It won't cool," replied the lean conjuror.

The tragedy queen now received a call from Cardinal Wolsey, to relieve Miss Narcissa Nimble-pins on the Pandean pipes and double drum. The little Melpomene assured Mr. Bosky of her high consideration, and, leaning on the mountebank messenger's arm, bobbed and backed out of the parlour very gracefully. But the motion-master would have been immoveable, had not his tawdry better-half, who had nothing of a piece but her tongue, hurried in with, the news that their stage-manager, having spitefully cut the wires, puppets and trade were at a stand-still.

The Lauréat being left solus, exhibited a disposition to compose himself over a cigar, an indulgence at which his eyes sympathetically winked. Should we draw aside the curtain between his box and ours?

A note from Mr. Bosky's nose

Seem'd to say,

"Away! away!

Leave me, leave me to repose!"

Our glasses were empty, and the fair was filling; so we took the hint and our hats, and were soon among the lions.

An Ancient Pistol-looking scarecrow with a cockaded something, between an old cocked hat, and an old hat cocked, on his shaggy pole; a black patch over one eye; a sham lame left leg; half a pair of half boots, and a jacket without sleeves, brandishing harlequin's wooden sword, and belabouring a cracked drum, beat up for recruits, and thus accompanied his tattoo.

With his brigade of brags

Captain Bobadil comes;

Soldiers furl your flags,

Crape and muffle your drums!

Let John Bull and the bell

Both be dismally told!

One, for a funeral knell;

One, the reward of the bold.

From Harry to Arthur, you

Britons! would conquer or die —

'Pon my soul it's true;

What will you lay it's a lie?

Bobadil trump'd up a story —

"Fighting's the time o' day!

All for honour and glory,

Provender, plunder, and pay.

It vastly better, by Jove, is

To be for liberty bang'd;

Than for prigging, my covies,

To stay behind and be hang'd!

Every man in his shoe

Looks as if he would die —

'Pon my soul it's true;

What will you lay it's a lie?

Limping London on pegs,

Crown'd with victory's palms,

Heroes without their legs

Now are asking for alms;

Cursing their liberal lot,

And Bob's grandiloquent whims;

Deuce in their locker a shot;

Tho' lots, alas! in their limbs!

We hardly know which to do;

Whether to laugh or to cry —

Ton my soul it's true;

What will y ou lay it's a lie?

Read me a comical riddle,

Paddy will say it comes pat —

Some men dance to the fiddle;

Bob's men dance to the cat.

Fine and flourishing speeches

Lads like Wellington, scoff;

They lead their troops on the breaches;

Bobadil, he pulls'em off!

Give the Devil his due.

Bob's a garrulous Guy —

Ton my soul it's true;

What will you lay it's a lie?

"Well, I never see such a low, frothy, horrid, awful, dandified, grandified, twistified, mystified, play-going, pleasure-taking, public-house set as these rubbishing Scaramouches! It would be quite a charity to send'em all to the Treadmill, or there's no mystery in mousetraps!"

"That little woman's tender mercies are cruel!" responded a voice behind, and leading captive a personage, who seemed to to wonder how the devil he got there! —a fierce, fidgety flounced madam, bounced past us with an air of inconceivable grandeur. It was Mrs. Flumgarten hooked on to the arm of Brummagem Brutus.

A sudden rush, from a "conveyancer" being escorted to the *Pied Poudre*, * brought us to that ancient seat of justice.

* Held at the Hand and Shears, the corner of Middle Street and King Street, Cloth Fair. The Pied Poudre was originally instituted to determine disputes regarding debts and contracts, when the churchyard of the ancient Priory contained the booths and standings of the Drapers and Clothiers. The beadle of Cloth Fair received the annual fee of 3s. and 4d. for measuring the yard-sticks. The officers of the Pied Poudre are two Serjeants at Maee for the Lord Mayor, two for the Poultry, and two for Giltspur Street Compters, and a constable appointed by the steward of Lord Kensington, to attend the court in his behalf. There was formerly an Associate, (the Common Serjeant, or one of the attorneys of the Lord Mayor's Sheriffs' Court,) but this officer has not attended for the last hundred and fifty years.

Some minor cases having been disposed of, Counsellor Rumtum rose, put on his green spectacles and "twelve children phisiognomy," (a most imposing gravity!) and opened his pleadings

"Gentlemen of the Jury, the plaintiff is Miss Andromache the Goddess of Wisdom, commonly called Minerva; the defendant is Mr. Andrew Macky, Merry Andrew and Bearward, who boasts the largest menagerie of well-educated monkeys in the fair. The plaintiff seeks to recover damages for an assault, perpetrated by the defendant's servant Jamboa, a belligerent baboon with a blue face. The Goddess had been stationed, like the Palladium of Troy, in a temple adjoining the defendant's caravan. The watchful cock was perched on her helmet, a waving plume descended to her heels, a magnificent breast-plate and royal robe adorned her imperial person, and armed with a spear and a shield, she presented all the fascinations which the ancients have attributed to Pallas. It is not in evidence, whether Miss Andromache had been transported by heroes like Diomedes and Ulysses; but it may be presumed that curiosity induced her to descend from her own palace to take a peep at Andrew Macky's menagerie. The Goddess was charmed with the intelligent visage and tall stately figure of the wild man of the woods, who sat quietly in a corner, leaning on his staff; and being desirous of ascertaining his exact altitude, (Wisdom, Gentlemen of the Jury, is ever on the lookout for new discoveries,) she roused him from his reverie, by propelling the sharp point of her spear to Jamboa's dextral hip-joint, to make him jump. Starting up furiously, he struck her immortal Ægis to the ground, inflicted with his grinders terrible havoc on her gorgeous trappings, smashed ferociously her invincible breast-plate; and imprinted on her royal person evident proofs of the piquant condition of his nails. For this assault and battery Andromache claims of Andrew Macky ample and liberal compensation; which, Gentlemen of the Jury, (here Counsellor Rumtum, tried the "soft sawder!") with your wonted gallantry, you will doubtless award her."

The Court, however, expressed an opinion, that the Goddess of Wisdom, by making an unprovoked sortie on so respectable a baboon, had not acted with her usual discretion, and directed Minerva to be nonsuited.

Look at the gay caps and bonnets in yonder balcony; and hark to the fifes and fiddles, accelerating the sharp trot to a full gallop! And now the volunteer vocalist, having frowned into nothingness a St. Cecilian on the salt-box, demands silence for this seasonable chant.

Don't you remember the third of September?

Fun's Saturnalia, Bartlemy fair!

Punch's holiday, O what a jolly day!

When we fiddled and danced at the Bear.

Romping, reeling it, toe and heeling it,

Ham and vealing it, toddy and purl —

Have you forgot that I paid the shot

I have not! my adorable girl.

With ranters and roysters we push'd thro' the cloisters,

Had plenty of oysters, of porter a pot;

I treated my Hebe with brandy, not (B. B!)

And sausages smoking, and gingerbread hot.

She whisper'd, "How nice is fried bacon in slices,

And eggs" —What a crisis! —Love egg'd me on —

"My dearest," said I, " I wish I may die

If we don't have a fry to-night at the Swan."

How we giggled when Pantaloon wriggled,

    And led a jig with Columbine down;

How we roar'd when Harlequin's sword

    Conjur'd Mother Goose into the Clown!

To Saunders's booth I toddled my Ruth,

    Saw Master and Miss romp and reel on the rope —

And it was our faults if we didn't both waltz,

    My eye! with old Guy, Old Nick and the Pope.

Rigging's rife again, fun's come to life again,

    Punch and his wife again, frolicksome pair,

Footing it, crikey! like Cupid and Psyche,

    Summon each rum'un to Bartlemy fair.

Trumpets blowing, roundabouts going,

    Toby the Theban, intelligent Pig!

His compliments sends, inviting his friends

    To meet the Bonassus to-night at a jig.

"Now my little lads and lasses! Shut one eye, and don't breathe on the glasses! Here's Nero a-fiddling while Rome was a-burning-and Cin-cinnatus a-digging potatoes. Here's Sampson and the Phillis-tines —Cain and Abel, and the Tower of Babel." This was sounded by a gaunt fellow (a stronger man than Sampson, for he lugged him in by the head and shoulders!) with a gin-and-fog voice and a bristly beard. His neighbour, a portly ogress with a Cyclopical physiognomy (her drum "most tragically run through!"), advertised a grunting giant, (a Pygmalion to his relations!) and backed his stupendous flitches against Smith-field and the world.

"Ladies and gentlemen," squeaked a little mountebank through an asthmatic trumpet, "walk in and see a tragical, comical, operatical, pantomimical Olla Podrida of Smiles, Tears, Broad Grins, and Horselaughs, called The Hobgoblin, or My Lady go-Nimble's Ghost; the Humours of Becky Burton and Doctor Diddleum; a Prologue by Lucifer and his imps; capering on his pericranium by *Signor Franchinello*; and dancing in a dark lantern by *Mynheer Von Tromping-tonverbruggenhausentiraliravontamen!*"

"Here's your dainty spiced gingerbread! that will melt in your mouth like a red hot brickbat, and rumble in your inside like Punch and his wheelbarrow!" —"And here's your Conjuration Compound, that if you bathe a beefsteak in it the over night, it will come out a veal cutlet in the morning!"

The fair was lighted up, and the fun grew "fast and furious" beginning with a loud chorus of acclamation, and so running on through the whole Sol fa of St. Bartlemy delight. There was a blended incarnation of kettle-drums, fifes, fiddles, French horns, rattles, trumpets, and gongs! A giantess of alarming dimensions, beaming with maternal ecstasy! reddened with deeper intensity from her painted show-cloth; and a miniature Lady-monster, a codicil to the giantess! peeped out imploringly from a wine-cooler in which some facetious crowned sconce had ensconced her at an after-dinner merriment to his Queen and Courtiers.

Original

The Mermaid had a long tail to exhibit and tell. Messrs. Rumfiz and Glumfiz, disciples of Zoroaster! began their magical incantations, swallowed knives and forks and devoured blue flame with increased voracity; the Fantoccini footed it with laudable vigour; the Conjuror would have coined his copper nose, only, winked the wag, "I knows and you knows Je n'ose pas!" the lions and tigers roared "Now or never!" and amidst this oratorio of discord and din, Harlequin, Othello, Columbine, Sir John Falstaff, Desdemona, Jim Crow, Cardinal Wolsey, and Scaramouch quadrilled on the outside platform of Richardson's Grand Booth, the gong (his prompter's tintinabulum!) sounding superabundant glorification.

We hastened to this renowned modern temple of the Smithfield drama, which was splendidly illuminated and guarded by tremendous pasteboard Genii, sphinxes, and unicorns, and saw our old acquaintance Bonassus (who looked like one of His Mandingo Majesty's Spanish liquorice guards!) enact Othello and Jim Crow. After much interpolated periphrasis and palaver, Mr. Bigstick darkly intimated that when he ceased to love the "gentle Desdemona," (Miss Teresa Tumbletuzzy!)

"Shay-oss is come agin"

At this moment the scenes stuck fast in the grooves-the halves of a house with an interstice of a yard or so between-when a lecturing mechanic bawled out from his sixpenny elysium,

"Ve don't expect no good grammar here, Muster Thingumbob, but, hang it! you might close the scenes!"

Mr. Bigstick being politely requested ("Strike up, Snow-drop! Go it, Day and Martin!") to "Jump Jim Crow" in triplicate, came forward, curvetting and salaaming with profound respect, and treated his audience with this *variorum version* of their old favourite.

Here's jumping Jim, his coat and skim-

-mer very well you know;

If you've a crow to pluck with him,

He's pluck'd you first! I trow —

Where'er he goes he gaily crows,

A Blackey and a Beau!

Reels about and wheels about,

And jumps Jim Crow.

O how the town ran up and down

To see the dancing Nigger!

If Jim's a flat, 'tis tit for tat!

For Jim thinks John a bigger

To (for a Yankee lean and lanky)

Shell his coppers so. —

What a noodle I —Yankee-doodle!

Rare Jim Crow!

Bull has fill'd his noddle full

Of learning, in profusion;

And Jim, with his long limping limb,

Has jump'd to this conclusion,

"A ninny and" —you understand!

When sitting all a-row,

Britons roar "Encore! Encore!

Jump Jim Crow!"

Jim's play'd his pranks-with many thanks,

He gives you now the hop;

Because, like his *Commercial Banks*,

He thinks it time to *stop!*

What Nigger Lad has ever had

Such lucky cards to throw?

Ever trump'd, or ever jump'd

Like Jump Jim Crow?

The pantomine of Hot Rolls, or Harlequin Dumpling, and the Dragon of Wantley concluded the performances; in which Mr. Bigstick's promising young pupil, Master Magnumdagnumhuggleduggle, by a *jeu de théâtre* bolted the baker; (bones, apron, night-cap and all!) set Old Father Thames on fire, exhibited the fishes frying in agony, and in his suit of spiked armour, like an "Egyptian Porcupig,"

> "To make him strong and mighty,
>
> Drank by the tale, six pots of ale
>
> And a quart of Aqua Vitæ!"

and marched forth fiercely to a ferocious fight with a green leather dragon stuffed with fiery serpents, that hissed and exploded to the tune of two-pence a time!

The Bartlemy fairities were in raptures. Master Magnumdagnumhuggleduggle, Mr. Big stick, the Tumblctuzzy and the Dragon were successively garlanded with broccoli-sprouts and turnip-tops! It was all round my hat" with Bonassus, who divided the Lion's share with the Dragon, and looked like a May-day Jack-in-the-green! The enthusiasm of the audience did not end here. They called for the Call-boy, and the Candle-snuffer, whose bliss would have felt no cc aching void" had a "bit of bacon" accompanied, by way of a relish, this kitchen garden of cabbage.

The bells of St. Bartholomew chimed the hour when churchyards and "Charlies" yawn; upon which the illuminations and mob went out, and away, and Momus looked as down in the mouth as a convolvulus. *

* Next morning's sun saw Smithfield restored to those polite
intelligences whose "talk is of bullocks" —with no greater
nuisance remaining, than its chartered brutes upon Jour
legs, beaten, goaded, tortured, and blasphemed at by its
greater brutes upon two!

The elephant booked his trunk and departed; the menagerie man returned to his dish of bird's claws and beaks, with a second course of shark's teeth and fish-bones; Punch and Judy were amicably domiciled with the dog, the devil, and the doctor; the Jacks-in-the-box, Noah's arks, Dutch dolls, and wooden Scaramouches, were stowed away pell-mell; the gingerbread kings, queens, and nuts, were huddled higgledy-piggledy into their tin canisters; a muddled chorister warbled "Fly not yet" to an intrusive "Blue-Bottle" that popped in the Queen's Crown and his own among a midnight dancing party of shopmen and Abigails, and a solitary fiddle, scraped by a cruel cobbler, squeaked the *Lay of the Last Minstrel!*

> Morn appearing, Nature cheering,
>
> Milkmaids crying "Milk!" for tea,
>
> Singing, joking; chimneys smoking,
>
> Bring, alas! no joys to me.

> Phoebus beaming, kettles steaming —
>
> Basso-hark I the dustman's bell,
>
> Obligato! —ff Sweep!" stoccato!
>
> *Old St. Bartle!* sound thy knell.

CHAPTER XIII.

Put out the light!" exclaimed Mr. Bonassus Bigstick, with a lugubrio-comic expression of countenance that might convulse a Trappist, to a pigeon-toed property-man and a duck-legged drummer, who were snuffing two farthing rushlights in the Proscenium.

"*Put out the light!*" and straightway he pocketed the extinguished perquisite. We were retiring from the scene of Mr. Bigstick's glory in company with two lingering chimney-sweeps, who had left their brushes and brooms at the box door, when our progress was arrested by a tap on the shoulder from Uncle Timothy.

"If you would explore the 'secrets of the prison-house,' I can gratify your curiosity, having an engagement with the great Tragedian to crush a mug of mum with him behind the scenes."

We were too happy to enjoy so novel a treat not to embrace the offer with alacrity. Mr. Bigstick welcomed us with a tragic hauteur, and carrying an inch of candle stuck at the extremity of Prospero's magic wand, lighted his party to the Green Room. As we passed along, the great Tragedian, who had the knack of looking everything into nothing, scowled an armoury of daggers at Harlequin, and Harlequin, if possible, looked more black than the Moor. On entering the sanctum sanctorum, Mr. Bigstick, striking an attitude and exclaiming "*Cara Sposa! Idol mio!*" introduced us to Teresa, the High-Dumptiness of St. Bartlemy, whom he dangled after like a note of admiration, he all mast, she all hulk; and when they parted, (with a Dolly Bull curtsy exquisitely fussy and fumy the Tumbletuzzy made her exit,) it was odd to see the steeple separated from the chancel.

"Ten thousand times ten thousand pardons, most divine bard! but having sunned myself in the optics of Teresa, my own became eclipsed to every object less refulgent. Gentlemen," — pulling forward a pipe-flourishing, porter-swigging personage who belonged quite as much to Bagfair as to St. Bartlemy, and looked as if he lived in everlasting apprehension of sibillations technically called, "Goose" —"Mr. Pegasus Bubangrub the Bartholomew Fair Poet, who may challenge all the Toby Philpots in Christendom to leap up to the chin into a barrel of beer, drink it down to his foot, and then dance a jig upon the top of it! Mr. Bubangrub edits a penny weekly; reports queer trials; does our Caravan *libretto*; answers my challenges; roasts my rivals, puffs his pipe-and Me! At present he is a mere dab-chick of literature; but let him start a rum name, and he shall cut the genteel caper, cut, too, his sky parlour, penny-a-lining and old pals; wonder, with amiable simplicity! what 'shooting the moon' can be, and diving for a dinner; and casting off his Toady's skin for the lion's, be feasted, flattered, paragraphed —'Purge, eat cleanly, and live like a gentleman!"

Mr. Bubangrub bowed, and respectfully hinted that every kingdom has its cabals, not excepting the realm of actors and actresses. That to soothe their petty jealousies; check the too-aspiring ambition of one, tickle the self-complacency of another-to be grave with the tragic; funny with the comic; patient with the ignorant and presuming, and on terms of eternal friendship with all-to come off victorious on that slippery ground

> "Where unfledg'd actors learn to laugh and cry,
>
> Where infant punks their tender voices try,
>
> And little Maximins the Gods defy,"

are difficulties that none but dramatic politicians of experience and discretion can surmount; and he advised every author to whom appetite offered a more powerful stimulant than genius, to make haste and possess himself of the important secret.

Mine host of the Ram now entered with a curiously compounded mug of mum, in which the great Tragedian (who was not particular from Clos Vougeot to Old Tom) drank the Stage that goes with and without wheels. Mr. Bosky, who had got scent of our "Whereabouts," arrived in time to propose the memory of Shakspere, and Mr. Bubangrub's longevity; Uncle Timothy gave Bonassus Bigstick and Bartlemy Fair; and Pegasus toasted the Tragic Muse and Teresa Tumbletuzzy. The Tragedian unbent by degrees; his adust countenance warmed into flesh and blood, and he grew facetious and festive.

"Bubangrub, my Brother of the Sun and Moon! my Nutmeg of delight! give us a song!"
The call was a command.

To pitch the tune Pegasus twanged from his Jew's-harp a chord, and apologizing for being "a little ropy," began, in a voice between a whistle and a wheeze,

> Ye snuff-takers of England
>
> Who sniff your pinch at ease,
>
> How very seldom you enjoy
>
> The pleasures of a sneeze!
>
> Give ear unto us smoking gents *
>
> And we will plainly shew
>
> All the joys, my brave boys!
>
> When we a cloud do blow.

* In 1585, the English first saw pipes made of clay, among the native Indians of Virginia; which was at that time discovered by Richard Greenville. Soon after they fabricated the first clay tobacco-pipes in Europe.
In 1604, James the First endeavoured, by means of heavy

imposts, to abolish the use of tobacco; and, in 1619, wrote his
"Counterblast" against what he accounted a noxious weed, and

ordered that no planter in Virginia should cultivate more than one hundred pounds.
In 1610, the smoking of tobacco was known at Constantinople.

To render the custom ridiculous, a Turk, who had been found smoking, was conducted about the streets with a pipe transfixed through his nose! And in 1653, when smoking tobacco was first introduced into the Canton of Appenzell, in Switzerland, the children ran after the Smokers in the streets; the Council likewise punished them, and ordered the innkeepers to inform against such as should smoke in their houses. —In 1724, Pope Benedict XIV. revoked the bull of excommunication, published by Innocent, because he himself had acquired the habit of taking snuff!=

The snuffer, buffer! raps his mull,

His nose it cries out "Snuff!"

The Smoker, Joker! puffs his full

In this queer world of puff!

The lawyer's gout is soon smok'd out; —

If in the parsons toe

It ends in smoke, say simple folk,

Just ends his sermon so!

The tippler loves his swanky, swipe;

The prince, the peer, the beau,

A pipe of wine-give me my pipe

Of Backy for to blow!

No pinch or draught drive care abaft

From folks a cup too low,

Like the joys, my brave boys!

When we a cloud do blow.

A penny-postman-like rap at the caravan door was answered by the great Tragedian with

"'Open locks whoever knocks!'" And, as the unexpected visitor became visible, he added, "Tom Titlepage! as thou art Tom, welcome; but as thou art Tom and a boon companion, ten times welcome!"

The Publisher's compromised dignity looked a trifle offended. He did not half relish being treated so familiarly.

"An infernal business this, Mr. Bigstick! The devil waits-the press stands still!"

"And why Tom, don't you? Here's a joint stool; sit down and quaff out of Lady Macbeth's gilt goblet. Egad you and the devil are in the nick of time to listen to and carry away such a Chapter of —"

Mr. Titlepage. Draw it mild!

Mr. Bigstick. As the moonbeams! —Gentlemen, lend me your ears; which, perhaps, you would rather do than your purses! Who steals mine, steals-what he will not grow inconveniently corpulent upon!

The Tragedian began to rummage an ancient hair-trunk that looked as raggedly bald as his own scalp; dislodging sceptres, daggers, crowns, spangled robes and stage wigs. In Dicky Gossip's bob * he discovered what he sought for; a dirty, torn, dog's-eared *disjecti membra*.

* Suett boasted a recherché and extensive collection of
stage wigs, comprising every variety, from the full-bottom,
to the Tyburn bob; which unique assortment was unfortunately
burned in a fire that happened at the Birmingham Theatre, on
Friday, August 13, 1792. This loss gave rise to several
smart epigrams, among which were the following.
"'Twas sure some upstart Tory in his rigs,

Who fir'd poor Suett's long-tail'd race of Wigs;
Ah! cruel Tory, thus his all to take,
Nor leave him one e'en for a hair-breadth 'scape."
"Raise your subscriptions, every free-born soul —
Stript of his wigs-behold a suffering Pole"
Dicky answered the doggrel, in a jingle of his own.
"Well-well may you joke, who perhaps have a wig,
But my loss is severe tho', for all this here gig;
For if spouse is dispos'd or to wrangle or box,
Alas! what will keep her from combing my locks?
My fortune's too ruin'd, as well as renown,
For in losing my wigs —I am stripp'd to a crown!"

Opening the bundle, and selecting at random, he bespoke the company's attention to a fragment
of

"THE AUTOBIOGRAPHY OF BONASSUS, OR THE BIGSTICK MEMOIRS."

"All the world's a caravan! and all the gentlemen and ladies Lions and Tigresses! For if a man be neither dwarf nor giant, but an unhappy medium between the two-if he be not upon boxing terms with a whole menagerie, and will not fisty-cuff-it and roar for an engagement, dam'me! he may whistle for one!"

Mr. Bigstick paused, glared ghastly terrible and ghostly grim.

"Yes, I'm too tall for a wonderful monkey, and too good-natured for an intelligent bull-dog. I can't drink sangaree out of my father's skull, nor beat the big drum with the bones of my grandmother!"

He then, after taking a deep draught at the mum, resumed his narrative.

"I was articled to the law, and Pump Court was the pabulum where I began to qualify myself for Lord Chancellor. But fearful is the dramatic furor of attorney's clerks. My passion was not for bills of costs, but for bills of the play; I longed to draw, not leases, but audiences; as for pleas, my ambition was to please the town; and I cared nothing for Coke, while Shakspere's muse of fire warmed my imagination! Counsellor Cumming soon found his clerk going. I quitted the Court, leaving my solitary competitor the Pump to spout alone."

A personable fellow * (for whom any lady might be proud to jump into the Serpentine, the jury finding a verdict of manslaughter against my good looks, with a deodand of five shillings on my whiskers!) 'I left my father's house, and took with me' —as much wardrobe as I could conveniently carry ow, and behind my back.

* A very different looking personage to Mr. Bigstick must
have been the unhappy young gentleman, aged twenty-two, (see
the "Times" 21st March, 1835,) who killed himself by poison,
and left this letter upon his table: —
"I die a Catholic —I leave my mortal remains to my father

and mother, regretting that they should have allowed the
growth and development of a creature of so disagreeable a
conformation as their son. Endowed with the most exquisite
feelings, my face has always frightened the fair sex. I go
to seek in Heaven a society which my aspect will not annoy;
for I imagine that, freed from its carnal covering, my
spirit will not dismay the inhabitants of the other world."

My first professional bow was in the Poor Gentleman, * and Raising the Wind, in a barn at Leighton Buzzard, where the Gods clambered up to the gallery by a ladder, through which many of the tippling deities could hardly see a hole!

* Another link in the dramatic chain is broken. Arthur
Griffinhoof has joined the jocund spirits of Garrick,
Hoadly, and the elder George.
Rejoice, ye witlings! for the lamp that dimmed your little

farthing rushlights, Death, the universal extinguisher, has
eclipsed for ever! Retailers of small talk, who fattened on
the unctuous crumbs of conceit that fell from the merry
man's table, make the most of your legacy: your master hath
carried his Broad Grins to Elysium. Ye select few, who
admired the wit and loved the man, mourn!
Thanks to the ghastly monarch! for he hath been a forbearing

creditor: —So large an amount of fun payable at sight, and
George a septuagenarian! Three days' grace-three score and
ten!
A day of mirth will it be on Styx, when the ferryman rows

over Mr. Merryman. Faith, Mr. Colman, you're a very droll
man!
What a coil attends the new comer! Churchill, Lloyd,

Thornton, Garrick, all inquiring about the modern Dram.
Pers. —"Ye jovial goblins," quoth George, "a Dram, per se!"
Whereupon Sam-not the lexicographer-marching forth his

wooden leg, accepts, with an approving chuckle, the pun as
Foote-ing, or garnish; they are hail spirit well met, and
become as merry as ghosts.
Life's a Jest; and a merrier one than thine, facetious

George, Time shall not crack till the crack of doom.

The stalls (the cart-horses having been temporally ejected) sparkled with the elite-sixpenny-worth of coppers being paid for sitting apart in aristocratical exclusiveness. My declamation might have electrified Gog and Magog, and made the Men in Armour start from their spears! The barn rang with applause, my success was triumphant, and my fate decided.

"I next joined Mr. Dunderhead, the Dunstable manager, on whose boards I had the supreme felicity of beholding, for the first time, the Tum-bletuzzy. She danced with the castanets (le Pantomime de Vamour); my heart beat to her fairy footsteps; the long sixes capered before my eyes, my pulse thumped a hundred and twenty per minute —I wooed, and had well nigh won her-when our Harlequin, a ci-devant, ubiquitous, iniquitous barber, all but dashed the nectared cup from my lip. I did not horsewhip him, 'for that were poor revenge,' —no! I shewed him up on my benefit night in a patter song."

"Bravo!" cried Mr. Bosky, "Let us, Mr. Bigstick, have the song by all means."

The great Tragedian, screwing, à la Mathews, his mouth a-jar, condescendingly complied.

> Stolen or stray'd my beautiful maid!
>
> Unlucky my ducky has met a decoy —
>
> As brown as a berry, as plump as a cherry,
>
> And rosy-cheek'd, very! and Jenny-so-coy!
>
> Baggage and bagging the Dunstable waggin
>
> Were popp'd by a wag in, hight Harlequin Lun —
>
> They, honey-moon hot, shot the moon like a shot;
>
> But I'll shoot the rascal as sure as a gun!

She sings like a linnet, she plays on the spinnet,

    A day's like a minute when she is in doors;

My aunt in the attic, my uncle extatic!

    Encore the chromatique my Philomel pours!

I lov'd her so dearly and truly, for really

    She cuts a mug * queerly, as Arthur's Queen Doll;

She beats the tol lol O of Molly Brown hollow,

    And sings like Apollo in Gay's pretty Poll.

I told her a rebus, I gave her a wee buss;

    She call'd me her Phoebus, her hero of pith;

Her caraway comfit, her prime sugar plumb, fit

    For lady's lip, rum fit! her Lollypop Smith!

* The Mugs out of which the violent politicians of Charles
the Second's time drank their beer, were fashioned into the
resemblance of Shaftsbury's face. Hence the common phrase,
"Ugly Mug!"

No more thought Teresa small tipple of me, sir,

    Than pretty Miss P., sir, our premiere danseuse,

lightsome, lenitive! philoprogenitive!

    Sukey with bouquet and white satin shoes!

To be, or not to be? is it a shot to be?

    Is it a knot to be, tied to a beam?

Death's but a caper, life's but a taper,

    A vision, a vapour, a shadow, a dream.

Hang melancholy! grieving's a folly!

Laugh and be jolly! there's nothing like fun!

I'll make Miss Terese cry "Yes if you please!"

And down on his knees shall Harlequin Lun."

"But the 'beautified Ophelia!' fickle, not false, and far less fickle than freakish! in all the tender distraction of Cranbourn Alley white muslin and myrtle, implored my forgiveness. Were her three-quarters' music and dancing to be thrown away upon a base barber?

'O ye, whose adamantine sorrows know

The iron agonies of copper woe!'"

Here the great Tragedian became overpowered, and cried a flood of stage tears very naturally.
"*Encore! encore!*" shouted Uncle Timothy.
Othello was at a loss whether or not to take this as a compliment, and weep a second brewing. He rubbed his eyes-but the Noes had it —
"Bigstick's himself again!"
"On the disbanding of our troop, we hied to Stoke-Pogeis with a letter of introduction to the manager. Mr. Truncheon (his wig 'in most admired disorder,') started and exclaimed, 'What the deuce could Dunderhead have been about to send you here?' The other night Dowager Mucklethrift bespoke 'Too late for Dinner,' I speculated on one upon the strength of it, and treated the company (who were as thin as our houses,) to a gallon of 'intermediate,' when, lo! and behold! in she tottered with her retinue (a rush of two!) to the boxes, and her deaf butler Diggory, esquiring some half-dozen lady patronesses, hobbled up to the threepenny gallery to grin down upon us!
"A man may as well bob for whale in the river Thames; for live turtle in the City Basin; for white-bait in the Red Sea; expect to escape choking after having bolted a grape-shot, or to elicit a divine spark from the genius of a mud volcano, as hope not to be ruined and rolled up among such sublime intelligences! There's a hole in the kettle, sir, and we are half starved!" Surrounded by Short's Gardens and dwelling in Queer Street, Teresa and myself began to diet on our superfluities. My Romeo last-rose-of-summer pantaloons were diluted into a quart of hot pea-soup, and Bobadil's superannuated cocked hat and Justice Midas's wig were stewed down in the shape of a mutton scrag, Juliet's Flanders' lace flounce furnishing the trimmings! At this extremity, when Mrs. Heidelburg's embroidered satin petticoat of my aunt's had gone to "my uncle's" for a breakfast, my friend Dennis O'Doddipool, * whose success at Cork had enabled him to draw one, and enjoy his bottle, invited us to Ballina-muck.
* An Hibernian member of a strolling company of comedians, in the north of England, lately advertised for his benefit,
"An occasional Address, to be spoken by a new actor" This excited great expectation among the towns-people. On his benefit night Paddy Roscius stepped forward, and in a rich brogue thus addressed the audience:
"To-night a new actor appears on the stage,

To claim your protection, and your patron-oge;
Now, who do you think this new actor may be?
Why, turn round your eyes, and look full upon me,
And then you'll be sure this new actor to see."
Qy. —Could this new actor be Mr. O'Doddipool?

We showered down as many benedictions upon Dennis as would stand between Temple Bar and Westminster, bundled up our 'shreds and patches,' levied tribute on the farmers' poultry, and when a goose fell in our way, made him so wise as never to be taken for a goose again! and arrived by short stages, in a long caravan, at Holyhead. Hey for Ireland! straight we bent our way to the land of praties and Paddies! O'Doddipool welcomed us with all the huggings and screechings of a German salutation; danced like Mr. Moses at the feast of Purim, * and cried —

* The feast of Purim, an ancient Jewish festival, held yearly on the 7th of March, is in commemoration of the fall of Hainan and his ten sons. This feast is generally spent in public rejoicing, such as masked balls, letting off fireworks, &c. At one time a Fair was held in the vicinity of Duke's Place; but which the authorities of the City of London have put down for several years past. Amongst the more respectable order, family parties are kept up to a very late hour. The tables are generally adorned with hung beef, to commemorate the hanging of Haman. On the evening of this feast, the Jews attend their synagogues, where the Reader chants the Book of Esther in the Hebrew language; and at one time, (the practice is now partially abolished,) whenever the Reader repeated the name of Haman, the younger branches of the congregation beat the seats, and otherwise created a noise, with small wooden hammers, which were designated Haman-clappers.

—like the French butcher, * for joy! I played first comedy before the lamps and second fiddle behind 'em-walking gentlemen and running footmen-bravos and bishops, ** —swept the boards with Tragedy's sweeping pall, and a birch-broom —

* A Slaughter-man, in the interval of killing, strolled from a neighbouring abattoir to Père la Chaise. Shedding tears like rain, and clasping his blood-stained hands, he stood before the tomb of Abelard and Eloisa; while ever and anon he blubbered out, "Oh! l'amour, l'amour!" He then wiped his eyes with his professional apron, and returned to business! This is truly French.

** Garrick was in the habit of employing a whimsical fellow whose name was Stone, to procure him theatrical supernumeraries. The following correspondence passed between the "Sir, Thursday Noon.

"Mr. Lacy turned me out of the lobby yesterday, and behaved very ill to me. I only ax'd for my two guineas for the last Bishop, and he swore I shouldn't have a farthing. I can't live upon air. I have a few Cupids you may have cheap, as they belong to a poor journeyman shoemaker, who I drink with now and then.

"Your humble sarvant,

"Wm. Stone."

"Stone, Friday Morn.

"You are the best fellow in the world. Bring the Cupids to

the theatre to-morrow. If they are under six, and well made, you shall have a guinea a piece for them. If you can get me two good murderers, I will pay you handsomely, particularly the spouting fellow who keeps the apple-stand on Tower-hill; the cut in his face is quite the thing. Pick me up an Alderman or two, for Richard, if you can; and I have no objection to treat with you for a comely Mayor. The barber will not do for Brutus, although I think he will succeed in Mat.
"D. G."

The person here designated the Bishop was procured by Stone,

and had often rehearsed the Bishop of Winchester in the play of Henry VIIIth, with such singular éclat, that Garrick addressed him at the rehearsal, as "Cousin of Winchester The fellow, however, never played the part, although advertised more than once to come out in it. The reason will soon be guessed from the two following letters that passed between Garrick and Stone on the very evening the Prelate was to make his début.
"Sir,

"The Bishop of Winchester is getting drunk at the Bear, and

swears he won't play to-night.
"I am, yours,

"Wm, Stone."

"Stone,

"The Bishop may go to the devil. I do not know a greater

rascal, except yourself.
"D. G"

—hissed in the centre region of a fiery dragon in some diabolical Jewiow-stration of dramatic diablerie, brandished a wooden sword-gallanted Columbine-blushed blue flame and brickdust in Frankenstein-plastered my head over with chalk for want of a Lord Ogleby white wig-and bellowed myself hoarse with tawdry configurations and claptrap vulgarities! And (*Punch* has no feelings'!) what my reward? A magnificent banquet of dry bread and ditch-water from O'Doddipool, ('Think on that, Master Brook!') peels, not of applause, but oranges! from the pit; and showers of peas (not boiled!) from the Olympus of disorderly gods. *
   * The custom of pelting actors and authors upon the stage is very ancient. Hegemon of Thasos, a writer of the old comedy, upon the first representation of one of his plays, came upon the stage with a large parcel of pebbles in the skirt of his

gown, and laying them down on the edge of the orchestra, gravely informed the spectators that whoever desired to pelt him might take them up and begin the attack; but if, on the contrary, they chose to hear with patience, and judge with candour, he had done his best to amuse them! The audience were so delighted with his play, that though its performance was interrupted by the arrival of very unfortunate news from Sicily, viz. the destruction of the Athenian Fleet, it was suffered to proceed; not one of them quitting the theatre, though almost every individual had lost a relation or friend in the action. The unfortunate Athenians could not refrain from shedding tears on the occasion; but such was their delicacy and honour with respect to the foreigners then present, that they concealed their weakness by muffling their faces in their mantles.

So finding, though in Ireland, my capital wasn't doubling, I gave the bog-trotters the "Glass of Fashion" (they never gave me a glass of anything!) to a sausage-maker's Polonius; took my leave and two and six-pence; bolted to Ballinamuck; (my Farce of Ducks and Green Peas never had such a run?) starred it from Ballinamuck to Bartlemy, and engaged with the man that lets devils out to hire, and deals in giants of the first enormity. My crack parts are Othello and Jim Crow; so that between the two, the lamp black never gets washed off my face, and I fear I shall die a Negro —

"Thus far," added the great Tragedian, rolling up the papers into a bundle and tossing them over to Mr. Titlepage, "the Autobiography of Bonassus! From Smithfield we march to the Metropolitans. 'The Garden' is sadly in want of a fine high comedy figure at a low one; and Drury, of a Tragedy Queen who can do Dollallolla. I smother a new debutante, Miss Barbara Bug-gins; beat Liston * hollow in Moll Flaggon; and put out of joint the noses of all preceding Mac-beths. The Tumbletuzzy opens in Queen Katherine (which she plays quite in a different style to Siddons)."

* Of an actor so extensively popular, let us indulge a few reminiscenees. We remember his first entrée upon the boards of old Covent Garden, in Jacob Gawky; but his present amplitude of face and rotundity of person were then wanting to heighten the picture; and flesh, like wine, does wonders. His voice, too, has Avaxed more fat and unctuous; and broader (like his figure) has grown his fun. The stage became possessed of a new character, such as humourist had never before conceived, or player played-Mr. Liston! —The town roared with laughter; actors split their sides at his deepening gravity; caricaturists, in despair, cast off invention, and trusted solely to his unique lineaments; our signs bore aloft his physiognomical wonders; and walking-sticks, tobacco-stoppers, snuff-boxes, owned the queer impeachment.
Liston! the Knight of the comieal countenance, where Momus

sits enthroned in every dimple, crying aloof to the sons of care and melancholy! He is the very individual oddity described in the epigram —
"Here, Hermes" says Jove, who with nectar was mellow,

"Go, fetch me some clay, I will make an odd fellow."

And forth sprang Liston, a figure of fun! Not for the

amusement of gods, but of men!
To Suett Ave owe our first impression of drollery, but his

glimmering spark was soon extinct. The sun of Liston has
been before us from its rising to its setting. We hailed its
grotesque ascension, basked in its-broad meridian, and now
(when time has somewhat sobered down its comet-like
eccentricities) sorrowfully contemplate its going down.
Liston's last season! and the cruel old boy looks so

provokingly hale and comical! What years of future laughter
are in his face, scored over with quips and cranks! drawn up
in farcical festoons! furrowed with fun!
Liston's last season! —Why should he retire? Are not the

times sad enough? —How will the world wag, wanting its
merriest one?

To this the satirical nosed gentleman nodded assent.
"With fifteen new readings to electrify the diurnal critics of Petticoat Alley and Blow-bladder Lane!"

Mr. Bubangrub guaranteed for the brethren. One new reading he would take the liberty of suggesting to Mr. Bigstick. John Kemble had entirely mistaken Shakspere's meaning. "Birnam Wood" comes not to "Dunsinane" a town; but to "Dunce inane" Macbeth! who was blockhead enough to put his trust in the witches. The great Tragedian danced with ecstasy at this "palpable hit," and promised pipes and purl for the critical party after the performance.

"Egg-hot," said he, "is not my ordinary tipple; but on this occasion (pardon egotism!) I will be an egg-hot-ist! And now, to the Queen's Arms for a supper, and then to Somnus's for a snooze!"

With a patronising air he conducted us down the ladder. To Uncle Timothy he said a few words in private, and our ears deceived us, if "gratitude" was not among the number.

We fancied that the jovial spirit of the good Prior, on a three days' furlough from Elysium, hovered over the holiday scene; and that a shadowy black robe and cowl, half concealing his portly figure and ruddy features, flitted in the moonlight, and disappeared under the antique low-arched door that leads to his mausoleum! *

* Each of the monks that kneel beside the effigy of Rahere has a Bible before him, open at the fifty-first chapter of Isaiah. The third verse is peculiarly applicable to his holy work. And as it was the Star that guided him to convert an unhealthy marsh, "dunge and fenny" on the only dry part of which was erected "the gallows of thieves," into a temple and a "garden of the Lord so it was his divine assurance that he would live to see, in his own case, the prophecy fulfilled; and hear the "voice of melody" echo through the sacred walls his piety had raised.
"The Lord shall comfort Zion: he will comfort all her waste

places; and he will make her wilderness like Eden, and her

desert like the garden of the Lord; joy and gladness shall be found therein, thanksgiving, and the voice of melody."

"Dreams are the children of an idle brain." Yet ours was a busy one through the live-long night. The grotesque scene acted itself over again, with those fantastical additions that belong to "Death's counterfeit." Legions of Anthropophagi; giants o'ertopping Pelion and Ossa; hideous abortions; grinning nondescripts; the miniature, mischievous court of Queen Mab, and the fiddling, dancing troop of Tam O'Shanter passed before us in every variety of unearthly combination. Clouds of incense arose, and the vision, growing dim, gradually melted away —a low, solemn chant leaving its dying notes upon the ear.

> Let gratitude's chorus arise,
>
> If gratitude dwell upon earth,
>
> To hymn thy return to the skies,
>
> Benevolent spirit of mirth!
>
> Long flourish thy frolicsome fair,
>
> Where many odd bargains are driven;
>
> And may peccadilloes done there,
>
> For thy merry sake be forgiven!

CHAPTER XIV.

The sentinel sleeps when off his post; the Moorfields barker enjoys some interval of repose; moonshine suffers a partial eclipse on Bank holidays among the *omnium gatherem* of Bulls and Bears; the doctor gives the undertaker a holiday; Argus sends his hundred eyes to the Land of Nod, and Briareus puts his century of hands in his pockets. —But the match-maker, ante and post meridian, is always at her post!

"The News teems with candidates for the noose: —A spinster conjugally inclined; a bachelor devoted to Hymen; forlorn widowers; widows disconsolate; and why not 'A daughter to marry?' Addresses paid per post, post paid! For an introduction to the belle, ring the bell! None but principals (with a principal!) need apply."

"Egad," continued Mr. Bosky, as we journeyed through the fields a few mornings after our caravan adventure, to pay Uncle Timothy a visit at his new *rus in urbe* near Hampstead Heath, "it will soon be dangerous to dine out, or to figure in; for a dinner may become an action for damages; and a dance, matrimony without benefit of clergy! But yesterday I pic-nic'd with the Muffs; buzzed with Brutus; endured Ma, was just civil to Miss; when early this morning comes a missive adopting me for a son-in-law!"

We congratulated Mr. Bosky on the prospect of his speedily becoming a Benedick.

"*Bien obligé!* What! ingraft myself on that family Upas tree of ignorance, selfishness, and conceit! Couple with triflers, who, having no mental resources or amusement within themselves, sigh 'O! another dull day!' and are happy only when some gad-about party drag them from a monotonous home, where nothing is talked of or read, but petty scandal, fashions for the month, trashy novels, mantua-makers' and milliners' bills! I can laugh at affectation, but I loathe duplicity; I can pity a fool, but I scorn a flirt. This is a hackneyed ruse of Ma's. The last coasting season of the Muffs has been comparatively unprolific. From Margate to Brighton Miss Matilda counts but five proposals positive, and half a dozen presumptive; in the latter are included some broad stares at Broadstairs from the Holborn Hill Demosthenes! and even these have been furiously scrambled for by the delicate sisters for their marriageable Misses! 'Everybody! says Lord Herbert of Cherbury, 'loves the virtuous, whereas the vicious do scarcely love one another."

An oddity crossed our path. "There waddles," said the Lauréat, "Mr. Onessimus Omnium, who thrice on every Sabbath takes the round of the Conventicles with his pockets stuffed full of bibles and psalm books, every one of which (chapter and verse pointed out!) he passes into the hands of forgetful old ladies and gentlemen whom he opines 'Consols, and not philosophy, console!' Pasted on the inside cover is his card, setting forth the address and calling of Onessimus! You may swear that somebody is dead in the neighbourhood, (the pious Lynx is hunting up the executors!) by seeing him out of 'the Alley' at this early time of the day."

Farther a-field, rambling amidst the rural scenes he has so charmingly described, we shook hands with Uncle Timothy's dear friend, the Author of a work "On the Beauties, Harmonies, and Sublimities of Nature." * Happy old man! Who shall say that fortune deals harshly, if, in taking much away, she leaves us virtue?

* To Charles Bucke,

On hearing that he is engaged upon another Work, to be entitled Man.

"Man!" comprehensive Volume! —busy Man —

A world of warring passions, hopes and fears;
Good, evil-all within one little span!
Pride, meanness; wisdom, folly; smiles and tears;
Th' oppressor, the oppress'd; the coward, brave;
Fate's foot-ball from the cradle to the grave!
These records of thy studious days and eves,

Thy musings and experience, are to me
A moral, that this sure impression leaves;
Man never yet was happy-ne'e?' can be!
The feverish bliss, my friend, that dreamers feign,
Binds him a prisoner faster to his chain.
The miser to his treasure, and the proud
To pride and its dominion; —to his gorge
The glutton; —and the low promiscuous crowd
To sordid sensualities, that forge
The unseen fetters, which so firmly bind,
Are all ignobly bound in body; —mind.
He only is a free man, who, like thee,
Does stand aloof, and mark the wild uproar
That shakes the depths of life's tempestuous sea;
And steers his fragile bark along the shore.
The swelling canvass and the prosperous gale
Herald the shipwreck's melancholy tale!
Nature, all beauteous Nature! —thou hast sung
In prose poetic, through each various scene;
And when thy harp upon the willows hung,
She kept thy form erect, thy brow serene;
And breathed upon thy soul; and peace was there:
The soft, still music of a mother's prayer.
She gave thee truth, humility, content;
A spirit to return for evil good;
A grateful heart for bliss denied, or sent;
And sweet companionship in solitude!
Candour, that wrong offence nor takes, nor gives;
A brother's boundless love for all that lives!
Pursue thy solemn theme. —And when on a Man
The curtain thou hast dropp'd, return once more
To Nature. She has Beauties yet to scan,
New Harmonies, Sublimities, in store!
She will repay thy love; and weave, and spread,
A garland-and a pillow-for thy head.
Uncle Timothy.

Winding through a verdant copse, we suddenly came in sight of an elegant mansion. From a flower-woven arbour, sacred to retirement, proceeded the notes of a guitar.

"Hush!" said the Lauréat, colouring deeply —

"breathe not! Stir not!" And a voice of surpassing sweetness sang

Farewell Autumn's shady bowers,

Purple fruits and fragrant flowers,

Golden fields of waving corn,

And merry lark that wakes the morn I

Earth a mournful silence keeps,

See, the dewy landscape weeps!

Hark! thro* yonder lonely dell

Gentle zephyrs sigh farewell!

Call'd ere long by vernal spring,

Trees shall blossom, birds shall sing;

The blushing rose, the lily fair

Deck sweet summer's bright parterre —

Flocks and herds, the bounding steed

Shall, sporting, crop the flowery mead,

And bounteous Nature yield again

Her ripen'd fruits and golden grain.

Ere the landscape fades from view,

As behind yon mountains blue

Sets the sun in glory bright —

And the regent of the night,

Thron'd where shines the blood-red Mars,

With her coronet of stars,

Silvers woodland, hill and dell,

Lovely Autumn! fare thee well.

Was Mr. Bosky in love with the songstress or the song? Certes his manner seemed unusually hurried and flurried; and one or two of his forced whistles sounded like suppressed sighs. So absent was he that, not regarding how far we had left him in the rear, he stood for a few minutes motionless, as if waiting for echo to repeat the sound!

We thought-it might be an illusion-that a fair hand waved him a graceful recognition. At all events the spell was soon broken, for he bounded along to us like the roe, with

"Jog on, jog on, the foot-path way,

And merrily hent the stile-a:

A merry heart goes all the day,

Your sad tires at a mile-a."

The laughing Autolicus! It was his blithesome note that first made us acquainted with Uncle Timothy!

The remembrance of boyhood is ever pleasing to the reflective mind. The duties that await us in after-life; the cares and disappointments that obstruct our future progress cast a shade over those impressions that were once interwoven with our existence. But it is only a shade; recall but one image of the distant scene, and the whole rises in all its freshness and verdure; touch but one string of this forgotten harmony, and every chord shall vibrate!

"Arma, vi-rump que cane-o!" exclaimed the Lauréat, pointing to his old schoolmaster, who was leaning over his rustic garden-gate, reading his favourite Virgil. And how cordial was their greeting! The scholar played his urchin pranks over again, and the master flourished a visionary birch. Mr. Bosky hurried us into the playground; (his little garden was still there, but it looked not so trim and gay as when he was its horticulturist!) led us into the school room, pointed out his veritable desk, notched at all corners with his initials; identified the particular peg whereon, in days of yore, hung his (too often) crownless castor; and recapitulated his boyish sports, many of the sharers of which he happily recognised in the full tide of prosperity; and not a few sinking under adverse fortune, whose prospects were once bright and cheering, and whose bosoms bounded with youth, and innocence, and joy!

"Let me die in autumn! that the withered blossoms of summer may bestrew my grave, and the mournful breeze that scatters them, sigh forth my requiem!"

These were the words of the poor widow's only son, at whose tomb, in the village church-yard, we paused in sorrowful contemplation. Its guardian angels were Love and Pity entwined in each other's arms. Uncle Timothy, after recording the name and age of him to whom it was raised, thus concluded the inscription: —

Mysterious Vision of a fitful dream!

Pilgrim of Time thro* Nature's dark sojourn!

Then cast upon Eternity's wide stream —

To Know Thyself is all thou need'st to learn:

And that thy God, omnipotent and just,

Is merciful, remembering thou art Dust!

—When the friends of our youth are fast dying away; when the scenes that once delighted us are fading from our view, and new connections and objects ill repay the loss of the old, how welcome the summons that closes our disappointments and calls us to rest! The mourners walk the streets, but the man is gone; the body dissolves to dust, but the spirit returns to Him that gave it!

The Village Free-School was at hand, (the morning hymn, chanted by youthful voices, rose on the breeze to heaven!) and the Alms-houses, where Uncle Timothy first met the poor widow and the good pastor. A troop of little children were gathered round one of the inmates, listening to some old wife's tale. 'Tis the privilege of the aged to be reminiscent: the past is their world of anecdote and enjoyment. Let us then afford them this pleasure, well nigh the only one that time has not taken away; remembering, that we with quick pace advance to the closing scene, when we shall be best able to appreciate the harmless gratification they now ask of us, and which we, in turn, shall ask of others.

The ancient church spire rising between the tall elms, and the neat Parsonage House gave an exquisite finish to the surrounding scenery. Happy England! whose fertile hills and valleys are spotted with these Temples of the Most High, where "the rich and the poor meet together, for the Lord hath made them all and the humble dwellings of the shepherds of his flock. The good pastor scattered blessings around him. His genius and learning commanded admiration and respect; his piety, and Christian charity conciliated dissent; and his life exemplified the beauty of holiness." He had confirmed the faithful; fixed the wavering; and reclaimed the dissolute.

> "The wretch who once sang wildly-danc'd and laugh'd,
>
> And suck'd down dizzy madness with his draught,
>
> Has wept a silent flood-reversed his ways —
>
> Is sober, meek, benevolent, and prays."

Place us above the sordid vulgar; light us on that enviable medium between competency and riches, and there we shall find the domestic virtues flourishing in full vigour and grace. In the rank hotbed of artificial life spring up those noxious weeds that choke and destroy them.

We now arrived at Uncle Timothy's cottage, reared in the midst of a flower garden. In a summer-house fragrant with roses, woodbine, and jessamine sat our host and the good pastor. A word of introduction soon made us friends; and from the minister's kind greeting, it was clear that

Uncle Timothy had not been niggard in our praise.

An old lady in deep mourning walked slowly up the path. Uncle Timothy went forth to receive her. It was the poor widow! The mother of that only son!

"Welcome, dear Madam! to this abode of peace. To-day —and what a day! so cool, so calm, so bright! we purpose being your guests."

"Mine?" faltered the poor widow, anxiously.

"Yours!" replied Uncle Timothy; "sit down, my friends, and I will explain all.

"My childhood was sorrowful, and my youth laborious. A near relation wasted my patrimony; and with no other resource than a liberal education, wrung from the slender means of my widowed mother, I began the world. In this strait, a generous friend took me by the hand; first instructing me in his own house of business, and then procuring me an eligible appointment abroad. From time to time I acquainted him with my progress, and received in return substantial proofs of his benevolent and watchful care. Years rolled away-fortune repaid my ardent endeavours-and I resolved to revisit my native land. I embarked for England; when, almost in sight of her white cliffs, a storm arose, the ship foundered, and I lost half my possessions. Enough still remained to render me independent. My mother and sister were spared to bid me welcome-my early oppressor (the infidel may laugh at retribution; but retribution begins, when a man is suspected in the society of others, and self-condemned in his own) had descended remorseful to the grave-and my noble benefactor —

> 'O grief had changed him since I saw him last;
>
> And careful hours, with time's deforming hand,
>
> Had written strange defeatures in his face —'

by pecuniary embarrassments, heightened by ingratitude, was brought very low. Cheerfully would I have devoted to him my whole fortune, and began the world again. For then I possessed strength and energy to toil. But ere I could carry this my firm resolution into effect, three days after my arrival,

'As sweetly as a child,

Whom neither thought disturbs nor care encumbers,

Tired with long play, at close of summer day,

Lies down and slumbers!'

he pressed his last pillow, requiting my filial tears with a blessing and a smile.

"My debt of gratitude I hoped might still in part be paid. My friend had an only daughter-Did that daughter survive?

"The most diligent inquiries, continued for many years, proved unsuccessful. On the evening of an ill-spent and wearisome day, Heaven, dear sir, (addressing the good pastor) led me to your presence while performing the sacred duty of comforting the mourner. What then took place I need not repeat. You will, however, remember that on a subsequent occasion, while looking over the papers of the widow's son, we discovered a sealed packet, in which, accompanying a mourning ring, presented to his mother, were these lines: —

Pledge of love for constant care

Let a widow'd mother wear;

Filial love, whose early bloom

Proves a garland for the tomb.

Ever watchful, ever nigh,

It breaks my heart, it fills my eye

To see thee hide the falling tear,

And hush the sigh I may not hear!

Heaven thy precious life to spare

Is my morning, evening prayer,

When I rise, and sink to rest,

'Tis my first and last request.

If, when deep distress of mind

Press'd me sorely, aught unkind

I have said or done, forgive!

Error falls on all that live.

Beneath the sod, where wave the trees,

And softly sighs the whispering breeze,

Fain I would the grassy shrine,

Mother! guard my dust and thine.

What are grief and suffering here?

Are they worth a sigh or tear?

What is parting? —transient pain,

Parting soon to meet again!

The second enclosure was the miniature of his grandfather. But that miniature! Gracious God! what were my sensations when I beheld the benignant, expressive lineaments of my early benefactor. The object of my long and anxious inquiries was thus miraculously discovered! 'Till that moment I had never felt true happiness. This cottage, dear Madam, with a moderate independence, the deed I now present secures to you; in return, I entreat that the miniature may be mine: and I hope some kind friend (glancing at his nephew) will, in death, place it upon my bosom."

"What darkness so profound," exclaimed the good pastor, "that the All-seeing Eye shall not penetrate? What maze so intricate and perplexed that our Merciful Father shall not safely guide us through? 'Throw thy bread upon the waters, and it shall return to thee after many days.'"

The village bells rang a merry peal; for the good pastor had given the charity children a holiday. They were entertained with old English fare on the lawn before the cottage, and superintended in their dancing and blindman's-buff by Norah Noclack and the solemn clerk. Nor were the aged inmates of the bountiful widow's Almshouses forgotten. They dined at the Parsonage, and were gratified with a liberal present from Uncle Timothy. And that the day might live in grateful remembrance when those who now shared in its happiness found their rest in the tomb, the Lauréat of Little Britain (some, like the sponge, require compression before they yield anything; others, like the honey-comb, exude spontaneously their sweets,) expressed his intention of adding two Alms-houses to the goodly number, and liberally endowing them.

Many a merrier party may have sat down to dinner, but never a happier one. It was a scene of deep and heartfelt tranquillity and joy. The widow-no longer poor-presided with an easy self-possession, to which her misfortunes added a melancholy grace.

Time passed swiftly; and the sun, that had risen and run his course in splendour, shed his parting rays on the enchanting scenery. Suddenly a flood of light illumined the chamber where we sat with an almost supernatural glory, beaming with intense brightness on the countenance of Uncle Timothy, and then melting away. Ere long in the distant groves was heard the nightingale's song.

"One valued relic" said the widow, addressing

Uncle Timothy, "I have ever carefully preserved. You, dear sir, were an enthusiast in boyhood: and when, as your senior, I once presumed to counsel you, this was your reply."

And she read to Uncle Timothy his youthful fancy.

Let saving prudence temper joy,

Curtail of wit the social day;

Excitement's pleasures soon destroy —

The spirit wears the frame away.

Thanks, gentle monitor! I greet

This friendly warning, well design'd;

For Stellas voice is ever sweet,

And Stellas words are ever kind!

I would not lose, to linger here,

One happy hour of wit and glee;

If e'er of death I have a fear,

It would with friends the parting be!

Then wear, my frame, and droop, and fade,

And fall, and dust to dust return; —

With friendship's rites sincerely paid,

'Tis sweeter to be mourned than mourn.

For mourn we must-it is a pain,

A penalty that man must pay

For dreaming childhood o'er again,

And sitting out last life's poor play.

Sad privilege! too dearly bought,

To sorrow over those that sleep;

Sadder, in apathy and naught,

To lose the will, the power to weep!

Ere thought and memory are obscur'd,

Let me, kind Stella! say adieu;

I would not ask to be endur'd,

No, not by e'en a friend like you!

Love, friendship, interchange of mind,

Celestial happiness hath given;

These glorious gifts she left behind,

Her foot-prints as she fled to Heaven!

"And so, Eugenio," said Uncle Timothy, "you intend to visit the Eternal City, and muse over the mouldering ruins of the palaces of the Cæsars. But rest not there-take your pilgrim's staff and pass onward to that Land made Holy by the presence of our Redeemer! Would that I could accompany you to the sacred hills of Zion!"

"O for such a guide!" exclaimed Eugenio. "But I should be too-too happy-and I may no more expect light without darkness, than joy without sorrow."

"If Uncle Tim goes, I go!" whispered the Lauréat. "With him I am resolved to live-with him it would be happiness —" the last few words were inaudible.

"Eugenio," said the good pastor, laying his hand on the young traveller's head, who knelt reverently to receive his blessing, "you are in possession of youth, health, and competence. How enviable your situation! —how extensive your power of doing good! Fortune smiled not on the widow's son-yet, to him belongs a far higher inheritance; the inexhaustible treasures of Heaven, the eternal affluence of the skies! A man's genius is always, in the beginning of life, as much unknown to himself as to others; and it is only after frequent trials, attended with success, that he dares think himself equal to certain undertakings in which those who have succeeded have fixed the admiration of mankind. Be then what our lost friend would have been, under happier circumstances. A stagnant, unprogressing existence was never intended for man. Action is the mind's proper sphere, ere time obscures its brightness and enfeebles its powers. And carry with you these truths, that the foundation of domestic happiness is faith in the virtue of woman; the foundation of political happiness is confidence in the integrity of man; the foundation of all happiness, temporal and eternal, is reliance on the goodness of God. If, amidst more important occupations, the Muse claim a share of your regard, let not the ribald scorn of hypercriticism discourage you on the very threshold of poetry —f Know thine own worth, and reverence the Lyre —'"

The night proved as lovely as the day. But with it came the hour of parting. Parting! —What a host of feelings are concentrated in that little word! The Lauréat bore up heroically. —The glare of the candles being too much for his eyes, he walked in the moonlight, while Eugenio sang —

Our sails catch the breeze-lov'd companions, adieu!

Farewell! —not to friendship-but farewell to you!

When Alps rise between us, and rolls the deep sea,

Shall I e'er forget you? Will you forget me?

Ah! no-for my hand you at parting have press'd,

In memory of moments my brightest and best!

How sad heaves my bosom this tear let it tell,

How falters my tongue when it bids you farewell!

Eugenio was on ship-board early the following morn. His friends attended, to wish him *bon voyage* and a safe return. And as the noble vessel moved majestically along the waters, high above the rest waved *adieu* the hand of *Uncle Timothy!*

CONCLUSION.

Thus, gentle reader, we have led thee through a labyrinth of strange sights, of land-monsters and sea-monsters, many of man's own making, others the offspring of freakish nature, of Jove mellow with nectar and ambrosia. If the "proper study of mankind is man," where can he be studied in a greater variety of character than in the scenes we have visited? The well-dressed automaton of a drawing-room, (a tailor made him!) fenced in with fashions and forms, moving, looking, and speaking but as etiquette pulls the wires, exhibits man in artificial life, and must no more be taken as a fair sample of the genus, than must pharmacy, in the person of the pimple-faced quack * mounted on his piebald pad, or charlatan's stage.

* "Quacksalvers and mountebanks are as easy to be knowne as an asse by his eares, or the lyon by his pawes, for they delight most commonly to proclaime their dealings in the open streets and market-places, by prating, bragging, lying, with their labells, banners, and wares, hanging them out abroade." Morbus Gallicus, 1585, by William Clowes. "In the yeare 1587, there came a Flemming into the cittie of

Gloceter (Gloucester) named Wolfgang Frolicke, and there hanged forth his pictures, his flagges, his instruments, and his letters of marte, with long labells, great tassels, broad scales closed in boxes, with such counterfeit showes and knackes of knauerie, coesining the people of their monie, without either learning or knowledge." A most excellent and compendious Method of curing Wounds, &c. translated by John Read, 8vo. 1588.

We have shewn thee to what odd inventions men are put to provide fun for their fellows, and food for themselves. Yet if we ascend the scale of society it will be found that the Merry-Andrew is not the only wearer of the Fool's coat; that buffoons and jesters are not exclusively confined to fairs; that the juggler, * who steals his five pecks of corn out of a bushel.

* The following description of an itinerant juggler of the olden time is exceedingly curious, and probably unique. "The third (as the first) was an olde fellowe, his beard

milkewhite, his head couered with a round lowe-crownd rent silke hat, on which was a band knit in many knotes, wherein stucke two round stickes after the jugler's manner. Hisierkin was of leather cut, his cloake of three coulers, his hose paind with yellow drawn out with blew, his instrument was a bagpipe, and him I knew to be William Cuckoe, better knowne than lou'd, and yet, some thinke, as well lou'd as he was worthy." Kind-Hart's Dreame. Hocus Pocus, junior, in his Anatomy of Legerdemaine, 1634,

mentions one "whose father while he lived was the greatest jugler in England, and used the assistance of a familiar; he lived a tinker by trade, and used his feats as a trade by the by; he lived, as I was informed, alwayes betattered, and died, for ought I could hear, in the same estate."

The nostrum-vender who cures all diseases in the world, and one disease more; the Little-go man and thimble-rigger have their several prototypes among the starred and gartered; the laced and tinselled "Noodles" and "Doodles" of more elevated spheres, where the necessity for such ludicrous metamorphoses does not exist; except to shake off the ennui of idleness-and idleness, said the great Duke of Marlborough, is a complaint quite enough to kill the stoutest General. How, gentle reader, has thy time been spent? If Utilitarian, * thou wilt say "Unprofitably!"

* "To set downe the jugling in trades, the crafty tricks of
buyers and sellers, the swearing of the one, the lying of
the other, were but to tell the worlde that which they well
knowe, and, therefore, I will ouerslip that. There is an
occupation of no long standing about London, called broking,
or brogging, whether ye will; in which there is pretty
jugling, especially to blind law, and bolster usury. If any
man be forst to bring them a pawne, they will take no
interest, not past twelue pence a pound for the month:
marry, they must haue a groat for a monthly bill, which is a
bill of sale from month to month; so that no advantage can
be taken for the usurie.
I heare say it's well multiplied since I died; but I

beshrewe them, for, in my life, many a time haue I borrowed
a shilling on my pipes, and paid a groat for the bill, when
I haue fetclit out my pawne in a day." William Cuckoe to all
close juglers, &c. "c. —Kind-Hart's Dreame. O the villany of
these ancient pawnbrokers!

If Puritan, "Profanely Presuming," however, that thou art neither the greedy, all-grasping nor the over-reaching, preaching second; but a well-conditioned happy being, with religion enough to shew thy love to God by thy benevolence to man, thou wilt regard with an approving smile the various recreations that lighten the toil and beguile the cares of thy humbler brethren; and thy compassion (not the world's —Heaven save them and thee from the bitterness of that!) will fall on the poor Mime and Mummer, whose antic tricks and contortions, grinning mask of red ochre and white paint, but ill conceal his poverty-broken spirit, hollow ghastly eyes, and sunken cheeks-and thou wilt not turn scornfully from the multitudes (none are to be despised but the wicked, and they rather deserve our pity) that such (perhaps to thee) senseless sights can amuse.

Self-complacent, predominant Self will be lost in generous sympathy, the electrical laughing fit will go round, and, though at the remotest end of the chain, thy gravity will not escape the shaking shock. Believing that thou art merry and wise; sightly, sprightly; learned, yet nothing loth to laugh; as we first met in a mutual spirit of communication and kindness, so we part. And when good fortune shall again throw us into thy company, not forgetting Mr. Bosky and the middle-aged gentleman with the satirical nose! we shall be happy to shake thy hand, ay, and thy sides to boot, with some merry tale or ballad, * ("Mirth, in seasonable time taken, is not forbidden by the austerest sapients,") if haply time spare us one to tell or sing. Till then, health be with thee, gentle reader! a light heart and a liberal hand.

* Henry Chettle, in his Kind-Hart's Dreame, gives the
following description of a Ballad Singer. "The first of the
first three was an od old fellow, low of stature, his head
was couered with a round cap, his body with a side-skirted
tawney coate, his legs and feete trust vppe in leather
buskins, his gray haires and furrowed face witnessed his
age, his treble violl in his hande assured me of his
profession. On which (by his con-tinuall sawing, hauing left

but one string,) after his best manner, he gaue me a
huntsvp: whome, after a little musing, I assuredly remembred
to be no other but old Anthony Now now." Anthony Munday is
supposed to be ridiculed in the character of cc Old Anthony
Now now the latter was an itinerant fiddler, of whom this
curious notice occurs in The Second Bart of the Gentle
Craft, by Thomas Deloney, 1598.
"Anthony cald for wine, and drawing forth his fiddle began

to play, and after he had scrapte halfe a score lessons, he
began thus to sing: —
"When should a man shew himselfe gentle and kinde? When

should a man comfort the sorrowful minde?
O Anthony, now, now, now,

O Anthony, now, now, now.

When is the best time to drinke with a friend?

When is the meetest my money to spend?

O Anthony, now, now, now,

O Anthony, now, now, now.

When goeth the King of good fellows away,

That so much delighted in dancing and play?

O Anthony, now, now, now,

O Anthony, now, now, now.

And when should I bid my good master farewell,

Whose bounty and curtesie so did excell?

O Anthony, now, now, now,

O Anthony, now, now, now.

"Loe yee now, (quoth hee,) this song have I made for your

sake, and by the grace of God when you are gone, I will sing
it every Sunday morning under your wives' window.* *
"Anthony in his absence sung this song so often in S.

Martin's, that thereby he purchast a name which he never
lost till his dying day, for ever after men cald him nothing
but Anthony now now."
Braithwait thus describes one of the race of "metre ballad

mongers."

"Now he counterfeits a natural base, then a perpetual

treble, and ends with a counter-tenure. You shall heare him
feigne an artfull straine through the nose, purposely to

insinuate into the attention of the purer brother-hood."

APPENDIX.

Well might Old England * have been called "Merrie," for the court had its masques and pageantry, and the people their plays, ** sports, and pastimes. There existed a jovial sympathy between the two estates, which was continually brought into action, and enjoyed with hearty good-will. Witness the Standard in Cornhill, and the Conduit in "Chepe;" when May-poles were in their glory, and fountains ran with wine.

   * The English were a jesting, ballad-singing, play-going people. The ancient press teemed with "merrie jests." The following oddities of the olden time grin from our

bookshelves. "Skelton's merrie Tales;" "A Banquet of Jests, Old and New" (Archee's); "A new Booke

of Mistakes, or Bulls with Tales, and Bulls without Tales;" "The Booke of Bulls Baited, with two Centuries of bold Jests

and nimble Lies "Robin Good-Fellow, his mad Pranks and merry Jests "A merry Jest of Robin Hood "Tales and quicke answers;" "xii. mery Jests of the Wyddow Edyth "The merry jest of a

shrewde and curste Wyfe lapped in Morrelles-skin for her good behavyour "Dobson's Drie Bobbes. Sonne and Heire to Scoggin, full of mirth and delightful recreation;" "Peele's Jests "Tarlton's. Jests "Scoggin's Jests "The Jests

of Smug the Smith;" "A Nest of Ninnies," &e. &e.

** There were not fewer than seventeen playhouses in and

about London, between 1570 and 1629.

A joyous remnant of the olden time was the coart-fool. "Better be a witty fool than a foolish wit." What a marvellous personage is the court-fool of Shakspeare! His head was stocked with notions. He wore not Motley in his brain.

   The most famous court-fools were Will Summers, or Sommers, Richard Tarlton, and Archibald Armstrong, vulgo Archee, jester to King Charles I. Archee was the last of the Motleys; unless we admit a fourth, on the authority of the well-known epigram.

> "In merry old England it once was a rule,
>
> The king had his poet and also his fool;
>
> But now we're so frugal, I M have you to know it,
>
> Poor Cibber must serve both for fool and for poet!"

Will Summers * was of low stature, pleasant countenance, nimble body and gesture; and had good mother-wit in him! A whimsical compound of fool and knave. He was a prodigious favourite with Henry the Eighth.

   * Under a rare print of him by Delarem, are inscribed the
following lines: —
"What though thou think'st mee clad in strange attire,

Know I am suted to my owne deseire:
And yet the characters describ'd upon mee,
May shewe thee, that a king bestow'd them on mee.
This home I have, betokens Sommers' game;
Which sportive tyme will bid thee reade my name:
All with my nature well agreeing too,
As both the name, and tyme, and habit doe."

That morose and cruel monarch tolerated his caustic satire and laughed at his gibes. When the king was at dinner, Will Summers 'would thrust his face through the arras, and make the royal gormandiser roar heartily with his odd humour and comical grimaces; and then he would approach the table "in such a rolling and antic posture, holding his hands and setting his eyes, that is past describing, unless one saw him."

Original

But Will Summers possessed higher qualities than merely making the Defender of the Faith merry. He used his influence in a way that few court favourites-not being fools! —have done, before or since. He tamed the tyrant's ferocity, and urged him to good deeds; himself giving the example, by his kindness to those who came within the humble sphere of his bounty. Armin, in his Nest of Ninnies, 4to. 1608, thus describes this laughing philosopher. "A comely foole indeed passing more stately; who was this forsooth? Will Sommers, and not meanly esteemed by the king for his merriment; his melody was of a higher straine, and he lookt as the noone broad waking. His description was writ on his forehead, and yee might read it thus:

"Will Sommers borne in Shropshire, as some say,

Was brought to Greenwich on a holy day,

Presented to the king, which foole disdayn'd,

To shake him by the hand, or else asham'd,

Howe're it Avas, as ancient people say,

With much adoe was wonne to it that day.

Leane he was, hollow-eyde, as all report,

And stoope he did too; yet, in all the court,

Few men were more belov'd than was this foole,

Whose merry prate kept with the king much rule.

When he was sad, the king and he would rime,

Thus Will exil'd sadness many a time.

I could describe him, as I did the rest,

But in my mind I doe not think it best:

My reason this, howe're I doe descry him,

So many know him, that I may belye him.

Therefore, to please all people one by one,

I hold it best to let that paines alone.

Only thus much, he was a poore man's friend,

And helpt the widdow often in the end:

The king would ever graunt what he did crave,

For well he knew Will no exacting knave;

But wisht the king to doe good deeds great store,

Which caus'd the court to love him more and more."

Many quaint sayings are recorded of him, which exhibit a copious vein of mirth, and an acute and ready wit. Upon a festival day, being in the court-yard walking with divers gentlemen, he espied a very little personage with a broad-brimmed hat; when he remarked, that if my Lord Minimus had but such another hat at his feet, he might be served up to the king's table, as between two dishes.

Going over with the king to Boulogne, and the weather being rough and tempestuous, he, never having been on ship-board before, began to be fearful of the sea; and, calling for a piece of the saltest beef, devoured it before the king very greedily. His majesty asked him why he ate such gross meat with such an appetite, when there was store of fresh victuals on board? To which he made answer, "Oh! blame me not, Harry, to fill my stomach with so much salt meat beforehand, knowing, if we be cast away, what a deal of water I have to drink after it!"

He was no favourite with Wolsey, who had a fool of his own, one Patch, that loved sweet wine exceedingly, and to whom it was as natural as milk to a calf. The churchman was known to have a mistress; Holinshed terms him "vitious of his bodie," and Shakspere says, "of his own body he was ill," which clearly implies clerical concupiscence. Summers improvised an unsavoury jest upon the lady, which made the king laugh, and the cardinal bite his lip. He was equally severe upon rogues in grain, for, said he, "a miller is before his mill a thief, and in his mill a thief, and behind his mill a thief!" and his opinion of church patronage was anything but orthodox. Being asked why the best and richest benefices were for the most part conferred on unworthy and unlearned men, he replied, "Do you not observe daily, that upon the weakest and poorest jades are laid the greatest burdens; and upon the best and swiftest horses are placed the youngest and lightest gallants?"

On his death-bed a joke still lingered on his lips. A ghostly friar would have persuaded him to leave his estate (some five hundred pounds —a large sum in those days!) to the order of Mendicants; but Summers turned the tables upon him, quoted the covetous father's own doctrine, and left it to the "Prince of this world," by whose favour he had gotten it.

Tarlton * is entitled to especial notice, as being the original representative of the court-fool, or clown, upon the stage. Sir Richard Baker says, "Tarlton, for the part called the clowne's part, never had his match, and never will have."

* Bastard, in his Chrestoleros, 1598, has an epigram to "Richard Tarlton, the Comedian and Jester" and, in Nash's Almond for a Parrot, he is lauded for having made folly excellent, "and spoken of as being extolled for that which all despise."
The music to "Tarleton's Jigge" is preserved in a MS. in the

Public Library, Cambridge (D d. 14, 24). This manuscript is one of six, containing a number of old English tunes, collected and arranged for the lute, by John Dowland, and among them are the music to many of Kemp's Jigs. "Most commonly when the play is done," says Lupton, in his London and the Countrey Carbonadoed and Quatred into seuerall Characters, 8vo. 1632,) "you shall haue a jig or a dance of all treads: they mean to put their legs to it as well as their tongues." According to the author of Tarltoris News out of Purgatory, the jig lasted for an hour. The pamphlet,

says he, is "only such a jest as his (Tarlton's) jig, fit
for gentlemen to laugh at an hour."

Original

He excelled in tragedy as well as comedy, a circumstance that has escaped the research of all his biographers. This curious fact is recorded in a very scarce volume, "*Stradlingi (Joannis) Epigrammata*," 1607, which contains verses on Tarlton. He was born at Condover in the county of Salop; was (according to tradition) his father's swineherd, and owed his introduction at court to Robert Earl of Leicester. Certain it is that Elizabeth took great delight in him, made him one of her servants, and allowed him wages and a groom. According to Taylor the water poet, ("Wit and Mirth") "Dicke Tarlton said that hee could compare Queene Elizabeth to nothing more fitly than to a sculler; for," said he, "neither the queene nor the sculler hath a fellow." He basked all his eccentric life in the sunshine of royal favour. The imperial tigress, who condemned a poor printer to be hanged, drawn, and quartered, for publishing a harmless tract, civilly asking her, when tottering and toothless, to name her successor, listened with grinning complacency to the biting jests and waggeries of her court-fool; grave judges and pious bishops relaxed their reverend muscles at his irresistible buffooneries; while the "many-headed beast," the million, hailed him with uproarious jollity. Here * I must needs remember Tarlton, in his time with the queen his soveraigne, and the people's generall applause.

"Richard Tarlton, ** for a wondrous plentifull, pleasant, extemporal wit, was the wonder of his time. He was so beloved that men use his picture for their signes."

"Let him *** (the fanatic Prynne) try when he will, and come upon the stage himself with all the scurrility of the Wife of Bath, with all the ribaldry of Poggius or Boccace, yet I dare affirm he shall never give that contentment to beholders as honest Tarlton did, though he said never a word."

* Heywood's Apology for Actors.
** Howes, the editor of Stowe's Chronicle.

*** Theatrum Redivivum, by Sir Richard Baker.

"Tarlton, when his head was onely seene,

The tire-house doore and tapistrie betweene,

Set all the multitude in such a laughter,

They could not hold for scarse an houre after." *

* Peacham's Thalia's Banquet, 1620.

In those primitive times (when the play was ended) actors and audiences were wont to pass jokes—"Theames," as they were called-upon each other; and Tarlton, whose flat nose and shrewish wife made him a general butt, was always too many for his antagonist. If driven into a corner, he, as Dr. Johnson said of Foote, took a jump, and was over your head in an instant. In 1611 was published in 4to. "*Tarlton's Jests, drawn into Three Parts: his court-witty Jests; his sound-city Jest's; his country-pretty Jests; full of delight, wit, and honest mirth.*" This volume is of extraordinary rarity. In the title-page is a woodcut of the droll in his clown's dress, playing on his pipe with one hand, and beating his drum with the other. In *Tarlton's News out of Purgatory*, the ancient dress appropriated to that character is thus described. I saw one attired in russet, with a buttoned cap on his head, a bag by his side, and a strong bat in his hand; so artificially attired for a clowne, as I began to call Tarlton's woonted shape to remembrance; and in Kind-Hart's Dreame (1592), "The next, by his suit of russet, his buttoned cap, his taber, his standing on the toe, and other tricks, I knew to be either the body or resemblance of Tarlton, who living, for his pleasant conceits, was of all men liked, and dying, for mirth left not his like." This print * is characteristic and spirited, and bears the strongest marks of personal identity. When some country wag threw up his "Theame," after the following fashion: —

"Tarlton, I am one of thy friends, and none of thy foes,

Then I prethee tell me how cam'st by thy flat nose:

Had I beene present at that time on those banks,

I would have laid my short sword over his long shankes."

The *undumpisher* of Queen Elizabeth made this tart reply: —

"Friend or foe, if thou wilt needs know, marke me well,

With parting dogs and bears, then by the ears, this chance

fell:

But what of that? though my nose be flat, my credit for to

save,

Yet very well I can, by the smell, scent an honest man from

a knave."

* Of the original we speak, which Caulfield sold to Mr. Townley for ten guineas! This identical print, with the Jests, now lies before us. Caulfield's copy is utterly worthless.

Once while he was performing at the Bull in Bishopsgate-street, where the queen's servants often played, a fellow in the gallery, whom he had galled by a sharp retort, threw an apple, * which hit him on the cheek: Tarlton, taking the apple, and advancing to the front of the stage, made this jest: —

"Gentlemen, this fellow, with his face of mapple, **

Instead of a pippin, hath throwne me an apple;

But, as for an apple he hath cast me a crab,

So, instead of an honest woman, God hath sent him a drab."

The people laughed heartily, for he had a queane to his wife. ***

Gabriel Harvey, in his "Four Letters and certain Sonnets," 1592, speaking of Tarlton's "famous play" (of which no copy is known) called "*The Seven Deadly Sins*," says, "which most deadly, but lively playe, I might have seen in London, and was verie gently invited thereunto at Oxford by Tarlton himselfe; of whom I merrily demanding, which of the seaven was his own deadlie sinne?

* Tom Weston, of facetious memory, received a similar
compliment from an orange. Tom took it up very gravely,
pretended to examine it particularly, and, advancing to the
footlights, exclaimed, "Humph! this is not a Seville (civil)
orange." On reference to Polly Peachem's Jests (1728) the
same bon-mot is given to Wilks.
** Mapple means rough and carbuncled. Ben Jonson describes

his own face as rocky: the bark of the maple being
uncommonly rough, and the grain of one of the sorts of the
tree, as Evelyn expresses it, "undulated and crisped into a
variety of curls."
*** It was the scandal of the time, that Tarlton owed not

his nasal peculiarity to the Bruins of Paris-garden,but to
another encounter that might have had something to do with
making his wife Kate the shrew she was.

He bluntly answered after this manner, 'the sinne of other gentlemen, letchery!'" Ben Jonson's *Induction to his Bartholomew Fair*, makes the stage-playur speak thus: "I have kept the stage in Master Tarlton's time, I thank my stars. Ho! an' that man had lived to play in Bartholomew Fair, you should ha seen him ha' come in, and ha' been cozened i' the cloth * quarter so finely!"

"There was one Banks (in the time of Tarlton) who served the Earle of Essex, and had a horse of strange qualities: and being at the Crosse-keyes in Gracious-street, getting money with him, as he was mightily resorted to; Tarlton, then (with his fellowes) playing at the Bell by, (should not this be the Bull in Bishopsgate-street?) came into the Crosse-keyes (amongst many people) to see fashions; which Banks perceiving, (to make the people laugh,) saies, f Signor,' (to his horse,) 'go fetch me the very est foole in the company.' The jade comes immediately, and with his mouth drawes Tarlton forth. Tarlton (with merry words) said nothing but 'God a mercy, horse!' In the end Tarlton, seeing the people laugh so, was angry inwardly, and said, 'Sir, had I power of your horse, as you have, I would doe more than that.' 'Whate'er it be,' said Banks, (to please him,) 'I will charge him to do it.' 'Then,' saies Tarlton, 'charge him to bring me the veriest wh —e-master in the company.' 'He shall,' (saies Banks,) 'Signor,' (saies he,) ' bring Master Tarlton the veriest wh —e-master in the company.' The horse leads his master to him.

* Cloth Fair, where the principal theatrical booths were
erected.

Then God a mercy, horse, indeed!' saies Tarlton. The people had much ado to keep peace; but Banks and Tarlton had like to have squared, and the horse by to give aime. But ever after it was a by-word thorow London, '*God a mercy horse!*' and is to this day."

"Tarlton, (as other gentlemen used,) at the first coming up of tobacco, did take it more for fashion's sake than otherwise, and being in a roome, set between two men overcome with wine, and they never seeing the like, wondered at it; and seeing the vapour come out of Tarlton's nose, cried out, 'Fire! fire!' and then threw a cup of wine in Tarlton's face." With a little variation, Sir Walter Raleigh is reported to have been so treated by his servant. There are some curious old *tobacco papers* extant representing the fact. It was a jug of beer, not a cup of wine.

"Tarlton being at the court all night, in the morning he met a great courtier coming from his chamber, who, espying Tarlton, said, 'Good-morrow, Mr. Didimus and Tridimus.' Tarlton being somewhat abashed, not knowing the meaning thereof, said, 'Sir, I understand you not; expound, I pray you,' Quoth the courtier, 'Didimus and Tridimus are fool and knave.' 'You overload me,' replied Tarlton, 'for my back cannot bear both; therefore take you the one, and I will take the other; take you the knave, and I will carry the fool with me.' And again; there was a nobleman that asked Tarlton what he thought of soldiers in time of peace?

'Marry,' quoth he, 'they are like chimneys in summer." Tom Brown has stolen this simile.

"Tarlton, who at that time kept a tavern in Grace-church-street, made the celebrated Robert Armin * his adopted son, on the occasion of the boy (who was then servant to a goldsmith in Lombard-street) displaying that ready wit, for which Tarlton himself was so renowned.

> "A wagge thou art, none can prevent thee;
>
> And thy desert shall content thee;
>
> Let me divine: as I am,
>
> So in time thou'lt he the same:
>
> My adopted sonne therefore he,
>
> To enjoy my clowne's suit after me.

"And so it fell out. The boy reading this, loved Tarlton ever after, and fell in with his humour; and private practice brought him to public playing; and at this houre he performs the same, where at the Globe on the Bank-side men may see him."

* Robert Armin was a popular actor in Shakspere's plays. He was associated with him and "his fellowes" in the patent granted by James I. to act at the Globe Theatre, and in any other part of the kingdom. He is the author of "The History of the Two Maids of More-clacke" 4to. 1609, in which he played Simple John in the hospital. His "true effigie" appears in the title-page: as does that of Green (another contemporary actor of rare merit), in "Tu Quoque."

Many other jokes are told of Tarlton; how, when he kept the sign of the Tabor, a tavern in Gracechurch street, being chosen scavenger, he neglected his duty, got complained of by the ward, shifted the blame to the raker, who transferred it to his horse, upon which he (Tarlton) sent the horse to the Compter, and the raker had to pay a fee for the redemption of his steed! And how he got his tavern bill paid, and a journey to London scot-free, by gathering his conceits together, and sending his boy to accuse him to the magistrates for a seminary priest! the innkeeper losing his time and charges, besides getting well flouted into the bargain.

In the year 1588 Tarlton gave eternal pause to his merriments. He was buried, September 3, in St. Leonard's, Shoreditch.

In the books of the Stationers' Company was licensed "A Sorrowful new Sonnette," intituled Tarlton's Recantation upon this Theame given him by a gentleman at the Bel Savage without Ludgate (now or els never) being the last Theame he songe; and Tarlton s repentance and his farewell to his friendes in his sickness, a little before his death."In "Wits Bedlam," 1617, is the following epitaph on him: —

"Here within this sullen earth

Lies Dick Tarlton, Lord of Mirth;

Who in his grave still laughing gapes,

Syth all clownes since have been his apes:

Earst he of clownes to learne still sought,

But now they learne of him they taught:

By art far past the principall,

The counterfeit is so worth all."

The following epitaph, quoted by Fuller,

"Hic situs est cujus poterat vox, actio, vultus,

Ex Heraclito reddere Democritum,"

is thus varied in Hackett's *"Select and remarkable Epitaphs"* —

"Hie situs est, cujus vultus, vox, actio posset

Ex," &c. &c.

Archibald Armstrong * in no way disgraced his coat of Motley; though the author of an epitaph on Will Summers speaks of his inferiority: —

"Well, more of him what should I say?

Both fools and wise men turn to clay:

And this is all we have to trust,

That there's no difference in their dust.

Rest quiet then beneath this stone,

To whom late Archee was a drone"

He was an attached and faithful servant, a fellow of arch simplicity and sprightly wit; and if he gave the public not quite so rich a taste of his quality as his predecessors did, let it be remembered that two religious factions were fiercely contending for supremacy, neither of which relished a "merrie jest" It seems, however, that Archee, who had outwitted many, was, on one occasion, himself outwitted.

* There are two rare portraits of Archee prefixed to
different editions of his Jests: one by Cecil, 1657; and one
by Gay-wood, 1660. Under that by Cecil are inscribed the
following lines: —
"Archee, by kings and princes graced of late,

Jested himself into a fayer estate;
And in this booke doth to his friends commend
His jeeres, taunts, tales, which no man can offend."
And under that by Gaywood, the following: —
"This is no Muckle John, nor Summers Will,
But here is Mirth drawn from the Muse's quill;
Doubt not (kinde reader), be but pleased to view
These witty jests: they are not ould, but new."

"Archee coming to a nobleman to give him good-morrow upon New-Year's day, he received a very gracious reward from him, twenty good pieces of gold in his hand. But the covetous foole, expecting (it seemes) a greater, shooke them in his fist, and said they were too light. The nobleman took it ill from him, but, dissembling his anger, said, 'I prithee, Archee, let mee see them again, for amongst them is one piece that I would be loath to part with.' Archee, supposing he would have added more unto them, delivered them back to my lord, who, putting'em up in his pocket, said, 'Well, I once gave money into a foole's hand, who had not the wit to keep it.'"

Archee was "unfrocked" for cracking an irreverend jest on Archbishop Laud, whose jealous power and tyrannical mode of exercising it, could not bear the laughing reproof of even an "allowed fool." The briefe reason of Archee's banishment was this: —A nobleman asking what he would doe with his handsome daughters, he (Archee) replyed, he knew very well what to doe with them, but hee had sonnes, which he knew not well what to doe with; he would gladly make schollars of them, but that hee feared the archbishop would cut off their eares! *

* "Archys Dream, sometime jester to his majestie; but exiled
the court by Canterburies malice," 4to. 1641.

These were the three merry men of the olden time, who, by virtue of their office, spoke truth, in jest, to the royal ear, and gave home-thrusts that would have cost a whole cabinet their heads. If their calling had no other redeeming quality but this, posterity would be bound to honour it.

THE END.

Lightning Source UK Ltd.
Milton Keynes UK
UKHW022355191121
394209UK00010B/2286